IN THE NAME OF HATE

IN THE NAME OF HATE

Understanding Hate Crimes

BARBARA PERRY

ROUTLEDGE

NEW YORK · LONDON

Published in 2001 by
Routledge
29 West 35th Street
New York, NY 10001

Published in Great Britain by
Routledge
11 New Fetter Lane
London EC4P 4EE

Routledge is an imprint of the Taylor & Francis Group.

Library of Congress Cataloging-in-Publication Data

Perry, Barbara, 1962–
    In the name of hate : understanding hate crimes / Barbara Perry.
        p. cm. —
    Includes bibliographical references and index.
    ISBN 0–415–92772–2 (hbk.) — ISBN 0–415–92773–0 (pbk.)
        1. Hate crimes—United States

HV6773.52 .P47 2001
364.1—dc21   00–062739

TO ALL THE OTHERS—MAY WE LIVE IN PEACE.

CONTENTS

LIST OF TABLES

ACKNOWLEDGMENTS

No piece of work springs unaided from the mind of a single academic. Rather, it is coaxed, cajoled, and molded by the advice and assistance of myriad others. This book is no exception to that pattern. From the early days when I first started to consider the dynamics of hate crime, I have benefited immensely from the intellectual and emotional support of others.

I am especially grateful to my colleagues in the Department of Criminal Justice at Northern Arizona University. I could not ask for more supportive or intellectually stimulating faculty. I have fed off of their energy and exploited their willingness to exchange ideas about culture, diversity, and violence. I owe a particular debt of gratitude to colleagues who have read and reread various parts of the manuscript over the years: Alex Alvarez, Marianne Nielsen, Ray Michalowski, Phoebe Morgan, and Nancy Wonders.

I must also acknowledge the students of NAU, who have assisted me in a variety of ways. Many of the ideas expressed in this book were the subject of great debate and discussion in a graduate course on hate crime. I thank the students who offered their perspectives and insights in that context. I also thank the graduate assistants who have helped to ease my burden by taking on some of the labor: research, editing, proof-reading, and so on. Many thanks to Kristen Jensen, Michael Muñoz, and Kathleen West.

I have also benefited from the help of colleagues outside NAU. In particular, while teaching at the University of Southern Maine, I took advantage of the opportunity to profit from the advice of Piers Beirne, Kimberly Cook, and Jim Messerschmidt. I have also benefited from many conversations with Mark Hamm. Claire Renzetti has been especially helpful and supportive of my efforts in the final stages of writing.

I would be remiss if I did not acknowledge my editor at Routledge, Ilene Kalish. From the beginning, Ilene was fully supportive of this project. Her energy and enthusiasm have seen me through the final sections and revisions of the book.

As always, my family has been my refuge. Although I don't see them nearly often enough, my parents, siblings, and nieces and nephew nonetheless always have been a source of energy for me. Much of what I do, I do with the aid of their endless support of my endeavors.

If it had not been for my husband, Michael Groff, I might never have begun this project. And, if it had not been for his unlimited encouragement, I might long ago have given it up. He is always my inspiration and my conscience. Thanks for keeping me on track.

INTRODUCTION The Violence of Hatred

We have all been programmed to respond to the human differences between us with fear and loathing and to handle that difference in one of three ways; ignore it, and if that is not possible, copy it if we think it is dominant, or destroy it if we think it is subordinate.

—Audre Lorde, *Sister Outsider*

The twentieth century appeared to close much as it had opened—with sprees of violence directed against the Other. The murder of Matthew Shepard, the dragging death of James Byrd, the dozens of school shootings, and the murderous rampage of Benjamin Smith all stand as reminders that the bigotry that kills is much more than an unfortunate chapter in United States history. Racial, gender, ethnic, and religious violence persist as mechanisms of oppression. It is a sad commentary on the cultural and social life of the United States that a book such as this remains timely as we enter the twenty-first century. The dramatic cases cited above are but extreme illustrations of widespread, daily acts of aggression directed toward an array of minority communities. I use the term communities purposefully here, since these acts are less about any one victim than about the cultural group they represent. Hate crime is, in fact, an assault against all members of stigmatized and marginalized communities.

Hate crime—often referred to as "ethnoviolence"—is much more than the act of mean-spirited bigots. It is embedded in the structural and cultural context within which groups interact (Young, 1990; Bowling, 1993; Kelly, Maghan, and Tennant, 1993). It does not occur in a social or cultural vacuum; rather, it is a socially situated, dynamic process, involving context and actors, structure, and agency. Ethnoviolence emerges within a network of enabling norms, assumptions, behaviors, institutional arrangements, and policies, which are structurally connected in such a way as to reproduce the racialized and gendered hierarchies that characterize the society in question. It is one of the five interrelated "faces of oppression" by which Iris Marion Young (1990) characterizes the experiences of minority groups. Oppressive violence is nested within the complex of exploitation, marginalization, powerlessness, and cultural imperialism. The first three of these mechanisms reflect the structural and institutional relationships that restrict opportunities for minority groups to express their capacities and to participate in the social world around them. It is the processes and imagery associated with cultural imperialism that supports these practices ideologically. Together, structural exclusions and cultural imaging leave minority members vulnerable to systemic violence, and especially ethnoviolence.

It is curious that hate crime has not been an object of extensive sociological or criminological inquiry. Conceptually, it lies at the intersection of multiple themes that are currently to the fore: violence, victimization, race/ethnicity, gender, sexuality, and difference, for example. In spite of the centrality of violence as a means of policing the relative boundaries of identity, few attempts have been made to understand theoretically the place of hate crime in the contemporary arsenal of oppression. It is not an area that has been examined seriously through a theoretical lens. This book is an attempt to address this void. Specifically, I offer an extended theoretical treatment of hate- and bias-motivated crime. I situate my work within the emerging theoretical framework identified by James Messerschmidt (1993) as structured action theory. Thus, I seek to explain violence against gays, lesbians, women, and racial, ethnic, and religious minority groups as resources for "doing difference."

From the dominant, white perspective, there are appropriate ways for subaltern groups to construct their race or gender or sexuality, ways that do not impinge on white male power. The problem arises when members of these groups resist—or are seen to resist—these externally applied criteria and opt to construct themselves according to their own images and ideals. Bias-motivated crime provides an arena within which white males in particular can reaffirm their place in a complex hierarchy and respond to perceived threats from challengers of the structure—especially immigrants, people of color, women, and homosexuals. Hate crime, then, is seen as an instrument of intimidation and control exercised against those who seem to have stepped outside the boxes that society has carefully constructed for them.

Clearly, this is not a new phenomenon, even in the United States. It is important to keep in mind that what we currently refer to as hate crime has a long historical lineage. The contemporary dynamics of hate-motivated violence have their origins in historical conditions. With respect to ethnoviolence, at least, history does repeat itself as similar patterns of motivation, sentiment, and victimization recur over time. Just as immigrants in the 1890s were subject to institutional and public forms of discrimination and violence, so too were those of the 1990s; likewise, former black slaves risked the wrath of the Ku Klux Klan when they exercised their newfound rights in the antebellum period, just as their descendants risked violent reprisal for their efforts to win and exercise additional rights and freedoms in the civil rights era; and women who demanded the right to vote on the eve of the twentieth century suffered the same ridicule and harassment as those who demanded equal rights in the workplace later in the century. While the politics of difference that underlie these periods of animosity may lie latent for short periods of time, they nonetheless seem to remain on the simmer, ready to resurface whenever a new threat is perceived—when immigration levels increase, or formerly powerless groups are suddenly empowered, or when relationships between groups shift for other political, economic, or cultural reasons.

STRUCTURE OF THE BOOK

In chapter 1, I situate my own work by addressing the diverse ways in which we currently define and measure hate crime. The extant literature generally does not treat the definition of hate crime as problematic. There is widespread consensus that legalistic definitions of the concept are acceptable and adequate. Thus, the common usage of the term assumes the commission of a criminal offense, a violation of an existing criminal code. For example, the federal Hate Crime Statistics Act of 1990 defines hate crime as "crime that manifests evidence of prejudice based on race, religion, sexual orientation or ethnicity." From a sociological standpoint, this definition is inadequate since it fails to encompass grievous violations which may nonetheless be legal (for example, the Holocaust). Moreover, legalistic definitions minimize the oppressive nature and intent of bias-motivated attacks.

Thus, chapter 1 will begin with the critical consideration of legalistic and sociological definitions of hate crime. Ultimately, I offer a definition which extends the scope of the term beyond the restrictive notions included in most state legislation. Inspired by Mark Hamm's (1994a, 1994b) discussions of "domestic terrorism" and David Theo Goldberg's (1990) discussion of "racist expressions," I construct a definition of hate crime that brings us closer to understanding the motives and impact of such hate-motivated violence. Thus, my working definition of hate crime is

> a mechanism of power intended to sustain somewhat precarious
> hierarchies, through violence and threats of violence (verbal or
> physical). It is generally directed toward those whom our society
> has traditionally stigmatized and marginalized.

From this perspective, hate crime is seen as an instrument that defends the gendered and racialized social ordering of American culture.

Chapter 1 is also concerned with the measurement of hate crime. How prevalent is this phenomenon? What are the characteristics of the victims and offenders? Unfortunately, the paucity of government data makes it difficult to answer these questions. It was not until 1990 that federal legislation mandated that states collect data on hate crime. The validity of these data, moreover, is weakened by jurisdictional inconsistencies in defining and recording hate crime.

Fortunately, there are a number of other sources of statistics on bias-motivated attacks. For example, the Anti-Defamation League and the National Gay and Lesbian Task Force provide rich data on anti-Semitic and homophobic violence respectively. And there is a small body of social science literature that enriches our knowledge of the victims and perpetrators of hate crime (for example, Hamm, 1994b; Levin and McDevitt, 1993). Taken together, these diverse sources allow us loosely to categorize the characteristics of both groups. It is these details that provide the empirical basis for the theoretical account which is to follow.

In the second chapter, I examine the inability of traditional criminological theory to account for hate crime as a cultural phenomenon. The emphasis is on strain theory, in particular, since it emerges implicitly in many discussions of hate crime where reference is made to rising rates of unemployment, job competition, and so on. However, as I argue, hate crime is not restricted to perpetrators who might be said to be experiencing "strain." On the contrary, hate crime is also perpetrated by those in relatively comfortable positions of strength (such as Ivy League students or police officers). Additionally, I examine the weaknesses of control theories, labeling theories, and contemporary critical criminological theories (perhaps the greatest disappointment). Wherever possible, I evaluate the utility of these theories through extant examples of work done within each tradition (for example, Hamm, 1994b; Levin and McDevitt, 1993).

In response to the noted limitations in theorizing hate crime, chapter 2 also offers an elaboration of Messerschmidt's work on structured action theory. Contrary to traditional role theorists, Messerschmidt argues that gender—whether masculine or feminine—is not a static category. It is not a given, natural property or master status which defines our identities once and for all. Gender is in fact an accomplishment: it is created through conscious, reflective pursuit and must be established and reestablished under varied situations. That is, gender is an activity concerned with "managing situated conduct" according to society's normative expectations of what constitutes essential maleness and femaleness (West and Zimmerman, 1987: 127). Moreover, the practice of gender occurs within the constraints of overlapping and competing structures, which are simultaneously conditioned by that practice. In particular, the structures of labor, power, sexuality, and culture all have significant implications for the process of doing gender.

Whereas Messerschmidt's emphasis is on doing gender (especially masculinity), I will extend it to include a discussion of hate-motivated violence in general, as a resource not only for doing gender, but race as well, following Candace West and Sarah Fenstermaker's recent exhortation to consider not just how we "do gender," but also race and class. It is from their work that I derive the more general term "doing difference."

Chapter 3 makes the argument that racially motivated violence is a mechanism that perpetuates the marginalization of racial and ethnic minorities. Clearly, this exercise of power has a diverse history, stretching from Native American ethnocide, to the forced importation of African slaves, to lynching of "freed" blacks, to the urban street violence of today. Depressingly little has changed since John Dollard observed in the 1930s that "white people fear Negroes. They fear them, of course, in a special context, that is, when the Negro attempts to claim any of the white prerogatives or gains. . . . By a series of hostile acts and social limitations the white caste maintains a continuous threatening atmosphere against the possibility of . . . demands by Negroes; when successful, the effect is to keep the social order intact" (Dollard, 1937: 316–317).

Violence against the racialized Other has long been part of the repertoire by which whites have reinforced their position of social and political superiority. bell hooks reminds us frequently of how—through word and deed—white people in the United States operationalize the ideology of white supremacy on a daily basis. Hate crime becomes a way to assert whiteness as a sign of privilege.

Correspondingly, hate crime is also a way in which people of color and other ethnic or religious minorities are reminded of "their place." Should they step—geographically or politically—outside the carefully established boundaries of permissible behavior, nonwhites are frequently confronted with a not-so-friendly reminder of their subordinate status. Whether in the form of a swastika on the door or a brutal beating, the message is the same: Conform to the standards set by the white majority, or risk its wrath.

In chapter 4, I argue that just as racialized violence is a practice of oppression vis-à-vis people of color, so too is gender-motivated violence a mechanism that perpetuates the marginalization of women, and gay men and lesbians. Moreover, gender-motivated hate crime also provides a very useful resource for doing gender, especially for accomplishing hegemonic masculinity. As an activity, it is tailor-made for this construction of masculinity, since it allows the visible demonstration of the most salient features of manliness: aggression, domination, and heterosexuality. "Uppity women" and gay men and lesbians undermine the hard-fought battles to define gender in essentialist terms. Thus, violence against women and homosexuals allows perpetrators to reaffirm their own aggressive heterosexuality in opposition to these nonconformist threats. Moreover, it becomes a very powerful means by which to forcefully remind "gender traitors" of their proper positionality in the gender hieararchy.

I argue in chapter 5 that our obsession with black-white and male-female conflicts has blinded us to other intergroup dynamics that might also play themselves out through hate-motivated violence. To the extent that hate crime involves the relational construction of identities, it should come as no surprise that it also has played a role in shaping the relationships between blacks and Jews, and blacks and Hispanics, for example. Consequently, this chapter explores the dynamics of violence among and between subordinated communities. I argue that such crimes are played out in the context of white domination, but nonetheless take on unique characteristics as groups seek to gain relative position and status.

Chapter 6 takes a look at entities that play a significant role in providing an environment in which hate crime is able to flourish: groups explicitly organized around principles of white supremacist, heterosexist patriarchal culture (to paraphrase bell hooks). While hate groups such as the Ku Klux Klan or White Aryan Resistance are directly responsible for only a small proportion of hate crime, they nonetheless provide an ideological framework within which perpetrators can legitimize their behavior. Thus I will examine both the activities and ideals of hate groups generally, in order to gain insight into the rhetoric that feeds hatred and violence concurrently.

The state also contributes to the legitimacy and the environment of hate and bias that underlies hate crime. Included in chapter 8 will be an examination of the extant rhetoric, policies, and statutes that facilitate violence against minority groups (such as sodomy legislation, the absence of hate crimes legislation, and so on), as well as practices within the state that could themselves be characterized as hate crimes (such as police brutalization of minority victims).

Hegemony implies its own potential demise, since any hegemonic formation is subject to strain, resistance, and transformation. It is a process of struggle. Such is the case with the contemporary tensions within the gender and racial hierarchies addressed herein. Thus, in the concluding chapter I will consider the limited efficacy of institutional and policy-oriented means of challenging hate crime. I also assess the utility of education and publicity, leading to enhanced tolerance, as solutions. While all of these responses are valuable and perhaps useful in the short term, they lack the transformative capacity that would release women and men, of all races and sexual orientations, from their subordination. Given that hate crime is so intimately connected to strongly entrenched gender and race hierarchies, it is painfully obvious that these phenomena must be resolved in tandem. While this might include education and institutional initiatives, it must also involve deeper structural changes which are intended to break down the hierarchical and dichotomous structures of race and gender. I argue in the conclusion that self-conscious social movements and coalitions will be the most effective instruments for long-term change.

ONE   Defining and Measuring Hate Crime

Such hate crimes, committed solely because the victims have a different skin color or a different faith or are gays or lesbians, leave deep scars not only on the victims but on our larger community. . . . They are acts of violence against America itself. And even a small number of Americans who harbor and act upon hatred and intolerance can do enormous damage to our efforts to bind together our increasingly diverse society into one nation realizing its full promise.

—President Bill Clinton, Radio Address, 1997

In 1990, then president George Bush signed into law the federal Hate Crime Statistics Act (HCSA), which mandated that the attorney general's office collect data on hate crime motivated by the victim's race, religion, ethnicity, or sexual orientation. This measure amounted to the public admission that this was not the "kinder, gentler nation" the president declared he sought. In fact, Bush signed the bill in the midst of an apparent upsurge of ethnoviolence.

As is typical of governmental decrees, the HCSA provides a narrow legalistic definition of hate crime:

> . . . crimes that manifest evidence of prejudice based on race, religion, sexual orientation or ethnicity.

For the most part, states that subsequently (or previously) introduced hate crime legislation have followed suit, adopting a similar definitional style. What differs across the nation is the breadth of protected classes. Minnesota, for example, records hate crime motivated by the victim's race, religion, national origin, sex, age, disability, and sexual orientation. In New Jersey, criminal violations of persons or property are designated as hate crimes where the victim's race, color, creed, ethnicity, or religion was a motivating factor. Oregon hate crime protections are extended to victims violated because of "perceived race, color, religion, national origin, sexual orientation, marital status, political affiliation or beliefs, membership or activity in or on behalf of a labor organization or against a labor organization, physical or mental handicap, age, economic or social status or citizenship of the victim." There is considerable variation in the victim populations addressed by state hate crime statutes. The common categories are reduced to race, religion, and ethnicity. Sexual orientation and gender, for example, appear in only a handful of statutes, as does country of origin (see Appendix I).

What these otherwise diverse statutes do share is an emphasis on the legal definition of "crime." That is, the term *hate crime* assumes the commission of a criminal offense, a violation of an existing criminal code. The hate crime designation may be applied only where a "predicate offense," or underlying crime, is committed as a result of bias or prejudice. While such a narrow restriction may be deemed necessary within the law enforcement community, it is not particularly satisfying from a sociological point of view. What of equally intimidating or injurious acts—motivated by prejudice—which are nonetheless legal according to state statutes? What of the gay man in Colorado who is legally denied an apartment or job because of his sexual orientation? This is legal, but arguably still a violation of his basic human rights. The HCSA, for example, explicitly upholds the legitimacy of acts of discrimination against gay men and lesbians (thanks to Jesse Helms). Section b(2) reads that ". . . nothing in this section creates a cause of action or a right to bring action, including an action based on discrimination due to sexual orientation." Or what of the nineteenth-century Native Americans, forced off the land, raped and murdered in their villages? Again, in many cases perfectly legal, but also heinous violations that were in fact part of the semiofficial program of westward expansion.

Therein lies the dilemma of defining hate crime. As with "crime" in general, it is difficult to construct an exhaustive definition of the term. Crime—hate crime included—is relative. It is historically and culturally contingent. As the above examples suggest, what we take as hate crime today in the United States, in another time, in another place, may be standard operating procedure. Ray Michalowski, for example, reminds us that it is a myth that "there exists some universally consistent definition of theft and violence as criminal acts"(1985: 15). On the contrary, both as a category and as a social phenomenon in and of itself, hate crime "is dynamic and in a state of constant movement and change, rather than static and fixed" (Bowling, 1993: 238).

Benjamin Bowling's (1993) comments suggest yet another important consideration in defining crime. That is, crime is best understood as a process rather than an event. It does not occur in a cultural or social vacuum, nor is it "over" when the perpetrator moves on. For this reason, we must define hate crime in such a way as to give the term "life" and meaning, in other words, as a socially situated, dynamic process involving context and actors, structure and agency. Bowling continues, presenting a comprehensive catalog of the elements to be taken into account when attempting to delineate hate crime:

> Conceiving of racial violence . . . as processes implies an analysis which is dynamic, includes the social relationships between all the actors involved in the process; can capture the continuity across physical violence, threat, intimidation; can capture the dynamic of repeated or systematic victimization; incorporates historical context; and takes account of the social relationships which inform definitions of appropriate and inappropriate behavior. (Bowling, 1993: 238)

While this is a heavy order for any single definition to fill, it is nonetheless possible to construct a conceptual definition that allows us to account for the predominant concerns raised by Bowling: historical and social context, relationships between actors, and relationships between communities. Seen in this context, it is apparent that our understanding of hate crime is furthered by a definition which recognizes the ways in which this particular category of violence facilitates the relative construction of identities, within a framework of specific relations of power. This allows us to acknowledge that bias-motivated violence is not "abnormal" or "anomalous" in the United States, but is rather a natural extension of the racism, sexism, and homophobia that normally allocates privilege along racial and gender lines. As expressions of hate, such acts of intimidation necessarily "involve the assertion of selves over others constituted as Other," where the self is thought to constitute the norm (Goldberg, 1995: 270).

A bare handful of social scientists point the way in efforts to construct culturally meaningful definitions of hate crime, which recognize its role in the "politics of difference." Leslie Wolfe and Lois Copeland contend that hate crime is

> violence directed toward groups of people who generally are not valued by the majority society, who suffer discrimination in other arenas, and who do not have full access to remedy social, political and economic injustice. (Wolfe and Copeland, 1994: 201)

This definition is useful in that it acknowledges that the predominant victims of hate crime are those already marginalized in other ways. Yet it fails to give a sense of how hate crime itself contributes to this marginalization. Carole Sheffield's definition is thus more fully developed:

> Hate violence is motivated by social and political factors and is bolstered by belief systems which (attempt to) legitimate such violence. . . . It reveals that the personal is political; that such violence is *not* a series of isolated incidents but rather the conse-

quence of a political culture which allocates rights, privileges and prestige according to biological or social characteristics.
(Sheffield, 1995: 438)

Sheffield explicitly addresses the importance of the political and social context that conditions hate crime, and, moreover, she highlights the significance of entrenched hierarchies of identity as precursors to hate violence. What is still missing here is a sense of the effect of hate crime on the actors—victim, perpetrator, and their respective communities.

Consequently, the preferred definition can begin with the principles identified by Wolfe and Copeland and Sheffield, yet extend them to account for the role of hate crime in coconstructing the relative identities and subject positions of both the victim and the offender, individually and collectively. Hate crime, then, involves acts of violence and intimidation, usually directed toward already stigmatized and marginalized groups. As such, it is a mechanism of power and oppression, intended to reaffirm the precarious hierarchies that characterize a given social order. It attempts to re-create simultaneously the threatened (real or imagined) hegemony of the perpetrator's group and the "appropriate" subordinate identity of the victim's group. It is a means of marking both the Self and the Other in such a way as to reestablish their "proper" relative positions, as given and repro-duced by broader ideologies and patterns of social and political inequality.

According to this definition, hate crime is a crime like no other. Its dynamics both constitute and are constitutive of actors beyond the immediate victims and offenders. It is implicated not merely in the rela-tionship between the direct "participants," but also in the relationship between the different communities to which they belong. The damage involved goes far beyond physical or financial damages. It reaches into the community to create fear, hostility, and suspicion. Consequently, the intent of ethnoviolence is not only to subordinate the victim, but also to subdue his or her community, to intimidate a group of people who "hold in common a single difference from the defined norm—religion, race, gender, sexual identity" (Pharr, cited in Wolfe and Copeland, 1994: 203).

Oftentimes, the specific victim is almost immaterial. The victims are interchangeable. Unlike actuarial or instrumental crimes, hate crimes are symbolic acts aimed at the people "watching" (Berk, Boyd, and Hamner, 1992). The target audience is not so much the victim as it is others like him or her. Richard Wright's words come easily to mind in this context: "The things that influenced my conduct as a Negro did not have to happen to me directly. I needed but to hear of them to feel their full effects in the deepest layers of my consciousness" (Wright, 1945: 21).

The intent of this book is to explore at length the role of hate crime in "influencing the conduct" of victims, offenders, and their correspon-ding communities. However, before I can accomplish this, it is necessary to establish the field. Specifically, I turn now to a consideration of how

we know what we know about hate crime. That is, I turn to a consideration of the limited sources of data which create for us some picture of
the empirical attributes of bias-motivated violence.

MEASURING HATE CRIME

There are few endeavors so frustrating as those intended to estimate the
extent of hate crime. While both academic and media reports make the
claim that ethnoviolence represents a "rising tide," the truth is we don't
know whether in fact this is the case. For the most part, existing method-
ologies are both too new and too badly flawed to give us an accurate picture of changes over time. As the introduction suggested, what we now
know as "hate crime" is not a new phenomenon. Violence motivated by
negative interpretations of difference and the demonization of the
Other is an age-old practice. The question of its increase or decrease is
less important than the basic fact that it exists, and as such, continues to
underline the continuity of intercultural tensions and hostilities. We
look at the data, then, not so much as a quantitative indicator of the magnitude of the problem, as of the contours of the problem. That is, the
data on hate crime can provide us with a glimpse into the patterns of
offending and victimization, and the dynamics of this brand of violence.

HATE CRIME STATISTICS ACT

With the passage of the Hate Crime Statistics Act (HCSA) in 1990, the federal government appeared to have committed itself to the task of collecting
"accurate" information on hate crime nationwide. The act mandated that
the "Attorney General shall acquire data, for the calendar year 1990 and
each of the successive four calendar years, about crimes that manifest evidence of prejudice based on race, religion, sexual orientation or ethnicity,
including where appropriate the crimes of murder, non-negligent
manslaughter, forcible rape, aggravated assault, simple assault, intimidation, arson, and destruction, damage or vandalism of property" (HCSA,
S(b)(1)). The data collected by individual law enforcement agencies would
be rolled into the Federal Bureau of Investigation's (FBI) Uniform Crime
Report (UCR). In 1994, two events occurred which resulted in the extension of the HCSA mandate. The Violent Crime and Law Enforcement Act
included an amendment to the HCSA, effectively adding crimes motivated
by bias against disability; and when the HCSA expired at the end of that
year, FBI Director Louis Freeh ordered that hate crime data collection continue. This was reaffirmed by the 1996 Church Arson Prevention Act which
eliminated the original statute's sunset clause, thereby making hate crime
data collection a permanent element of the UCR.

The limits of the federal government's commitment to hate crime
data collection are immediately apparent in S(b)(1) itself. Efforts are
constrained by the narrow definition of both the protected groups and

the enumerated offenses. Only five grounds for motivation and eight offenses are to be counted in the UCR. This leaves a lot of ground uncovered. Other criminal offenses and equally injurious noncriminal offenses are left uncounted. Similarly, victimization on the basis of gender, or political orientation, for example, are excluded. Moreover, this brings to mind the problem of inconsistency among reporting agencies. Not all states recognize the same categories of bias in their legislation. Some states do not include gender in their hate crime legislation, some don't include sexual orientation, yet others include such anomalous categories as "whistle blowers." These discrepancies have obvious implications for the abilities of law enforcement agencies to collect and record what is seen by the UCR as relevant data. Add to this the disparities in police training in the identification of hate crime, and the frequent resistance to recognizing the phenomenon, and you have a recipe for imprecision (Bureau of Justice Assistance, 1997).

Because the hate crime data are collected in the same way as the other UCR data, they are fraught with the same deficiencies. In addition to the limitations imposed by law enforcement agencies are those presented by trends in public underreporting. In fact, some argue that hate crimes are even more dramatically underreported than other UCR offences (Berrill, 1992; Weiss, 1993). Gay victims, for example, may fear that the admission of their victimization is concomitantly an admission of their sexual orientation. Reporting an anti-gay crime to the police is tantamount to "outing" themselves—an event for which they may not be prepared. Similarly, the undocumented foreign laborer may fear the repercussions of his or her status being revealed. Moreover, victims may well fear secondary victimization at the hands of law enforcement officials. At the very least, they may perceive that police will not take their victimization seriously. And perhaps they would be correct on both counts. It is not unheard of for police to further berate stigmatized victims—gay men and lesbians, female and male victims of domestic violence, people of color. The case of Abner Louima, the Haitian immigrant sodomized by New York City police officers, attests to the extremes to which officers have been willing to go in an effort to (re)assert dominance.

Louima's case highlights another reason why hate crime may go unreported: distrust of law enforcement agencies, either on the basis of experiences within the United States, or for immigrants, in their country of origin. Given the hostile relationships between state authorities and minority communities, it is not surprising that victims of ethnoviolence are skeptical about the willingness of police officers to respond to their victimization. Similarly, the black South African immigrant whose early experience with state authority might have included nighttime "visits" and "disappearances" is unlikely to welcome any interaction with police in this country.

TABLE 1 Sample Comparisons of Uniform Crime Report Hate Crime Data to Those Collected by Antiviolence Organizations, 1992–1998

| | ANTI-ASIAN | | ANTI-SEMITIC | | ANTI-GAY | |
	UCR	NAPALC	UCR	ADL	UCR	NGLTF/AVP*
1992	217	NA	1,017	1,730	250	2,102
1993	258	335	1,143	1,867	832	2,136
1994	211	452	915	2,066	671	2,064
1995	355	458	1,058	1,843	984	2,212
1996	355	534	1,109	1,722	1,001	NA
1997	347	347	1,087	1,571	990	2,245
1998	359	295	1,145	1,611	1,426	2,552

Sources: Anti-Defamation League, 1993; 1994; 1995; 1996; 1997; 1998; 1999. Antiviolence Project, 1998, 1999. Federal Bureau of Investigation, 1993; 1994; 1995; 1996; 1997; 1998; 1999. National Asian Pacific American Legal Consortium, 1996; 1999. National Gay and Lesbian Task Force, 1993; 1994; 1995; 1996; 1997.

* In 1995, the NGLTF ceased to distribute data on anti-gay violence. The task was assumed by the Antiviolence Project in 1997.

A significant qualitative shortcoming of the UCR is that it provides little more than numbers. How many incidents? How many assaults? How many offenders? How many Asian victims? It tells us nothing of the process involved. What motivated the offender? What is the relationship between the victims' and offenders' communities? What emotions prevailed? What words were exchanged? For these crucial subjective elements, we must look elsewhere.

That the UCR data underrepresent the magnitude of hate crime is evident from the discrepancies between the report and the numbers published by antiviolence organizations. Table 1 provides a glimpse into representative cases. For all three categories of bias motivated violence, the number of incidents recorded in the UCR is far below those reported to the specific agencies. This disparity is especially evident in the comparison between the UCR and the National Gay and Lesbian Task Force (NGLTF) Antiviolence Project (AVP) data, which represents only nine cities across the country. In 1992, for example, the UCR recorded little more than one-tenth of the incidents recorded by the NGLTF; the data converged only slightly by 1994, when the UCR recorded nearly one-third as many incidents as the NGLTF. It is apparent, then, that the aforementioned limitations restrict the accuracy of the UCR.

In spite of these limitations, the UCRs are of some use. They represent the most comprehensive data base in the country in terms of geographical coverage, and in terms of the motivations they reflect. While inaccurate in absolute numbers, the data nonetheless may be useful as a source of information on general trends and patterns.

Table 2 provides a summary of UCR data from 1991 to 1996. The

TABLE 2   Hate Crime by Bias Motivation, 1991–1998

	1991	1992	1993	1994	1995	1996	1997	1998
Race	**2,963/62.3%**	**4,,025/60.8%**	**4,732/62.4%**	**3,545/59.8%**	**4831/60.8%**	**5,396/61.6%**	**5,898/59.9%**	**5,360/58.3%**
Anti-White	888/18.7%	1,342/20.3%	1,471/31.1%	1,010/17.0%	1,226/15.4%	1,106/12.6%	1,267 /12.9%	989/10.8%
Anti-Black	1,689/35.5%	2,296/34.7%	2,815/59.5%	2,174/36.6%	2,988/37.6%	3,674/41.9%	3,838/39%	3,573/38.9%
Anti-American Indian	11/0.2%	26/0.4%	27/0.5%	22/0.4%	41/0.5%	51/0.6%	44/0.4%	66/0.7%
Anti-Asian/Pacific Islander	287/6.0%	217/3.3%	258/5.4%	211/3.6%	355/4.5%	355/4.1%	437/4.4%	359/3.9%
Anti-Multiracial Group	88/1.9%	144/2.2%	161/3.5%	128/2.2%	221/2.8%	210/2.4%	312/3.2%	373/4.1%
Ethnicity	**450/9.5%**	**669/10.1%**	**697/9.2%**	**638/10.8%**	**814/10.2%**	**940/10.7%**	**1,083/11%**	**919/10.0%**
Anti-Hispanic	242/5.1%	369/5.6%	472/6.2%	337/5.7%	516/6.5%	564/6.4%	636/6.5%	595/6.5%
Anti-Other Ethnicity	208/4.4%	300/4.5%	225/3.0%	301/5.1%	298/3.7%	376/4.3%	447/4.5%	324/3.5%
Religion	**917/19.3%**	**1,162/17.5%**	**1,298/17.1%**	**1,062/18.0%**	**1,277/16.1%**	**1,401/16.0%**	**1,483/15.1%**	**1,475/16.0%**
Anti-Jewish	792/16.7%	1,017/15.4%	1,143/15.1%	915/15.4%	1,058/13.3%	1,109/12.7%	1,159/11.8%	1,145/12.5%
Anti-Catholic	23/0.5%	18/0.3%	32/0.4%	17/0.3%	31/0.4%	35/0.4%	32/0.3%	62/0.7%

continued on the next page

Table 2: Hate Crime by Bias Motivation, 1991-1998, continued from previous page

	1991	1992	1993	1994	1995	1996	1997	1998
Anti-Protestant	26/0.5%	28/0.4%	30/0.4%	29/0.5%	36/0.5%	75/0.9%	59/0.6%	61/0.7%
Anti-Islamic	10/0.2%	15/0.2%	13/0.2%	17/0.3%	29/0.4%	27/0.3%	31/0.3%	22/0.2%
Anti-Other Religion	51/1.0%	69/1.0%	63/0.8%	67/1.1%	102/1.2%	129/1.5%	173/1.8%	138/1.5%
Anti-Multireligious Group	11/0.2%	14/0.3%	14/0.3%	14/0.2%	20/0.3%	24/0.3%	26/0.3%	45/0.5%
Anti-Atheist/Agnostic	4/0.1%	1/ 0.0%	3/0.1%	3/0.1%	1/0.0%	2/0.0%	3/0.0%	2/0.0%
Sexual Orientation	**425/8.9%**	**767/11.6%**	**860/11.3%**	**685/11.5%**	**1,019/12.8%**	**1,016/11.6%**	**1,375/14%**	**1,439/15.7%**
Anti-Homosexual	421/8.9%	750/11.3 %	830/10.9%	664/11.2%	984/12.4 %	991/11.3%	1,351/ 13.7%	1,407/15.3%
Male	NA	557/8.4%	516/8.1%	501/8.4%	735/9.2%	757/8.6%	912/9.3%	972/10.6%
Female	NA	93/1.4%	121/1.6%	100/1.7%	146/1.8%	150/1.7%	229/2.3%	265/2.9%
Anti-Heterosexual	3/0.1%	14/0.2%	28/0.4%	14/0.2%	17/0.2%	15/0.2%	14/0.1%	13/0.1%
Anti-Bisexual	1/0.0%	3/0.1%	2/0.1%	7/0.1%	18/0.2%	10/0.1%	10/0.1%	19/0.2%
Total	**4,755**	**6,623**	**7,587**	**5,932**	**7,947**	**8,759**	**9,839**	**9,193**

Sources: Federal Bureau of Investigation, 1992; 1993; 1994; 1995; 1996; 1997; 1998; 1999.

data seem to confirm a number of trends that anecdotal evidence has long suggested:

1) The most frequent motivation consistently is race. Racial bias typically accounts for nearly two-thirds of all incidents; when ethnicity is included, the proportion rises to over 70 percent.

2) African Americans are the most likely victims of racially motivated violence. While making up less than 15 percent of the population, they represent approximately one-third of the victims of ethnoviolence.

3) Jews are the second most frequently victimized cultural group, representing the vast majority of religious bias victims and well over 10 percent of all victims.

4) Gay men, and to a much lesser extent lesbians, are also frequent victims of hate crime. The cumulative data also suggest that their "share" of the victimization increased rapidly over the 1990s.

Turning to table 3, we get a sense of the other side of the equation, that is, characteristics of the suspected offenders. As one might expect, white offenders are in the majority. However, we must take these data with a grain of salt, since such a large proportion of offenders are typically unknown.

Table 4 reveals a number of trends associated specifically with racially and ethnically motivated violence. Most intriguing here are the disparities between crimes against the person and crimes against property. It is apparent that hate crime—relative to "normal" street crime—is much more likely to involve physical threat and harm to individuals, rather than property. This table also reveals the impact of changes in reporting on the data. In 1991—the first year for which data were available—only 2,771 agencies reported; by 1996, over 10,000 were participating, with a corresponding leap in the number of total incidents reported.

Finally, a word about the geographic distribution of reported hate crime (see Appendix II). California, New York, New Jersey, and Massachusetts tend to be "leaders" in terms of the number of hate crimes reported. However, this may reflect to some extent differences in recording practices. At least with respect to California, New York, and Massachusetts, these states have also been leaders in establishing bias crime units, and in training officers to identify hate crime effectively.

Overall, the UCR provides a starting point for any discussion of hate crime. However, we are well advised to supplement this information with that available from the growing number of non-governmental bodies devoted to tracking and responding to hate crime. Generally, these agencies tend to gather information specific to one target group—the Anti-Defamation League (ADL) on anti-Semitism, or the NGLTF on anti-gay violence for example. Again, we must recognize that each of these bodies brings with it unique strengths and weaknesses.

TABLE 3 Racially/Ethnically Motivated Violence by Suspected Offender's Race, 1991–1998

	1991	1992	1993	1994	1995	1996	1997	1998
White	1,679	2,612	2,813	2,939	3,361	4,892	NA	2,988
Black	769	1,381	1,312	1,139	1,209	1,258	NA	759
American Indian	12	14	30	32	40	50	NA	55
Asian/Pacific Islander	47	36	53	51	97	106	NA	61
Multiracial	77	98	133	135	98	177	NA	164
Other/Unknown	1,974	1,773	3,246	2,966	2,377	2,211	NA	2,252

Sources: Federal Bureau of Investigation, 1992; 1993; 1994; 1995; 1996; 1997; 1998; 1999.

TABLE 4 General Trends in Racially/Ethnically Motivated Violence

	1991	1992	1993	1994	1995	1996	1997	1998
Participating Agencies	2,771	6,181	6,551	7,356	9,584	11,355	11,211	10,730
Total Incidents	4,558	6,623	7,587	5,932	7,947	8,734	8,049	7,755
Incidents Motivated by Race/Ethnicity								
# Incidents	3,413	4,694	4,732	3,545	5,645	5,396	5,898	5,075
# Offenses	NA	5,914	5,786	4,431	7,192	6,767	9,861	9,235
# Victims	NA	6,078	6,011	4,540	7,482	6,994	10,255	9,722
# Known Offenders	NA	6,939	6,258	4,356	6,709	6,122	8,474	7,489
# Crimes Against Person	3,321	4,695	4,415	3,382	5,539	4,953	6,873	6,305
# Crimes Against Property	1,434	1,219	1,371	1,049	1,639	1,814	2,973	2,905
Racial/Ethnic Bias Motivation								
Anti-White	888	1,342	1,471	1,010	1,226	1,106	1,267	989
Anti-Black	1,689	2,296	2,815	2,174	2,988	3,674	3,838	3,573
Anti-American Indian/Alaskan Native	11	26	27	22	41	51	44	66
Anti-Asian/ Pacific Islander	287	217	258	211	355	355	437	359
Anti-Hispanic	242	369	472	337	516	564	636	595
Anti-Multiracial Group	88	144	161	128	221	210	312	373
Anti-Other Ethnicity	208	300	225	301	298	376	447	324

Sources: Federal Bureau of Investigation, 1992; 1993; 1994; 1995; 1996; 1997; 1998; 1999.

Perhaps the most firmly entrenched antiviolence project is the Anti-Defamation League of B'Nai B'Rith. Since 1979, the ADL has been generating annual audits of anti-Semitic violence, not only in the United States but worldwide. The purpose of these audits is well expressed in the Audit of Anti-Semitic Incidents, 1994: "to provide the community and its elected and law enforcement officials with an accurate and reliable measure of overt anti-Semitic activity, and thus a basis for response, evaluation and counteraction regarding a troubling and dangerous problem" (ADL, 1995: 18). The mandate of the ADL goes much further than that of the FBI's UCR program. ADL includes among its data "incidents" that may not fit the traditional definition of crime. Rather, "in developing criteria for evaluating these incidents, ADL has tried to be professional but not coldly bureaucratic, dispassionate without being aloof from the painful realities and emotional trauma behind the statistics" (ADL, 1995: 18). To this end, the ADL tracks murder, assaults, and arsons to be sure, but this is supplemented with attention paid to harassment, petty and serious vandalism, anti-Semitic slurs, and the distribution of neo-Nazi literature. Consequently, the audits are more comprehensive in scope than those of the UCR.

Another valuable contribution made by the ADL audits is that they provide the context and detail lacking in the UCR. Not only do they "count" ethnoviolence, but they also situate the data by providing summaries of illustrative cases. It is from these synopses that we gain valuable insight into hate crime as a process, specifically as a process which separates "us" from "them." Here we get some sense of the motive and source of the hostility. It is these details which help us to better understand the dynamics of this phenomenon.

Of course, the audits are not without flaws. The determination of what is to be considered anti-Semitic is subjective at best. The ADL (1995) readily acknowledges this as problematic. The organization recognizes the shades of gray involved in anonymous reports, anti-Semitic remarks directed toward non-Jews, or violations of Jewish property (such as synagogues) motivated by greed rather than bias, for example. While efforts are made to corroborate all reports, and while the ADL seeks to remain professional, invariably some incidents are included erroneously in the audits. More problematic are the means by which the ADL gathers its data. The audits are based on a combination of data from law enforcement agencies, and reports or complaints filed directly with the ADL. Since both types of reports are voluntarily made by victims, it is clear that the ADL also undercounts the extent of anti-Semitic violence.

Looking at table 5, one especially disturbing fact leaps immediately to the fore: since 1991, anti-Semitic violence has been increasingly more likely to involve personal rather than property crimes. Historically, this

TABLE 5   Anti-Semitic Violence by Selected Offense Type, 1990–1998

	1990	1991	1992	1993	1994	1995	1996	1997	1998
ADL Data									
Harassment, threats, assaults	758	950	874	1,079	1,197	1,116	941	898	715
Vandalism	927	929	856	788	869	727	781	673	896
Total	**1,685**	**1,879**	**1,730**	**1,867**	**2,066**	**1,843**	**1,722**	**1,571**	**1,611**
Campus anti-Semitic incidents	95	101	114	122	143	NA	NA	NA	NA
FBI (UCR) Data	**NA**	792	1,017	1,143	915	1,058	1,109	1,159	1,145

Sources: Anti-Defamation League, 1991; 1992; 1993; 1994; 1995; 1996; 1997; 1998; 1999. Federal Bureau of Investigation, 1992; 1993; 1994; 1995; 1996; 1997; 1998; 1999.

has been a group victimized by crimes against property, such as synagogue or cemetery desecrations. However, the tide has turned in recent years. Additionally, the decline in the number of anti-Semitic incidents beginning in 1995 has corresponded to an increase in the intensity of the violence associated with the incidents. In 1995, for example, an arson in New York City resulted in several deaths. In November of that year, the FBI fortunately foiled an attempt by the TriState Militia to bomb several ADL offices.

Another disturbing trend is the growth in campus incidents of anti-Semitism. Institutions of higher learning, in particular, have seen an alarming growth in the amount of anti-Semitic violence, vandalism, and leafleting. It is disheartening to imagine this generation of students as the next generation of leaders. They will set the tone for the rhetoric and policies of tolerance or intolerance.

RACIALLY MOTIVATED VIOLENCE

In contrast to the monitoring of anti-Semitic violence, there is no national, coherent audit of racially motivated violence in the United States. The Southern Poverty Law Center's *Intelligence Report* includes "For the Record," a catalog of bias incidents drawn from media sources, public reports, and initial police reports (table 6). However, these are neither verified, consistent, nor exhaustive. The emphasis is on events that involve activities associated with hate groups, although individual acts of violence are considered as well. Moreover, while the majority of incidents concern racially motivated violence, offenses against gays often are included. Thus the primary value of the SPLC date is that it, too, offers brief narratives describing the incidents. Consequently, the reports are qualitative supplements to the UCR data.

There are some regional organizations committed to collecting hate crime data in their area or state. North Carolinians Against Racist and Religious Violence, for example, monitors media sources as a means of tracking hate crime trends. The Northwest Coalition Against Malicious Harassment also monitors and reports bias-motivated activities in its *Northwest Beacon*. Alternatively, some local and national organizations have been involved in survey research oriented around hate crime. The National Institute Against Prejudice and Violence has been at the forefront of these initiatives, publishing reports on workplace and campus ethnoviolence, for example. Indeed, the institute has discovered that violence in both of those settings is much more widespread than was anticipated. More narrowly, the Los Angeles County Office of Education (1995; online) recently released a research report documenting a 53 percent increase in racial hate crime between 1989 and 1992. While valuable to their immediate constituents, such localized data obviously are limited in the extent to which their findings might be generalized.

Two national organizations have emerged in recent years specifically as a response to the perceived increase in anti-Asian violence. Established in 1980, the Arab American Anti-Discrimination Committee (ADC) "publishes information on issues of concern to Arab Americans, and provides educational materials on Arab history and culture, as well

TABLE 6   Estimates of Racially/Ethnically Motivated Violence by Offense Type, 1996–1998

	1996	1997	1998
Murder	0	11	25
Assault	148	107	117
Arson/Conspiracy	31	17	8
Bombing/Conspiracy	3	4	13
Cross Burning	49	23	36
Threat	22	33	34
Harassment	53	55	44
Intimidation	18	23	43
Vandalism	101	125	131
Leafleting	22	59	81
Total	458	457	532

Sources: Data are collated from the Southern Poverty Law Center's *Intelligence Reports* (#85, winter 1997; #86, spring 1997; #87, summer 1997; #88, fall 1997; #89, winter 1998; #90, spring 1998; #91, summer 1998; #92, fall 1998; #93, winter 1999). "For the Record" is prefaced with the caveat that "Incidents of apparent hate crimes and hate group activities listed here are drawn from media sources and initial police reports, not all of which have been verified by the Intelligence Project. Because hate crimes often are not reported, this listing understates the true level of bias incidents."

as the ethnic experiences of Arabs in the United States" (ADC, 1996: I). The latter is best expressed in the Annual Reports on Anti-Arab Racism, which document anti-Arab hate crime, discrimination, and defamation. Like similar reports, they too provide extensive materials, including narratives, which contextualize hate crime. Moreover, the ADC explicitly has expressed its observation that Arab Americans consistently have been targeted with ridicule, even violence, in the aftermath of crises in the Middle East. Most recently, such an increase was readily apparent during and after the Gulf War.

The National Asian Pacific American Legal Consortium (NAPALC) is the other relative newcomer to the monitoring of racial bias. As the NAPALC notes in a recent annual report, its audit is the only "comprehensive, nationwide, non-governmental compilation and analysis of anti-Asian violence in the United States" (1996: 3). The range of its sources of data is broad and varied: telephone and intake sessions, newspaper reports, community-based organizations, churches, human rights commissions, bar associations, and government agencies. Its annual audits are veritable treasure troves of information. They provide summary numbers, synopses of cases, information on legal actions taken by NAPALC, analyses of regional and national trends, and extensive policy recommendations. Again, absolute numbers are inaccurate, but the trends and analyses are informative (table 7). Their data confirm what anecdotal evidence and intuitive observations have suggested: riding the wave of anti-immigrant and anti-Asian sentiment, anti-Asian violence remains a consistent threat. Moreover, table 8 points to an issue I will take up in a later chapter: the relationships between minority groups are increasingly strained. This is evident from the relatively high proportion of hate crime perpetrators and suspects who are of African-American or Hispanic descent.

ANTI-GAY/ANTI-LESBIAN VIOLENCE
Second only to the ADL in consistency of reporting and longevity is the National Gay and Lesbian Task Force (NGLTF). This national organization for gay rights and advocacy has been preparing and issuing annual reports on anti-gay and anti-lesbian violence since 1984. Early reports (1984–1989) reflected data from participating local advocacy and victim witness services across the country. Beginning in 1990, representative cities were selected as the focus for national tracking programs. The cities were selected on the basis of the maturity and professionalization of their victim service agencies. As of 1996, nine cities were included in the national tracking program. Additionally, these national data are frequently supplemented by the inclusion of the findings from local and regional victimization prevalence surveys. In 1996, the NGLTF suspended the collection of data. This task was assumed by the AVP in 1997, using much the same methodology.

TABLE 7   Anti-Asian Violence by Selected Offense Type, 1993–1998

	1993	1994	1995	1996	1997	1998
Total Incidents (NAPALC)	**335**	**452**	**355**	**370**	**144**	**295**
Vandalism	17%	9%	16%	29%	32%	31%
Threats/Intimidation	9%	5%	13%	16%	17%	15%
Police Abuse	7%	4%	3%	NA	NA	NA
Harassment	4%	12%	7%	22%	19%	17%
Assault	28%	26%	28%	33%	31%	32%
FBI (UCR) Data	**258**	**211**	**355**	**355**	**437**	**359**

Sources: National Asian Pacific American Legal Consortium, 1996; 1999. Federal Bureau of Investigation, 1994; 1995; 1996; 1997; 1998; 1999.

TABLE 8   Suspected Perpetrators of Anti-Asian Violence by Race of Offender, 1994–1995

	1994		1995	
	NAPALC	**FBI**	**NAPALC**	**FBI**
White	125	91	125	241
African American	44	36	48	57

Sources: National Asian Pacific American Legal Consortium, 1996; 1999.

Clearly, the NGLTF and AVP reports are not exhaustive. They reflect victimization only in the cities covered by the report. Moreover, the data collected in the included cities are not accurate measures, given the consistent problem of underreporting. Just as few victims report their victimization to police, few report even to the victim advocacy organizations in their area. Similarly, the prevalence studies are limited by their sample populations. Many surveys are distributed through gay and lesbian organizations or publications, which many closeted gays avoid. In addition, those involved in such organizations may be more activist, more visible, and therefore more at risk than might otherwise be the case.

In spite of these limitations, NGLTF is justified in its claim that "the many years of consistent, uniform and continuous collection of data which contribute to the national profile does [sic] provide an accurate reflection of the characteristics of anti-lesbian/gay violence and trends over time" (NGLTF, 1995: ii). Both the national tracking program of the NGLTF and AVP and the many prevalence studies emerging in recent years provide important details about the dynamics and trends associated with anti-gay violence. They provide chilling evidence that such victimization is widespread. Moreover, they represent much-needed data supplementary to the UCR. Looking at the comparison between NGLTF data and UCR data (table 9), the need for this is evident. The discrepancy between the two data sets is staggering. Each year the six or nine cities consistently report more anti-gay violence than the UCR reports for the entire nation. The data from New York City alone nearly outpace the national UCR data.[1]

Together the NGLTF and the many prevalence studies paint a distressing picture of anti-gay violence (Comstock, 1991; Berrill, 1992; see table 10 and table 11). Hate crime perpetrated against gays is extensive. The prevalence surveys, for example, consistently find upward of 60 percent—often as high as 80 or 90 percent of subjects experiencing verbal abuse; physical abuse is as high as 30 percent. Moreover, rates of victimization, and the proportion of all victimizations involving assaultive offenses are dramatically higher than for the general population. In fact, anti-gay violence tends to be the most brutal of all such victimizations (Berrill, 1992; 1993).

MISOGYNISTIC VIOLENCE

On December 6, 1989, Marc Lepine lined up female engineering students against a wall, opened fire and killed fourteen while shouting his intent to "kill the feminists." On April 23, 1990, the U.S. Congress signed into law the Hate Crime Statistics Act mandating the collection of data on crime motivated by prejudice on the basis of race, ethnicity, religion, and sexual orientation. In light of the former, the failure of the latter to include gender is a distressing irony. Perhaps more clearly than any other case, the Lepine murders demonstrate that much violence against women is indistinguishable from other hate crimes. It, too, is intended to intimidate and control a larger class of people—women—not just the victims.[2]

Owing to this exclusion, it is worthless to turn to the UCR, or even the National Crime Victimization Survey (NCVS) for data on ethnoviolence perpetrated against women. Neither addresses domestic violence or family violence; even the measure of rape documented by these reports is distorted by limitations of definition and operationalization. Consequently, the two dominant measures of crime are not very valu-

---

1. One contributing factor here is that not all incidents reported to cooperating agencies fit the UCR profile of the eight index offenses. Additionally, in some jurisdictions, some offenses are not classified as "crime," e.g., harassment.

2. The debate as to whether violence against women constitutes hate crime is taken up more fully in chapter 4.

TABLE 9 Anti-Gay Violence Recorded by the FBI for Six Cities, Compared to That Recorded by the National Gay and Lesbian Task Force, 1990–1998

	1990	1991	1992	1993	1994	1995	1996	1997	1998
National Total (FBI)	NA	421	750	832	671	984	1,001	1,081	1,407
Boston	147	209	238	187	234	173	161*	228	145
Chicago	198	210	252	204	177	82	96	49	NA
Minneapolis/ St. Paul	112	338	311	153	190	218	NA	288**	235
New York City	507	592	662	587	632	625	575	658	616
Portland, OR	NA	NA	NA	99	106	47	NA**	NA	NA
San Francisco	425	473	435	366	324	324	415	402	395
City Totals (NGLTF)	1,389	1,822	1,898	1,596	1,663	1,470	1,247	1,625	1,391

Sources: Antiviolence Project, 1998; 1999. Federal Bureau of Investigation, 1991; 1992; 1993; 1994; 1995; 1996; 1997; 1998; 1999. National Gay and Lesbian Task Force, 1991; 1992; 1993; 1994; 1995; 1996; 1997.

* Beginning in 1996, the AVP collected and reported data for Massachusetts, rather than data only for Boston.

** Beginning in 1997, the AVP collected and reported data for Minnesota, rather than data for only Minneapolis/St. Paul.

*** The AVP ceased to collect and report data on anti-gay violence in Portland, OR.

TABLE 10 Anti-Gay/Lesbian Victimization, 1990–1998

	1990	1991	1992	1993	1994	1995	1996	1997	1998
Boston	147	209	238	187	234	173	161	228	145
Chicago	198	210	252	204	177	82	96	49	NA
Columbus	NA	NA	NA	NA	149	181	186	206	199
Denver	75	89	204	229	156	NA*	NA	NA	31
Detroit	NA	NA	NA	84	96	90	116	120	130
Minneapolis/ St. Paul	112	338	311	240	190	218	NA	288	235
New York City	507	592	662	587	632	625	575	658	616
Portland, OR	NA	NA	NA	99	106	47	NA	NA	NA
San Francisco	425	473	435	366	324	324	415	402	395
Total (NGLTF)	1,464	1,911	2,102	2,136	2,064	1,741	1,549	1,951	1,751

Sources: Antiviolence Project, 1998; 1999. National Gay and Lesbian Task Force, 1991; 1992; 1993; 1994; 1995; 1996; 1997.

* The AVP ceased to collect data for Denver in 1995; in 1998, the Project began collecting and reporting data for Colorado.

TABLE 11 Prevalence Studies of Anti-Gay/Lesbian Victimization

Type of Victimization	A N=234 (M=150; F=84) %	B N=1,363 (M=796; F=561; UNK=6) %	C N=234 (M=113; F=121) %	D N=291 (M=461; F=260) %	E N=721 (M=461; F=260) %	F N=542 (M=314; F=228) %	G N=395 (M=unk; F=UNK) %
Verbal abuse	79	84	91	–	87	–	–
Threats of violence	45	45	–	–	48	37	–
Property damage	22	14	27	16	18	–	–
Targets of objects	–	25	28	21	27	25	–
Followed or chased	38	34	41	32	31	–	13
Spat upon	–	15	12	7	15	–	–
Punched, hit, kicked	24	20	24	18	19	17	9
Weapon assault	9	7	7	7	10	–	–
Victimized by police	–	16	30	–	22	–	–
Sexual assault	–	9	–	8	6	–	5
Victimized in school	–	–	–	–	49	–	–
Familial verbal abuse	–	–	–	–	22	24	–
Familial physical abuse	–	–	–	–	5	8	–
Any familial abuse	–	–	–	–	23	–	–
Fear for safety	–	–	–	–	–	–	–
Expect future harassment	–	–	–	–	–	–	–
Know others victimized	–	–	94	–	–	–	56

NOTE: A=Utah (Aaron, 1991); B=Massachusetts (LeBlanc, 1991); C= 36 states, DC, and Canada (Platt, 1990); D=31 states and the District of Columbia (Comstock, 1989); E=Pennsylvania (Gross, Aurand, & Adessa, 1988; data cited derived through secondary analysis of original report); F=Baltimore, Maryland (Morgen & Grossman, 1988); G=District of Columbia (District of Columbia Lesbian and Gay Anti-Violence Task Force, 1988).

Source: Berrill, 1992.

able resources for documenting hate crime perpetrated against women. More so than is the case for violence motivated by race, ethnicity, or sexual orientation, then, data documenting the dynamics of violence against women must be derived from the many antiviolence projects to have emerged in recent years (Jenness and Broad, 1997). Wolfe and Copeland (1994) note four organizations that explicitly monitor hate crime against women: the Women's Project of Little Rock, the Texas Council on Family Violence, the National Clearinghouse on Marital and Date Rape, and the Clearinghouse on Femicide. Consistently, the data gathered by these and other local agencies reveal that women are not safe on the streets, in their homes, or even among friends and family. Violence and the threat of violence are part of the daily experience of millions of women in the United States.

The diversity and limitations of available data sources make it virtually impossible to accurately estimate the extent of violence against women. Regardless of their origin or nature, data gathering strategies tend to seriously undercount the number of victimizations. Victims of domestic violence or sexual assault, for example, are reluctant to report not only to police, but even to interviewers (Bachman and Saltzman, 1995; Wolfe and Copeland, 1994). Nonetheless, even these limited estimates paint a staggering picture of the extent to which "the risk factor is being female" (Heise, 1989: 6).

While women continue to report violent victimization at two-thirds the rate of men, recent trends indicate a pattern of convergence over the last two decades. That is, as violence against men appears to be decreasing, violence against women is increasing (Craven, 1996; Weisburd and Levin, 1994). Moreover, just as violence against men tends to be committed by other men, so too is violence against women committed by men. In 1991, of every ten killings in which the victims were women, nine were committed by men (Cybergrrl, online; 1996), and those were most likely to be men known to the victim, either intimately or as an acquaintance. In 1992–1993, for example, less than 23 percent of female victims of violent crime reported that the offender was a stranger. In contrast, men were as likely to be victimized by a stranger (49 percent) as by someone they knew (51 percent) (Craven, 1996). On average, women experience eight to ten times more violence at the hands of intimates than do men (see table 12). In 1996, of the approximately 1,800 cases of lethal violence among intimates, three out of four victims were women. Moreover, women's risk of lethal and nonlethal violence is elevated when they attempt to leave an abusive relationship. This is reflected in the findings that up to 50 percent of women who attempt to leave their abusers are followed, harassed, assaulted, sexually assaulted, or murdered by their former partners (Browne, 1995; Browne and Williams, 1993; Tjaden and Thoennes, 1998; Weisburd and Levin, 1994).

TABLE 12   Violent Victimizations Committed by Intimates by Sex of Victim, 1992–1996

	1992	1993	1994	1995	1996
Male #	145,650	163,558	176,168	115,483	147,896
Rate/1,000	1.4	1.6	1.7	1.1	1.4
Female #	952,188	1,072,072	1,003,116	953,683	837,899
Rate/1,000	8.8	9.8	9.1	8.6	7.5

Source: Chaiken, 1998.

The extreme pole on the continuum of violence against women is, of course, homicide—often termed "femicide" or "gynocide" because of the explicitly gendered nature of the violence (Caputi and Russell, 1992; Caputi, 1993). Hundreds of women are murdered yearly, most by men, and most by men they know. Historically, serial killers have tended to target women (Caputi and Russell, 1992).

Nonlethal forms of sexist violence—especially sexual assault—are even more far-reaching in their impact. However, given the levels of underreporting, it is difficult to estimate rates of sexual assault in the United States. This is complicated by the lack of consensus as to what constitutes sexual assault. Historically in this and other Western cultures, rape has been restricted to forced vaginal penetration of a woman by a man who is not her husband. However, this fails to account for the spectrum of sexual violence experienced by women and girls. Consequently, we must attend to the sexual violence constituted by spousal/partner rape, acquaintance rape, "date rape," and stranger rape (rarest of all), as well as forms of nonconsensual sex that do not involve physical force, such as sexual harassment.

A recent report revealed that some 500,000 women report rape and sexual assault annually (Bachman and Saltzman, 1995). Contrary to popular wisdom, less than one-quarter of these are committed by strangers. The largest proportion (50 percent) are committed by friends or acquaintances, and the remaining 25 percent are committed by intimates (Bachman and Saltzman, 1995). The extent to which women are at risk of sexual assault is highlighted in a 1992 report filed by the Congressional Caucus for Women's Issues. Among their findings:

- One in three women will be a victim of rape during her lifetime.
- Every hour, sixteen women confront rapists; every six minutes a woman is raped.
- Over the past decade, the rape rate has risen four times as fast as the total crime rate.
- 60 to 80 percent of rapes are date or acquaintance rape.

- One in seven college women will be raped before they graduate, and 90 percent will know their attacker.
- An estimated one in seven married women will be raped by their husbands (see also Center for Women Policy Studies, 1991).

As the final statistic suggests, gender violence within the home is pervasive. Moreover, women are by far the most frequent victims, and men the most frequent perpetrators of domestic violence. Like other gender-motivated violence, that which occurs in the home and within intimate heterosexual relationships comprises the full spectrum from ongoing verbal disparagement, to harming pets, to rape, to homicide. Battering is, in fact, the leading cause of injury to women, far outstripping accidents, muggings, and rape (Cybergrrl, online; 1996). In any given year, approximately four million women will be battered by their male intimates (Women and Violence, 1990). In introducing the Violence Against Women Act in 1993, Senator Joseph Biden informed his colleagues that 21,000 women weekly report to police that they have been beaten in their homes (Biden, 1993). The data on domestic violence are staggering; they reveal a scenario in which millions of women live in fear of abuse, harassment, sexual assault, even homicide within their homes. Moreover, as noted earlier, the risk of such violence increases rather than decreases when they attempt to leave that situation.

Sexual harassment of women is also prevalent in the workplace. However, the historical lack of legal recourse and public recognition of the problem have served to render sexual harassment invisible. It is only with the highly publicized cases of Tailhook, Clarence Thomas, and President Bill Clinton that it has been put on the public agenda. Consequently, like other forms of gender violence, there is a remarkable discrepancy between the number of occurrences and the number of reported cases (Gratch, 1995). Moreover, sexual harassment occurs most frequently where women are in nontraditional—that is, "masculine"—occupations such as policing or the military (Gratch, 1995; Martin and Jurik, 1996). A recent study of federal employees reveals that reports of sexual harassment have increased dramatically since 1980, so that in 1994 approximately 15 to 30 percent of federal employees (depending on the agency) reported that they had experienced sexual harassment on the job (U.S. Merit Systems Protection Board, 1995). The vast majority of victims were women. The same report cited comparative figures from studies of agencies outside the federal workforce which also reveal distressingly high rates of sexual harassment of women. A study of female executives at the rank of vice president or higher found that two-thirds had experienced harassment; a study of female attorneys found that over one-third of those surveyed had such experience.

What this cursory overview suggests is that, on account of their gender, women are at risk of violence on the streets, on their campuses, in their workplaces and in their homes. While not all of that violence is bias motivated, it is likely that a substantial proportion is conditioned by narrowly defined gender expectations at least, misogyny at worst.

EMERGENT TRENDS

A small body of literature has begun to identify consistent trends in the dynamics and patterns associated with hate crime—what we might refer to as the "empirical attributes" across categories of ethnoviolence. Jack Levin and Jack McDevitt (1993) offer a concise list of four such characteristics: excessive brutality, stranger victimization, interchangeableness of victims, multiple offenders.

As noted earlier, hate crime victims are more likely to experience assaultive incidents than offenses against property. This is an inversion of trends for the general population. Consequently, such victims are also more likely to be at the receiving end of excessively brutal violence. To the extent that hate crime perpetrators are motivated by fear, hatred, mistrust, or resentment of their victims, for example, they are more likely to engage in extreme violence—violence which is beyond that necessary to subdue the victim. In the case of anti-gay violence, for example, homicide records indicate an elevated risk of multiple stabbings, genital mutilation, or torture, where the intent is to "rub out the human being because of his (sexual) preference" (Mertz, cited in Berrill, 1992: 25).

These brutal acts of violence are commonly perpetrated on strangers—people with whom the perpetrator has had little or no personal contact. The victim simply represents the Other in generic terms. That he or she is a member of the hated or demonized group is enough to leave them vulnerable to attack. Further knowledge of their identity, personality, or intent is unnecessary. Neither Michael Griffith nor Yusuf Hawkins was known to his assailants. That they were black was motive enough for their murders. Additionally, both of these cases reinforce the observation that hate crime often involves multiple offenders. This is a group activity, involving ratios as dramatic as ten to one, but more often in the neighborhood of three to one. A glance at the SPLC Klanwatch *Intelligence Report* catalog of hate crimes also provides evidence of the tendency of pairs or groups of offenders to act together. It is, perhaps, this tendency that also helps to account for the brutality involved in hate crime.

As the UCR data presented earlier suggest, there is a consistent pattern of risk of victimization. The most prevalent bias motivation is race, with African Americans the most vulnerable targets. Next in line are Jews and gay men. Moreover, victims are most likely to experience personal rather than property victimization. The exception to this appears to be violence motivated by religion (especially anti-Semitism), wherein victimization is more likely to involve damage to property.

What little information is available with respect to hate crime perpetrators appears to paint a fairly consistent image[3] as well: they are overwhelmingly young white males. Virtually every data collection method reinforces this perception. The profile is evident in UCRs, NGLTF reports, ADL audits, NAPALC audits, as well as in anecdotal measures such as the catalog offered by the SPLC *Intelligence Reports*. In short, young members of the dominant hegemonic bloc consistently are responsible for the victimization of subordinate groups.

---

3. Victims are often unable to provide much information about their offenders, either because they did not see them (e.g., vandalism, telephone harassment), or because they were too overwhelmed to notice much about them.

## TWO

Accounting for Hate Crime:
       Doing Difference

We believe all kinds of things about: what real men really are what women must want
what black people feel and smell like what white people do and deserve how rich people
earn their comforts and cadillacs how poor people get what's coming to them
O we are all racist we are all sexist some of us only some of us are the targets of racism
of sexism of homophobia of class denigration but we all all breathe in racism with the
dust in the streets

—**Rosario Morales,** *We're All in the Same Boat*

A nineteen-year-old junior at Harvard paints a swastika in the dormitory room of a Jewish classmate. A thirty-five-year-old construction worker beats his black coworker. A fifty-year-old supervisor verbally harasses her lesbian receptionist. A sixteen-year-old high school dropout shoots the East Indian owner of a local restaurant.

What are the common denominators here? How do we make sense of the disparate motives, dynamics, and characteristics of these offenders, their actions and their victims? This is the role of theory in criminology and sociology: to identify and make sense of patterns in human behavior and experience. Unfortunately, the events described here have not been adequately accounted for. Criminology has failed to provide a coherent framework for understanding the diverse phenomenon that we refer to as "hate crimes."

The last half decade has produced a few journalistic explorations of hate crime. While these include intriguing anecdotes, case studies, and even some graphic representations of white supremacist propaganda, they are bereft of sophisticated explanations for the phenomenon of hate crime. Perhaps the most visually striking of these is Leo Regan's *Public Enemy*. Through photographs and interviews, Regan reveals the anger, the hatred and the violence of a group of British neo-Nazi skinheads. But the best example of this genre is James Ridgeway's *Blood in the Face*. It is a comprehensive catalog of prominent U.S. hate groups that provides rich detail on the history, organization, and ideologies of the far-right hate groups. Kenneth Stern's *A Force Upon the Plain* (1996) offers a similar historical survey of the rapid growth of the militia movement. Using the Oklahoma City bombing as a point of reference, Stern traces the origins and impact of this country's widespread militias. Like Ridgeway, he examines the ideological links shared by the different factions of this movement. This volume explores the relationship between the paranoia of these "ultrapatriots" and their tendency to engage in brutal acts of bigotry against their perceived enemies, whether they be ZOG government agents, immigrants, Jews, or others supposedly threatening to take over the country. Again, however, the account is atheoretical. No attempt is made to connect the growth of the militia movement to its broader sociopolitical environment.

All of the above-mentioned studies are rich in detail. In this respect they provide fodder for further social inquiry. They expose the broad interconnections both between groups and between ideological beliefs and practical action. It soon becomes clear how a particular reading of the Bible, for example, can legitimate violence against Jews or gays. However, what does not become clear is why such a reading emerges. Journalistic renderings on hate crime promote a sensational image of hatemongers, without fully accounting for the source of their hatred. Moreover, by focusing on hate groups, these authors promote the inaccurate assumption that hate crime is a carefully orchestrated, premeditated activity carried out by angry, sometimes psychopathic, members of a definable organization. This is to overstate the proportion of hate crimes committed by skinheads or Klansmen, for example. Conversely, it understates the often random acts of individual bigotry. This is a common shortcoming of popular depictions of hate crime. The focus tends to be on organized hate groups, rather than on the broader everyday dynamics of hate crime.

To date, one of the richest descriptive accounts of hate crime is that found in Levin and McDevitt's *Hate Crimes: The Rising Tide of Bigotry and Bloodshed* (1993). Even here, the theoretical framework is implicit rather than explicit. It is secondary to the authors' coverage of concrete case studies. This volume provides researchers with a wealth of data about the nature of hate-motivated violence. It is replete with specific examples of assaults motivated by race, gender, religion, ethnicity, and sexual orientation. In some cases, drawing on newspaper accounts or police and court files, it provides the context and rationale for the perpetrator's actions, as well as the impact on the victims. *Hate Crimes* is also a valuable source for those interested in policies and practices to curb the "rising tide." One-third of the text is devoted to consideration of legislation, law enforcement training, and coalition building as practical means by which to combat hate crime.

Levin and McDevitt succeed in their pledge to provide a "typology that differentiates various kinds of hate offenses" (1993: x). Thus, while conceding that hate crime generally arises out of bigotry, they nonetheless categorize hate crime according to four secondary motives: as an expression of resentment; as thrill-seeking behavior; as a reaction to personal threat; as part of a mission to eliminate "inferior" populations.

To their credit, Levin and McDevitt situate all types of hate-motivated violence within the context of the (re)emerging culture of hate that characterizes the United States. Within such an environment, intolerance, bigotry, and violent expressions of these sentiments are not only acceptable, but encouraged by the likes of rap music, sexist humor, racist campaign ads, and action-adventure movies. Is it any wonder, they ask, that "hatred is hip"?

Because it is grounded in strain theory, Levin and McDevitt's account is inherently subject to weaknesses that I will discuss in more detail below. While alienation and economic instability underlie some occasions of hate crime, they are only a partial explanation. Levin and McDevitt seem to have forgotten their initial assertion that hate crime is grounded in a *culture* of hate, not a subculture. Yet the latter is the picture that emerges. The implication is that there is a subculture of bigotry, much like Albert Cohen's subculture of delinquency; or that lower-class culture and experience specifically gives rise to not only Walter Miller's gang delinquency, but also hate crime. However, as the later critique of strain theory will make clear, there is much left unexplained by this approach.

The same can be said of most traditional criminological theories. The discipline has failed to seriously address the sociocultural underpinnings of the violent oppression of subordinate communities. Where criminology touches on the experiences of marginalized populations, the emphasis rarely has been on victimization motivated by prejudice. Rather, the focus has been on the criminality and criminalization of minority groups. As the following brief consideration of select theories will reveal, traditional criminological theories lack sufficient explanatory power in the context of hate crime.

SOCIAL CONTROL THEORY

According to Travis Hirschi's variant of control theory, criminal offenders are those for whom the "bonds" to conventional society have been loosened. That is, the constraints that ordinarily inhibit deviant behavior have, by some unidentified process, deteriorated to an extent that the perpetrator lacks the incentive to abide by the law. In Hirschi's words, "Delinquent acts result when an individual's bond to society is weak or broken" (1969:16).

Specifically, Hirschi identifies four elements that constitute the social bond. The first, *attachment*, refers to one's affective ties to significant (conventional) others. Here, he prioritizes the importance of family ties as a brake on delinquency. *Commitment* to conventional society likewise inhibits criminal behavior. To the extent that one has a stake in society (for example, a job, a strong G.P.A.), one is unlikely to risk that position by engaging in a sanctionable behavior. *Involvement* in conventional activities evokes two related inhibitors: people who are actively engaged in Little League or the Parent-Teachers Association or the local city council have little time to be involved in criminal activities; moreover, these same activities may in fact reinforce commitment to conventional norms and values. Finally, where individuals hold a strong *belief* in the legitimacy of the prevailing order and its constituent legal codes, they will abide by those rules.

It is unlikely that we can make sense of hate crime within this framework. If it were the case that perpetrators of racially or religiously motivated crimes, for example, were free of parental pressure, or free of religious dogma, then perhaps we could stretch control theory to account for hate crime. However, this does not seem to be the case. There is little that distinguishes hate crime offenders from their nonoffending peers. In fact, it may be the case that youths who engage in hate crime are attached and committed and involved and strong in their beliefs. But in spite—or even because—of these bonds, they are prone to violence against those whom they identify as different. That is, the social bond *allows* rather than inhibits hate crime!

Among the conventional organizations that Hirschi identifies as crucial to maintaining conformity is organized religion. Consequently, those with strong faith in a deity, or a set of theological principles, would be expected to refrain from engaging in illegal activities, including hate crime. However, it is readily apparent that this does not stand up to empirical testing. Some of the most heinous and brutal acts of violence have been carried out in the name of religion and religious beliefs. Native American ethnocide can be attributed to the efforts of Europeans to Christianize the "savages." The recent spate of abortion clinic violence, especially as evidenced by John Salvi's attacks in New England, are likewise motivated by religious zeal. Many of the burgeoning hate groups also draw their inspiration and ideologies from very narrow scriptural interpretations. Some of the most violent and militant of the right-wing extremist groups (such as Aryan Nation; Covenant, Sword and Arm of the Lord; the Order) are saturated in the principles of Christian conservatism and Christian Identity. Their readings of scripture identify a hierarchy of race and gender that serves explicitly to justify their assaults on the Other.

Even beyond this, there is reason to question the utility of social control theory with respect to hate crime. While hate crime offenders can be said to be violating the criminal code, it is not so apparent that they are violating normative standards in the United States. For Hirschi, it is the internalization of norms that inhibits criminal activity. In the case of hate crime, it is the internalization of norms that encourages criminal activity. In a generally racist, sexist, homophobic culture, violence motivated by hatred is not deviant behavior. In fact, it conforms to what is a normatively unjust value system. It is an affirmation of the gendered and racialized hierarchy that constitutes the "legitimate" social order.

STRAIN THEORY

At the heart of strain theory, as developed by Robert Merton, is the notion of anomie. According to Merton, deviant behavior emerges as a result of a disequilibrium, or a dissociation between culturally prescribed goals and the socially structured means by which to achieve them. A "deviant adjustment" is in fact a response to a situation in which "those institutionalized procedures which promise a measure of successful attainment of the goals are not available to the individuals" (Merton, 1938: 676). In short, frustration of one's efforts to achieve "success" (however defined by the culture in question) gives rise to aberrant behavior.

In U.S. culture, the American Dream prevails as the shared cultural goal. Success comes to be defined by the accumulation of wealth, material goods, and status. People are expected to strive for the ideal of a comfortable suburban lifestyle, replete with three-bedroom house, two-car garage, the weekday Buick and the weekend Bronco, savings in the bank, and an outing to the theater every Thursday night. And, of course, it is "agreed" that the appropriate means for attaining such a state is by adherence to the Protestant work ethic: get an education, get a good job, work hard, work honestly.

Therein lies the rub. In a society as hierarchically structured by race, class, and gender as the United States, access to resources is unequally distributed. Not all members of society are readily able to succeed by legitimate means. There are those who are structurally unable to compete for scarce material and social resources. The resultant strain is most dramatically experienced among those in the lower class, for whom education and employment opportunities are limited.

This anomie, then, leads to one of five modes of adaptation. *Conformists* continue to subscribe to both the cultural goals and norms, regardless of their perceived level of success. *Innovators*, on the other hand, maintain an allegiance to culturally defined goals but—faced with substantial obstacles to success—they resort to alternative illegitimate means (such as theft). *Ritualists* abandon any hope of ever achieving great wealth and status, but nonetheless retain a formalistic adherence to the institutionalized norms of society and the workplace. *Retreatists* and *rebels* are both characterized by rejection of the prevailing ends and means. The former, unable to succeed by legitimate or illegitimate means, simply withdraw from the broader society into a world of their own. The latter explicitly denounce the prevailing order and seek to impose an altogether different synthesis of goals and means.

It is possible to "slot" hate crime perpetrators into at least two of Merton's deviant modes of adaptation. Some might be considered innovators, to the extent that they seek their thwarted status rewards through victimization and subjugation of others. Indeed, many variants of strain theory—such as those proposed by Miller, Cohen, or Richard Cloward and Lloyd Ohlin—explicitly argue that lower-class youths generally resort to crime and violence as an alternative means of achieving the status and prestige denied them in the broader culture. Hate crime perpetrated against minorities, then, is one means by which these young men can prove their toughness, their strength. In analyses like that of Levin and McDevitt, the emphasis is generally on a youth subculture characterized by alienation, downward mobility, economic uncertainty, and loss of turf or privilege. Singly and in groups young men attempt to adapt to their immediate environment by lashing out at the Other, by constructing and then victimizing the "cause" of their weakened position. However, this doesn't explain why they select powerless victims specifically.

Alternatively, strain theorists might attribute a rebel identity to hate crime offenders. While this culture extols equality as a valued principle, hate-motivated offenders would seek to overturn this platform in favor of white supremacy or white domination. Consequently, they are willing to resort to whatever means necessary—harassment, violence, and so on—to eliminate the "inferior races." In place of diversity, they would enforce uniformity of race, creed, and color. This philosophy underlies many organized hate groups, such as White Aryan Nation, or the Order. The preamble to the Aryan Nation's Oath of Allegiance makes this explicit: "I, as a free Aryan man, hereby swear an unrelenting oath upon the green graves of our sires, upon the children in the wombs of our wives, upon the throne of God almighty, sacred is His name, to join together in holy union with those brothers in this circle and to declare forthright that from this moment on I have no fear of death, no fear of foe; that I have a sacred duty to do whatever is necessary to deliver our people from the Jew and bring total victory to the Aryan race" (cited in Ridgeway, 1995: 107).

The majority of scholarly (and journalistic) accounts of hate crime and hate groups to have emerged in recent years are at least implicitly driven by strain theory. There is a tendency to argue that hate crime is symptomatic of the general malaise, the sense of threat felt by those who see themselves as victims of affirmative action. From this perspective, hate crime (illegitimate means) is an outgrowth of enhanced economic competition for jobs (legitimate means). Hate offenders are said to blame their economic instability or lack of job security on the immigration of "foreigners" or the global financial conspiracy of the Jews, for example. Levin and McDevitt draw attention to such resentment as a possible motive in hate crime. Robert Kelly introduces his collected edition on hate crime with the assertion that hate crimes are "occasioned by systematic unemployment and poverty that lives side by side with colossal affluence" (1993: 4). William Zellner (1995) likewise relies explicitly on Merton to explain the existence and ideologies of white supremacist groups.

Initially, this is an appealing take on hate crime, especially to the extent that—contrary to control theory—it recognizes crime as a structurally and culturally mediated process. Moreover, there is no doubt that hate crime occurring in the historical (recession) and sociogeographical (inner city) context of economic instability may be in part a response to perceived strain. Those facing downward mobility may indeed lash out against scapegoats whom they hold to be responsible for their displacement—women, immigrants, African Americans, and so on. However, not the least of the inconsistencies here is that if strain accounted for hate crimes, then those most prevalent among the victims would instead be perpetrators! Who is more disadvantaged—economically, socially, and politically—than women and racial minorities? Yet these groups are much more likely to be victims than offenders.

Levin and McDevitt are not entirely accurate when they state that "although hate mongers may grow up learning the conventional culture, they are *abnormal* with respect to their lack of power and prestige in mainstream society . . . these kids may be in school, but they are not successful in school" (1993: 534). This statement raises two interrelated weaknesses associated with strain theory. First, it is distinctly possible that hate crime occurs not in spite of "conventional culture" but because of it. Hate crime is not abnormal; rather, it is a normal (albeit extreme) expression of the biases that are diffused throughout the culture and history in which it is embedded. In other words, "seeing hate as an extreme expression that arises only in moments of cultural tension encourages us to ignore its role with subtle negotiations that take place daily in complex modern society, indulging the comfortable notion that hate is a pathological practice of others" (Whillock and Slayden, 1995: ix–x).

Acts of racially motivated violence—hate crimes—differ little in intent or impact from "legitimate" political discourse such as the Republicans' use of the Willy Horton ads in 1992. The same homophobia which gives rise to hate crime also maintains state sodomy legislation. Hate crime, then, is anomolous only to the extent that acceptably racist or sexist perceptions are expressed in socially unacceptable ways. The sentiments are legal; only the assault is illegal.

The second faulty assumption underlying Levin and McDevitt's assertion is that hate crime perpetrators are powerless. A large proportion of hate crime is accounted for by white working-class males; so at least on the class continuum, they can be said to be powerless. But there is another side to this as well. In relative terms, it is apparent that hate crime offenders are not at all "powerless." While hate-motivated acts may represent a rare opportunity to exercise power otherwise unavailable to them, it can also be said that hate crime represents the maintenance of power in relation to subordinate racial, ethnic, or gender groups (Goldberg, 1995). Racial or homophobic graffiti reminds the subordinate Others of their place in the cultural hierarchies, to the advantage of the perpetrators. It is thus an act of domination rather than resistance or rebellion.

Moreover, hatemongers are not all alienated, deprived youth. It is also the case that hate crime knows no class boundaries. Richard Girnt Butler, a recent leader of Aryan Nations, was an aerospace engineer; Robert Miles, who has played leadership roles in many white supremacist groups (including grand dragon of the KKK) was a manager for an insurance company. Hamm's investigation of U.S. skinheads reveals that they are in fact "working class conformists with a hyperactive commitment to the goals and means of the dominant American culture. They are often multi-talented; they seem to be dedicated workers and responsible students" (Hamm, 1994a: 130). Moreover, a recent article in *The Advocate* catalogs the growing trend in anti-gay violence in the workplace. Supervisors and coworkers alike harass and assault gay victims almost daily.

Hate crime is increasingly likely to occur in places of privilege such as the workplace and college campuses. The ADL (1989) notes with concern the paradox between the commitment to diversity in postsecondary education, and the dramatic increase in bias-motivated incidents on campuses nationwide. Here are people already advantaged by their access to education, who nonetheless opt for the victimization of minority peers. Even Harvard and Yale—those bastions of white upper-class privilege—have not been immune to violence motivated by "difference."

The gulf between white students and minorities is evident in polls conducted by the National Institute Against Prejudice and Violence. These surveys of university students consistently find that smaller proportions of white students than black students perceive discrimination against racial and ethnic minorities to be a problem on campus. Similarly, while the majority of black and Jewish students typically are aware of specific racist incidents, the majority of their white, non-Jewish classmates are often unaware of any such activities (Ehrlich, 1994; Ehrlich, Larcom, and Purvis, 1994).

The most damning counterevidence, however, is that concerning secondary victimization of minorities. As legitimate agents of social control, police officers are the very embodiment of social power in our culture. Yet with all their available legitimate means and instruments of control, police are still very likely to resort to the exercise of harassment and brute force against not just criminals but also those deemed unworthy of their protection—such as gays, black youths, and so on. Joseph Harry has referred to this process as "derivative deviance," or victimization of people "who because of their deviant status, are presumed unable to avail themselves of civil protection" (1982: 546). Gary Comstock (1989), Steven Rosen (1992), Amnesty International (1994), and Gregory Herek (1992) are among those who have documented the tendency of police officers (not to mention prosecutors and judges) to harass and even physically assault gay men or lesbians. This may take the form of unnecessary or overzealous prosecution under anti-gay legislation (sodomy legislation, for example), or further victimization of gay victims. Some officers go out of their way to assail gays. The latter is illustrated by the experience of a gay reporter for the *Village Voice*. "As we crossed 4th Street, a police car spotted us holding hands and spewed out a barrage of hatred . . . (B)oth officers got out of the car, clutching their billy clubs, continuing a barrage of verbal abuse. . . . The younger officer took my notebook, tearing out the pages with his car and badge identification numbers" (cited in Rosen, 1992).

Documentation of secondary victimization—and outright brutality—against racial minorities is even more readily available. The 1994 Mollen Commission on police corruption in New York City revealed some telling findings with respect to police violence against minorities, as did the 1991 Christopher Commission in Los Angeles. Frankie Bailey (1991) traces the "evolution" of mistreatment of racial minorities at the hands of the criminal justice system. Flowers (1990) similarly details the historical context of secondary victimization of minorities, as well as its contemporary prevalence. Ronald Flowers's conclusions about the use of violence by police highlights the extent to which this is an expression of power, rather than powerlessness: "it is still not uncommon for police officers to use excessive force in arresting minority suspects, particularly when arrestees are verbally abusive, the victims are not minorities, the crime has taken place in a predominantly white area, or the complainant is white" (1990: 154). Hate crimes perpetrated by officials of the state, then, also serve as a reminder of the "proper and subordinate" place of minority citizens. They are processes by which the hegemonic white community is preserved from despoliation at the hands of rogue minorities.

In sum, strain theory fails as a satisfactory account of hate crime, since it acknowledges neither the cultural diffusion of prejudice and bigotry, nor the use of hate violence as an exercise of power by both the powerless and the empowered. In this sense, it shares the primary weakness of control theory: an inability to account for the inclusion of otherwise conformist and integrated individuals in the ranks of hate offenders. Both theories also fail to address the cultural meaning of hate crime. That is, neither considers the question of the role that hate crimes play in assigning meaning and identity to social beings. In this respect, labeling theory appears at first glance to hold some promise.

LABELING THEORY

Concerned as it is with issues of marginalization and stigmatization, one would expect labeling theory to provide some insights into this particular brand of criminality. From this perspective, deviance is a social construct arising out of a process of "tagging" or labeling those deemed—by the audience—in some way defective or deviant. "The deviant is one to whom the label has successfully been applied; deviant behavior is behavior that people so label" (Becker, 1963: 8). Or to use Tannenbaum's inspiring words: "The process of making the criminal, therefore, is a process of tagging, defining, identifying, segregating, describing, emphasizing, making conscious and self-conscious, it becomes a way of stimulating, emphasizing and evoking the very traits that are complained of" (1938: 19).

Crime and deviance are explained as a social process by which a negative identity is applied and assumed. That is, both the social audience and the newly designated "deviant" come to identify that individual according to the "master status" associated with their norm violation. Social control—whether informal or formal—consequently has the paradoxical effect of enhancing the commitment to deviance because the constitutive labeling process cyclically reinforces a deviant self-image. This negative identity might also be understood as a stigma, a sign of disrepute—"an attribute that is deeply discrediting" (Goffman, 1963: 3). According to Erving Goffman, those who have been stigmatized as "different" in some socially relevant way are reduced to a "tainted and discounted" image (1963: 3). These discredited subjects may then further immerse themselves in their deviance.

The foremost strength of labeling theory is that it encourages us to see criminal activity as a process, rather than a static event. It is the result of actions, reactions, and interactions between human agents. We are made to acknowledge that these actions thus have long-ranging meaning for the victim, the offender, and the broader social audience, including the reference communities of both.

Moreover, labeling theory has been used creatively to account for deviant identities (see, for example, Becker, 1963). Donald Black and Albert Reiss (1970) offer a classic analysis of police officer–delinquent interactions in this light; Goffman (1963) examines the stigmatization of a range of "deviant" identities including Jews, blacks, prostitutes, and homosexuals; Mary McIntosh (1968) confronts the marginalization of gays as a labeling process. Essentially, these accounts have addressed the ways in which socially marginalized communities have been forced into that position. It is argued that the attributes associated with blacks, Jews, or gays, for example, motivate their exclusion from conventional society. One might "stretch" this and thereby conclude that it is their deviant designation—the stigma—which makes them vulnerable to official and unofficial acts of oppression.

But this is less than satisfying, since it explains only the "secondary deviance" of the victims, not the offenders. Moreover, hate crime offenders may meet with less negative censure than the victims of their violence. The "criminality" of those motivated by hatred of the Other often inspires acclaim rather than condemnation, as when the secondary victimization of gays is supported by a homophobic police department, or when a Nazi executes a Jew. Even on a more basic level, it is apparent that in a culture as chauvinistic as that of the United States, persecution of minority victims often goes unpunished. Ultimately, then, there is no process of stigmatization, of negative identification with respect to hate crime offenders.

Labeling theory also suffers from a failure to explicitly concretize the context in which crime occurs. What are the structural and cultural inhibitors and facilitators of hate crime? While labeling theory does address the issue of power, it often does so from a pluralist standpoint. That is, it implies that "society is composed of a variety of interest groups or segments, and that power is spread among a number of groups or segments" (Lynch and Groves, 1989: 46). Thus, it fails to address the impact of the carefully constructed hierarchies of race, class, and gender, which are so crucial to an understanding of hate crime. Empirically, labeling theorists have been much more interested in examining the "sensational" deviants, rather than the effects of specific exercises of power and domination in the context of interactions between those who are structurally advantaged and those who are not.

These shortcomings notwithstanding, there is yet a glimmer of hope to be derived from the interactionist perspective of which labeling theory is a part. It bears repeating that the processual understanding of crime is indispensable in helping us to understand hate crime. Additionally, interactionist approaches turn our attention to the importance of the construction of meaning and identity through interaction—this too is a useful insight to bear in mind when analyzing hate crime. This particular crime does in fact assert the hegemonic identity of the offender, at the same time that it reaffirms the subordination of the victim.

CRITICAL CRIMINOLOGY

Critical criminology is a useful corrective to the tendencies of theory to neglect the political dimensions of crime, since it explicitly is concerned with the importance of power in the context of crime and social control. Similarly, it provides the structural grounding that is often absent in labeling accounts. It behooves us to recall Marx's famed assertion that "it is not the consciousness of people that determines their existence, but their social existence that determines their consciousness."

While Marxist-inspired analyses of gender have been prevalent for at least two decades, similar attention to other non-class divisions such as race, ethinicity, or sexual orientation has been lacking. Cornel West has asserted, not infrequently, that the stuff of hate crime—racism, nationalism, homophobia, sexism, xenophobia—has been undertheorized by Marxists. This is overwhelmingly the case in criminology, where the most neglected field of inquiry has been "the relationship of crime and minority groups within society" (Flowers, 1990: xiii).

This is especially disturbing given that radical or critical criminology emerged out of the civil rights movements of the 1960s. Marxist criminology aligned itself not with the "Establishment" as had traditional mainstream criminology. Rather it assumed an oppositional stance, more in sync with the liberationist struggles of the day. That is, critical analyses were rooted in the experiences and perceptions of the oppressed. In spite of this, there has been little scholarly consideration of the relationship between minority status and crime. Feminist criminology recently has begun to gain influence within the discipline; the same cannot be said for "racial criminology" or "gay criminology." Moreover, with respect to race and ethnicity, at least, criminologists are most likely to examine patterns of offending and criminal justice processing of minority offenders, rather than their victimization. And they are unlikely to examine victimization based on the victim's status.

Before proceeding, it is important to keep in mind that critical criminology is anything but a unified approach. One characteristic that is shared is a direct or indirect link to Marxist analyses of capitalism. Various perspectives differ, however, in the extent to which they break with the Marxist past. Nonetheless, it is probably accurate to say that critical criminologists are interested in the links among and between the cultural and structural dimensions of capitalism, inequalities, and crime.

Due largely to internal reflection and assessment, critical criminology has evolved from its initial instrumentalist stance, which "simply exposes the horrors of capitalism and the injustices of criminal justice" (Platt, 1982: 44). Early critical criminological accounts differed little from the principles derived explicitly from Marx and Engels. Thus, the focus in the early work of scholars such as Richard Quinney and William Chambliss was on the way in which criminal law supported and perpetuated capitalism either in the short or long term. Law was seen as a way to control the "dangerous classes" or to encourage them to acquiesce to a legitimate social order.

With respect to causes of crime, the emphasis likewise has been on structural incentives. In particular, class inequalities in wealth, status, and power differentially shape life chances and opportunities. Those at the low end of these continua are most likely to resort to crime. In short, crime is best understood in terms of the class relationships associated with capitalism.

As Barbara Hudson (1993) reflects, critical criminology in recent years has highlighted relative deprivation and marginalization as primary determinants of crime. It is in this context that the connection between minority status and crime can be addressed. Quite simply, minority youth are the most dramatically affected by both processes, and therefore more prone to crime: "Black unemployment rates, black residence in areas of urban decay, black exclusion from the political and cultural milieu would all lead to an expectation of high black crime rates" (Hudson, 1993: 13–14). Moreover, the same class relations that condition black involvement in crime also are said to explain differential social control. That is, even racialized social control is "overdetermined by class relationships and labor market conditions" (Hudson, 1993: 16). Where minority communities are deemed a threat to capitalism, they will be subject to intensified repression. Stewart Tolnay and E. M. Beck explain lynching as a response to the fact that Southern blacks were "transformed from personal property to potential *competitors*" (1992:34). Ronald Takaki (1989) has made similar arguments with respect to turn-of-the-century violence and legislative control exercised against Chinese workers. It is, for these theorists, the changing nature and intensity of economic competition within the working class that accounts for victimization of minorities.

One of the most sophisticated efforts to account for race, within the margins of Marxist theorizing, was that found in Stuart Hall et al. (1978). Central to this work was the question of how the "race problem" and the "crime problem" in Britain were constructed so as to be perceived as a seamless web. Hall and his coauthors attempted to unpack the way in which an economically and politically threatened state deployed ideologies and practices of racism to construct the black mugger as a scapegoat. A similar examination of the racialization of both the recession and urban disorder by John Solomos et al. demonstrates how "race is easily depicted as the common denominator of the full range of social pressures: too many immigrants, high birthrates in black communities mean too many people chasing too few jobs; unstable black family patterns means excess demands for housing and welfare services; black culture and personality traits mean excess crime" (cited in Hudson, 1993: 22).

Critical criminology has a great deal to recommend it as an explanatory framework for hate crime. It explicitly confronts at least two of the primary conceptual "facts" associated with the phenomenon: marginalization and power. Both themes are crucial to a fully political understanding of hate crimes, given that they are themselves exercises of power intended to assert the marginal status of victims and, simultaneously, the relatively privileged status of the offenders. Moreover, the understanding of hate crime requires consideration of the specific sociohistorical context in which it emerges—an approach that is also a hallmark of recent critical theorizing. For Paul Gilroy this involves paying attention to "the construction, mobilization and pertinence of different forms of racist ideology and structuration in specific historical circumstances" (1982: 281) In so doing, critical criminology points to the official ideologies and practices that might make minorities vulnerable to popular forms of repression as well.

However, critical analyses of minorities and crime remain relatively underdeveloped. There is still a stubborn tendency to prioritize class and economic relations as determinant of crime and criminalization. This is an inadequate account, especially when dealing with hate crime. In many ways, critical criminology suffers from the same flaws as strain theory. It too, is unable to account for the relative lack of hate crime offenses by those who are most marginalized—people of color, women and gays. Conversely, it also fails to make sense of hate crimes perpetrated by the least marginalized—white, middle-class males, police officers, criminal justice officials, and so on.

Critical criminology is most concerned with the way in which marginalization contributes to crime. What of the obverse? What of the way in which crime contributes to marginalization? This is what hate crime accomplishes. It constructs the relative identities of both offender and victim by simultaneously asserting one and subordinating, if not annihilating another.

Marxist-informed analyses of crime also fail as an explanatory schema in another crucial respect. Although seen as an outcome of broader socioeconomic processes, crime itself is not regarded as a process. The criminal event itself is seen as a static, singular event. While situated in its broad historical context, crime is not also placed in its immediate subjective context. It is crucial to examine hate crime in terms of the meanings it has not just for the impersonal structural imperatives of capitalism, but also for the perpetrator, victim, and their respective reference communities. This latter ability does not inhere in critical criminology.

The most sophisticated critical exegesis on hate crime is undoubtably Mark Hamm's (1994a) exploration of U.S. skinheads. This is an explicit attempt not only to expose the skinhead culture, but also to theorize its motives and structure. Hamm is unafraid to approach the issue in an innovative and eclectic manner, both methodologically and theoretically. The very nature of the skinhead subculture required an unorthodox style of research. Hamm was faced with the task of overcoming the paranoia, resistance, and violence of this movement. What emerged, then, was a rich ethnography that drew its sample from a diverse range of sources. For ten interviews, Hamm approached skinheads on the streets of U.S. cities. Seventeen telephone interviews resulted from letters sent to "known skinheads" as identified by Tom Metzger's White Aryan Resistance (WAR) mailing list (two of these subjects were interviewed twice). He was also able to conduct three "bonus" interviews, which resulted from unsolicited contact from skinhead leaders who apparently learned of the research. Two subjects were solicited through Metzger's WAR electronic bulletin board. Finally, two skinheads serving time for alledged hate crimes joined the sample. Ultimately, then, Hamm's creative subject search yielded thirty-six interviews. The structured interview was constructed so as to glean data that could be linked theoretically to elements of functionalist, differential reinforcement and neo-Marxist cultural theories. To that end, Hamm solicited information on "class, goals, school, family, politics, style, music, television, literature, computers, religion, drugs, guns, group dynamics and hate crime" (1994a: 103).

A complex and surprising picture of the skinhead subculture emerges from Hamm's interviews. His theoretical interpretation is correspondingly complex, since it integrates elements of the three perspectives noted above. While skinhead culture appears to be a working-class phenomenon (subcultural), it is also characterized by *synanomie* rather than *anomie*. That is, skinheads appear to be "hyperactively bonded to the dominant social order" (Hamm, 1994a: 212). This is apparent in their commitment to school and to blue-collar employment.

It is via the mechanisms of differential reinforcement that these working-class youths enter the terrorist subculture. In particular, exposure to White Power music and to WAR media (zines, electronic bulletin boards) seems to be the dominant factors in explaining the "conversion" to neo-Nazism. The bonding within skinhead groups is completed by the adoption of a shared, readily identifiable, countercultural style. However, unlike their European counterparts, in the United States "most terrorist skinheads do not look like skinheads at all" (Hamm, 1994a: 130). Skinheads in the United States have adopted a style of their own that is more indebted to Levi-Strauss than Doc Marten. Two cultural objects complete the style and prepare the skinheads for terrorism: the Smith & Wesson .357 and beer. The latter, while unanticipated, plays a central role as a trigger to the "berserking" that can include minority victimization. No cases of violence uncovered by Hamm were committed in the absence of massive quantities of beer.

Hamm's analysis is the first of its kind. It is, to date, the only ethnographic and theoretical exploration of organized hate violence. It is worthy of praise on this basis alone. However, it is also outstanding in terms of the novel and unexpected insights it allows into the skinhead subculture. These are not the alienated, disenfranchised misfits of the media stereotypes. Rather, they are relatively successful "hyperconformists" who use beer as a catalyst for violence. This in itself forces us to reevaluate popular conceptions of hate crime offenders.

While inspiring this question, Hamm's account does not necessarily provide a generalizable response. Hamm falls short of providing a comprehensive approach to hate crime generally. Not all perpetrators resemble skinheads in manner or motivation. Not all are exposed to the vitriole of Metzger. Not all are committed to the philosophy of neo-Nazism. To be fair, this was not Hamm's intent. His research was explicitly motivated by an interest in understanding terrorist youth subcultures. What Hamm offers, then, is a starting point for analysis, based on the recognition that skinheads represent a "subculture whose rituals and symbols reveal a basic truth about the values of society at large" (Hamm, 1994a: 215). Subsequent theorizing must make clear what that "basic truth" is, and how it informs the bigotry and actions of those not associated with organized hate groups.

SUMMING UP

As the foregoing critique has implied, criminology has yet to come to terms with the phenomenon we have come to know as hate crime. Existing theory tends to neglect the structural underpinnings of hate crime and the situated process that it entails. As my earlier definition of hate crime (chapter 1) suggests, to understand hate crime, one must put it in its sociocultural context. In particular, hate crime—often referred to as "ethnoviolence"—must be understood as one among an array of mechanisms by which deeply ingrained sets of power relationships are maintained. It is, in short, constituted of and by difference. In fact, as this chapter and the remainder of the book will argue, hate crime is a vitally important mechanism for "doing difference."

ACCOUNTING FOR HATE CRIME: DOING DIFFERENCE

Both historical and contemporary patterns of stratification in the United States give lie to the myths of the "melting pot" and "We the People." On the contrary, this is a nation grounded in deeply embedded notions of difference that have been used to justify and construct intersecting hierarchies along lines of sexuality, race, gender, and class, to name but a few. In other words, difference has been socially constructed, but in ever-changing ways across time and space. Nonetheless, these constructions have reinforced similarly changing practices of exclusion and marginalization. The secret to the success of these social constructs is that they are virtually invisible, to the extent that the divisions appear "natural"; they are taken for granted. Michael Omi and Howard Winant articulate this notion with respect to race, although it is an equally apt assessment of gender or sexual identity: "Everyone learns some combination, some version, of the rules of racial classification, and of her own racial identity, often without obvious teaching or conscious inculcation. Thus we are inserted in a comprehensively racialized social structure. Race becomes 'common sense'—a way of comprehending, explaining and being in the world" (1994: 60).

The systems of classification to which Omi and Winant refer tend to presume essentialist, mutually exclusive categories of belonging. They assume an either/or understanding of identity: one is either a man or a woman; either white or black or Asian or Native; either Christian or Jew or Muslim. Given this conceptualization of identity, one is forced to choose "a side." In some contexts, the choice is given, since differences in race or gender, for example, are assumed to be innate, biological, that is, "natural." Whatever the case, discrete boundaries are assumed. One can belong to only one side of the equation; the borders are held to be impermeable. Consequently, identity formation is often concerned with "drawing boundaries, engaging in boundedness, configuring rings around" the categories of difference (Weis, Proweller, and Centrie, 1997: 214). The task of difference, then, is to police the borders between categories. There is no room for divergence, since this would threaten the "natural" order.

Associated with these closely guarded divisions are corresponding assumptions about the members within each category. That is, particular traits and abilities are associated with each group. Generally, these traits are posed in oppositional terms, such that the social construction of one group necessarily implies the construction of its opposite. Michelle Fine refers to these opposites as "nested," or as forming a "coherent system" (1997: 58). Lois Weis, Amira Proweller, and Craig Centrie similarly refer to the "parasitic construction" of self and Other (1997: 214). Neither could exist independently without the other. In creating the self, in carving out an identity, we necessarily create its antithesis. However, as Frankenberg reminds us, this coconstruction is not symmetrical (1993: 236). It implies dominance, normativity, and privilege, on the one hand, and subordination, marginality, and disadvantage on the other.

What is most significant about this positioning of self and Other is the fact that it implies the normativity of a hegemonic form, what Audre Lorde refers to as a "mythical norm": "Somewhere, on the edge of consciousness, there is what I call a *mythical norm*, which each of us within our hearts knows 'that is not me.' In america, this norm is usually defined as white, thin, male, young, heterosexual, Christian and financially secure. It is with this mythical norm that the trappings of power reside within this society" (1995: 192).

Historically in the United States, difference has been constructed in negative relational terms. A dominant norm such as that suggested by Lorde has been established, against which all others are (unfavorably) judged. This is the case whether we speak in terms of race, class, gender, sexuality, beauty, or any other element of identity. So it is those who are not white or male or Christian or moneyed who are marked or stigmatized as different. They are the alien Others who fall outside the standardized boundaries.

Also implicit in this construction of difference is the assumption of a good/bad opposition. Not only is the Other different; by definition s/he is also aberrant, deviant, inferior. Structures of oppression operate through a set of dualisms—such as good/evil, superior/inferior, strong/weak, dominant/subordinate—wherein the second half of the binary is always marked as deficiency relative to the superior capacities and privileges of the norm.

We must keep in mind here that difference does not inherently imply inferiority. That evaluation is imposed on the Other by the dominant center. The marking of the Other as deviant is an interpretive act: "It is assigning a value to a particular difference in a way that discredits an individual or group to the advantage of another that transforms mere difference into deficiency" (Rothenberg, 1995a: 11). The marking of difference as deficiency is a social, political process that has the effect of creating hierarchies along divisions such as race, sexuality, and class. Once a group has been defined as inferior or defective or substandard, it is necessarily assigned a subordinate place in society. This construction of the Other facilitates the unequal distribution of resources and power in such a way that it appears natural and justifiable. Racism, sexism, and homophobia all are predicated upon such negative valuations of difference. Women, for example, are deemed inferior by virtue of their "weakness" or "irrationality"; Asians by virtue of their "hyperrationality."

This "oppressive meaning of difference," as Young (1995a) expresses it, suggests that social systems prioritize some versions of identity over others, so that subordinate individuals and groups are sure to stay in that position. Catharine MacKinnon's observations with respect to gender might just as easily be applied to race or class, for example: "gender is not difference; gender is hierarchy. . . . The idea of gender difference helps keep male dominance in place" (cited in Rothenberg, 1992: 60).

While I have been speaking in general terms here, it is important to bear in mind the diversity of forms of difference and corresponding structures of oppression in the United States. At the very least, we must attend to distinctions grounded in race, class, sexuality, and gender, although this is not to deny the existence of differences in religion, age, and political affiliation to name a few. Moreover, Stephanie Wildman and Adrienne Davis rightly point out the specificity of the structure of power associated with each of these: "Within each power system, privilege manifests itself and operates in a manner shaped by the power relations from which it results. White privilege derives from the system of white supremacy. Male privilege and heterosexual privilege result from the gender hierarchy" (1995: 574).

While each of these dimensions retains its own specificity and internal (il)logic, Margaret Anderson and Patricia Hill Collins (1995) and Candace West and Sarah Fenstermaker (1995) remind us that they are interlocking structures of domination. Thus it is both the independent and combined effects of these dimensions that condition actions, interactions, opportunities, and privilege. Nonetheless, the salience and impact of these interactive structures of power is situationally specific. In different contexts, in different institutional settings, one may be more visible or dramatic in its impact; or different combinations might prevail. In other words, from situation to situation, the nature and depth of the interactive effects of race, class, sexuality, gender, and age, for example, will be distinct. So while gender may come to the fore in the context of the family, the combination of race and gender may be more salient in the criminal justice system, or sexuality may be the most relevant dimension at a gay pride parade. It is up to the social scientist, then, to unpack the salience of each structure of domination for the situation in question.

INSTITUTIONALIZING DIFFERENCE

Structures of power and oppression permeate society. They inform and are reinforced by myriad institutional forms. Moreover, power and privilege are unequally allocated along hierarchies shaped by such dimensions as race, class, and gender. Hegemonic visions of "how the world should be" find substance and support most strongly in dominant structures: labor, power, sexuality (Connell, 1987; Messerschmidt, 1993, 1997), and culture (Martin and Jurik, 1996). In other words, relations of difference are sorted and constructed in and through these overarching institutions. These are what Stephen Cornell and Douglas Hartmann refer to as "construction sites," each of which

> is a place where social actors make claims, define one another, jockey for position, eliminate or initiate competition, exercise or pursue power, and engage in a wide array of other activities that variously encourage or discourage, create or transform, and reproduce or ignore identities. . . . Our concern is with the arenas where boundaries are established, where some identities become more elaborate or comprehensive and some less, and where patterns of intergroup stratification are established or change, altering the advantages and disadvantages that different identities carry. (Cornell and Hartmann, 1998: 154)

It is these contexts—labor, power, sexuality, and culture—that specifically condition human action, identity, and place in such a way that hierarchies of difference may be maintained or challenged. Difference is expressed and reaffirmed within each of these structures, in very distinct yet parallel ways.

LABOR

Because categorical differences between groups are assumed to be accompanied by differences in capacities, there are also dramatic discrepancies in the place and treatment of groups in the context of labor.

Thus, the social division of labor represents a valuable support for prevailing structures of inequality (Connell, 1987, 1995; Pharr, 1995). Moreover, as Suzanne Pharr notes, "The method is quite complex: limit education and training opportunities for women and people of color and then withhold adequate paying jobs with the excuse that people of color and women are incapable of filling them" (1995: 483).

The oppressive and exclusionary definition of difference discussed earlier reaches into the social division of labor. On the basis of presumed abilities (or lack thereof), those who are marked as different or inferior or deficient are correspondingly assigned productive and reproductive roles that are held to be in line with their "natural" tendencies. Predictably, the opportunities are limited to a very narrow range of relatively powerless positions, thereby maintaining and reinforcing their subordinate place. Moreover, job segregation into low-wage jobs ensures the unequal distribution of income that is also a hallmark of these relations of domination. Access to material resources—including education, employment, income level—places groups and individuals in relation to one another within the racialized or gendered hierarchy, for example. This distribution across labor categories ensures that "group identity construction is one eminently possible outcome" (Cornell and Hartmann, 1998: 160). The division of labor thus becomes a potential source of identification and of empowerment, or conversely, disempowerment (Messerschmidt, 1993).

POWER

The importance of power as a cornerstone of the politics of difference goes beyond purely economic concerns. "Power" is a much broader concept, encompassing "the ability to impose a definition of the situation, to set the terms in which events are understood and issues discussed, to formulate ideas and define morality, in short, to assert hegemony" (Connell, 1995: 107). Power, then, consists in the ability to set the terms of discourse and action, and to impose a particular type of order. Again, we might link this to the negative politics of difference, in that it seeks effectively to deny the authority of marked Others. Consequently, relations of power might be conceptualized in economic, social, political, or cultural terms. It is because it manifests itself in such a range of locations that power becomes such an important structural feature of the relations within and between groups.

While the exercise of power may be backed by force, it is most effective if exercised in more "legitimate" or acceptable forms—through ideological means, for example (I will return to this theme in the later discussion of culture as structural support). Whatever the dynamics that underlie the exercise of power, however, it remains an often contested means by which to maintain relations of subordination and domination.

Foucault stressed the importance of recognizing that each form of power contains its own corresponding forms of resistance. Those relations of inequality must consistently be reproduced in the midst of struggle and contestation.

SEXUALITY

Another major axis upon which structural patterns of inequality rest is sexuality. To the extent that a hegemonic form of masculinity exists in any historical period, it serves to create a hierarchy around sexual values and practices. In short, each culture can be characterized by a series of definitions of "appropriate" and "inappropriate" sexual forms. Specifically, those definitions "provide permissions, prohibitions, limits and possibilities" with respect to activities, partners, and objects of sexuality (Messerschmidt, 1993: 73).

Given these definitions—which might include prohibitions on racial or gendered couplings—certain behaviors and identities become marginalized at best, stigmatized and demonized at worst. Again, whatever is outside the norm is considered deviant, the negative Other, and therefore subordinate on the hierarchy of sexuality. Conversely, the enactment of hegemonic forms of sexuality reinforces the exercise of other forms of power.

CULTURE

Similarly, cultural artifacts and practices intersect with other structural patterns to give rise to relations of inequality. Speaking of the production of culture, John Fiske contends that "all meanings of self, of social relations, all the discourses and texts that play such important cultural roles can circulate only in relation to the social system. . . . Culture . . . and meanings . . . are centrally involved in the distribution and possible redistribution of various forms of social power" (cited in Apple, 1997: 124). Culture, then, is a crucial object in the construction of structural patterns of inequality. It is informed by, and in turn informs, other structures, such as power and sexuality. It is in the process of culture that we find the meanings, the significance, and the roles assigned to self and other.

Culture is a vast complex, encompassing political discourse, ideological constructs, media representations, and religious dogma. In the most coherent, and perhaps authoritarian cultures, each of these would correspond exactly. However, in Western culture—presumed to be more "open" and "democratic"—the fit is much looser; there remains more autonomy among and between the various forms. Nonetheless, even in the United States, it is possible to detect a relatively consistent discursive formation as described by Goldberg: "a totality of ordered relations and correlations—of subjects to each other and to objects; of economic production and reproduction, cultural symbolism, and signification; of laws and moral rules; of social, political, economic or legal inclusion and exclusion. The socio-discursive formation consists of a range of rules: 'is's' and 'oughts,' 'do's' and 'don'ts,' 'cans' and 'cannots,' 'thou shalts' and 'thou shalt nots'" (1990: 297).

Culture acts to disseminate and in fact normalize particular representations of groups independently and in relation to others—in ways that reinforce hierarchical structures. Thus, those characteristics of groups, those "natural" predispositions, those rules of sexuality, find expression in cultural processes. They are institutionalized in ideologies and stereotypes of racial or gender inferiority, in laws that marginalize or exclude particular groups and individuals, in media depictions that demonize the Other. Culture takes up the content of those other structural supports and gives them tangible substance.

STRUCTURAL CRISIS TENDENCIES

While each of the structural patterns addressed herein carries tremendous weight in constructing and maintaining difference, none is without its inherent contradictions. Connell (1995) refers to "crisis tendencies" in the hegemonic politics of gender, characterized by threats to the prevailing order. Historically, such tendencies have challenged and often altered gender relations, and especially the place and definition of diverse masculinities. However, the tendency toward flagging legitimacy is also characteristic of other relations of difference. We might also identify crisis tendencies in racial, sexual, or class orders, for example. Here, too, reactionary behavior meets the challenges posed by alternative systems of meaning.

As with any hegemonic formation, the structures of domination around gender, race, and sexuality are constantly subject to counter-hegemonic activity. Those Others recognizing their subordination or marginalization periodically seek to improve their position through the imposition of alternative visions of "what should be." They openly resist their enforced position of inferiority by making claims to equality or recognition. To the extent that this is so, such dynamics have transformative potential. This may be the case even if the hegemonic groups responds forcefully. Generally speaking, in the presence of strong challenges, the social order is unlikely to remain exactly as it was. Resistance historically has been met with some mutation—either progressive or reactionary. At the very least, such a disruption in the stability of the social system "destroys the taken-for-grantedness of . . . authority on which the simple reproduction of power inequalities rests" (Connell, 1987: 160).

DOING DIFFERENCE

While the foregoing analysis accounts for the sociocultural meaning and place of varied identities, it tells us little about how—at the level of human agency—we construct these identities as an individual or group. This is where the notion of structured action (Messerschmidt, 1993; 1997) becomes useful. From this perspective, the structures of oppression and their supporting institutional patterns provide the context and constraints within which we "do difference" as human actors. Moreover, it is the "interactions between individuals and groups (that) is the medium for much institutional functioning" (Acker, 1992: 568). It is these structural arrangements that define the standards to which we hold ourselves and others accountable with respect to the appropriate enactment of categories of difference (West and Fenstermaker, 1997). It is this accountability to race or gender, for example, that maintains existing racial and gender orders.

The distinction between structure and action is a false one. They do not represent an either/or opposition; rather, together they represent a coherent framework within which humans construct their identity. In other words, human action and interaction within these structural contexts are not merely determined; they are also determinant. Structures of domination are both context and outcome, constitutive of and by human behavior and interaction. In seeking to construct individual and collective identities we tend to re-create the conditions that maintain existing relations of power. Identity becomes "real" when we enact it in such a way that calls attention to the hegemonic ideologies that shape it, either by reaffirming it or challenging it. By engaging in "inappropriate" racial or gender behavior, for example, we actively challenge, perhaps alter, those arrangements. It is in the process of "doing difference" that the instability—the crisis tendencies—mentioned earlier are played out. In short, human action and interaction constitute, reconstitute, and periodically transform structures of difference.

Race, gender, sexuality—all those dimensions of identity discussed throughout—represent what West and Fenstermaker (1997) refer to as an "ongoing accomplishment" (see also Messerschmidt, 1993; 1997). Identity is created through conscious, reflective pursuit and must be established and reestablished under varied conditions. In other words, identity construction is an activity concerned with "managing situated conduct" according to socially normative expectations of what constitutes the "essence" of one's race or gender, for example (West and Zimmerman, 1987: 127).

The construction of identity is an interactive accomplishment by which actors perform their "manliness" or "womanliness," their "whiteness" or "blackness" or "Asian-ness." They do so with an eye to how their behavior will be interpreted or evaluated by others. Central to this conceptualization is the notion of "accountability." At all times, in all situations, actors are concerned with whether their behavior *will be seen to be* in accordance with approved standards for their assigned identity. Consequently, "To the extent that members of society know their actions are accountable, they will design their actions in relation to how they might be seen and described by others" (West and Fenstermaker, 1997: 25). Since this enactment is situated within existing relations of power, the conduct will generally repeat and thus support those relations (Winant, 1995: 505). Conventional culture is consumed with ensuring our awareness of and commitment to traditional notions of gender, sexuality, race, and so on. Movies, advertising, the legal order, even the organization of department stores take for granted the *essential* differences between groups noted earlier. It is in this context that we are continually expected to "account" for our gendered behavior, for example.

Within the essentialist understanding of identities, there is very little space for ambiguity, or crossing the boundaries between categories of difference. Speaking of gender, specifically, West and Zimmerman contend that "a person engaged in virtually any activity may be held accountable for performance of that activity as a *woman* or a *man*, and their incumbency in one or the other sex category can be used to legitimate or discredit their other activities" (1987: 136). In other words, accountability involves the assessment of behavior as either conforming or deviating from culturally normative standards. Whenever we "do difference"— which is a recurring effort—we leave ourselves open to reward or censure. So it is that we are discouraged from the "attempt to cross the line, to transgress, desert or quit" (Bourdieu, cited in Fine, 1997: 58).

To the extent that individuals or groups "perform" in a way that corresponds to the "mythical norm" or in ways that correspond to normative conceptions of one's identity construct, they are held to be doing difference appropriately (Messerschmidt, 1997). In so doing, they uphold the boundaries that separate them from the Other, and ultimately the social relations of power. Conversely, when individuals or groups cross those boundaries, when they fail to perform their identity in normative ways, they are held to be doing difference inappropriately, and thereby leave themselves open to censure. In situations such as this, where subordinate groups attempt to redefine difference, for example, they may become vulnerable to attack. With this in mind, Jean Miller's questions can be answered: "when does . . . confrontation with difference have negative effects: when does it lead to great difficulty, deterioration, and distortion, and to some of the worst forms of degradation, terror and violence—both for individuals and for groups—that human beings can experience?" (1995: 57). The answer: when boundaries are threatened, when subordinate groups seek to redefine their place, when they do difference inappropriately. Miller in fact answers her own questions in a similar way: "when subordinates show the potential for, or even more dangerously, have developed other [non-normative] characteristics—let us say intelligence, initiative, assertiveness—there is usually no room available within the dominant framework for acknowledgement of these characteristics" (1995: 60). The threat must be repressed, and the dominance of the hegemonic group reaffirmed. It is in this context that hate crime emerges as a resource for doing difference, and punishing those who do difference inappropriately.

DOING DIFFERENCE, DOING HATE CRIME

To summarize: when we do difference, when we engage in the process of identity formation, we do so within the confines of structural and institutional norms. In so doing—to the extent that we conform to normative conceptions of identity—we reinforce the structural order. However, not everyone always performs "appropriately." Frequently, we construct our gender or race or sexuality in ways that in fact challenge or threaten sociocultural arrangements. We step out of line, cross sacred boundaries, or forget our "place." It is in such a context that hate crime often emerges as a means of responding to the threats. The tensions between hegemonic and counterhegemonic actors may culminate in violent efforts to reassert the dominance of the former and realign the position of the latter.

Moreover, it is important to keep in mind the earlier assertion that identity is shaped relationally. Both the perpetrator and the victim of hate are continually engaged in the process of constructing their identities: "It is not only the racist or sexist who constructs difference, but the victim of each or both who seeks to create difference as well. At times, the 'victim' has done so in response to the racism and/or sexism in the society in order to survive, but at other times movements made up of these 'victims' have sought to redefine difference as part of a struggle for power and personhood" (Rothenberg, 1992: 48). Such alternative constructions of difference challenge the carefully molded perceptions of how the world should be, and what each person's or each group's place is in that world. When confronted with such novelties, one means by which to "put things right" is through violence. Consequently, hate crime provides a context in which the perpetrator can reassert his/her hegemonic identity and, at the same time, punish the victim(s) for their individual or collective performance of identity. In other words, hate-motivated violence is used to sustain the privilege of the dominant group, and to police the boundaries between groups by reminding the Other of his/her "place." Perpetrators thus re-create their own masculinity, or whiteness, for example, while punishing the victims for their deviant identity performance.

A paradox is apparent here. On the one hand, hate crime perpetrators are said to be punishing victims for inappropriate performances of sexuality or race, for example. So a black man engaged in a relationship with a white woman is victimized for having transcended both the boundaries of sexuality and race. On the other hand, he also is being punished for engaging in what is *perceived* to be race-appropriate behavior: he is living the stereotype of "black-man-as-predator," which has long been used to justify the inferior position of black males. What this suggests is a "lose-lose" situation. Victims may be punished for *transcending* normative conceptions of relevant categories of difference; but they also may be sanctioned for *conforming* to relevant categories of difference.

Where the popular image of the Other is constructed in negative terms—as it frequently is—group members may be victimized on the basis of those perceptions. Hate crime is thus "bolstered by belief systems which (attempt to) legitimate such violence" so as to "limit the rights and privileges of individuals/groups and to maintain the superiority of one group" (Sheffield, 1995: 438–439). Members of subordinate groups are potential victims *because of* their subordinate status. They already are deemed inferior, deviant, and therefore deserving of whatever hostility and persecution comes their way. In sum, they are "damned if they do and damned if they don't." If they perform their identities on the basis of what is expected of them, they are vulnerable. If they perform in ways that challenge those expectations, they are equally vulnerable.

Hate crime, then, is a forceful illustration of what it is to engage in situated conduct. The interactions between subordinate and dominant groups provide a context in which both compete for the privilege to define difference in ways that either perpetuate or reconfigure hierarchies of social power. Simultaneous and oppositional efforts to do difference set up tensions in which the act of victimization coconstructs the victim and perpetrator. This confrontation is informed by the broader cultural and political arrangements that "allocate rights, privilege and prestige according to biological or social characteristics" (Sheffield, 1995: 438). Perpetrators attempt to reaffirm their dominant identity, their access to resources and privilege, while at the same time limiting the opportunities of the victims to express their own needs. The performance of hate violence, then, confirms the "natural" relations of superiority/inferiority. It is a form of interpersonal and intercultural expression that signifies boundaries. And, significantly, the boundary is "capable of organizing personal interactions in sometimes lethal ways" (Cornell and Hartmann, 1998: 185).

The sort of sociological and cultural analysis of hate crime suggested herein allows us to recognize the oppression that it represents as residing in a structural complex of relations of power grounded simultaneously in race, class, gender, and sexuality. It is also important to recognize, as Messerschmidt (1993) implies, that the salience of each of these grounded subject positions varies across time and across situations. That is, any particular act of hate crime may involve the relative racial or gender or sexual identities of the actor involved, or even some combination of these.

THREE   Defending the Color Line:
Race, Difference, and Hate Crime

I was expected to act like a black man—or at least like a nigger. I shouted a greeting to the world and the world slashed away my joy. I was told to stay within my bounds, to go back where I belonged.

—Franz Fanon, *The Fact of Blackness*

Throughout most of the history of the United States, there was little question of who "the American" was. *He* was undoubtably and unquestionably white. So much was this taken for granted that white people have rarely seen themselves as racial creatures (Frankenberg, 1993). Only the Other belonged to what has culturally been defined as a "race." Unlike people of color, white people do not generally look through a filter of race when they gaze upon the world. Whiteness is conceived as the norm, and its attendant privileges are rendered invisible.

The normalization of whiteness constructs racialized boundaries that assume whiteness as the standard against which all others are judged. It divides white from nonwhite, "unraced" from "raced." As with gender, there is an ideological presumption of innate, biological differences between races, which is then extrapolated to cultural and ethical differences. One's biological race is understood to determine one's "essence," to the extent that physical characteristics are linked to all other elements of one's identity. It is the *mark* of race that gives rise to distinctions between groups, not the *reality* of race. As Elizabeth Spelman so elegantly put it, "The existence of racism does not require that there are races; it requires the belief that there are races" (1988: 208). So powerful is this belief in the United States that particular races have been excluded from immigration, excluded from political participation, excluded from citizenship, excluded from personhood—all on the basis of the prevailing credo of white supremacy and nonwhite inferiority.

This construction of racial difference subsequently justifies the above-mentioned exclusions and other marginalizing tendencies through racial ordering along hierarchical lines. As mentioned previously, difference has been understood negatively in the United States, so that it comes to signify deficiency or deviance. Consequently, "nonwhite" is equivalent to difference and inferiority. Nonwhite is the antithesis of white, and must necessarily remain subordinate to white. Such race-based juxtapositions are central to legitimating and rationalizing the marginalization of the Other who stands outside the boundaries of whiteness: "The attempt to racially define the conquered, the subjugated, or enslaved is at the same time an attempt to racially define the conqueror, the subjugator, or the enslaver" (Lopez, 1995: 199). Racial categorization, then, represents the placing of racial groups within unequal relations of dominance and subordination. Moreover, the resultant hierarchy—while the object of resistance—nonetheless is continually reconstituted in and through multiple social forms: discourse, power, policy, and patterns of ownership, for example. In other words, a web of racial projects is informed by interlocking cultural and structural forms (Omi and Winant, 1994).

Hate crime can be seen as one such racial project, in that it connects the structural meanings and organization of race with the cultural construction of racialized identity. On the one hand, it allows the perpetrators to reenact their whiteness, thereby establishing their dominance. On the other hand, it coconstructs the nonwhiteness of the victims, who are perceived to be worthy of violent repression either because they correspond to a demonized identity, or, paradoxically, because they threaten the racialized boundaries that are meant to separate "us" from "them." And all of this occurs within the institutional contexts of what is known to be the appropriate place of victim and victimizer.

It is in this sense that I refer to situated action: hate crime takes its meaning and its impact from the broader array of social and institutional patterns. As with any human activity, racial violence is mediated by and enacted within culturally available forms. Each of us is held accountable to our race category as we perform in diverse settings. Our racial performances "can be used to justify or discredit other actions; accordingly, virtually any action can be assessed in relation to its race category" (West and Fenstermaker, 1995: 22). So, for example, a Hispanic youth who excels in school is perceived by the majority to be crossing established racial boundaries. He is "discredited" to the extent that he has forgotten his place. Consequently, a white youth who victimizes this "upstart" will be justified and in fact rewarded for his efforts to reestablish the racialized boundaries between himself and his victim. Both actors have been judged for their actions, with predictable and reconstitutive consequences. Race—for both actors—has been (re)accomplished, the boundaries preserved.

In the quote that prefaced this chapter, Franz Fanon acknowledges his own "situated" experiences of "doing race." Fanon was no stranger to racialized violence. As an active and outspoken critic of Western racial politics, he often found himself accused of racial transgressions. bell hooks similarly attests to the violent potential inherent in the game of racial accountability. She observes that the daily violence experienced by so many black people "is necessary for the maintenance of racial difference. Indeed, if black people have not learned our place as second-class citizens through educational institutions, we learn it by the daily assaults perpetuated by white offenders on our bodies and beings that we feel but rarely publicly protest or name. . . . Most black folks believe that if they do not conform to white dominated standards of acceptable behavior they will not survive" (1995: 15). There is—as many black or Asian or Native American or Hispanic people know—danger in nonconformity and in challenging borders. The white gaze is upon them, judging them against their own whiteness, but also against those imposed standards to which hooks refers. Racial violence, then, becomes justifiable as a punishment for some transgressions of institutionalized codes of conduct. I turn now to a consideration of those structured patterns that tell us "where we belong." I will address the racialized contours of culture, power, labor, and sexuality, their implications for "doing race," and how racially motivated hate crime emerges as a supplementary means of constructing racial identity and difference within those institutional settings.

THE CULTURE OF RACISM

While racism constitutes a structured pattern of relationships between groups, it simultaneously might be understood as a cultural field of discourse in support of that structure. The practices of racism encompass exclusion, marginalization, subordination, and not least of all violence. But these patterns are predicated upon legitimating ideologies and images that mark the Other, and the boundaries between self and Other, in such a way as to normalize the corresponding inequities. Racist discourse, then, provides "a reservoir of procedural norms that not only tacitly inform routine activity, but are also able to legitimate more purposive, explicitly racist practices" (Smith, 1989: 150). It is within the cultural realm that we find the justifications for inequities, and for ethnoviolence. For it is this body of discourse that articulates the relations of superiority/inferiority, thereby establishing a hospitable environment for openly racist activity.

At the heart of this cultural field of discourse, one discovers "the American"—a deep-seated (albeit often contested) presumption of what it is to be American. As I noted earlier, for the dominant majority, this invariably suggests whiteness (Frankenberg, 1993; Wellman, 1993). Or perhaps David Wellman's characterization is more precise, since he suggests that the American identity revolves around "a conception of America that defines what it is not" (1993: 245). Culturally, white Americans construct themselves in negative relational terms. Their normative whiteness is created on the backs of the Other. The American is *not* raced, is *not* black or Asian, is *not* even ethnic. Language reinforces this exclusive categorizing in that the norm of whiteness is implicit in such terms as "black author," "Pakistani doctor," or the distinction between white "hired hands" and black "servants." Simultaneously, white Americans stand on this self-perception as a means of both constructing their identity and marginalizing, even denigrating, that of nonwhites.

Ethnoviolence becomes understandable in this context, as an arena in which the primacy of whiteness can be re-created, and in which the boundaries between what is and is not American can be reaffirmed. Xenophobic violence is especially acute with respect to immigrants and their descendants. Chinese, Koreans, Indians, and other people of color are perceived as "perpetual foreigners" who will never assimilate and become "American." They will forever be outsiders. The National Asian Pacific American Legal Consortium (NAPALC) cites a talk show host's complaints that world-class figure skaters Kristi Yamaguchi and Michelle Kwan—both second-generation Americans—were not "real" Americans (1995: 4). A New York City police officer acted on these sentiments when he beat a Pakistani cab driver. The assault was accompanied by the exclamation, "You immigrants think we're stupid. . . . This is my country, I'll teach you a lesson" (NAPALC, 1995: 7).

Violence predicated upon the "un-American" identity of the victim permits the perpetrator to reassert the normativity of the white American. It publicizes the perpetrator's message that he represents the ideal and that people of color fail to meet the standard. The white offender is the permanent insider, the victim the permanent outsider, who forever must be reminded of his or her relative status positions. This becomes particularly urgent when the dominant group feels insecure in its position, when the "American" is no longer easily identified. That this has been the case over the past decade and a half helps to account for the flurry of hate crime activity over that time period.

Howard Winant shares this contention, observing that "once, U.S. society was a nearly monolithic racial hierarchy, in which everyone knew his place. Today, nobody knows where he or she fits in the U.S. racial order" (1997: 41). The traditional primacy and privilege of whiteness has been seriously challenged if not eroded since the onset of the civil rights movement. As Winant's assertion suggests, we are now in the midst of a cultural shift, in which identity politics has thrown into question the historical correlation of Americanness and whiteness. Minority groups have asserted claims to inclusion and participation, that is, to the status of American. Such challenges to hegemonic cultural identities have—not surprisingly—engendered considerable anxiety and hostility. In other words, "trying to renegotiate a new American national identity and culture that no longer has the certainty of fixed race, class and gender categories creates change, confusion and often violence. When people are wronged, they can use violence as a weapon; thus the degree of violence can be linked to the issue of a changing American national identity" (Anderson and Collins, 1995: 361).

That national identity has undergone dramatic change in the past two decades. Immigration patterns have reshaped the demographics of the United States, so that by 2050, it is estimated that whites will represent a mathematical minority of the population. And with numerical strength has come political expression. Beginning with the black and Native American civil rights movements of the 1960s, racial and ethnic minority groups have mobilized, demanding a place and a voice that represents their identity. They are "in America's face" (Wellman, 1993: 246). This activism has created a sense of insecurity and uncertainty among the traditional white majority. And this has been accompanied by a reactionary ethos that often culminates in violence.

Paradoxically, perpetrators of hate crimes, who are motivated by fears of cultural changes, construct themselves as victims of these transformations. They are the "new minority," vulnerable to the threat presumed to be represented by people of color. From the perpetrators' perspective, their violence is legitimate, since they are protecting themselves and "their" country from the threat of outsiders—from the invasion by the "darkened hordes." The offenders become the champions of the race as they reassert the relative belongingness of whites in contrast to the outsider status of others.

Equally important as the reestablishment of whiteness as Americanness is the role hate crime plays in punishing those Others who have attempted to overstep their boundaries by assuming they, too, are worthy of first-class citizenship. Again, this is evident in anti-immigrant sentiment and its corresponding violence. But it is also apparent at more localized points of contact where whites feel their identity—or safety—threatened by unwelcome intrusions of people of color. Weis et al. (1997) uncovered such a sense of community loss in their interviews with white working-class men. These subjects expressed a "felt assault," a sense of "no longer belonging" in their own neighborhoods—sentiments they attributed to the influx of minorities "who they clearly position as the other" (Weis et al., 1997: 218). Similar perceptions underlie the violence associated with New Jersey's "Dot Busters," who sought to discourage the invasion of Pakistani and Indian residents. They, too, articulate a sense of loss in the midst of a "foreign" presence.

There are those who "belong" in a community—whether national or local—and those who do not. When the latter transgress the boundaries, they are held to be enacting their racial identities in unacceptable and threatening ways. The consequences of their violations are apparent in such tragic cases as the recent rash of racially motivated violence in Denver, Colorado, where one of the alleged murderers claimed, "Drank a little bit. I'm a deep thinker. Walked through town with my gun in my waist, saw the black guy and thought he didn't belong where he was at" (Time, 1997: 53). Similar motives were in play in the murders of Yusuf Hawkins in Bensonhurst and Michael Griffith in Howard Beach. Both had committed the unpardonable sin of entering white territory. One of Griffith's attackers led the assault shouting, "There's niggers on the boulevard. Let's kill 'em" (cited in Levin and McDevitt, 1993: 5). The implication was that they had no right to be present in that area and deserved to pay with their lives, as Griffith did. And the perpetrators could claim the support of their community. Many residents of Howard Beach, for example, expressed the sentiment that Griffith and the two other black youth who were assaulted deserved their fates. They were held responsible, since they had crossed the "color line." Illustrative of the community's justification for the attackers' actions are the following statements: "We're a strictly white neighborhood. They (the blacks involved in the attack) had to be starting trouble" and "Puerto Ricans and coloreds have no business here after 8 P.M. The (white) kids had no right to start trouble, but the black men never should have been here" (cited in Pinkney, 1994: 44–45). Similarly, Bensonhurst residents demonstrated remarkable racial solidarity in their support for the killers of Yusuf Hawkins. Hundreds of white residents met those demonstrating against racial violence with more of the same. They consistently harassed the marchers, greeting them with chants of "Niggers go home" and placards expressing racial slurs. Residents of both of these communities, and the perpetrators themselves, performed their whiteness through the denigration and persecution of blacks who happened into the neighborhoods. In an effort to be positively evaluated, as one Bensonhurst youth described, "You go on missions to impress your friends. You get a name as a tough guy who is down with the neighborhood and down with his people" (cited in Wellman, 1993: 240). In this way, the youths of such white communities can prove themselves accountable to their racial class.

But what is the basis for such exclusionary conceptions of Americanness and belongingness? Why and how are the racialized Others distinct from white America? We might look for a response to these questions in the realm of stereotypes and popular images. It is these portrayals that justify and underlie the hostile treatment of racial minorities. In line with an essentialist understanding of racial classification, the overriding ideology is that of inscribed traits, wherein "the stereotypes confine them to a nature which is often attached in some way to their bodies, and which thus cannot easily be denied" (Young, 1990: 59).

Stereotypes that distinguish the racialized Other from white subjects are thus grounded in what are held to be the identifying features of racial minorities. They help to distance white from not white. The latter is to be feared, ridiculed, loathed for its difference as recognized in the popular psyche. Almost invariably, the stereotypes are loaded with disparaging associations, suggesting inferiority, irresponsibility, immorality, and nonhumanness, for example. Consequently, they provide both motive and rationale for injurious verbal and physical assaults on minority groups. Acting upon these interpretations allows dominant group members to re-create whiteness as superiority, while castigating the Other for their presumed traits and behaviors. The active construction of whiteness, then, exploits stereotypes to legitimate violence.

No minority racial group can escape the application of labels that are held to apply to the group as a whole. Most communities of color share the unfortunate fate of being characterized as dishonest and deceitful. In some cases, this takes on the extreme of painting the whole group and especially males as criminal: violent, thieving, sexual predators. This is most likely to be associated with blacks and Hispanics, and increasingly with Chinese youth. Similarly, Jews and Asians (especially Koreans) are held to be dishonest in their business dealings. Blinded by greed, "those people" are not above manipulating and swindling honest white folks out of their hard-earned money. Several racial groups are also identified as lazy and unambitious. While these labels have long been applied to African Americans, in contemporary discourse they have been extended to Native Americans and Mexican Americans. The high unemployment rates of these groups are taken as a sign of their unwillingness to work, rather than the structural discrimination that precludes them from rewarding and high-paying jobs.

Beyond the stereotypes common to many groups like those examples above, particular groups are targets of more specific images. African Americans, for example, are deemed to be oversexed, to lack intelligence, and to be consumed by the need to entertain themselves. Native Americans are held not only to be lazy, but to be drunks as well. Asians—lumped together as one group in spite of their many regional distinctions—are marked by the stigma of being too serious, cunning, and yet submissive. Arabs in recent years have suffered dramatically in the cultural realm in the United States. The Arab world has become the "evil empire," with its people characterized as "violent, barbaric sex maniacs," always plotting a violent takeover of the United States (Sabbagh, 1990: 2). Asians are the one group that also consistently evokes a positive stereotype, as the "model minority." However, this too becomes the basis for hostility when whites perceive Asians to represent unfair competitors in business and employment.

Individuals enter each social interaction carrying with them the baggage that holds these stereotypical images. Whether a particular member of a minority group corresponds to these is almost immaterial. It is assumed—via gross generalizations—that all blacks are criminal, or all Asians are submissive, or all Jews are greedy. Violence motivated by these preconceptions becomes an effort to prove one's whiteness— racial solidarity—relative to the defiled Other. It is a claim to superiority, which is meant to establish once and for all that the white perpetrator is not black, is not Asian, is not Jewish. Rather, the perpetrator removes himself from the victim group by engaging in violence directed against it—surely one would not seek to harm the self, only the Other.

The self-righteousness with which white perpetrators proclaim their identity is implicit in a recent case of anti-Asian violence. In San Francisco, a Chinese-American woman's yard was scattered with garbage and dog feces, her car scratched, and her garage door marked with racist graffiti. The perpetrators marked their "obvious" virtue by calling attention to the negative difference represented by the woman's racial categorization: among the slurs on the door was: "These chinks and gooks steal and eat pets" (NAPLAC, 1995: 30). By marking the Chinese with these stigmata, white perpetrators are simultaneously marking themselves as the opposite: moral, humane, honest, law-abiding; in short, as the ideal representatives of humanity.

Similarly, when the youths of Bensonhurst and Howard Beach attacked their victims, they did so within the context of a mind-set that distinguished "us" from "them." The black youths were to be excluded from the neighborhood because they were presumed to be "looking for trouble." In contrast to the white defenders of the race, the black victims were constructed as threats to the physical and economic security of the white residents of the neighborhoods—of course they had robbery or murder or sexual assault on their minds, since "all black men" are criminals. Again, attacking these youths provided the offenders with proof of their masculine role of defenders, to be sure; but it also provided them with proof of their racial purity and solidarity. They were not like their victims. Rather, they were the virtuous ones: their actions were inscribed with the mark of the moral supremacy of whiteness. As Fine comments in another context, "Among these white adolescent men, people of color are used consistently as a foil against which acceptable moral, and particularly sexual, standards are established. The goodness of white is always contrasted with the badness of black—Blacks are involved in drugs, Blacks are unacceptable sexually, Black men attempt to "invade" white sexual space. . . . The binary translates in ways that compliment white boys" (1997: 57). Violence is an important mechanism through which these "translations" are made. It helps to reestablish the natural hierarchy of goodness and evil, strength and weakness, morality and immorality. It ensures that whites and people of color will inhabit their appropriate places in physical and cultural terms.

RACIALIZED SEXUALITY

As the preceding quote implies, from the perspective—historical and contemporary—of white Americans, one of the most palpable realms of difference between "us" and "them" lies in sexuality. And it is in this context that people of color often are subject to the most vicious opprobrium and hostility precedent to racial violence. While they are perceived generally as threatening—in economic, political, and social terms—they are especially to be feared, ridiculed, and censured on the basis of their presumed sexualities. Black male sexuality, frequently Jewish male sexuality, and occasionally Asian male sexuality are constructed as "dangerous, powerful and uncivilized force(s) that (are) hazardous to white women and a serious threat to white men" (Daniels, 1997: 93). Yet it is also the case that people of color are held up to ridicule and hostility because of the opposite assumption: that they are asexual or undersexed, a myth commonly associated with Asian males, for example. Thus, their masculinity is thrown into question. Moreover, women of color are feared and reviled on the same basis: they are racialized, exotic Others who do not fit the Western ideal of womanhood. Additionally, whether male or female, whether cast as over- or undersexed, people of color are most at risk when they visibly cross the racialized sexual boundaries by engaging in interracial relationships.

On the basis of these controlling images of people of color, white women and especially white men are fearful and suspicious of the sexualities of the Other. Speaking of the white fear of black bodies in particular, Cornel West contends that this "fear is rooted in visceral feelings about black bodies and fueled by sexual myths of black men and women . . . either as threatening creatures who have the potential for sexual power over whites, or as harmless, desired underlings of a white culture" (1993: 199). In this context, hate crime functions to reinforce the normativeness of white sexuality while punishing people of color for their real or imagined sexual improprieties. It is a means of degrading the bodies of the Other, with an eye to controlling them. Hate crime emasculates the sexual threat, thereby firmly establishing the essential boundaries between groups.

As noted previously, white Western culture has long held to para-doxical controlling images of the sexualities of people of color. Foremost among these has been the tendency to imagine people of color as "excessive, animalistic, or exotic in contrast to the ostensibly restrained or civilized sexuality of white women and men" (Frankenberg, 1993: 75). At different times, in different contexts, most nonwhite groups have been perceived as sexual predators, guided by their animal-like instincts. Since all but the white race were historically held to be subhuman creatures anyway, it was a small step to paint the Others' sexuality in similar terms. Unlike their white superiors, people of color had not learned to tame their sexual desires, nor to direct them toward "appropriate" objects, that is, members of their own race.

The "exotic" Chinese male laborer of the nineteenth century, for example, was feared to be sex-starved, predatory, and lascivious. Thus he was seen as a threat to white women. This perceived risk was but one of the motives underlying the anti-Asian sentiment and violence at the turn of the century. However, nowhere have white fears been more pal-pable than in their historical relationship with black males. No other group has been so narrowly defined by its sexuality than have black males. This was clear under slavery, where "bucks" were valued for their breeding capacity, but also where black male subordination was justified on the grounds of his savage and beastly nature. As Messerschmidt (1997: 23) contends, black masculinity was irrevocably defined in terms of black sexuality, which in turn was seen as "animalistic and bestial" (1997: 23). Thus, the unrestrained instincts and desires of black men could be reined in only through the use or threat of violence.

The sexualized image of black males was reproduced in postbellum culture. In fact, to the extent that African Americans' sexual independ-ence was correlated with their economic and political freedom, they presented an even greater threat to white masculine superiority. The fact that alleged black rapists were as often castrated as lynched suggests an attempt to emasculate the "savage" by symbolically (and literally) erasing his identity—much as one would control a wild dog. The vicious punishment meted out to black males served to highlight their animal nature, at the same time that it reinforced the power and hegemony of white males. Consequently, "Both race and masculine difference were reproduced through the practice of lynching and castration and ulti-mately emasculating the African American male body" (Messerschmidt, 1997: 36).

The presumption of black male as sexual predator continues to underlie racial difference and racial violence in the contemporary era. In fact, the myth of rapacious and insatiable black sexuality is perhaps one of the most enduring themes in United States culture. It emerged in the 1988 Willie Horton ads; it was evoked even by Clarence Thomas's claim that he was the victim of a "high-tech" lynching; and it ensured Mike Tyson's conviction for sexual assault. The image of the black sexual predator is the cultural lens through which whites perceive blacks. As such, it provides the context for racially motivated violence: violent people are worthy of violent repression.

The thread that binds these historical processes together—and that makes hate crime such a valuable resource—is the coconstruction of the black sexual predator and the white savior. At the height of white resistance to black citizenship, South Carolina Senator Bill Tillman expressed the black threat and the white response: "The white women of the South are in a state of siege. . . . Some lurking demon who has watched for the opportunity seizes her; she is ravished, her body prostituted, her purity destroyed, her chastity taken from her. . . . So far as I am concerned he has put himself outside the pale of the law, human and divine. . . . We revert to the impulse to 'kill, kill, kill'" (cited in Wiegman, 1993: 237–238). Only through avenging the "defilement" of the white woman can the white male reclaim his appropriate position as the "protector" and "savior" of white women. This simultaneously casts the black male in the image of "evil" and the white male in the image of "goodness" (and, of course, white women as defenseless).

Fine et al. uncovered contemporary evidence of this dichotomization in their interviews with white male high school students, who proclaimed both their right and duty to preserve the chastity of white girls, for themselves: "Much expressed racism centers on white men's entitled access to white women, thus serving the dual purpose of fixing black men and white women on a ladder of social relations. . . . This felt need to protect white girls translates as a code of behavior for white male students. It is the fact that *Black* men are invading *White* women, the property of *White* men, that is at issue here" (1997: 57–58).

In defending their white girls from the unrestrained sexuality of black boys, the white boys are also defending themselves—that is, the sanctity of their own carefully restrained, "civilized," normative sexuality. These youths are reacting to messages received from the broader culture. Few other interpretations are available to them when a high school principal can ban interracial dating with the disclaimer that "It is not that I have anything against interracial dating. . . . It's just that those black boys really want our white girls" (cited in Fine et al., 1997: 59).

Moreover, these codes of behavior often rest on violence as a means of policing the relative identities. Yusuf Hawkins, for example, was a proxy for eighteen-year-old Keith Mondello, evidently aggravated by the revelation that a former girlfriend had dated black and Hispanic men. Mondello was further disturbed on the night he formed the group that killed Hawkins when the girl told him that she had planned to celebrate her birthday with a group of black and Puerto Rican friends. The anger and hostility of Mondello and his predominantly Italian peers were so evident that the party was canceled. Deprived of direct targets of their wrath—the potential partygoers—Mondello and his friends turned their anger on three other, interchangeable black youths who had happened to be in the neighborhood. One of Mondello's accomplices is said to have exclaimed, "Let's not club the niggers, let's shoot them and show Gina," presumably as a means of reminding Gina and any black males with an interest in white women that their "unnatural" desires would not be tolerated.

In contrast to the fear and hostility with which the black male predator is met, ridicule is the sentiment often directed toward other men of color. Yen Espiritu (1997) points out the fact that the image of Asian males as sexually rapacious is generally overshadowed by the opposite extreme: the image of Asian men as undersexed or effeminate. Espiritu traces this tendency historically to the anti-Asian, exclusionary immigration policies of the turn of the century. By restricting the entry of women, such policies created all-male Asian enclaves that subsequently "reversed the construction of Asian masculinity from 'hyper-sexed' to 'asexual' and even 'homosexual'" (Espiritu, 1997: 90). Just as castration emasculated black males, so too did the enforced bachelorhood of Asian males emasculate them. The absence of Asian women meant, first and foremost, that Asian men could not "engage" with women. But it also meant that they were pushed into feminized labor: they were responsible for the household labor. Later, World War II internment of the Japanese deprived their men of the breadwinner role in such a way as to once again throw all areas of masculinity—including sexual prowess—into question. The perceived emasculation of Asian men continues to be reflected in the model minority stereotype, with its presumption of passivity and subordination.

While such a passive picture of Asian men does not engender much in the way of hostility or antagonism, it nonetheless does present an opportunity for engaging in hate crime as a means of policing the relative sexual identities of perpetrator and victim. *Because* of their reputation for passivity, Asian men are seen to be easy victims on which to practice domination; *because* of their reputation as a model minority, Asian men are seen to be legitimate victims; *because* of their reputation as sexual eunuchs, Asian men are not "real men" and thus represent a weak link in the chain of masculine domination; *because* of their racial difference and all that entails, Asian men must also be refused access to white women, lest they threaten the purity of the race.

Jewish men also occupy an uncertain place on the racialized hierarchy of sexuality. For the most part, Jews are not regarded as a direct threat in the way black males are. They are, rather, presumed to be asexual—apparently their financial desires overwhelm their sexual desires.

However, Jewish men are presumed to represent a more insidious sexual threat. From their positions of cultural and political power, Jews are in fact suspected of encouraging homosexuality as a means of weakening the hegemony of white, heterosexual, Christian males. Jessie Daniels refers to this as the "feminizing influence of Jewish men on white men" (1997: 112). It is the Jews, according to white supremacist rhetoric, who have spawned the current wave of "degeneracy" and "homosexuality" (1997: 112). In so doing, they have created a cultural phenomenon that threatens to minimize not only the sexual dominance of heterosexual white men, but also their political and economic power. Moreover, this process is exacerbated by the corresponding tendency of Jews to encourage whites to engage in interracial relationships. Once again, this deprives white men of their sexual rights to white women; but at the same time, it weakens the white race by introducing "impurities" into the bloodlines.[1]

The hostility toward interracial relationships and interracial sexuality ultimately is grounded in the essentialist understanding of racial difference. Boundary crossing is thus not only unnatural, but threatening to the rigid hierarchies that have been built around these presumed differences. This sentiment is evident in a letter to the editor written in response to a photo of black and white youths dancing together: "Interracial marriages are unbiblical and immoral. God created different races of people and placed them amongst themselves. . . . There is nothing for white Americans to gain by mixing their blood with blood of other peoples. There will only be an irreversible damage for us" (cited in Mathabane and Mathabane, 1992: 186).

(DIS)EMPOWERING RACE

An obvious hallmark of racism as a structure of domination is the restriction of the power of nonwhite racial groups. To this end, racial minorities have historically been limited in terms of social, political, and economic power (the latter will be addressed explicitly in the next section). In 1965, Kenneth Clark suggested the boundaries within which racial minorities circulated. His metaphor remains apt now, thirty years later: "The dark ghetto's invisible walls have been erected by the white society, by those who have power, both to confine those who have *no* power and to perpetuate their powerlessness. The dark ghettos are social, political, educational, and—above all—economic colonies" (cited in Pinkney, 1994: 7).

---

1. As I suggested, Jewish sexualities are rarely a direct motivating factor in anti-Semitic violence with respect to isolated hate crime perpetrators. However, I will discuss in a later chapter how the perception of the Jewish conspiracy to encourage homosexuality and miscegenation is of paramount importance in the rhetoric of many organized hate groups.

The ghetto to which Clark refers is not only a geographical location. It is, metaphorically, a social process by which minorities are marginalized—ghettoized—relative to legitimate sources of empowerment. The sorts of racial constructions and categorizations discussed earlier are the stuff of which social exclusions are built, to the extent that they legitimate discrepancies in access to opportunities and privilege. The power that is wielded—physical and social—by whites is exercised in such a way as to "develop, evolve, nurture, spread, impose, and enforce the very myths . . . that underlie racism" (Fernandez, 1996: 160).

Historically in the United States, power cautiously has been guarded by imposing restrictions on citizenship and its correspondent rights. Taking Dee Cook's interpretation of Marshall's taxonomy of rights as a starting point, we can examine how minority groups in the United States have been denied inclusion: "To possess citizenship is to be a full member of the community and to enjoy the civil, political and social rights which constitute membership" (1993: 156).

Whether through formal policy or informal practice, racialized minorities have consistently been disenfranchised as a means of limiting their voice and position in the United States. Slavery, for example, effectively denied the humanity and thus eligibility for citizenship of black men and women. This institution constructed whiteness as personhood and blackness as property—as chattel. At the very moment when democracy and liberty were heralded, slavery sentenced blacks to a rightless existence. Consequently, blacks were restricted from the exercise of political (voting, holding office), civil (giving testimony against whites), and social (access to public buildings, right to choose one's employment) empowerment until well into the twentieth century.

While not subject to slavery, most other racial minority groups nonetheless have suffered a similar lack of access to citizenship resources. Native Americans, for example, were not only denied voting rights and other forms of political expression; efforts were made to "deculturate" them by removing children from their families and placing them in foster homes or boarding schools where they could be re-created in the image of the dominant white culture. The earliest Chinese immigrants—welcomed as a source of cheap labor—nonetheless were excluded from enjoying privileges of citizenship by the Chinese Exclusion Act of 1882. Japanese Americans likewise were barred from citizenship (until 1952), as well as from owning or buying land. For a brief period of time, they were restricted from residing in West Coast states. The latter was a fallout of World War II resettlement and incarceration of West Coast Japanese, or what amounted to a total deprivation of civil liberties.

While no ethnic or racial group legally is excluded from attaining United States citizenship at this time, it does not necessarily follow that all groups are able to enjoy the privileges associated with this status. Racial minorities continue to be marginalized by their inability to gain full access to political, civil, and social rights, such that inclusion is still constituted of and by "whiteness," not "color." Collectively, Native Americans' sovereignty continues to be thwarted by the failure of the state to recognize treaty rights. As a group, Natives are limited in political and economic terms. Civil rights violations of an array of racial and ethnic groups are endemic. The 1992 beating of Rodney King and the 1997 sodomizing of Abner Louima—both by police officers—are but the tip of the iceberg. Similarly, the 1997 sweep of Chandler, Arizona, illustrated and reinforced the subordinate status of people of color. This search for undocumented Latino/Latina immigrants constituted a dramatic breach of the civil rights and liberties of the dozens of "apparently" Hispanic *citizens*—people randomly stopped and ordered to produce their "papers," solely on the basis of their presumed race. Similarly, housing and mortgage discrimination continues to be a determining factor in the persistence of racial and ethnic segregation (Hacker, 1995; Smith, 1995). And, while the political power of minorities has increased somewhat over the past couple of decades, all such groups are still underrepresented in the formal machinery of politics.

Racially motivated violence is directly implicated in efforts to maintain these unequal relations of power. It is itself a mechanism of social power by which white males in particular assert a particular version of hegemonic whiteness. It is not difficult to trace the history of racially motivated violence during periods when the power of whites was perceived to be at risk—periods in which this identity was reconstructed through the exercise of violence as a resource for "doing race." Nor is it difficult to identify contemporary illustrations.

Violence in general long has been accepted as a means of flexing one's muscles, both literally and figuratively. Racially motivated violence, specifically, continues to be a mechanism for doing so in such a way as to reinforce the privilege of whiteness and the subjugation of color. It represents a "will to power" by which the very threat of otherwise unprovoked acts of violence "deprives the oppressed of freedom and dignity" (Young, 1995: 83). Conversely, both the threat and use of violence by white perpetrators enhance their authority in the eyes of the communities of both the victim and the offender. Violence is empowering for its users: physical dominion implies a corresponding cultural mastery, as indicated by Gunner Lindberg's letter boasting of his killing of a Vietnamese man, Thien Minh Ly: "Oh I killed a jap a while ago. I stabbed him to death at Tuslin High School . . . I walked right up to him and he was scared . . . he got happy that he wasn't gona get jumped. Then I hit him . . . I stabbed him about 7 or 8 times he rolled over a little so I stabbed his back out 18 or 19 times then he layed flat and I slit one side of his throat on his jugular vein . . . I stabbed him about 20 or 21 times in the heart" (cited in Phan, online: 2).

The murderer's use of the derogatory label "jap" implies the racial distancing and animosity that underlie Lindberg's motive. He signifies his dominant whiteness by derogating Ly's Asian identity. That Ly was in fact Vietnamese and not Japanese further confirms Lindberg's presumption of superiority and hauteur. It is enough to know that Ly was Asian—no need to discern his true ethnicity or national origin. Any Asian could be at risk. Thus, the entire community is put on notice. Moreover, Lindberg's awareness that his racial identity was reinforced by his acts is clear in his pretentious statement within the letter: "here's the clippings from the newspaper, we were on all the channels." Lindberg assumes that his audience—upon learning of his exploits in the media—will judge his whiteness and not find him lacking. He is appropriately accountable to his race, given his eagerness to destroy the Other. No race traitor there; rather Lindberg announces through his actions that he is in solidarity with the white race, thereby preserving white privilege and position.

Such racial constructions, however, are dynamic and relational. Not only does this example illustrate how perpetrators empower whiteness through violence. It is also suggestive of the opposite: disempowerment of the victims' communities. Ly's death—like other hate-motivated assaults—also represents an effort to render impotent the targeted group. Individual assaults are a warning sign to others like the victim: you could be next. As we saw earlier in Richard Wright's description of the vicarious experience of racial violence: "The things that influenced my conduct as a Negro did not have to happen to me directly; I needed but to hear of them to feel their full effects in the deepest layers of my consciousness." A black person or a Korean person or a Hispanic person need not have been a victim personally. Like Wright—like bell hooks, cited previously—they are all too aware of their constant vulnerability because of their race. The immutability of their racial identity invokes hopelessness—they are victimized for reasons they cannot change. In the midst of the "Dot Busters" campaign of terror against Asian Indians in Jersey City, an open letter made clear the generalized vulnerability of a group: "If I'm walking down the street and I see a Hindu and the setting is right, I will just hit him or her" (cited in "Racial Violence Against Asian Americans," 1993). Thus, hate crimes have the potential to throw an entire community into paralysis, forcing it to withdraw further into itself. The victimized group redefines itself as powerless in the face of the racist onslaught. William Marovitz observes that "By making members of minority communities fearful, by making them suspicious of other groups, and of the power structure that is supposed to protect them, these incidents can damage society and polarize our communities" (1993: 50). Such violence reaffirms the subordinate status of minority communities. At its extreme, it discourages social and political participation, by keeping potential victims off the streets and out of the public eye. Moreover, when perpetrated at the hands of police officers, or with their tacit approval, it even minimizes the enjoyment of civil rights.

Paradoxically, efforts to render minority communities impotent—whether through the mechanism of hate crime or other repressive means—can backfire. Rather than hobbling the victim group, they may in fact mobilize the community. This was the case in New York City, for example, where Haitians accompanied by other Caribbeans demonstrated angrily, vocally, and visibly against the racist violence represented by Louima's brutal beating at the hands of police officers. While innumerable victims had previously remained silent out of fear and intimidation, the publicity surrounding Louima's victimization galvanized the community into action.

A decade earlier, other New York neighborhoods witnessed similar rallies. The racially motivated murders of Michael Griffith in Howard Beach and Yusuf Hawkins in Bensonhurst both resulted in flurries of organizing and demonstrating. An organization created after the first murder—New York City Civil Rights Coalition—was still available to lend its support to those involved in prosecuting the Hawkins case. Both incidents inspired widespread demonstrations condemning the racism of the perpetrators' communities, as well as the racist culture of New York City generally. Clearly these cases stimulated rather than disabled the communities.

Unfortunately, this posture of empowerment often is seen as an affront to white dominance. The victim community is perceived to be violating the anticipated rules of behavior. Instead of accepting their subordination, they resist it. In such a context, incidents of hate crime may escalate in retaliation. Consider the case of Farmington, New Mexico, in the mid-1970s. In response to the vicious murders of three Indian men, local Navajo activists established the Coalition for Navajo Liberation. While the immediate cause of the coalition was to see justice done in the prosecutions for the offence, it soon expanded to address the broader patterns of discrimination and victimization experienced by Natives in the border town. As the coalition dug in its heels and intensified its demands for justice, the antagonism of the white community became clear. Rather than discourage anti-Navajo violence, the activism of the Coalition for Navajo Liberation seemed to inspire it, as evident in the increase in the number of drive-by shootings at hogans, and at sheep tended by Navajo people (Barker, 1992).

Similarly, in Bensonhurst and Howard Beach, demonstrations were met with vicious racial slurs, flying bottles, and vandalized cars.

Activism—a sign of strength—begets animosity. Depressingly little has changed since John Dollard observed in the 1930s that "white people fear Negroes. They fear them, of course in a special context, that is, when the Negro attempts to claim any of the white prerogatives or gains. . . . By a series of hostile acts and social limitations, the white caste maintains a continuous threatening atmosphere against the possibility of . . . demands by Negroes; when successful, the effect is to keep the social order intact" (cited in Doob, 1993: 75). Seen in this light, hate crime is a reactionary tool, a violent and extreme response to the Other who is out of control, who has overstepped his or her social or political boundaries, thereby challenging the entrenched hierarchies.

THE ECONOMICS OF RACE

The presumption of racial hierarchies has had, and continues to have, a profound impact on the place of minority groups within the labor process. In particular, people of color traditionally have been marginalized and exploited as free, cheap, and malleable labor (Young, 1990). Thus, while the political and social gains made by minorities in recent years threaten white cultural identity, economic gains represent a more direct and tangible threat to white economic security. People of color who presume to advance on the economic ladder are perceived as unfair and undeserving competitors, and takers of "white" jobs. People of color are seen to have "overstepped" the economic boundaries which have long contributed to their marginalization. Consequently, it is in the context of economics that white fear and resentment are most frequently and viciously translated into racial violence.

Where once whiteness guaranteed status and security, this is no longer the case. Gone are the days when minorities legitimately could be excluded from rewarding job opportunities. Gone, too, are the days of plentiful industrial and manufacturing jobs that offered white males the resources for constructing dominant racial and gender identities: family wage and physical labor. The massive economic restructuring that has taken place in the United States over the last two decades has resulted in a shift from industrial to service jobs, the latter providing significantly less opportunity for constructing an aggressive and masterful white masculinity.

Few working-class men acknowledge the role that corporate elites have played in this reconstruction (Weiss, Proweiller, and Centrie, 1997). Instead, they blame their perceived loss of privilege on the undeserving Other, who usually is constructed in racial terms. It is African Americans, Asian Americans, Hispanic Americans, and immigrant minorities who are thought to attain "privilege" through affirmative action and welfare, for example. Consequently, the racialized Other is viewed with hostility and resentment. It is in this contradictory space that hate crime often emerges as a means of reasserting white racial privilege, while punishing people of color for what is perceived to be their unearned winning of privilege.

Many white men now picture and present themselves as the "new minority." They experience a sense of displacement and dispossession relative to people of color. This imagery of "white-man-as-victim" gives voice to the insecurity of white men in a weakened economy. It also provides an ideological rationale for re-creating people of color as legitimate victims. Thus, perpetrators of ethnoviolence are akin to the young white men interviewed by Fine, who act or "speak for a gendered and racial group whose privilege has been rattled and whose wrath is boiling over" (Fine et al., 1997: 66).

Where have all the jobs gone? From the perspective of many disaffected white workers, the answer is clear enough. They have not been relocated offshore, or replaced by technology. Rather, they have been stolen from them by lesser and unfit beings: those uppity Others who have won the ears of politicians and employers alike. The most visible manifestation of this inverted preference for minorities is the bogey of affirmative action. There is a widespread consensus emerging that affirmative action policies have resulted in the displacement of qualified white workers by unqualified minority workers (Fine et al., 1997; Weiss et al., 1997). In a curious inversion of history, many white males imagine an array of signs stating "Whites Need Not Apply." This is particularly frustrating in the context of the cultural constructions of blacks, Hispanics, and Native Americans, for example, as lazy and undisciplined. Where white workers imagine themselves at the opposite pole—hardworking and dedicated—the backdrop is set for a volatile response.

"Reverse discrimination" provides the motive and rationale for harassment and assaults of minority workers. This has become evident in the studies of workplace ethnoviolence carried out by the Prejudice Institute, which find relatively high rates of harassment and defamation of people of color, in other words, those who "don't belong" (Weiss, Ehrlich, and Larcon; 1991–1992; Ehrlich, 1998). Successive reports of the U.S. Commission on Civil Rights (1990; 1992a; 1992b; nd) also reveal the links between hostility toward affirmative action and violence against minorities. An especially brutal illustration of this connection occurred in Novato, California, in 1995, when a man named Robert Page attacked Eddy Wu, a Chinese American, at a supermarket. He stabbed him twice in the parking lot, then followed him back into the store where he stabbed him several times more. Wu was left with multiple injuries, including a punctured lung. Page later testified that he had consciously set out to "kill me a Chinaman" because "they got all the good jobs" (NAPALC, 1995: 8). A 1990 Commission on Civil Rights summary report cites Gurr's conclusion that "most of the historical episodes of anti-democratic action occurred in times, in places and among people who suffered from economic dislocation. . . . Their grievances in those circumstances tend to focus on the Federal government and on minorities . . . because they are believed to receive unfair advantage from Government programs" (15–16). Ethnoviolence is an attempt to reclaim the advantages of whiteness. It is an assertion of racial superiority and, more important, proprietorship: to the white man, not some "third world invader," belong the spoils. Violence motivated by the resentment of labor competition provides the perpetrator with the opportunity to publicly announce his indignation and, correspondingly, his "right to work." This is the essence of white masculinity after all: the ability to provide. If he is to distinguish himself from minorities of color, he must forcibly resist the latter's access to equitable conditions of employment.

This disaffection has been a boon to the white supremacist movement, which has exploited the growing backlash against affirmative action. There is a convergence between public animosity and the white supremacist rhetoric that poses the white male as victim. This has become a common theme in the groups' calls to arms. White Nationalist leader Yggdrasil is explicit in his condemnation of the empowerment of racial minorities: "Now black and brown people are not fools, they know they are being rewarded for raising a rukus [sic]. So far, they keep getting the same rewards for it. More rukus [sic] leads to more benefits, more advantages, more tribute, and more humiliation of the average White by their own elite" (online). In response to oppositional racial identities, white supremacists lash out against the usurpation of "their" place. Minorities—conspiring with the federal government—have blurred the economic boundaries that traditionally marginalized people of color. White supremacists would have us put racial minorities back in their place—whether this is defined as another country, the menial labor pool, the emergency room, or the morgue. "White Nationalism" or "White Power" provides the solutions to the dispossession of white workers. The politics of white racialism provides a forum for white men to reconstruct themselves in their proper form: as superior racial beings, legitimately benefiting from their racial identity economically, politically, and socially.

Part of this agenda to regain control involves a similar backlash against immigrants. While immigrants historically have been associated with moral and cultural threats, they also have been targets of racial animus on the basis of their perceived economic threat. Immigration, then, is seen as another part of the explanation for white job loss. What makes the current wave of immigrants even more threatening than those in the past is that they are perceived to be inassimilable—people of color. Again, the notions of their undeservingness and their unfair competition emerge, as we see in the following statement from American Dissident Voices, which contrasts the undisciplined immigrants of today with their previous counterparts: "The immigrants of the last century were nearly all Europeans and were assimilated to our culture and institutions quickly and *they proved their mettle by hard work by which they built our Western Civilization* across a nearly empty wilderness" (online, emphasis added). Implicit in this analysis is the assumption that immigrants will not work hard, but will nonetheless steal valuable employment opportunities from white workers. Interestingly, even as immigrants attempt to reproduce for themselves a productive racial identity, they are demonized. Rather than reward their initiative, the white "hosts" punish them through harassment and violence. In recent years, those of Hispanic and Asian descent have taken the brunt of the anti-immigrant violence, for slightly different reasons.

Hispanics—Mexicans in particular—often are held responsible for the dual threats of wage depression and competition for unskilled and semiskilled jobs. Based on the erroneous assumption that the vast majority of Hispanics are undocumented, many white males accept the view that these immigrants are working illegally and therefore at very low wages. Joe Feagin reminds us that the situation is more complicated than this; Mexican immigrants, especially, "mostly take low-wage jobs in textile, construction, agriculture and service firms, and, as happened in earlier decades, the competitive job situation causes resentment from native-born workers. This is the case even though most immigrants have little effect on the employment situations of native-born workers because they mostly fill low-wage jobs that would not otherwise have been filled or created" (1997: 29).

There is an abundance of examples to illustrate the link between job competition and racially motivated violence. Hispanic day laborers and those living in migrant worker camps are frequent victims. In 1992, six white males armed with baseball bats beat a Hispanic man in an Alpine, California, migrant workers' camp. They later bragged about "kicking Mexican ass" (SPLC, 1997: 223). It was not only the particular victim that was being admonished. The beating also served notice that Mexicans as a class were not welcome. The victim was but one symbol of the unwillingness of his people to stay in their place—in other words, across the border.

An equally dramatic case occurred in 1996 at the University of California at Davis where a Mexican woman threatened to overstep her boundaries. She was a successful engineering student, an intern for a state legislator lobbying for humane immigration policies. Two white males attacked her, punching her, cutting her hair, and writing on her body with black marker "Wetback" and "Go home illegal." They later warned her that, if she reported the assault, she and her "wetback friends" would be killed (Martinez, 1997: 238). This woman represented the dual threat posed by Mexican immigrants: occupational success and activism on behalf of her people. Clearly, she had violated the geographical and cultural boundaries that separate "us" from "them." The violence that greeted her is a common means by which to redefine the boundaries of "acceptable" behavior on the part of immigrants. Activism and mobility on the part of people of color are not to be tolerated.

This theme emerges frequently wherever Hispanics have attempted to improve their lot. In efforts to minimize their own economic exploitation, Mexican Americans and Mexican immigrants actively have been involved in labor organizing in many of the low-wage occupations in which they find themselves. That this construction of a challenging and oppositional identity has been perceived as a threat is evident in the assaults—especially in the 1970s and 1980s—against Cesar Chavez and the United Farm Workers. Dozens of organizing farm workers were murdered by state officials and civilians alike. It is not unheard of in United States history for racially and ethnically identified labor movements to become victims of repressive violence (Young, 1990). Such organizing subverts the racially normative distribution of labor and must therefore by condemned. Mexican-American employment in menial labor and their unwillingness, collectively, to accept the terms of this employment facilitates the development of an active, empowered, and resistant cultural identity. From the perspective of the white working class, however, they are guilty of ethnic transgressions. Their violation of the "rules of the game" leaves them vulnerable to the wrath and violence of native-born workers.

The economic activity—not necessarily activism—of Asians and Asian Americans provokes similar resentment. However, in this case, it emerges out of hostility toward the perceived success of the "model minority." Regardless of their diversity and uneven performance in the United States, Asians are inscribed with the mantle of prosperity, in spite of their "perpetual foreignness." Because they are not seen as "Americans," Asians risk reprisal when they become viable, if not superior competitors. In Queens, New York, for example, four men broke into a Pakistani-American home, stealing over $10,000 in cash and jewelry. One of the assailants told the family "You Indian people come here and take our jobs. We are fighting for our country" (NAPALC, 1995: 31). The months of violence, harassment, and intimidation experienced by Vietnamese shrimpers in Texas also illustrates the point. Supported by the KKK, local white shrimpers engaged in a campaign of violence from 1979 to 1980, which included sinking the boats belonging to the Vietnamese, cutting their fishing nets, assaults, and harassment. Gilbert Pampa, then director of the federal Community Relations Service, observed, "There was displeasure on the part of the other fish-ermen concerning the overindulgence of refugees. [The American fish-ermen] did not feel that the refugees were competing in the American way. The refugees worked on Sundays, stayed longer hours on the bay, and sometimes caught shrimp outside certain demarcated areas of the bay. [The Americans] felt that this was unfair to them, and the competition turned to open conflict" (cited in the U.S. Commission on Civil Rights, n.d.: 51).

This conflict, too, is part of a historical pattern. Asians often have been singled out as scapegoats during times of economic stress. In the 1870s and 1880s, for example, Chinese laborers were viciously attacked, burned out, and murdered by gangs of white laborers and unionists. To the white workers, Asian laborers have the appearance of overachievers who must be curbed if white workers are to retain their image as disciplined and worthy laborers. When held up to the imagined standard of the Asians, native-born workers lose their place in the racial labor hierarchy.

It is not only individual immigrants and Americans of Asian descent who are held responsible for this loss of place. Asian nations (often viewed as interchangeable) represent a global economic threat. Although this "menace" is mitigated in the 1990s, the legacy of the violence of the 1980s remains part of the contemporary social fabric. The lengthy trade deficit with Japan has had serious repercussions on industry, employment, and intercultural relationships. In his statement to the U.S. Commission on Civil Rights, Congressman Robert Matsui argued that "in recent years, most of the industries that have suffered the worst have been hurt by imports from countries in South East Asia. As anger develops against nations of Asia, that anger is transferred to Americans of Asian ancestry who appear to be quick and "easy" targets" (n.d.: 63). The 1982 murder of Chinese-American Vincent Chin in Detroit, Michigan, is but the most extreme in an ongoing series of such attacks on Asian Americans. Two white men engaged Chin in an argument in a bar, referring to him as "Nip" and "Chink." After leaving the bar, the men chased Chin with a baseball bat. When they caught up with him, they delivered a series of blows to his head, knee, and chest that resulted in Chin's death four days later. That this example fits the pattern is evident in two facts of the case: the assailants were laid-off autoworkers; and one was reported to have said, "It is because of you that we are out of work" (U.S. Commission on Civil Rights, nd: 43).

Other less dramatic cases nonetheless support the link between hostility toward Asian nations and violence directed toward those of Asian descent:

Los Angeles, California: Cars carry bumper stickers that read, "Toyota—Datsun—Honda—and Pearl Harbor" and "Unemployment made in Japan."

Flint, Michigan: A display at an automobile exhibit included a car featuring a Japanese caricature, dropping a bomb on Detroit. (U.S. Commission on Civil Rights, n.d.)

Queens, New York: Three white males called a Chinese-American man a "chink." When he challenged them on it, one answered, "I have a problem with slanty-eyed yellow bastards. I don't want you chinks thinking you own the world." The three men then pushed him down and beat him, leaving the man with injuries requiring several stitches. (NAPALC, 1995: 30)

Fearing a loss of domestic and global hegemony, white perpetrators of racially motivated violence seek to redeem their status through repressive and retaliatory acts of violence. They seek to enhance their own stature and mastery by vanquishing the Other who has overstepped geographical and economic boundaries. The viciousness of both the verbal and physical attacks attests to their rage at the loss of relative advantage. Rather than appear meek and accepting—the very antithesis of hegemonic, white masculinity—white males assert themselves through misdirected violence. Better to be seen as active agents of their own destiny than victims of the encroachment of inferior Others.

## FOUR

Doing Gender and Doing Gender
Inappropriately: Violence against Women,
Gay Men, and Lesbians

I identify as a woman. Whatever insults women insults me.
I identify as gay. Whoever insults gays insults me.
I identify as feminist. Whoever slurs feminism slurs me.

—Gloria Anzaldúa, *La Prieta*

Gender, like race, is not a static category. It is not a given, natural property or master status that defines our identities once and for all. It is in
fact an accomplishment: it is created through conscious, reflective pursuit and must be established and reestablished under varied situations
(West and Zimmerman, 1987; West and Fenstermaker, 1993;
Fenstermaker, West, and Zimmerman, 1987; Messerschmidt, 1993;
Connell, 1987). That is, gender is an *activity* concerned with "managing
situated conduct" according to society's normative expectations of what
constitutes essential maleness and femaleness (West and Zimmerman,
1987: 127). Moreover, gender is a means by which actors express their
manliness or womanliness. They do so with an eye to how their behavior is interpreted or evaluated by others. Central to this conceptualization is the notion of "accountability." At all times, and in all situations,
actors are concerned with whether their behavior *will be seen to be* in
accordance with approved standards for their assigned sex.
    Within this essentially dichotomous understanding of sex, there is
very little space for ambiguity, or for blurring the line between masculinity and femininity. On the contrary, "a person engaged in virtually
any activity may be held accountable for performance of that activity as
a *woman* or a *man*, and their incumbency in one or the other sex category can be used to legitimate or discredit their other activities" (West
and Zimmerman, 1987: 136). In other words, accountability involves the

assessment of behavior as either conforming or deviating from culturally normative standards. Whenever we do gender—which is a recurring effort—we leave ourselves open to reward or censure.

Accomplishing gender is not solely an individual or even interpersonal process. It is also institutional, to the extent that it is reinforced by broader social relationships and structures. Consequently, "If we do gender appropriately, we simultaneously sustain, reproduce and render legitimate the institutional arrangements that are based on sex category. If we fail to do gender appropriately, we as individuals—not the institutional arrangements—may be called to account [for our character, motives, and predispositions]" (West and Zimmerman, 1987: 146).

The practice of gender occurs within the constraints of overlapping and competing structures which are simultaneously conditioned by that practice. As noted previously, the structures of labor, power, sexuality, and culture all have significant implications for the process of doing gender. They provide the context in which we "do gender." First, the sexual division of labor defines for us what is considered appropriate work for "essential" males or females, or more important, what is *not* appropriate. Issues involving both the allocation and organization of work (such as job segregation, training and pay differentials, workplace and household technologies) provide important markers and instruments for engaging in masculinity or femininity. To be an engineer or work with heavy machinery or make management decisions is to be masculine; to be a nurse or work with a typewriter or follow orders is to be feminine. To do gender appropriately, one must labor appropriately.

One must also pay homage to established relationships of power. Whether we are speaking of the restricted roles of women in decision making, or their control of institutional resources, or the nature and likelihood of access to social and political institutions, it is consistently the case that women have been disadvantaged as men seek to maintain their own privilege. Women's lived experience of unequal personal and structural power affects and limits their opportunities in all spheres of life.

Gender is accomplished in the context of patterns of sexuality and emotional attachment, or the "social patterning of desire," as well (Connell, 1987: 112). This dimension is predicated on a hierarchy of sexualities, arrayed beneath the hegemonic pattern of the heterosexual couple. The heterosexual ideal generally is characterized by an unequal relationship wherein the male is dominant. Moreover, alternative sexualities (homosexuality, interracial couplings) are subordinated if not vilified.

Underlying, often supporting, these gender structures is an array of cultural constructs that serve to define "masculine" and "feminine." Consistently, such imagery reinforces the presumed strength, aggressiveness, and mastery of the former, and the presumed weakness, passivity, and enslavement of the latter. Media images (such as Ally McBeal), legal constructs (such as female dependency), humor (such as "dumb blonde" jokes), and an array of other cultural icons reproduce feminine ideals that highlight women's sexed position in U.S. society.

Just as parallel structural and cultural scripts condition racialized violence, so too do they condition gendered violence. Moreover, while not all violence against women is necessarily bias motivated—just as not all violence against people of color is bias motivated—much of it is inspired by the anxieties and frustrated expectations of "woman's place." It is meant to teach women, both individually and collectively, a lesson about remaining accountable to their femininity.

GENDER-MOTIVATED VIOLENCE:
KEEPING WOMEN IN "THEIR PLACE"

Gender-motivated violence is predicated upon widespread assumptions regarding gender and gender-appropriate deportment. In particular, these assumptions revolve around constructions of gender that represent polar extremes inhabited by masculine and dominant men, and feminine and subordinate women. Violence is but one means by which men as a class enforce conformity of women as a class. Moreover, it is not necessary for all men to engage in violence against women, since the very threat of violent censure is constantly with women. Violence against women, then, is indeed a "classic" form of hate crime, since it too terrorizes the collective by victimizing the individual. In so doing, hate crime against women reaffirms the privilege and superiority of the male perpetrator with respect to the female victim.

Feminist scholars acknowledge the parallel between violence against women—especially sexual violence—and the lynching of black males as means to exert control and create identity (Brownmiller, 1974; Rothschild, 1993; Pendo, 1994). There is little difference in the motives. Both groups are victimized because of their identity, often for very similar illusionary "violations": "for being uppity, for getting out of line, for failing to recognize 'one's place,' for assuming sexual freedoms, or for behaving no more provocative than walking down the wrong road at night in the wrong part of town and presenting a convenient isolated target for group hatred and rage" (Brownmiller, 1975: 281). Just as racially motivated violence seeks to reestablish "proper" alignment between racial groups, so too is gender-motivated violence intended to restore men and women to "their place." Victims are chosen because of their gender and because of the assumptions about how they should enact their gender. The gender polarization that permeates U.S. culture is taken as a "natural," "given" fact, wherein women are expected to enact deference, men dominance. This dichotomy presupposes mutually exclusive scripts for males and females—scripts that constrain everything from modes of dress and social roles to ways of expressing emotion and experiencing sexual desire. It also defines any person or behavior that deviates from these scripts as problematic: unnatural, immoral, biologically anomalous, or psychologically pathological. Gender-motivated violence is a key means by which men and women rehearse their scripts, ensuring that women act "like women" in the bedroom, in the kitchen, in the workplace, and on the street.

GENDER, POWER, AND VIOLENCE

In each of these domains, gendered relations of power are enacted, albeit in slightly disparate forms. What unites the home, the workplace, and the street is that each historically has been a crucial site in efforts to establish an "appropriate" hierarchy in which men are dominant, women subordinate. Each has been the locus of struggles that have contributed to the empowerment of men and the relative disempowerment of women.

The United States is a male supremacist society wherein gender difference is constructed as gender inferiority and, ultimately, gender disadvantage. Consequently, women garner less power, prestige, and economic reward than men, who have consistently retained leadership and control in government, commerce, and family matters (Lorber, 1994). This is readily apparent in the legal history that has helped shape gendered relations of power. Male privilege has long been guaranteed by legal proscriptions and silences that have simultaneously excluded women from involvement in the public sphere, while failing to protect them in the context of their private lives (Taub and Schneider, 1990). On the one hand, legal exclusions on women's enfranchisement, ownership of property, and employment (in law and medicine, for example) have meant that until well into the twentieth century, women were unable to participate fully in politics or the economy. Even today, restrictions on access to abortion or to social security provisions, for example, limit the participatory power of women.

On the other hand, law has also enabled the subordination of women within the home. The same nineteenth- and twentieth-century provisions that limited (married) women's ownership of property meant that married women, in particular, ceded autonomy to their husbands upon marriage. The historical tendency to exclude from criminal proceedings husband's rapes or assaults on wives similarly ensured the dominance of men who were merely exercising their "marital rights." The continued failure to recognize the value of women's domestic labor through some form of income support likewise helps to maintain women's economic dependence on men, both during and subsequent to marriage. This is exacerbated by inequitable divorce settlements and the intractable wage disparities between men and women.

At least with respect to family and domestic violence, men's perceived sense of "ownership" continues to provide a context for the victimization of girls and women. The structured inequality of women leaves them vulnerable to the presumption of male control by whatever means necessary. It establishes an environment in which men freely manipulate the terms of a relationship. Violence becomes one such means for him to prove that he is "the man" and therefore in control. This even extends to relationships with daughters, as in the case of incestuous assaults. Research consistently suggests that child sexual abuse within families is disturbingly common (Baskin and Sommers, 1998; Belknap, 1996). It is not unlike woman battering in the home, to the extent that it too is a display of men's control over women, and especially women's sexuality. As Elizabeth Stanko (1985) contends, incestuous assaults are an assertion of male "rights" of access to and control of the powerless female. Young girls especially are vulnerable to such victimization due to their place in the family, their lack of experience, and their femaleness, which Stanko equates with powerlessness.

The extensive research of R. Emerson Dobash and Russell Dobash has led them to identify four interrelated "sources of conflict" that, they argue, are most predictive of woman battering: "men's possessiveness and jealousy; men's expectations concerning women's domestic work; men's sense of the right to punish 'their' women for perceived wrongdoing; and the importance, to men, of maintaining or exercising their position of authority" (1997: 268). Uniting these four triggers is the sense that the man has the right, perhaps the duty, to express his masculine power through violent repression. The female partner in such a relationship is seen to have challenged the masculine authority of her partner. She is seen to have transcended the boundaries of appropriate behavior and deference—perhaps she spoke too long with another man, or sought employment outside the home, contrary to the "demands" of her partner. Such behaviors throw into question the masculinity of the perpetrator. If he cannot control "his woman," perhaps he is not really a manly man after all. By striking out in violence, he reasserts his dominant and aggressive masculinity.

This male concern with taking charge and taking control of the heterosexual relationship emerges repeatedly in research on domestic violence (Websdale and Chesney-Lind, 1998; Weisburd and Levin, 1994; Wolfe and Copeland, 1994; Dobash and Dobash, 1997). This is especially true for patriarchal and usually lower-class families. In such situations, the "essential" nature of the patriarch is interpreted as the responsibility to "dominate and control their wives, and wife beating serves both to ensure continued compliance with their commands and as a resource for constructing a 'damaged' patriarchal masculinity. Thus, wife beating increases (or is intended to do so) their control over women" (Messerschmidt, 1993: 147).

That a great deal of domestic violence is in fact motivated by a presumed loss of control and ownership is apparent in the increased likelihood of victimization as women attempt to exit a relationship. When women seek to empower themselves, when they seek to achieve some personal autonomy by escaping an abusive relationship, they often become dangerously vulnerable to stalking, assault, even murder (Browne, 1995; Chaiken, 1998; Tjaden and Thoennes, 1998). In many relationships, separation is the moment when the quest for control becomes lethal. Browne's interviews with battered women who killed their partners revealed the extent to which men's attempts to retain control outlast the relationship. One participant maintained that "we were separating but I don't think that would have solved anything. Don always said that he would come back around—that I belonged to him" (Browne, 1995: 232). The spouse of another of Browne's subjects once wrote in his journal, "Every time, Karen would have ugly bruises on her face and neck. She would cry and beg me for a divorce, and I would tell her, 'I am sorry. I won't do it again. But as for the divorce, absolutely not. If I can't have you for my wife, you will die. No one else will have you if you ever try to leave me'" (Browne, 1995: 232). Men who batter attempt to assert their proprietary masculinity through violence. It is as if they fear that all appearance of masculinity, of dominance, of control is lost in the face of women's challenges to their authority. Their violence simultaneously reestablishes the appropriate place of the male and female partners; it is both male prerogative and female punishment.

Moreover, not all men need to engage in battering for it to have a debilitating effect on women. Indeed, the power of domestic violence is that—like other forms of bias-motivated violence—it is embedded in a systemic pattern of real and potential violence against women. The violence against a particular woman in the home is a reminder that any woman in society is subject to violent control by men. In other words, "Men's power is not an individual, but a collective one. Women's lives are bounded by it. The threat of male violence outside the home . . . is an acutely intimidating reality to women who endure violence within their own homes" (Stanko, 1985: 57). Men correspondingly enact their "will to power" outside the home. Assaults, rapes, or homicides that are outside the bounds of an intimate relationship tend to be directed at individual women as proxies for the combined threats to masculine domination represented by women as a class. In their daily lives, all women, at any time, may be vulnerable to gender-motivated harassment, intimidation, and violence because they are women and because they represent the devalued, often threatening Other. Wherever a particular act lies on the continuum of violence, it is a "ritual enactment of domination, a form of terror that functions to maintain the status quo" (Caputi, 1993: 7).

As with racially motivated violence, gender-motivated violence often emerges in the context of what is perceived by men as a loss of relative position. Challenges to the collective hegemony of men often are met with aggressive attempts to reassert the "natural" dominance of men. It is, in these terms, a reactive expression of insecurity in the face of reconstituted femininities. It is no coincidence that violent crime perpetrated against women has risen so steadily in the three decades corresponding to the rise of the women's movement. Marilyn French (1992) and Susan Faludi (1991) carefully document what they refer to as the "War Against Women" and the antifeminist backlash, respectively. Both authors point to the increasing harassment and intimidation of women through violence and the threat of violence. As women have collectively striven to redefine themselves as autonomous actors, some men have been compelled to meet the challenge by resorting to the readily available resource of violence.

Marc Lepine is a case in point. On December 6, 1989, Lepine entered a classroom at Montreal's Ecole Polytéchnique, systematically separated the male and female engineering students, and opened fire on the women. Before he killed himself, Lepine had murdered fourteen women and seriously injured nine others. In his verbal harangue during the shooting and in his suicide note, Lepine made it clear that his assault was intended to punish the feminists he held responsible for his personal failures—in particular, his inability to get into engineering school. Lepine's response was extreme, but nonetheless illustrative of the male response to the "erosion of white male exclusivity and privilege" (Caputi and Russell, 1992: 13).

WORKING TOWARD VIOLENCE

Lepine's case also is illustrative of one of the greatest sources of male trepidation and hostility: the reconfiguration of the gendered division of labor. This is a central component within which gendered relations of power are embedded. Misogynistic hostility often finds its roots and its focus in what are perceived to be distortions in the "natural" division of labor between men and women. Gender-motivated violence, in other words, is very likely in the context of local and global patterns that empower women with respect to the distribution and organization of work.

As noted earlier in this chapter, there is a social perception that there is "men's work" and "women's work"; each provides the structured opportunities and resources for what is deemed the appropriate performance of labor to which each gender is "naturally" suited. At the highest level of generality, this means that "woman's place" is in the home—bearing, nurturing, and raising the children, and acting as companion and sexual partner for her spouse. "Man's place" is in the corridors of the capitol, or the office, or the shop floor—making the "hard" decisions, doing the "hard" work, and providing the paycheck. Beyond this illusory ideal are arranged an array of other less-valued options that reproduce the gendered relations of reproduction and production. Even in the workforce, women are expected to behave like women, occupying subordinate, nurturing, and supportive roles as secretaries, as nurses, as (elementary) schoolteachers. Correspondingly, men are expected to act like men in their capacity as leaders, managers, and manual laborers.

The gendered division of labor is manifest in a number of identifiable patterns, including wage differentials, job segregation, and uneven patterns of reproductive labor in the home. Each of these can be traced back to the deeply embedded ideologies of "gender-appropriate" labor. Not only is the work women do devalued. Traditionally, it has also been viewed as secondary. Labor inside the home is invisible and unrecognized; work outside the home is merely something she does until married, or to earn pin money. In contrast, "men's work" is deemed essential to the operation of both the national and the family economy. His is the "real" work, which earns a "real" paycheck. Consequently, women's labor tends to be both underacknowledged and underpaid (if not unpaid), while that of men tends to be highly recognized in both social and economic terms.

In concrete terms, this means that women in the United States still earn only about 75 cents to every dollar men earn. In spite of equal-pay legislation, even in similar jobs men's wages outpace those of women. This holds regardless of educational level attained. In 1991, men with less than eight years of schooling earned, on average, $19,632 annually, or $300 more than women who had completed high school ($19,336). Men without a college degree earned $33,758, or $600 more than women with a bachelor's degree or above (U.S. Department of Commerce, 1993).

Moreover, the fact that "women's work" is less prestigious contributes to low wages industrywide in those areas dominated by women. Typically, the higher the concentration of women in a particular job, the lower the median wage. In fact, some studies estimate that as much as 35 to 40 percent of the income disparity between men and women can be accounted for by occupational sex segregation (Reskin, 1993; Rosenfeld and Kalleberg, 1991). For example, in 1990, 99.1 percent of all secretaries were female and their median weekly wage was $343; 96.1 percent of all child care workers were women, and their weekly income was $203. In the same year, women represented only 13.4 percent of all police officers, who earned $645 per week, and 3.1 percent of all airline pilots or navigators, who earned $898 per week (U.S. Department of Labor, 1991).

The dual labor market that characterizes the U.S. economy maintains women in low-wage, low-prestige ghettos of service work, while simultaneously maintaining the male privilege of lucrative, skilled, and professional positions. Moreover, in keeping with the "natural" superiority of men over women, even when men are employed in traditionally female areas, the positions they occupy are more powerful. For example, while women constituted 98 percent of all clerical staff in 1992, over 40 percent of the clerical supervisors—the bosses—were men (U.S. Department of Commerce, 1993).

The gendered division of labor is reproduced in the household. In spite of the dramatic increase in women's labor force participation, they continue to bear a disproportionate share of the burden of homemaking (Ferree, 1987). The parallel construction of a gendered division of labor in the home means that "just as there is a wage gap between men and women in the workplace, there is a 'leisure gap' between them at home. Most women work one shift at the office or factory and a 'second shift' at home" (Hochschild, 1995: 444). Consequently, traditional male privilege also tends to be reproduced in the home: women's unequal structural and economic power finds its counterpart in her unequal access to personal power within the home.

It is women's "essence," after all, to nurture. This expectation lies at the heart of the sexual division of labor. What Robert Connell (1987) refers to as emphasized femininity is enacted through women's commitment to household labor: cleaning, cooking, and attending to the needs of husband and children alike. Regardless of the reality, the idealized image of femininity might resemble something from the black-and-white episodes of *Pleasantville* or *Leave It to Beaver*, or the full-color television ads of today. A nicely dressed Mommy mops the (already spotless) floor of a tidy and ordered house, then prepares a full-course meal for her provider husband and well-behaved and -coiffed children. One moment she is overseeing the children's homework, the next she is a fiery vixen satisfying her husband's sexual fantasies.

Of course, this is a simplified and monolithic vision. There is remarkable variation across class, race, and ethnicity with respect to the extent to which women are held accountable to the ideal. For example, Scott Coltrane's (1995) interviews with dual-income Chicano couples found an asymmetrical division of labor to be more prevalent among both lower-class and upper-middle-class couples than among white-collar and working-class Chicanos. A. S. Barnes's (1985) examination of African-American couples suggests also that men at the extremes of educational and occupational hierarchies rejected housework as a threat to their masculinity.

There is some consistency in gender expectations that cuts across all other lines of difference. There continue to exist "patriarchs" of all classes and races who enact their masculinity through concentrated attempts to define the terms of the labor "contract" in heterosexual relationships. As much as the "culture of fatherhood" may have changed in recent years, the "conduct of fatherhood" has not kept pace (La Rossa, 1995). In other words, in spite of the popular belief that contemporary family life is more egalitarian, the reality is that many women continue to negotiate their identities in relationships that are oppressive and decidedly unequal.

Recent years have witnessed remarkable disruptions in the traditional patterns of the public and private division of labor. Changes in the distribution and organization of work have robbed men of the predictable context and resources for the exhibition of their manly characteristics: autonomy, risk taking, mastery of humans and nature. At the same time, gains of the women's movement have blurred the gendered labor lines. Together these patterns have created anxiety among those who are left without evidence of their masculinities. Kenneth Karst expresses this uneasiness in colorful terms when he asserts, "In an economy that has not produced jobs to keep up with the pool of prospective workers, a lot of men, especially young men, have become nervous about more than their flaccid incomes" (1993: 144–45). Because the labor realm has for so long been a site for the visible construction of dominant and patriarchal masculinity, recent challenges posed by resistant and empowered femininities in search of autonomy have provoked considerable backlash. All too often, women's efforts to redefine femininity in the context of their work have been countered by violence intended to remind them of the appropriate gendered balance of labor. The blurring of gender lines has proven disquieting to many who see male preserves crumbling. The working-class men interviewed by Fine et al. (1997) voiced their concerns about their diminished abilities to exercise masculine prerogatives. The traditional mechanisms in and through which they could enact aggressive and patriarchal masculinity have faded in the 1980s and 1990s, "a time when the women they associated with got independent, their jobs got scarce, their unions got weak and their privileged access to public institutions was compromised by the success of equal rights and affirmative action" (Fine et al., 1997: 66). As beneficiaries of equal rights and affirmative action, women are among the blameworthy. They are seen, by virtue of their engagement in "inappropriate" labor activities, to have impinged on men's opportunities to "do gender" without interference or competition.

One very visible reaction to these perceived threats and improprieties is evident in the ubiquitous practice of sexual harassment. Laura O'Toole and Jessica Schiffman observe that women's presence in nontraditional fields is associated with an elevated risk of harassment (1997: 134). Stanko (1985) similarly notes that the more highly educated a woman is the more likely she is to be harassed. In this context, workplace harassment becomes a frequent response to women's invasion of male bastions. It is a means to simultaneously create a particular masculinity and enforce a particular exclusive feminity. Carol Brooks Gardner's (1995) interviews with men revealed explicitly that men often perceived sexual harassment of women as a well-deserved response to their economic and professional advances. Their encroachment into male realms interferes with, indeed calls into question, men's ability to prove themselves to be men by the work they do. If women can do the job, then what does that say about the masculinity of the role players?

Sexual harassment allows for the reassertion of masculinity and femininity, and especially the "natural" differences between the two. It sexualizes the workplace, so as to reassure the men that they are at once heterosexual and empowered, and to remind the women that they are sexual objects, not laborers. The differences between masculinity—aggressive, in control, dominant—and femininity—passive, sexual, submissive—are made explicit through sexual jokes, grabbing or sexual assaults aimed toward women. The message that accompanies the acts is that women "don't belong," that they are "out of place," in short, that femininity cannot be constructed appropriately in male-dominated workplaces. This becomes very clear in the study of workplace sexual assault conducted by Beth Schneider (1993). Interestingly, she found that in approximately one-half of the incidents of workplace sexual assaults reported by respondents, the offenders coerced their victims through "challenges to femininity." In other words, they expressed the sentiments that "real women" would welcome the sexual advances. In light of their employment in male-dominated fields, women were asked to prove their femininity through sexual conduct. Perpetrators' sought to reinstate their victims' femininity by coercing them to make themselves available sexually.

That women hear the punitive message loud and clear is often evident in their reactions to the harassment. While many don't bother to report their harassment to supervisors, a disconcerting number of women leave or change jobs in the face of ongoing harassment (U.S. Merit Systems Protection Board, 1995; Gardner, 1995; Stanko, 1985). Gardner's female subjects reported that they often began to feel "untraditional" and that they did not belong in the workplace. One women who quit after a lengthy period of harassment stated that her experience "proved men are right when they say women still belong at home, because I do and now that's where I am. I should never have tried [to take a job outside the home]" (Gardner, 1995: 61).

Short of quitting their jobs, some women who stay in the workplace nonetheless reassess their self-presentation so that they might be seen as conforming to some minimum standard of "appropriate femininity"

(Gardner, 1995). They act "less bitchy" or "less sexy" or even less competent or intelligent. In this way, they may become accountable to the ideal of emphasized femininity. Where this is the response, the male harasser has been effective in reaffirming the proper, or at least acceptable boundaries between men and women. As long as women remain in the workplace, they are expected to do so within redefined but nonetheless circumscribed boundaries of acceptable workplace behavior set by male workmates and superiors. In this way, the harasser resumes control of the situation. *He* takes a stand; *he* engages in behavior that renders women powerless in the workplace. By displaying his own power, and emphasizing his own aggressive heterosexuality, the harasser takes advantage of sexual harassment as "an effective (albeit primitive) resource for solidifying, strengthening, and validating a specific type of heterosexual shop-floor masculinity, while simultaneously excluding, disparaging and ridiculing women" (Messerschmidt, 1993: 132). Moreover, women are peculiarly vulnerable to sexual harassment in the workplace. Earlier in this chapter, we saw how men are positioned structurally to exploit the labor market as a place of empowerment. In the public mind, paid employment traditionally has been the locus for the construction of masculinities rather than femininities. More important, however, where women have entered the workforce, it has been in a position of relative inferiority and subordination. Women's entry into the workforce has been on unequal terms. Consequently, men can engage in sexual harassment of women with virtual impunity. Such behavior is all too often perceived as a typical, normative interaction between unequals. Women are rarely in a position to effectively challenge their harassers who are their political, social, and usually economic "betters."

To the extent that workplace harassment is intended to make women feel like they don't belong, it parallels the intent of much violence in the home. Woman battering, too, often finds its roots and its motivation in a desire to confirm the traditional division of (domestic) labor. Disputes over whether and how women will labor outside the home, and the distribution of labor within the home, go to the heart of patriarchal violence behind closed doors. The challenge to male authority is not restricted to the workplace. As Fine et al. (1997) indicated, men also fear an erosion of their ability to perform as "real men" in their homes. They fear emasculation in the face of multiple and alternate constructions of femininity, few of which correspond to the passive and nurturing ideal.

Add to this the deskilling and loss of autonomy associated with the contemporary workplace. The resultant situation is one in which a whole class of men envision themselves with limited traditional means of testing and proving their masculinity. Violence directed toward their female partners represents a remaining weapon in the dwindling arsenal of resources available for presenting a masculine face to the world. Powerless in the workplace, he assumes power in the home. The assumption of this authority is held to extend to the violent enforcement of "his woman's" compliance to a rigid essence of femininity. It is when she resists such compliance that she is likely to become vulnerable to assault within the household. In this way, the struggle to define the terms of the domestic division of labor provides a context for both partners to do gender on relative, often antagonistic terms.

Neil Websdale and Meda Chesney-Lind's (1998) review of recent domestic violence literature reveals the consistency with which researchers are able to identify a relationship between patriarchal ideals and wife battering. For example, studies by Dobash and Dobash have revealed that battering is most likely to occur where women challenge their partners about household (economic) decisions, and where women are perceived as having failed in their "wifely duties"—refusing sex, serving cold meals, or neglecting the vacuuming. In other words, violence is a reactive performance of masculinity in the face of oppositional performances of femininity.

Interviews with batterers and their victims are illuminating in this regard. Often, both are very much aware of the existence of shared patriarchal beliefs, and the role of violence in enforcing them. A Kentucky woman interviewed by Websdale makes astute observations on the consequences of her "inappropriate" performance of an oppositional form of femininity:

> Tamara: The man is the head of the household. The woman has no say. It doesn't matter about her morals and her feelings. Nothing.
> Websdale: Was your husband like that?
> Tamara: He tried to be. That was our biggest problem. I talked back. I had an opinion and I wasn't allowed to have an opinion. And I'd say, "I don't care if you agree or not, honey, that's how I feel." That's one reason I was hit.

Male batterers express the same ideological position, as is the case with this abusive male interviewed by Peter Adams, Alisa Towns, and Nicole Garvey:

> Well, you got the male and you got the [laughing] female. And the male earns the bread and the woman brings up the family and that. . . . And it's a fact of life that only women can be a mother. There's no, there's no other way around it. And the man's still gotta go and earn the bread and the woman's still gotta have the children. (1995: 390)

Interviews with both battered women and their partners conducted by Dobash and Dobash (1998) reflect the paramount importance men place on their needs and their partners' ability to fulfill them. Often the only provocation to violence was the woman's failure to anticipate or fulfil her partner's expectations of her domestic femininity. One woman reported that

> He was late and I'd started cooking his meal but I put it aside, you know, when he didn't come in. Then when he came in I started heating it. I was standing at the sink and he just came up and gave me a punch in the stomach. . . . It was only because his dinner wasn't ready on the table for him. (1998: 147)

This theme appears again in Diana Russell's interviews with victims of marital rape. One participant revealed that

> Oftentimes, he'd ask "where's my supper?" If it wasn't there, he'd hit me, even though I never knew when he'd be home because he was out with other women. (1990: 129)

A final illustration of the relationship between patriarchal beliefs and gendered violence is cited by Jane Caputi and Diana Russell:

> In 1989, Curtis Adams was sentenced to 32 years in prison for tor-turing his wife in a ten-hour attack. After she refused anal sex, Adams handcuffed his wife, repeatedly forced a bottle and then a broomstick into her anus and hung her naked out the window— *taking breaks to make her read biblical passages adjuring women to obey their husbands.* (1992: 18, emphasis added)

In such patriarchal relationships, male batterers use violence to simultaneously prove their manliness and remonstrate "their women" for failing to prove their corresponding womanliness. An essential nature and set of roles is assumed for each, and when they are not forth-coming—when his ability to be a real man is thwarted by her refusal to be a real woman—violence often ensues. The enactment of violence is an enactment of masculine power and control, where it might otherwise be eroding.

Intuitively, this analysis implies that domestic violence perpetrated against women of color may be especially problematic. Christine Rasche (1995) maintains that many of the ethnic communities that have shaped the United States—Latinos, African Americans, Asians, and Native Americans in particular—are structured by rigid patriarchal norms that tend to render familial violence tolerable, if not invisible. However, Kimberlé Williams Crenshaw (1994) highlights the problem-atic nature of this assumption in light of the academic neglect of the "intersection of racism and patriarchy." What Crenshaw does make clear is that women of color are uniquely vulnerable to gendered violence because of their multiply determined structural disempowerment. They are often simultaneously oppressed by their class, gender, and racial position. That this is the case is also suggested by recent trends toward increasing domestic violence among the Navajo of the Southwest, for example (Zion and Zion, 1996). The traditionally egalitarian nature of these people has been distorted by their more recent history of racial discrimination and disempowerment. Racial and economic disadvantage, coupled with the incursion of Anglo gender ideals, has dramatically altered the place of Navajo women. Increasingly, like their white counterparts, Navajo women are expected to perform the rituals of domestic femininity as a complement to the male performance of patriarch.

Contrary to popular mythology, African-American gender politics are characterized by neither the extreme matriarch nor the extreme patriarch. Rather, the performance of gender historically has been fluid. According to Beverly Greene (1997), rigid expectations of femininity and masculinity have been "impractical" against the backdrop of economic marginalization of black men. While the importance of the family has been a constant, idealized notions of masculinity and femininity nonetheless have varied by class, region, and ethnicity.

This is not to say that domestic violence has not also been a constant. hooks' volumes consistently draw attention to the sexism that seems to permeate African-American culture, even where patriarchal performances of masculinity are not in question. hooks agrees that male-as-breadwinner has not always been a viable option as a resource for most young black males. Proof of masculinity instead is embedded in their aggression, their sexuality, or in their ability to discipline the family. Combine these options with the tendency to share with white males a devalued and disdainful perception of women, and the climate is ripe for domestic violence against "uppity black women" (hooks, 1981; 1992). Contemporary African Americans also can find legitimation for their violent subjugation of women in the Muslim glorification of the "feminine ideal." Women are expected to defer to men's natural superiority. Violence in this context allows men to exercise at once their aggressiveness, dominance, and holiness (hooks, 1981).

Espiritu's (1997) examination of the gender politics of Asian Americans also highlights the intersection of race, gender, and class. In contrast to what is often a very traditional division of labor and power in their homeland, Asian immigrants to the United States find that their abilities to maintain such boundaries are compromised. As Espiritu contends, Asian-American women are more likely to be employed, albeit in low-wage occupations, than either their counterparts at home or their male partners in the United States. Consequently, they assume an elevated position in the family as breadwinner and decision maker—a clear threat to the masculinity authority and place of their husbands. As in the parallel white patriarchal family, violence can come to represent a leveling influence. One immigrant male expressed his dissatisfaction with his situation in the United States:

> In Korea [my wife] used to have breakfast ready for me. . . . She didn't do it any more because she said she was too busy getting ready for work. If I complained, she talked back at me, telling me to fix my own breakfast. . . . I was very frustrated about her, started fighting and hit her. (Espiritu, 1997: 75)

Asian immigrant males' inability to sustain traditional patriarchal identities and women's challenges to an idealized and subordinate femininity have resulted in elevated rates of family violence among these families (Civil Rights Commission, 1992a). Such violence is a readily available means to resurrect "normal" relations of power, whereby women are reminded that, regardless of economic contributions, their true place is in the kitchen, their true occupation is the care of the family.

SEXUALITY AND VIOLENCE

Paralleling the presumption of a normative division of labor, there exists the presumption of normative sexualities. The latter is especially crucial in helping us to understand sexual violence as gendered violence. Sexual assault serves a particularly dramatic role in the policing of gender boundaries and the control of women's sexuality, for it is the place wherein women become objectified as predominantly sexual beings in the service of men.

To the extent that women are sexualized—in the workplace, on the street, in the home—they are held accountable to a femininity that requires sexual responsivity to men's advances. Just as the relative performance of masculinity and femininity assumes male proprietary rights, so too does it assume that sex with the woman of his choice is a man's right. Herein lies the context for gender-motivated sexual violence. As one rapist put it,

> Rape is a man's right. If a woman doesn't want to give it, the man should take it. Women have no right to say no—women are made to have sex. That's all they're good for. (Curran and Renzetti, 1994: 207)

Just as a sense of entitlement underlies domestic violence, so too does it underlie sexual violence within and outside intimate relationships. As the above quote suggests, sexual access to women as a class is perceived as the inalienable right of men as a class. Sexual assault, then, is an institutionalized, rather than aberrant, means by which men can perform their masculinity while "symbolizing and actualizing women's subordinate position" (MacKinnon, 1991: 1302). Women's sexuality is a ready commodity, available to all. In other words, "all women are whores and, therefore, fair game; sexual violence is normal and acceptable" (Caputi and Russell, 1992: 18).

Entitlement takes on a special meaning in the context of sexual assault by intimates—both rape in marriage and acquaintance rape. In these situations, sexual assault takes on an additional validity, reinforcing the gendered power of men to control even the most intimate dimensions of women's lives. Earlier, I discussed the family as a preeminent site for the regulation of the sexual division of labor, through violence if necessary. The marital relationship is no less important for the regulation of sexuality, and women's sexuality in particular. It is the site at which men most readily and forcefully exercise their (hetero)sexual rights to a woman's body. Women are expected to "exchange" their sexual favors for a share of their husbands' paychecks, or for the dinner and a movie provided by their dates. This, according to tradition, is the appropriate way for a woman to express her gratitude, and of course, her femininity. Should she adopt an oppositional femininity—by saying "no"—she becomes vulnerable to violent reprobation. Such is the normativity of sexual entitlement, that rapists—and their victims—often don't acknowledge intimate rape as rape. Robin Warsaw (1994) reports that 84 percent of men who had committed date rape asserted that their actions definitely did not constitute rape. A victim of rape clearly articulates her victimizer's failure to recognize the severity of his assault:

> He left me a note with one of those smile faces drawn on it. The note read "Denise, I woke up and you were gone. Catch ya later! Have a nice day. Bob." Minutes later, the phone rang. The voice belonged to a cheerful Bob. I think I called him a bastard or a fucker and I told him not to ever call me again, and then hung up. He called back, sounding surprised, asking, "Hey, what's the matter?" (Warsaw, 1994: 91).

Similar assumptions of the unobstructed right of men to women's bodies is evident in sexual assault within cohabiting and marital relationships. Even more so than dates or boyfriends, husbands hold their wives to the presumption of unrestricted sex-on-demand. That is part of her "role" as prescribed by narrow and rigid constructions of femininity. She is the sexual companion, often sexual property, of her mate. When women rebel against such prescriptions, they become vulnerable to the violent reassertion of their partners' aggressive sexuality and manhood, in a way that also is intended to remind them how they are expected to perform. This was the interpretation of rape offered by many of Russell's (1990) subjects:

I consented to sex with him when I didn't want to. . . . It was out of duty, I guess you'd say. He somehow conveyed to me that he expected it of me because I was his wife. (52)

With a husband, you feel forced. I have an obligation to my husband which is very bad. It's always been a man's world. (81)

He used to call me at work to come to him at once because he wanted sex. I used to work on Saturday and he didn't so he wanted me home. (92)

It was a very brutal marriage. He was so patriarchal. He felt he owned me and the children—that I was his property. In the first three weeks of our marriage, he told me to regard him as God and his word as gospel. If I didn't want sex and he did, my wishes didn't matter. (123)

Women and men learn very young that male sexual access to women is "naturally" unrestricted. In some cases, this lesson is learned in the home, when young girls become the victim of child sexual abuse. This practice normalizes sexual assaults against women. It also sexualizes them very early on, so that they become defined by their "sexual capital"; girls learn that their most valuable and manipulable asset is their sexuality. As Stanko puts it, "One basic part in some children's lives, however, can be a source of confusion: as part of the pink world, incestually assaulted children learn that their female role also entails sexual availability to men" (1985: 20). Perhaps, then, it is no accident that those victimized as children are vulnerable to revictimization as adults (Belknap, 1996).

These lessons are reinforced as girls and boys enter adolescence. Barrie Thorne's (1994) work on gender socialization in school settings suggests that adolescent girls are encouraged to cultivate a "culture of compliance and conformity" with respect to boys that may very well leave them vulnerable to sexual victimization. Conversely, boys begin to develop a sense of self that is predicated on mastery of their environment, including girls.

If women have not learned during earlier courtships that "their sexuality is not their own," the lesson often is driven home after marriage (Stanko, 1985: 73). In fact, sexual assault is the ultimate abrogation of women's choice, autonomy, and self-determination. Forced sex reproduces masculine dominance and control like few other activities. It victimizes women in ways to which they are "uniquely vulnerable" (Rothschild, 1993: 270). Men's ability to overpower women sexually— by right—establishes them as master.

O'Sullivan's comparison of gang rapists and batterers suggests that in some respects, there are remarkable similarities in the dynamics of marital rape and gang rapes. Both appear to turn on "general beliefs in male supremacy, hostility toward women, and different standards for sexual behavior in men and women" (O'Sullivan, 1998: 89). However, there is also a crucial difference: "Gang rape is 'about' the relationship among men doing it rather than their relationship to they woman they are abusing. . . . [Marital rape] is more instrumental than expressive, with the goal of regulating the relationship between the man and his wife" (O'Sullivan, 1998: 105). In other words, gang rape has a different audience in mind, with a slightly different purpose. It is a display of sexual prowess for the group. It is a communal exercise whereby men degrade women while simultaneously proving their solidarity, their sexuality, and their manhood. They share in one another's sexuality through their sharing of the victim (O'Sullivan, 1998; Martin and Hummer, 1995; Sanday, 1998). Moreover, that gang rapes are especially likely in college fraternities should not come as a surprise, since these groups tend to be consumed with constructing and displaying masculinity. Few contexts are so meticulously orchestrated around a conception of hegemonic masculinity that "stresses competition, athleticism, dominance, winning, conflict, wealth, material possessions, willingness to drink alcohol, and sexual prowess vis à vis women" (Martin and Hummer, 1995: 473). In brief, few contexts provide such a ready recipe for gang rape as a display of heterosexuality, misogyny, and loyalty.

Just as in other situations involving coerced sex, gang rapists perceive their victims as sexual commodities. Patricia Yancey Martin and Robert Hummer's (1995) investigation of fraternities suggests that sexual violence against women is seen by members as a sport or game in which women collectively are pawns, and in which the goal is to score sexually. Non-fraternity rapists share this notion of using a woman—any woman—as a vessel for a group adventure. The challenge is to perform for the group, regardless of the wishes of the interchangeable victim. As expressed by one such rapist,

> We felt powerful, we were in control. I wanted sex and there was peer pressure. She wasn't like a person, no personality, just domination on my part. Just to show I could do it—you know, macho.
> (Scully and Marolla, 1993: 39)

Male sexual prowess is performed at the expense of the victim's autonomy. The victims are natural and ready outlets for the satisfaction of males' "explosive" or "insatiable" sexual appetites (Sanday, 1998; Messerschmidt, 1993). While men voluntarily and enthusiastically enact what is for them normal masculinity, their female victims are involuntarily and unwillingly forced to play the feminine role into which the culture has cast them: sexual conduits whose own pleasure is unimportant.

Women who are victims of gang rape are not in a position to exercise their autonomy. The sheer fact of being outnumbered by two, three, or seven men is itself an obstacle to resistance. Peggy Sanday cites one such case, where the victim was virtually paralyzed with fear:

The 17–year-old freshman woman went to the fraternity "little sister" rush party with two of her roommates. The roommates left early without her. She was trying to get a ride home when a fraternity brother told her he would take her home after the party ended. While she waited, two other fraternity members took her into a bedroom to "discuss little sister matters." The door was closed and one of the brothers stood blocking the exit. They told her that in order to become a little sister she would have to have sex with a fraternity member. She was frightened, fearing they would physically harm her if she refused. She could see no escape. Each of the brothers had sex with her, as did a third who had been hiding in the room. During the next two hours, a succession of men went into the room. There were never less than three men with her, sometimes more. (1998: 498)

Alternatively, the victim's ability to consent may be compromised by her state of intoxication, a factor that is unfortunately often used to "blame the victim." If she had been a "good girl," if she had acted "like a lady," she would not have put herself in the position to be so dramatically violated. Chris O'Sullivan traces this to the cultural perception that women who do not adhere to their roles as gatekeepers of sexuality are "fair game for exploitation" (1998: 85). Such popular interpretations, however, deny the complicity of the offenders in providing the liquor and in exploiting the victim when she is vulnerable.

The literature on campus gang rape, in particular, reveals the normativity of alcohol use as a precedent to gang rape (O'Sullivan, 1998; Sanday, 1998). Offenders often plan and coordinate their victims' excessive consumption of alcohol. One fraternity member boasted that

We provide them with "hunch punch" and things get wild. We get drunk and most of the guys end up with one. . . . Hunch punch is a girl's drink made up of overproof alcohol and powdered Kool-Aid, no water or anything else, just ice. It's very strong. Two cups will do a number on a female. (Martin and Hummer, 1995: 477–478)

The "number" that such drinks do on women is to render them incapable of resistance, either because of a loss of coordination or a loss of consciousness. That women are but the vessel of men's sexuality is especially evident here, where women could not possibly be expected to attain any pleasure from the act. This bothers the participants not at all;

it is in fact seen as an extension of women's normative sexual passivity. A couple of examples will suffice to illustrate the dynamics whereby fraternity men take advantage of their intoxicated victims.

> In the Florida State case, the ringleader met the victim at an off-campus drinking club and invited her back to his fraternity for a "party." . . . At the fraternity house, her host gave her a bottle of wine, which she finished. He carried her unconscious to the communal shower room and summoned three other men. His best friend left his own date waiting downstairs in the hall to join in the assault. After sexually assaulting her, the four classy men wrote fraternity slogans and "hatchet gash" on her thighs, dumped her in the entry hall of another fraternity and called 911. At the hospital, her blood alcohol level was found to be potentially lethal and semen from several different men was found in her vagina. (O'Sullivan, 1998: 101)

> It was her first fraternity party. The beer flowed freely and she had much more to drink than she had planned. It was hot and crowded and the party spread out all over the house, so that when three men asked her to go upstairs, she went with them. They took her into a bedroom, locked the door and began to undress her. Groggy with alcohol, her feeble protests were ignored as the three men raped her. When they finished, they put her in the hallway, naked, locking her clothes in the bedroom. (Sanday, 1998: 498)

Whether drunk or sober, the victim's sexuality often is invoked to justify the perpetrator's behavior. As noted previously, victims often are portrayed as "whores" or "sluts" who have violated the standards of femininity, and so deserve to be themselves violated for their impropriety. In such contexts, women are presumed to enjoy gang rape. This allows the construction of the perpetrators as men involved in the legitimate performance of heterosexuality with willing participants. Their behavior is a natural reaction to the seductress in their midst. It is not they who have schemed to assault the victim, but the victim who has somehow schemed to "fire them up." The following example illustrates the presumption of consent:

> A 19–year-old woman student was out on a date with her boyfriend and another couple. They were all drinking beer and after going back to the boyfriend's dorm room, they smoked two marijuana cigarettes. The other couple left and the woman and her boyfriend had sex. The woman fell asleep and the next thing she knew she awoke with a man she didn't know on top of her trying to force her into having sex. A witness said the man was in the hall

with two other men when the woman's boyfriend came out of his room and invited them to have sex with his unconscious girlfriend. (Sanday, 1998: 498)

That victimized women are presumed to be always willing, available, and receptive to male "advances" also is apparent in the rationales of gang rapists interviewed by Diana Scully and Joseph Marolla (1993). Rapes of women hitchhikers were justified under the pretext that they must have been prostitutes and therefore "enjoyed it." Gang date rape involved the planned communal assault of one group member's date. This, too, was rendered acceptable by impugning the sexual promiscuity—read inappropriateness—of the victims: "Usually the girl had a bad reputation, or we know it was what she liked" (Scully and Marolla, 1993: 40). One participant admitted to committing twenty or thirty such assaults on "girls who were known to do this kind of thing." He also believed that "it might start out as rape, but then they [the women] would quiet down and none ever reported it to the police" (Scully and Marolla, 1993: 40). Obviously, the women "enjoyed" or even "invited" their victimization. Consequently, men imagined themselves to have established their sexual prowess by their demonstrated ability to satisfy even a protesting woman.

Such demonstrations are at the core of gang rapes. To themselves and their peers, such behavior is not deemed aberrant or deviant. Quite the contrary, it is a show of manliness and comaraderie among friends. Again, it is apparent that the intended audience is not the woman involved. She is a secondary player, interchangeable with any other available woman. What is important is that the men involved solidify their individual and collective identities as heterosexual performers. The show is for the coparticipants. The communal activity permits the concurrent display of sexuality, fearlessness, and comaraderie. O'Sullivan expresses the value of gang rape to its participants as "a performance put on for other men, proving one's masculinity through heterosexual dominance and exploitation of women. It is a way of co-operating and competing with male friends through a shared risky and risqué, socially sanctioned (in the sense that it's something to brag about among men, although not something to write home to mother about) behavior" (1998: 105). Gang rape signifies the commitment of the participants to the group and to masculine norms of behavior. It is a very public enactment of loyalty to the brotherhood of Man over Woman. And it is a confirmation of the aggressive sexuality of each of the group members. That it is seen as a crucial test of one's heterosexual mastery is evident in the finding that those who refuse to participate are branded "unmanly," possibly homosexual (Sanday, 1998; Martin and Hummer, 1995).

An implicit thread has run throughout this discussion of gender-motivated violence: cultural permission to hate and to victimize women is typically bestowed upon men. Abundant myths, stereotypes, images, and ideologies simultaneously support gendered and unequal relations of power, labor, and sexuality as well as the resultant gender-motivated violence. Cultural assumptions about men, women, and the relationships among and between them condone and often encourage victimization of women as women, because they commonly objectify and minimize the value of women. In other words, "men physically and emotionally abuse women because they *can*, because they live in a world that gives them permission" (Pharr, 1988: 14). For example, actual and potential victims of sexual violence are all too often portrayed as fantasizing about and therefore enjoying their victimization. Movie images, pornographic magazines, even commercial advertising often paint a portrait in which women may initially resist, but ultimately willingly and enthusiastically participate in their own violation. Hence, "No Means Yes" and other such rape myths abound to distance the offender from culpability. "Boys will be boys," after all!

This discussion of gender-motivated violence began with the acknowledgment that our culture assumes a masculine and feminine essence—traits, characteristics, capacities that clearly distinguish Man from Woman. Part of that binary is the construction of women as either "good" or "bad," depending upon their adherence to their prescribed role (Sheffield, 1987). If femininity is enacted through nurturing, submissive, passive behavior, then the woman is good; if it is enacted through selfishness, aggression, promiscuity, or resistance, the woman is bad and so deserves whatever she gets by way of violent retribution. The Bad Woman is herself to blame for male violence directed at her: "women who are beaten by their intimate partners, raped by strangers or acquaintances, or even killed somehow deserve their victimization because of their own fallibility, misjudgement or provocation" (Miller, 1994: 232–233).

Cultural constructs surrounding women's experiences of violence overwhelmingly lay blame on the victim. If only she had not been out alone; if only she had prepared a hot, appetizing meal; if only she had not dressed so provocatively, she would not have been assaulted, battered, or raped. In other words, if she had "done femininity" appropriately rather than oppositionally, she would not have suffered. Violence is a predictable response to women who violate the gender order. In contrast, the male offender is exonerated, often rewarded. He is "doing masculinity" normally; he is performing masculinity in a socially sanctioned, legitimate manner, in accordance with his right and duty to chasten non-conforming women.

Sheffield (1989) identifies what she refers to as "gender violence myths" that perform this function of releasing males from culpability. Rape myths include:

- all women want to be raped
- no woman can be raped if she doesn't want it
- she asked for it
- she changed her mind *afterward*
- she said no but meant yes
- if she's going to be raped, she may as well lie back and enjoy it

Among the wife-battering myths:

- some women need to be beaten
- a good smack will straighten her out/shut her up
- she needs a beating to keep her in line
- she must have provoked it

Sexual harassment is often justified because:

- she was seductive/flirting
- she was in a workplace where she didn't belong
- she misunderstood "friendliness"

In the context of a culture that holds so tenaciously to these sorts of excuses, women who are assaulted become suspect. She must have done something "inappropriate" to incite the violence. Moreover, it is not just the perpetrators who cling to the popular mythologies. Friends and family of the victim are likely to question her role in the process; police officers carry the assumptions into their investigation of reports of gender-motivated violence; and judges and attorneys are infamous for their tendency to try the victim rather than the offender in cases of sexual assault and domestic violence.

Sheffield (1987) argues elsewhere that the good/bad woman dichotomy is especially problematic for women of color, who, according to strictures of the racial hierarchy, can never achieve "goodness." It is the presumption of the inherent inferiority of black women that long left them vulnerable to unpunished and unpunishable rape at the hands of white men. That black women are uniquely vulnerable to gendered violence is implicit in Opal Palmer Adisa's observation that "African American women are more likely to be raped than any other woman, are least likely to be believed, and most often watch their rapists treated with impunity or mild punishment" (1997: 196). Women of color typically are not viewed as "real" victims. More so even than white women, women of color are characterized as inviting violent assault. The latitude allowed them for enacting femininity is even more circumscribed than that allowed white women. African-American women, for example, are "safe" only when enacting the roles of "mule" or "Mammy." So narrow are these notions of black womanhood that few women could possibly live up to them. Consequently, black women are assigned the label—often by black and white cultures alike—Jezebels, matriarchs, or uppity black women. It is this intersection of race, gender, and sexuality that shapes the victimization of black women and other women of color (Crenshaw, 1994; Collins, 1993). As noted earlier, it is the Jezebel image of the black prostitute that is perhaps most damning. It constructs black women as sexually promiscuous and therefore enticing, seductive. It is "impossible" to rape a prostitute since she is always on the job.

Aída Hurtado confirms the contrasting imagery of white and black femininity. While the former share in the privilege of white men through their enactment of emphasized femininity, the latter are denied such access and are instead the objects of white masculine power and aggression:

> In many ways the dual conception of women based on race—"white goddess/black she-devil, chaste virgin/nigger whore, the blond blue-eyed doll/the exotic 'mulatto' object of sexual craving"—has freed women of color from the distraction of the rewards of seduction. Women of color "do not receive the respect and treatment— mollycoddling and condescending as it sometimes is—afforded to white women." (Hurtado, 1989: 846; quoting Joseph, 1981)

In other words, race conditions the gender imagery to which women are held accountable, especially in terms of their sexuality. While both white women and women of color are vulnerable to gendered violence, the cultural permission for such victimization varies dramatically. As argued above, white women are often victimized because they are perceived to have crossed some boundary of appropriate feminine behavior; women of color because they are perceived to be, "by nature," sexually available and provocative. In short, white men's subordination of white women and women of color "involves holding them accountable to normative conceptions of essential womanly nature in different ways" (West and Fenstermaker, 1993: 168).

ANTI-GAY VIOLENCE AND THE CONSTRUCTION OF GENDER

As the foregoing discussion suggests, the contemporary practices of gender politics result in a situation where *men in general* benefit from the subordination of women. Clearly, a dominant masculinist project is the subordination of women by men. However, no less important is the "denial of authority to some groups of men" (Connell, 1987: 109). Significantly, the intersection of the division of labor, power, sexuality, and culture, as outlined above, means that there also exists a hierarchy of masculinities in which some are subordinated to others. Relations of power operate between masculinities and femininities, but also between an array of masculinities. Not all men share in the ability to exercise control at either the macro- or microsocial level. Below a hegemonic masculinity are arrayed a series of subordinated masculinities. Working-class men are subordinate to capitalists; black men to white; homosexuals to heterosexuals. Goffman may have overstated the case only slightly when he identified ideal—or "hegemonic"—masculinity as "a young, married, white, urban, northern, heterosexual Protestant father, of college education, fully employed, of good complexion, weight and height, and a recent record in sports. . . . Any male who fails to qualify in any of these ways is likely to view himself—during moments at least—as unworthy, incomplete and inferior" (1963: 128). The crucial point here is that the nonqualifiers not only "feel" inferior, but are so judged. This is the standard according to which the hierarchy of masculinities is created, resulting in stigmatized and marginalized "out-groups." It is among these subordinated masculinities that we find homosexuals.

Herek explicitly places homophobic violence in its sociocultural context: "Anti-gay violence is a logical, albeit extreme extension of the heterosexism that pervades American society. *Heterosexism* is defined here as an ideological system that denies, denigrates and stigmatizes any nonheterosexual form of behavior, identity, relationship or community" (1992: 89). From this point of reference, Herek goes on to trace the ideological and institutional practices that serve to denigrate and marginalize gay men and lesbians. From the exclusion of gays from civil rights and hate crime protections, to biblical condemnations of homosexuality as "unnatural," to curricular constraints on positive presentations of homosexuality, heterosexism is transmitted through cultural institutions (Herek, 1992: 90). The implication of this is that gays are subsequently rendered invisible at best, worthy of persecution at worst.

As one potential resource in the accomplishment of gender, gay-bashing plays the dual role of reaffirming the perpetrator's ability to "do gender," while simultaneously punishing the victim's propensity to "do gender inappropriately." At one and the same time, this practice serves to define, regulate, and express sexuality. It is a forceful resource by which young men, in particular, can regulate challenges to the binaries of gender and sexuality. In short, both hegemonic and subordinate forms of masculinity are shaped and maintained through active homophobia. In particular, hegemonic masculinity is accomplished through the simultaneous valuation of aggressive heterosexuality and the denunciation of homosexuality.

GAY-BASHING AS A RESOURCE FOR CONSTRUCTING MASCULINITIES
Violence against homosexuals is not a new problem (Bensinger, 1992). Historically, it has been a legally sanctioned policy, as in medieval

Europe or the colonial United States where sodomy was punishable by various forms of mutilation, or even death. Homosexuals were imprisoned and exterminated alongside German Jews in Nazi death camps (Herek and Berrill, 1992: 1). Some American "liberators," noting the pink triangles worn by gay men in the camps, returned the "deviants" to their prisons in sympathy with the Nazis' intentions (Grau, 1995; Heger, 1980; Plant, 1986). The McCarthy era in the United States was a period of extensive legal and extralegal persecution of gay men and lesbians (Duberman, 1993; Adam, 1995).

While most (but not all) American states have eliminated legislation that would criminalize the sexual practices of gays and lesbians, the gay community continues to suffer as victims of hatred, harassment, and violence. Moreover, attacks against homosexuals tend to be among the most brutal acts of hatred. They often involve severe beatings, torture, mutilation, castration, and sexual assault. They are also very likely to result in death (Comstock, 1991; Levin and McDevitt, 1993). NGLTF annual audits consistently report disproportionate evidence of "overkill" in gay-related homicides (1996; 1997; 1998). In fact, more than 60 percent of such homicides show evidence of "rage/hate-fueled extraordinary violence . . . (such as dismemberment, bodily and genital mutilation, use of multiple weapons, repeated blows from a blunt object, or numerous stab wounds)" (NGLTF, 1995: 18). Frequently, the mutilation or dismemberment follows death, as if to wipe out the victim's identity.

What accounts for the persistence of violence against gays? Perhaps a consideration of the common traits shared by its perpetrators provides some insight. Consistently, the data show that they are "predominantly ordinary young men" (Comstock, 1991: 2; Hamm, 1994). In particular, they are young white men or adolescents, often from working-class or middle-class backgrounds (Berk, Boyd, and Hamner, 1991; Berrill, 1992; Hamm, 1994a). With this in mind, Comstock is quite right to insist that sociological and sociocultural, rather than psychodynamic, processes are at work. It is vital to recognize anti-gay violence as an active exercise in the construction of gender. Such an understanding allows us to examine hate crime in its immediate subjective context by drawing attention to the interactions and implied meanings of actors and their audiences. Yet it also demands that we consider the historical and cultural contexts that inform those meanings, so that we might understand the ways in which identities are shaped both by our engagement with others and by our structural background.

Gay-bashing provides young men in particular with a very useful resource for doing gender, especially for accomplishing hegemonic masculinity. It is an interesting paradox that while masculinity is assumed to be "natural," it also appears to be so fragile "that one must always guard against losing it" (Hopkins, 1992: 123; Kaufman, 1995). Gay-bashing thus allows perpetrators to reaffirm their own masculinity, their own aggressive heterosexuality, in opposition to this noncon-formist threat. As an activity, it is tailor-made for this construction of masculinity, since it allows the visible demonstration of the most salient features of manliness: aggression, domination, and heterosexuality.

Recall West and Zimmerman's (1987) contention that gender is sit-uationally managed. Doing gender is to be understood in the context in which it occurs. The task of gender is reaccomplished in a diversity of social settings, each of which may demand different accountable activi-ties. Thus, "even though one is recognized as a man (or boy) prior to evidenced masculinity, evidence must also be forthcoming in order to merit that continued 'unproblematic' status" (Hopkins, 1992: 124). In this context, the practice of violence against gays provides one such sit-uational resource for men to establish their masculinity. And it does so in both negative and positive terms: by establishing what a man *is not* and what he *is*.

Gay-bashing provides proof of manhood, which is especially impor-tant for young males who are constantly challenged to prove their viril-ity. The perpetrator proves, by his actions, that he is unafraid to fight, as any real man must be. And, he is unafraid of engaging in illegal attacks on his victims—again a sign of his manhood.

Like all social actors, gay-bashers act with an eye to their audience (Herek, 1992a; 1992b). How will they be evaluated? What is the message their actions carry? In part, violence against gays provides visible, docu-mented proof of offenders' unquestionably straight sexuality. As Messerschmidt contends, physical violence against gay men in front of other young, white, working-class men reaffirms what they define as nat-ural and masculine sex—heterosexuality (1993: 100). Karen Franklin takes a similar position, arguing that "in group assaults the homosexual victim can be seen as fundamentally a dramatic prop, a vehicle for a rit-ualized conquest through which assailants demonstrate their commit-ment to heterosexual masculinity and male gender norms" (1998: 12). Gay-bashing provides a resource through which young men can con-firm not only what is natural, but what is culturally *demanded* of them in performance of their particular style of masculinity.

Thus, while violence against gays serves as a verification of the per-petrator's bravery and machismo, it also serves as a disclaimer of his homosexuality. The taunts the young adolescent males often favor—such as, "What are you, a fag?"—are frequent reminders of the inviola-bility of the artificial boundaries between the sexes. Hostility against homosexuals can be accounted for as an assertion of its opposite, that is, heterosexuality. The gay-basher could not possibly be mistaken for a homosexual, since he willingly assaults homosexuals. The active substantiation of his homophobia simultaneously removes any doubt about the offender's sexuality. Similarly, the epithets cast by the perpetrator distance him from the dreaded Other, once again offering obvious proof that he is of the "in-group" rather than the "out-group" constituted by homosexuals. The Blue Boys, an avowed homophobic group of young men interviewed by Michael Collins, offer an extreme illustration of this point:

> We chose the blue baseball bat because it's the color of the boy. The man is one gender. He is not female. There is no confusion. Blue is the color of men, and that's the color that men use to defeat the anti-male, which is the queer. (1992: 193)

As this statement implies, gay-bashing also provides the ideal context in which young men can conclusively establish what they *are*, in other words, manly, virile men. Recall the importance of accountability here: one must be seen (and interpreted) to be masculine in the prevailing sense of the term. And violence is a tried and true means to this end. However, many forms of violence carry significant risks: that of losing a fight, that of injury, that of arrest. The dynamics of gay-bashing, on the other hand, offer few such risks. Given its frequent group nature, there is little risk of loss or injury. In light of victims' fear of reporting, as well as police indifference, there is little risk of arrest (Harry, 1992). Ultimately, gay-bashing allows males to flex their muscles, to prove their masculinity with few of the hazards normally attendant with violent engagements. A youth interviewed by Eric Weissman supports this interpretation:

> We were trying to be tough to each other. It was like a game of chicken—someone dared you to do something and there was just no backing down. (1992: 172)

Similarly, a confirmed gay-basher assured Collins that his group (the Blue Boys)

> are *real* men searching for real solutions. We can't expect help from nobody but ourselves when it comes to cleaning the streets of the faggot and dyke scum. (1992: 193)

"Real men" can take care of themselves and those around them. One way of defending this circle is to eliminate the threat—in this case, homosexuals—through violence. Simultaneously, the offender can demonstrate his strength and his capacity to defend his territory, as must all hegemonic males.

The Blue Boys, and even less extreme "typical" gay-bashers are most at pains to prove the very essence of their masculinity: heterosexuality. To quote the same member:

I tell you, (the) Blue Boys are male. We're heteros. We have girl-friends and wives. We're out there fucking chicks every night and we have nothing to do with any fag shit. (Collins, 1992: 193)

Young men's attempts to assert a particular form of sexuality in a public manner can take many forms—"cruising for chicks" or boasting of their (hetero)sexual exploits. In the case of violence against homo-sexuals, denial of the "unnatural" reinforces the "natural" heterosexu-ality of their emerging masculinity. Ironically, then, gay-bashers are not so much *violating* the norms of society (re: violence), as they are *reaf-firming* a much more important set of norms revolving around sexuality. Their activities reflect the performance of the most salient features of a culturally approved hegemonic masculinity: aggression, domination, and heterosexuality.

GAY-BASHING AS A RESPONSE TO DOING GENDER INAPPROPRIATELY

Any performance of masculinity typically involves more than one audi-ence. Perpetrators are playing to their peers, and to whatever other elements of "conventional" society happen to be watching. For them, the message is "Look at me! I'm a real man!" A very different message is transmitted to the most adversely affected audience: the victims. What they hear is "Real men are heterosexual. By definition, *you are not a real man!*" Simply put, gays are seen to be doing gender inappro-priately. Thus, while violence against gays affirms the hegemonic mas-culinity of the actor(s), it also disparages the masculinity of homosexuals, whose behavior is no less accountable, no less open to interpretation and evaluation.

Gay men are, in fact, doing gender, just as are heterosexuals. They are constructing their own masculinity, albeit an alternate form of mas-culinity that is culturally subordinate to its heterosexual counterpart. On this basis, they are vulnerable to social disapprobation because they are seen to be gender traitors. Thus, while traditional hegemonic masculinity demands aggression and heterosexuality, it also requires the repression of the challenge represented by homosexuality. Violence against gays is a very powerful means by which this subordination can be maintained.

First and foremost, there is an extensive cultural mythology that facilitates anti-gay sentiment and activity. It is a mythology that con-structs gay identities as dangerous and wicked. Contemporary imagery and stereotypes surrounding gay men, in particular, often resurrect the historical construction of homosexuality as sin and illness. The domi-nant Western perspective has been shaped by the social and moral agenda of the Euro-Christian majority. Drawing on the English com-mon law, the colonial state determined that "what was sinful in the eyes of the church was illegal in the eyes of the state" (Biery, 1990: 10). So it was that "sodomy" and "buggery" came to be seen as immoral acts, and "crimes against nature."

While there are still proponents of the "homosexuality as sin" perspective, this religiously grounded view has been supplemented, if not supplanted, by the more "scientific" view of same-sex relations as "illness." This interpretation, "which also sees homosexuality as wrong and deviant, maintains that sexual acts are symptoms of a sickness. In contrast to the sin conception, the sickness view sees the desire to engage in homosexual activity inhering in the individual's identity" (Editors of the *Harvard Law Review,* 1990: 4).

Whether grounded in religion or science, an immutable stigma is applied to gay identity, which is perceived as a moral and physical threat to the public's well-being. By engaging in "unnatural" sexual behavior, gays are said to thwart God's law; they promote a "deviant lifestyle" to the young and pliable; they carry disease and degeneracy like rats carry the plague. Homosexuals of both sexes are perceived to be predatory and menacing. Moreover, the unspoken threat is that they are gender traitors, because they have broken ranks with dominant males, thereby threatening to destabilize carefully scripted gender relationships. Long-standing gender boundaries are uncomfortably blurred by homosexuality.

Given such pervasive negative sentiments, it is perhaps not surprising that gay men (and lesbians) still suffer considerable legal discrimination and exclusion. The anti-gay mythology is embedded in the legal order. Restrictions on their sexuality, relationships, and civil rights means that gay men and women typically do not enjoy the same freedoms as their heterosexual counterparts. *Bowers v. Hardwick,* is held to be the most significant contemporary legal statement of the status and rights of gays (Editors of the *Harvard Law Review,* 1990; Mohr, 1988; Leiser, 1997). In that case, the Supreme Court upheld the constitutionality of Georgia's sodomy statute. In his majority opinion, Chief Justice Warren Burger concluded that "to uphold that the act of homosexual sodomy is somehow protected as a fundamental right would be to cast aside millennia of moral teaching." With these words, he denied the legal right to private, consensual same-sex sodomy. Twenty states continue to criminalize same-sex sexual relations, referring to them variously as "sodomy," "unnatural intercourse," "deviate sexual conduct," "sexual misconduct," "unnatural and lascivious acts," and "crimes against nature."

While prosecutions under these sodomy statutes are rare, their presence nonetheless has a dramatic impact on gay men and lesbians. Symbolically, the legislation and its terminology marginalize and stigmatize a whole community. They send the message that same-sex activity is "unnatural," "deviant," and not to be tolerated. At the practical level, these laws are "frequently invoked to justify other types of discrimination against lesbians and gay men on the ground that they are presumed to violate these statutes" (Editors of the *Harvard Law Review*, 1990: 11). So, for example, the "criminality" of gay men or lesbians has been used to refuse parental rights, or the right to adopt, or the right to marry. The legally ambiguous status of gay men and women even can be invoked as a means of denying them freedom from discrimination in employment and job benefits (domestic partner benefits, for example). Ultimately, the persistent criminalization of homosexual behavior leaves gay men and lesbians vulnerable to public and private persecution, including violence. This designation of "deviant" has long facilitated the persistence of the criminalization and pathologizing of same-sex relations. Consequently, gay men and women have been harassed, persecuted, and disempowered for their difference: they continue to be marked as the sexual Other.

As outlined previously, "doing gender" explicitly is concerned with structuring differences between males and females, with creating "essential" natures specific to each gender. Consequently, contemporary sexuality (and marriage) is predicated upon the normalcy of opposite-sex relationships. Homosexuals apparently refuse to play this game. They do not sufficiently accomplish either maleness or femaleness; they have not even attempted to become one of the "natural" sexes. Homosexuals refuse to be forced into these binary categories of masculine or feminine. Thus, by definition, homosexuality transcends the boundaries our culture has so conscientiously erected between the genders, lapsing into the category of deviance. Additionally, gays violate the sanctity, the "naturalness" of established gender identities. That is, they are sanctioned for *presumably* failing to practice either absolute femininity or masculinity. Such violations ultimately make them vulnerable to stigmatization and finally to violent repression. William Hassel's two teenage assailants clearly were hostile to his refusal to "be a man." Throughout the attack—at knifepoint—the pair challenged his masculinity, beating him for crossing the gender line, for being a failed man. They threatened to complete his emasculation physically. According to Hassel's account,

> They made me address them as "Sir." They made me beg them to be made into a real woman. They threatened to castrate me. They threatened to emasculate me. They called me "Queer," "Faggot." One of them urinated on me. They threatened me with sodomy. (1992: 144–145)

This patterning of sexuality—cathexis—is a major axis of the sexual power relations of which gender accomplishment is so integral a part. Homosexuals' "unnatural" sexual attractions threaten the dichotomous sexual ideals. They are seen to have crossed the acceptable boundaries of sexuality. Homophobia and gay-bashing thus can be explained by "the degree to which the fact of homosexuality threatens the credibility of a naturalized ideology of gender and a dichotomized social world" (Connell, 1987: 248). Violations of the normative rules of cathexis provide an important motive for violence against gays. In West's terms, homosexuals are "called to account for" their failure to do gender as prescribed (West and Zimmerman, 1987).

It bears repeating that gender constitutes a hierarchical structure of domination not only between but within genders. This structure of power is also a constitutive part of the broader pattern of sexual power relations, in which heterosexual masculinity comes to the fore. The hierarchy of masculinities valorizes this narrow, hegemonic form of masculinity, while denying or limiting the power of "lower" forms of masculinity (and all forms of femininity). Consequently, "a series of masculinities becomes subsumed under one form of masculinity that becomes 'masculine'" (Kinsman, 1987: 104).

Because homosexuality challenges the fundamental assumptions of what it is to "be a man," it inevitably is assigned an inferior status in this gender hierarchy. The institutional norm of heterosexual masculinity is affirmed in the media, legislation and social policy, and police practices, to name but a few (Kaufman, 1987; Carrigan et al., 1987). The 1978 Briggs Initiative was an early attempt to expel homosexuals from the education system. Restrictions on "domestic partner" benefits disadvantage gay couples. And tax status is based on the traditional heterosexual marriage—doubly problematic since most states outlaw gay marriages.

At the level of the informal social order, gay-bashing serves a no less effective, but certainly more violent, disciplinary mechanism. Violence is used as a tool of subordination intended to maintain the powerlessness of homosexuals. Tim Carrigan et al. are worthy of a lengthy quotation on this point:

> The history of homosexuality obliges us to think of masculinity not as a single object with its own history but as being constantly constructed within the history of an evolving social structure, a structure of sexual power relations. It obliges us to see this construction as a social struggle going on in a complex ideological and political field in which there is a continuing process of mobilization, marginalization, contestation, resistance, and subordination. It forces us to recognize the importance of violence, not as an expression of subjective values or of a type of masculinity, but as constitutive practice that helps to make all kinds of masculinity. (1987: 89)

Violence simultaneously conditions both hegemonic and subordinate masculinities. As such, it is an integral weapon within the structure of power relations. This is especially obvious when gays collectively challenge their subordination. The last decade has seen a dramatic increase in the activity and visibility of a vibrant gay and lesbian movment. This visibility has been a two-edged sword. On the one hand, it has resulted in valuable gains in gay rights. On the other hand, it has engendered great hostility and backlash. Just as Native Americans and women, for example, are at increased risk of victimization during periods of activism, so too are gays more vulnerable when they find their voice. This is evident in the increased violence leading up to gay rights referenda in Maine, Colorado, and Oregon. Kathleen Sarris's experiences in Indiana are not atypical. She had played a leadership role in Justice, Inc.'s efforts to promote pro-gay activities. Following a widely publicized press conference, Sarris suffered weeks of telephone harassment and hate mail. The harassment culminated in a brutal beating and sexual assault by a man claiming to be

> acting for God; that what he was doing was God's revenge on me because I was a "queer," and getting rid of me would save children and put an end to the movement in Indiana. (Sarris, 1992: 202)

Such assaults are indicative of a perceived loss of white male privilege—privilege that instead has been offered up to "undeserving" gays. A white male convicted of murdering a gay man in Texas justified his crime with reference to this relative imbalance. He bemoaned the fact that, while he had worked hard all his life, he nonetheless was unable to find a decent job, and yet

> here they [homosexuals] are, they're doing something that God totally condemns in the Bible. But look at everything they've got. . . . They've got these good jobs, they've got money. They've got the cars, they've got the apartments. They've got all the nice stuff in 'em. So, yeah, I resented that. (cited in Franklin, 1998: 18)

This assailant raises another crucial element underlying gay-bashing. He articulates quite openly the common perception that gay men have benefited unjustly from meaningful and profitable employment. This is in spite of the fact that gay men often are perceived to be doing gender inappropriately in terms of its final dimension, that is, in labor. As Connell (1987) explains, the sexual division of labor amounts to the historical constitution of gender-appropriate categories and processes of work. Consequently, we are left with cultural ideals with respect to who is capable of and who should perform what tasks. Moreover, actors' performance of these tasks provides an important means for demonstrating their essential masculinity or femininity. Men make decisions, women follow orders; men are professionals, women are support staff; men work with their hands, women look nice.

According to popular stereotypes, homosexuals contravene this comfortable arrangement as well. Just as they refuse to abide by the rules of gendered sexuality, so too do they buck conformity in their employment. The work of male homosexuals is not that of "manly men" but of passive, effeminate men. Again, according to popular stereotypes, gay men are hairdressers, dancers, or interior designers. Given the cultural association between homosexuality and feminine weaknesses, gay men are thought to be incapable of the "tough," "demanding" jobs like construction, or even management. We don't want "them" teaching our children, since they might seduce them. We don't want "them" raising children of their own, since they would reproduce another generation of gays.

The sexual politics of labor have little room for the sort of gender ambiguity presumed of homosexuals. The gay community, in many states, is still without statutory protection against job discrimination. Like women, who similarly are ghettoized and subordinated in the gender hierarchy, homosexual men often are left with few high-paying options and few opportunities for significant professional advancement. This economic violence complements the physical violence of gay-bashing in a number of ways. First, homosexuals who are not "out" may fear the publicity associated with reporting their victimization. That is, the risk to their job status, family affections, and so on appears greater than the benefits to be derived from reporting violence perpetrated against them. In the absence of consistent reporting, there is little to deter potential offenders. Second, there are frequently additional (social) injuries when victimization is reported, either with or without the victim's consent. Rather than winning sympathy, as do most victims of crime, homosexuals often are further victimized after the initial assault—experiencing harassment from neighbors or coworkers, even threats of job loss or demotion. Anti-gay violence in the workplace only recently has begun to receive the attention it deserves (NGLTF, 1996, 1997, 1998; Bain, 1995). A Boston victim advocate observed in an interview with an *Advocate* reporter that while such cases are not necessarily as violent or brutal as others,

> there is something especially frightening nonetheless about harassment at work, because the victims don't have the freedom to leave; it's happening in the place where they make their living. The situation can be agonizing over time, especially if the harassment is coming from a supervisor. (cited in Bain, 1995: 31)

The dynamics parallel the experiences of women harassed on the job. The implied—sometimes explicit—message is that the victims don't belong. They don't deserve the job or position they hold because they don't "fit." That is, like women in "men's" jobs, gays in the workplace represent a direct threat. Physical violence or ongoing harassment makes the victim's workplace experiences unbearable, often forcing them to seek employment elsewhere.

Ultimately, then, gay-bashing is a practice motivated by the discomfort, even hostility toward those Others who cross the gender boundaries of sexuality, power and labor, who refuse to "do gender appropriately." In almost Durkheimian fashion, violence against gays reasserts the normative order around gender by rewarding the perpetrators (explicitly or implicitly) for accomplishing masculinity in a "manly manner" while punishing the victims for refusing to do so.

MASCULINITIES, FEMININITIES, AND ANTI-LESBIAN VIOLENCE

If gay men are victimized for their failure to appropriately construct their masculinity, are lesbians subject to violence for their failure to appropriately construct their femininity? To be sure, lesbians are often victims of homophobic violence, but at a much lower rate than gay males (Berrill, 1992; Comstock, 1991; NGLTF, 1992, 1993, 1994). In part, these findings may reflect women's greater tendency not to report homophobic violence (NGLTF, 1994). Additionally, Kevin Berrill identifies several pragmatic reasons why lesbians may appear to be at lower risk of victimization: the fact that men, in general, are at a greater risk of violence; the higher visibility of gay men as opposed to gay women; the earlier recognition and "outing" of gay men; gay women's greater tendency to alter behavior, and therefore vulnerability to assault; the difficulty in distinguishing anti-woman violence from anti-lesbian violence. (1992: 28)

Theoretically, this last point is significant. Beatrice von Schulthess's (1992) study of anti-lesbian violence in San Francisco reveals close links between anti-woman and anti-lesbian violence. In fact, she argues that anti-lesbian violence is an extension of misogynistic sentiment generally. Thus the two are difficult to untangle. This confusion may, in fact, deflate the numbers of *reported* anti-lesbian hate crimes. Victims and law enforcement authorities alike often are unable (or unwilling) to identify assaults as anti-lesbian. They may, instead, be perceived as anti-woman. Women in general become conditioned to gender harassment at work, in the home, on the street (von Schulthess, 1992; NGLTF, 1995). Victoria Brownworth (1991) cites three dramatic examples where anti-lesbian sentiment was apparent in the perpetrators' actions or testimony, yet none was officially defined as homophobic violence. Similarly, she quotes a lesbian victim, who makes clear the difficulty of distinguishing the motive in this context:

> Was my attack anti-lesbian? Or was it anti-woman? . . . I was raped because as a woman I'm considered rapeable, and as a lesbian I'm considered a threat. How can one separate these two things? (1: 52)

Lesbians and non-lesbians alike frequently report this confusion (Pharr, 1988; NGLTF, 1994). Sexual harassment—wolf whistles and "come-ons," for example—often escalates into lesbian baiting and, worse, violence. In the immediate context of the rejection of his sexual overtures, the perpetrator's masculinity is threatened—his sexual attractiveness and prowess are thrown into question. In general then, this form of social control as punishment is most likely to occur when

> our behavior is not acceptable, that is when we're being independent, going our own way, living whole lives, fighting for our rights, demanding equal pay, saying no to violence, being self-assertive, bonding with and loving the company of women, insisting upon our authority, making changes that include us in society's decision-making. (Pharr, 1988: 19)

Consequently, lesbians—and women erroneously identified as lesbians—are subject to similar social censure as gay males. Pharr reminds us that "to be a lesbian is to be *perceived* as someone who has stepped out of line, who has moved out of sexual/economic dependence on a male, who is woman identified" (1988: 181). Lesbians also may be punished for doing gender inappropriately. As a lesbian, she has forfeited all "womanly" rights to protection; she is left vulnerable to the harassment and violence that mark her as deviant and "out-of-line."

However, it remains the case that lesbians appear to be less frequent victims of anti-gay violence than men. How are we to explain the fact that while the dynamics of lesbian- and gay-bashing are similar in kind they differ in degree? Connell (1987) provides a potential line of response. He contends that the gender hierarchy demands slightly less conformity of women than of men. Whereas men are arrayed relative to a hegemonic masculinity, women are held accountable to a less rigid norm of "emphasized femininity." Thus, failures to accomplish "appropriate" masculinity are likely to elicit stronger negative social sanctions than are similar challenges to femininity: "All forms of femininity in this society are constructed in the context of the overall subordination of women to men. For this reason there is no femininity that holds among women the position held by hegemonic masculinity among men. . . . No pressure is set up to negate or subordinate other forms of femininity in the way hegemonic masculinity must negate other masculinities" (Connell, 1987: 187; see also Harry, 1992). In other words, there is slightly more latitude for gender nonconformity—especially in terms of sexuality and expression—among women than among men. Same-sex bonding, affection, and physical contact are much more readily accepted for women than men—the former may even be titillating for men to observe, as evidenced by the amount of lesbian activity pictured in magazines such as *Playboy* and *Penthouse*. Thus, women's homosexuality does not threaten the status quo in quite the same way as that of men. They can retain their femininity in spite of their sexual orientation, since they are still perceived as sexual objects. Gay men, on the other hand, do not have the same appeal. In fact, gay men threaten the very fiber of the gender hierarchy. Their violations touch the basic assumptions on which the hierarchy is predicated: that of the primacy of the heterosexual male.

Whether one speaks of anti-woman or anti-gay violence, one is speaking of action oriented around the reaffirmation of a hegemonic formation. Such violence represents efforts to keep men and women in appropriate alignment, along the axes of labor, power, sexuality, and culture. Until equality between genders is achieved, until we all can blur the boundaries between genders, we will continue to force people into rigid categories of male/female, straight/gay, normal/deviant. And we will continue to devalue and persecute the "negative" half of the equation.

## FIVE

Beyond Black and White:
               Minority-on-Minority Violence

Now we often march in opposite directions or face each other across an abyss. Now our
two communities clash regularly over issues of power, priorities, competitive oppression
and conflicting self-interest.

                    —Pogrebin and Hutchinson, *A Dialogue on Black-Jewish Relations*

It is ironic that at the same time that policymakers, scholars, and com-
mentators point to the increasing diversity of the United States, they
stubbornly persist in collapsing racial and cultural relations into a black-
white binary. If we are to make sense of the current state of racial and
cultural conflict, it is imperative that we broaden our understanding to
recognize the United States for what it is: a multicultural, multiracial,
and multiethnic community, characterized by multiple and crosscutting
coalitions and cleavages. The politics of difference, in other words, is
also inscribed in the interethnic relations of oppressed groups. Cornel
West insists that "although this particular form of xenophobia from
below does not have the same institutional power of those racisms that
affect their victims from above, it certainly deserves attention as a struggle within the politics of identity formation" (1994: 109).

It is particularly important to acknowledge this in our conversations
about hate crime, where minority-on-minority violence is not unheard
of. Two recent conflicts highlight this often overlooked reality: the
Crown Heights violence between blacks and Jews in 1991, and the black-
Asian-Hispanic conflicts that exploded in the Los Angeles riots of 1992.
While obviously signs of the long-standing tensions among and between
these similarly marginalized groups, these incidents represent efforts to
negotiate identity and place in the United States. These events—and

others like them—present the actors with opportunities to do difference, and especially race, through violence.

This chapter represents a tentative exploration of the phenomenon of intercultural violence among and between oppressed groups. This task is made difficult by the lack of literature in this area. As noted at the outset, scholars have been slow to address hate crime within this context. Thus what follows is a speculative analysis, in which I've drawn from the fields of anthropology (such as Amaguer, 1995), social work (such as Greene, 1997), and cultural studies (such as hooks, 1990; 1995). I will present three illustrative sets of relationships: African American–Asian American; Jewish–African American; and gay men within communities of color.

CAN WE ALL GET ALONG?

The same diversity that threatens the white majority—and thus underlies hate crime—similarly causes ruptures and discomfort among this nation's oppressed groups. These ruptures ultimately revolve around identity and recognition. Yet such struggles for recognition take place on different terms vis-à-vis oppressed groups, as opposed to those involving white-minority relations. The white majority excludes or marginalizes subordinate groups. However, within the politics of interethnic minority conflicts, there emerges an opportunity to acquire or sustain recognition. The motivation here is that "while the subject desires recognition as human, capable of activity, full of hope and possibility, she receives from the dominant culture only the judgement that she is different, marked and inferior" (Young, 1990: 60). One way to overcome, indeed overturn, this negation is to extrapolate the "rules of the game" to the context of subordinate ethnic conflict, to mark another as "different, marked, inferior." Only in this way can the subordinate establish some semblance of dominance, demanding of other oppressed groups that which is not forthcoming from the hegemonic majority. Punished, repressed, and reprimanded for asserting their ethnic identity within view of the majority culture, members of subordinate groups can opt to engage in hate crime as an alternative resource for constructing their identities.

Consequently, minority-on-minority violence also can be viewed within the framework of "doing difference," since it too is suffused with hierarchical conflict. Interethnic violence among and between subordinate groups "becomes a 'field of possibilities' for transcending class and race discrimination," that is a critical instrument for doing race, in particular (Messerschmidt, 1993: 103). But it is important to interpret such violence within the master narrative of white, heterosexual, masculine hegemony. That is, minority-on-minority hate crime is not only about Korean–African American conflict, or African American–Jewish conflict. Rather, it is about how these tensions play out in the context of relations of racial, ethnic, and gender subordination. As Lisa Ikemoto contends, "If you experience racism as one marginalized by it, then you may use racism to explain your relationship with other groups and their members" (1995: 307). Even in their relationships with one another, members of subordinate groups are "dependent on the will and left-overs of a dominant group" (Ikemoto, 1995: 308). Ultimately, hege-monic constructions of race or gender identity infuse the experiences and interactions of subordinate groups as well.

One might expect the common experiences and marginality of oppressed groups to provide the basis for solidarity rather than division. It is not unreasonable to suppose that they might recognize and exploit their common hardships. Gay men and lesbians share with recent immi-grants and native-born racial minorities discrimination, harassment, and violent victimization. All are subject to ongoing daily patterns of (mis)treatment that seek to maintain their inferior status.

In contrast, what emerges is not a shared commitment to racial or gender justice, but instead shared antagonisms and hostilities directed toward one another. Their rage at their continued disempowerment is misdirected downward or sideways toward those who are similarly vic-timized, rather than upward toward those who seek to exploit the cleav-ages. The Los Angeles riots were a clear illustration of this tendency, representing as they did "a multiracial, trans-class, and largely male dis-play of justified social rage. For all its ugly xenophobic resentment, its air of adolescent carnival, and its downright barbaric behavior, it signi-fied the sense of powerlessness in American society" (West, 1993: 255). Ironically, the common "powerlessness" becomes the basis for conflict rather than community. Even in Los Angeles, the combatants generally attacked one another, rather than posing any direct threat to their white oppressors.

Evidence of these divisions is apparent in opinion polls, which illus-trate the negative perceptions that oppressed groups hold of one another (Oliver and Johnson, 1984). There are chilling parallels between dominant and subordinate groups' readings of other minority groups. In fact, hegemonic systems of meaning construction are repro-duced in the context of interethnic relations. Melvin Oliver and James Johnson summarize research findings that revealed interethnic antago-nisms founded upon perceptions of power and unfair employment opportunities accruing to other minority groups. Similarly, Steven Holmes reports the findings of a national poll commissioned by the National Conference of Christians and Jews (1994: B8). The results sug-gest strongly that blacks, Asians, and Hispanics generally hold even more negative views of one another than do whites. Forty-six percent of Hispanics and 42 percent of blacks saw Asians as "unscrupulous, crafty and devious in business." Sixty-eight percent of Asians and 49 percent of blacks agreed that Hispanics "tend to have bigger families than they are able to support." Thirty-one percent of Asians and 28 percent of Hispanics believed that blacks "want to live on welfare."

These findings are indicative of the hostilities between groups. Yet they also are indicative of the extent to which all members of society are susceptible to dominant viewpoints. They reinforce the assertion that the society of the United States is grounded in constantly shifting hierarchies of oppression. In other words, they "revealed the power of racist rhetoric between politically, economically, and culturally disadvantaged groups" (Chun, 1996: 3). Perhaps we should not have expected solidarity after all. Subordinate groups are not immune to the power of hegemonic ideologies. They too are a crucial part of the audience, having listened to, observed, and lived within the structures of inequality: "We must remember that racial minorities, having been socialized in a society that sees them as inferior to whites, are equally likely to believe in the inferiority of racial groups other than their own" (McClain and Stewart, 1995: 149). Even immigrants arrive here with prepackaged ideas of how race and gender operate in the United States, having been "informed" by American media outlets worldwide. This is especially important in understanding the relationship between African Americans and other minority groups. White supremacy is reinscribed in the hostility with which other people of color greet blacks in this country:

> In race talk, the move into mainstream America always means buying into the notion of American blacks as the real aliens.
> Whatever the ethnicity or nationality of the immigrant, his nemesis is understood to be African American. . . . Often people of color . . . hold black people responsible for the hostility they encounter from whites. It is as though they see blacks as acting in a manner that makes things hard for everybody else. (hooks, 1995: 198–199)

This is what distinguishes minority relations from majority-minority relations: the sense that all Others are in competition for the favors of the white majority; they are in a struggle to assign blame for their relative positions of inferiority. The struggle for economic, political and cultural empowerment becomes a struggle to disempower "the competition," through violence if necessary.

AFRICAN AMERICAN–ASIAN CONFLICT

The black and Hispanic victimization of Korean shop owners in the aftermath of the Rodney King verdict illustrates the potential for violence when subordinate groups—especially those with a long history in the United States—are threatened by what is perceived as the empowerment of another oppressed group. In this light, Koreans are seen to have "jumped the queue" in the struggle for political and economic opportunities. This makes them vulnerable to the opprobrium and resentment of the oppressed communities they serve, as was clear in the response of one black youth asked in a television interview to explain the looting: "Because we hate 'em. Everybody hates them" (Frontline, April 27, 1993).

This racial animosity springs from a number of sources within the context of both African Americans' and Asian Americans' efforts to construct their racial identities. Like all other members of U.S. society, each of these groups perceives the other through the lens of cultural mythologies. Asians see African Americans as criminals, as welfare cheats, as threats to their economic and physical well-being. African Americans see Asians as "perpetual foreigners," as unsavory businesspeople. These tendencies are exacerbated by ongoing media coverage, which highlights the tensions rather than efforts at reconciliation. This was the case in the 1990 boycott of Korean businesses in Flatbush, New York, where the media coverage was deemed to be "inflammatory and polarizing" and "overly simplistic and in some cases blatantly racist" (U.S. Commission on Civil Rights, 1992: 37). It was also the case in the treatment of the 1992 Los Angeles riots, in which the mainstream media contributed to the animosity by "spotlighting tensions between African Americans and Koreans above all efforts to work together . . . [and] by exploiting racist stereotypes of Koreans as unfathomable aliens, this time wielding guns on rooftops and allegedly firing wildly into crowds" (Kim, 1993: 221).

Such divisive mechanisms encourage blacks and Asians to adopt an oppositional stance relative to one another—they are portrayed as inevitable enemies rather than allies. Unfortunately, they all too often accept these externalized interpretations of their relationship, as evidenced by their long-term animosities. Moon Jo (1992) catalogs the charges and countercharges levied by blacks and Asians as each group attempts to construct itself as the wronged party. Korean shopowners in particular are said to be rude, exploitive, unwilling to hire blacks, and unfairly advantaged by government programs. African Americans are said to be unwilling to cooperate or understand, criminal threats, unreliable workers, and unfairly advantaged by government programs (see also McClain and Stewart, 1995).

Nowhere is the racial animus of blacks and Asians more apparent than in the low-income, predominantly black communities where so many Koreans have established "mom-and-pop" businesses. As newcomers to the United States, Korean employment opportunities often are blocked by language, educational, and of course racial barriers. They turn instead to self- and family employment in the retail trade. In cities like New York, Los Angeles, and Atlanta, more than 30 percent of Koreans are small-business owners. In this capacity, they assume the role of commercial "middlemen" between corporations reluctant to locate in the inner city and their low-income, nonwhite clientele. The entrepreneurial stance adopted by Koreans is not welcomed by the African Americans inhabiting these communities. Quite the contrary: from the perspective of African Americans, Koreans are "foreign" interlopers who have, first of all, forced out black business owners and, second, engaged in exploitative practices.

Black hostility toward these shop owners apparently has inspired anti-Asian violence as a means of recouping their lost prominence in the community. A seven-block black neighborhood in Washington, D.C., has seen nine firebombings of Korean businesses since 1984. In Los Angeles, more than twenty Korean shop owners have been killed in black communities since 1990. During the Los Angeles riots, three hundred Chinese businesses were looted and burned; in all, 40 percent of the businesses lost were Asian owned (Cho, 1993). Moreover, anti-Asian violence and harassment are endemic in these communities (U.S. Commission on Civil Rights, 1992).

In large measure, black perpetrators of anti-Asian hate crime are reacting to the particular way in which Asian Americans construct their racial identity in the context of a white supremacist culture. Asians' assigned role as "middlemen" is taken as a sign of their "preferred status" in United States society. They are held accountable—and found guilty— as illegitimate interlopers who entered "the game" very late, yet nonetheless managed to vault over the heads of native-born African Americans.

The dual image of Asians as middlemen and as the model minority further divides them from African Americans. Their efforts to assimilate and advance are taken as arrogance that must be met with hostility. Perhaps even more than the dominant white culture, African-American, inner-city poor are threatened by the perceived success of Asian Americans. In addition to the economic competition represented by the latter is the competition for place and status relative to the white power structure. Asian Americans are exploitable as a wedge against native-born blacks, who are told to look to Asians as an indication that the American Dream is open to all, *if only you are willing to work for it.* Korean shop owners, Chinese entrepreneurs, and Japanese executives are held up as models of the potential for assimilation and advancement—with the implied message that African Americans just don't work hard enough. Consequently, Asians become caught between the racism of whites and the racialized resentment of blacks:

> The model minority myth plays a key role in establishing a racial
> hierarchy which denies the oppression of Asian Americans while

simultaneously legitimizing the oppression of other racial minorities and poor whites. (Chang, 1995: 329)

Violence is a readily available outlet for this misdirected hostility. It is a means of empowerment for blacks who see themselves losing ground relative to newly arrived immigrants—losing ground, that is, in economic, political, and cultural terms. Violence directed toward Asian Americans is an effort to reclaim some of this loss in status, while simultaneously seeking to remind Asians of their appropriate place in the racialized pecking order.

JEWS AND AFRICAN AMERICANS

Joshua Price poignantly expresses one source of intergroup hostility among oppressed groups when he states that "although Jewish, I understand myself as an almost-insider to Anglo culture in the United States" (cited in Lugones and Price, 1995: 113). He is not alone in seeing himself and American Jews as "almost insiders," quite like Asians. This provokes anger toward what many perceive as a "privileged minority." Price further admits to complicity in white dominance, in exchange for inclusion in their ranks. He too is asked—and often agrees—"to maintain solidarity and loyalty—often in order to break, exclude, violate, exploit and deny those people who are outside the inner circle" (113). Much like African Americans throughout their history in the United States, Jews experience a "double consciousness," described by W. E. B. Du Bois as the simultaneous construction of identity within the context of both dominant and subordinate cultures. Understandably, this causes insecurity and discomfort all around. Cornel West also speaks to this uneasy positioning of Jews relative to subordinate blacks and dominant whites when he observes that

> The images of black activists yelling "Where's Hitler when we need him?" and "Heil Hitler," juxtaposed with those of David Duke celebrating Hitler's birthday seem to feed a single line of intolerance burning on both ends of the American candle, that threatens to consume us all. (1994: 111)

More so even than Asians, American Jews occupy a paradoxical position in the racialized hierarchy of power and place. And, more so than Asians, they are seen as conspirators in the plot to maintain the subordination of blacks. Consequently, they are held accountable by black Americans to a construction of racial identity that is seen as oppositional and threatening. To an alarming extent in some quarters, Jews are held to be complicit in the formation and maintenance of a racialized hierarchy which subordinates blacks. Anti-Semitic violence then becomes a mechanism for transcending racial domination and, simultaneously, an important resource for constructing relational identities.

This uneasy relationship between blacks and Jews has a lengthy history, punctuated by periods of conciliation. In many ways, black anti-Semitism has paralleled that of the white Christian majority. Nineteenth-century religious teachings portrayed Jews as protagonists, as in black catechisms, for example:

Q. Who killed Jesus?
A. The wicked Jews.
Q. The wicked Jews grew angry with our Savior, and what did they do to Him?
A. They crucified Him. (Dinnerstein, 1994: 198).

Similar sentiments are expressed in many black spirituals of the time, which make such claims as "Virgin Mary had one son, The cruel Jews had him hung" (Dinnerstein, 1994: 198). As often as not, prejudices grounded in religious teachings were accompanied by secular stereotypes that further vilified the "wicked Jews" as greedy, insatiable, and conniving in their quest for wealth. A turn-of-the-century article in *Colored America* insisted that Jews were "parasitical and predatory rather than conservatory and constructive in tendencies—preying upon and devouring the substance of others" (cited in Dinnerstein, 1994: 199).

Little has changed in this century. Black Americans still share with white Americans the perception of Jews as Christ killers, predators, and greedy financiers:

This is part of the way racism works—it is easier to scapegoat Jews . . . than to target larger structures of white supremacy. . . . It is a distortion of reality to act as though any form of black anti-Semitism, however virulent, exists in isolation from the anti-Semitism that is learned whenever anyone absorbs without question the values of mainstream white culture. (hooks, 1995: 210)

Yet the relationship between blacks and Jews in the United States retains its own specificity in light of the relative economic and political positions of the two groups. On the one hand, both are "not white" and therefore outsiders. But Jews are both "not white" and "white," or at least "almost white." By virtue of the latter, they are also insiders, sharing the white skin privilege—something African Americans can never accomplish.

In this vein, West (1993) identifies the predominant cultural and structural dynamics that condition relations between blacks and Jews, and that set the stage for interethnic violence. First, he contends, black anti-Semitism reflects black anti-whitism. Jewish complicity in the politics and economics of racism in the United States is seen to reinforce the subordination of the nation's black community. There is a sense among some blacks that Jews could only become "white" in America because of the existence of blacks. Thus, Jewish-black relationships reproduce broader white-black relationships of power, which assume a paternalistic, often exploitative face in that they "have almost always been as philanthropist to recipient, shopkeeper to customer, landlord to tenant, employer to employee, teacher to student, welfare worker to client, and so forth" (Dinnerstein, 1994: 224).

The perceived role of Jews in the continued oppression of black America is taken as a sign of betrayal between "natural allies." West (1994) holds that blacks have heightened expectations of Jews in light of the similarity of their historical experiences of oppression and earlier coalitions around civil rights. Blacks and Jews alike have experienced (at different times and places) enslavement, ghettoization, subjugation, diaspora, and violence. In light of these similarities, then, black Americans are embittered by the perception that their allies have become their enemies. As evidence of this betrayal, they point to Jewish resistance to affirmative action and state social security provisions, for example.

This sense of betrayal is enhanced by the corresponding fear that Jews, like Asians, like Hispanics, like all other subordinate groups, have vaulted past African Americans in economic and political strength. The result is a case of "underdog resentment and envy directed at another underdog who has 'made it' in American society" (West, 1994: 151). Jewish appeals to the aforementioned similarity of oppression, then, ring hollow in the ears of African Americans who have been surpassed in power, left behind by Jewish success. Moreover, whatever measure of success is achieved by Jews is seen as a further evidence of Jews as co-conspirators in white racism. It is success won, not through effort and initiative, but by white nepotism.

While the social and economic malaise of black Americans provides the background for black anti-Semitism, the Nation of Islam in recent years has provided its public forum. The rhetoric of Islam—as preached by Louis Farrakhan, for example—provides a menu of ideologies which coconstruct blacks as the chosen people and Jews as the worst of all "white Devils." Just as white supremacist groups condition and encourage hate-motivated sentiment and activity, so too does the anti-Semitism of Farrakhan. Jews are to be blamed for alcohol and drug abuse in black communities, for negative stereotypes of blacks in entertainment media, for black poverty. *The Secret Relationship Between Blacks and Jews* provides much of the fodder for this virulence, holding Jews accountable for slavery and black genocide in general. Muhammad's and Farrakhan's frequent references to "Jew York City," "Jewnited Nations," and "Columbia Jewniversity" highlight the perception of the breadth of Jewish control and manipulation. In a recent interview, Farrakhan exploits the image of Jews as usurious leeches: "In the '20s, '30s and

'40s, up into the '50s, the Jews were the primary merchants in the black community. Wherever we were, there they were. What was their role? We bought food from them; we bought clothing from them; we bought furniture from them; we rented from them . . . Sucking the lifeblood from our own community" (Farrakhan, 1996: 53).

In the context of the structural and cultural relationship between blacks and Jews, interethnic violence persists as a resource for the establishment and reestablishment of racial and ethnic identity. This is especially important for poor, African-American youth who lack access to alternative means by which to compete with Jews. Resentment toward Jewish progress is manifest in bias-motivated harassment and victimization, which enhances the status of the perpetrator(s), while seeking to disempower the victim(s). It attests to the group alliance of the perpetrators, and especially to their "insider" status. Conversely, it reconstructs the Jewish victims as perpetual "outsiders." This is a curious—but important—inversion of the groups' relative positionality in the broader culture, where blacks are always the outsiders, while Jews are seen to traverse the boundaries between insider and outsider at will. This is at the heart of what Shelby Steele refers to as the "unseen problem" between blacks and Jews: the "presumption by the larger society that we make up a brotherhood of outsiders . . . and we fight against each other to prove it wrong, to show that we have no such brotherhood" (1994: 180).

These dynamics were readily apparent in the violence that followed the death of Gavin Cato in Crown Heights, New York. The long simmering antagonism toward the neighborhood's Hasidic Jews boiled over into a week of violence, which included the stabbing death of Yankel Rosenbaum. Here, too, the black community espied evidence of preferential treatment and white racism, as when Hasidim were accompanied by police escorts, or allowed to organize street patrols that harassed black community members. In response, spurred by Cato's death, blacks sought to preserve both the geographical and racialized boundaries between themselves and the Other by violence, harassment, and vandalism, accompanied by exclusionary messages that included "Heil Hitler" and "Get the Jews Out."

For the black community of Crown Heights, the Hasidim were "out of place" both in geographical and political terms. They had betrayed their "allies" by siding with the white majority. Consequently, the killing of Cato lit a fuse that had long lay in wait. His death provided the context and the motive for black demonstrations of racial solidarity, even across ethnic groups (Haitians and Jamaicans, for example).

To humiliate, devalue, and victimize the identifiable "white Jewish devil" is simultaneously to proclaim the positive collective identity of the African American, very much in contrast to the negative identity generally assigned blacks in this culture. It is, moreover, a means of distancing oneself from the Other. Anti-Semitic violence reinforces the differences rather than the similarities between these two differently oppressed groups. It reasserts the particular and unique suffering of blacks in the United States. There is a certain resentment toward the Jewish assumption of shared oppression. The language and activities of anti-Semitism make that resentment clear (Lester, 1994: 172).

GAY MEN AND COMMUNITIES OF COLOR

Intercultural violence is not necessarily restricted to conflict between ethnic and racial groups. Anti-gay violence crosscuts ethnicity. Violence perpetrated against gays by men of color crosses the axes of race, gender, and sexuality. In other words, regardless of race or ethnicity, masculinity, in particular, assumes heterosexuality. hooks (1990, 1992, 1994, 1995) returns again and again to the tendency of black males, for example, to demand compulsory heterosexuality. In this sense, gay men, especially black and Chicano gay men, are further marginalized within their racial communities, since they are simultaneously "race traitors" and "gender traitors." hooks cites the lamentation of a black gay writer, who claims that "nobody wants to know my name, or hear my voice" (1992: 113). Gay men of color are "outsiders" on both the axes of gender and racial identity.

The complexity of attempts to simultaneously negotiate ethnic and sexual identities remains dramatically underdeveloped both theoretically and empirically. What follows, then, is a tentative exploration of how men of color may or may not use "gay-bashing" as a resource in their own performance of a racialized gender identity. Again, as with interracial violence, it is imperative to consider anti-gay violence by people of color in the context of broader patterns of patriarchal white supremacy. It is these interlocking structures of inequality that condition and delimit the resources available to men of color as they seek to establish themselves in U.S. society. Yet the effects of inequality on each cultural group retain a specificity, depending on historical and cultural position of each. For far too many gay men and women, being black or Jewish or Hispanic among like others offers no refuge when one is gay. Where they might expect solidarity on the basis of their ethnic identity, they may instead suffer stigmatization, persecution, and violence on the basis on their performance of their gender and sexual identity.

Many traditional Native American cultures would have no call to denigrate homosexuality in their midst. More so than most groups in the United States, Native Americans often hold to a flexible, fluid conceptualization of sexuality. Behavior is more likely to be evaluated according to the appropriateness of the context, rather than the behavior itself. Thus, there is no rigid proscription against homosexuality. On the contrary, many Native traditions refer to the "Two Spirited" as one who is valued because of the inherent combination of both the male and female spirits. This dualism allows the Two Spirited to see and perceive the world from a much clearer, much more complete perspective. Rather than defining sexuality in binary terms, then, many Native cultures see one's sexual identity along a mutable continuum: "If one takes the line of male/female, gay/straight, and bends it into a circle, there are an infinite number of points. Just so, there are theoretically an infinite number of points of gender and sexual identity for an individual that can shift and differ over time and location" (Tafoya, 1997: 8).

Some Asian cultures share elements of this tolerant outlook on sexual diversity. Historically, same-sex relationships have permeated the upper echelons of Japanese society, including the wealthy urban classes, Buddhist clergy, and the military. In fact, homosexual practices known as *nanshoku* ("male colors") or *shudo* ("way of companions") were so intimately connected to the warrior society that they were often referred to as the "pastime" of the Samurai—a manly bunch if ever there was one! Clearly, then, masculinity did not require unfailing performances of heterosexuality. However, while this tradition was readily accepted for centuries, it seems to have become latent since the turn of the century, a phenomenon Miller (1995) attributes to the Westernization of Japan—a process that included a transition in sexual morality.

Nonetheless, there remains a significant distinction between Asian and Western reactions to homosexuality. Miller (1995) and Greene (1997) both assert that Asian resistance is grounded not in homophobia, nor in heterosexism, but in pressure to marry. Asian-American men, in particular, are held accountable more to family than to gender expectations. Homosexuality is thus a punishable threat to the family line and name. Where a male renounces this obligation and traditional obedience to the family, efforts to regulate his behavior may include violence, even death. Hence, this violence constitutes an attempt on the part of male family members (not judgmental strangers) to reassert their dominance in the familial relationship; at the same time, it is a penalty intended to ensure compliance with the interests of the family. Consequently, anti-gay violence in this context is not an attempt by strangers to assert their aggressive masculinity. Rather it is a weapon for ensuring family honor. This may be especially important for Asians living in the United States, where the Western culture generally poses a threat to the continuation of the traditional Asian family line and values.

Family also provides a context for anti-gay violence among Latinos, yet in a different—and generally more intense—manner (Greene, 1997). In traditional Latino cultures, masculinity is rigidly enacted through the patriarchal family and associated roles of provider and protector. Homosexual men, on the other hand, are regarded as effete, and both incapable and unwilling to assume these roles. Consequently, they are labeled as traitors to the family as well as to the culture itself. Cherrie Moraga argues that the rigidity of Latino conceptions of masculinity is stronger than virtually any other culture in the United States: "Because they [gay Latino men] are deemed inferior for not fulfilling the traditional role of men, they are more marginalized from mainstream heterosexual society than other gay men and are especially vulnerable to male violence" (1996: 299). As a result, gay or effeminate Latino men are subject to persistent violence as punishment for their betrayal. They have transgressed an inviolate boundary, thereby threatening the solidarity and dominance of Latino men as a group.

However, this virulent homophobia is not without its contradictions, especially among Chicano men. Drawing on anthropological evidence, Almaguer (1995) asserts that the Chicano understanding of homosexuality revolves around sexual acts rather than sexual preferences per se. Specifically, a distinction is drawn between *activo* and *pasivo*, with stigmatization and ridicule reserved for the *pasivo*. The latter is deemed to be enacting a passive, subservient, feminine identity, very much out of line with the favored *activo*, who is by definition active, aggressive, and very "male." The *activo* may in fact gain status through his dominance of the weaker recipient who is judged to be a feminized man: biologically male, but not really a man (Almaguer, 1995).

The *pasivo*, or more vulgarly termed *joto* or *puto*, does not meet the standards established for the construction of the aggressive, heterosexual dominant male. On the contrary, he is accused of having betrayed the Chicano's proscribed gender and sexual performance. As a consequence of this, he is constantly vulnerable to the violence of other Chicanos, who are simultaneously affirming their solidarity for all to see. It is left to the perpetrators of anti-gay violence to reassert masculine privilege and heterosexuality by the negation of the threat: "The openly effeminate Chicano gay man's rejection of heterosexuality is typically seen as a fundamental betrayal of Chicano patriarchal cultural norms. He is viewed as having turned his back on the male role that privileges Chicano men. . . . Those who reject these male prerogatives are viewed as non-men" (Almaguer, 1995: 425).

The dynamics of Latino intolerance for homosexual men take on a special significance in the United States. Here, traditional resources for enacting masculinity are limited by structures of inequality—racism and classism—that inhibit the Latino male's ability to express his manhood through the familial roles of provider and protector. Elevated rates of unemployment, underemployment, and impoverishment have meant that many of Mexican, Puerto Rican, or Cuban heritage, for example, continue to find that their ability to support a family is dramatically undermined (Feagin and Feagin, 1996). This predisposes them to judge harshly those who "choose" not to struggle beside them to preserve the family, and concomitantly, the culture. Moreover, curtailed economic success leaves aggressive heterosexuality as a paramount residual means through which to construct their manliness. Yet here, too, homosexual men fail to meet the standard.

If this holds true for Latino males, it is perhaps doubly true for African-American men whose capacity to enact masculinity has been even more thoroughly circumscribed. Greene (1997) postulates that homophobia among African Americans generally may be more pronounced since it is multiply determined by sexism, Christian religiosity (especially Southern Baptist), and external and internalized racism. By virtue of their long experiences within a white Christian society, African Americans have also internalized the norms and values associated with white patriarchal notions of masculinity; yet by virtue of their class and race subordination, poor black male youths, in particular, do not have access to the resources by which they might "appropriately" enact the hegemonic form of masculinity. Consequently, African-American males have adopted alternative versions of what it is to be "a man." This perspective is aptly summed up in Richard Majors and Janet Billson's analysis of the "cool pose" as a method for constructing an aggressive masculinity in the face of ongoing racism. The cool pose is a response to a key dilemma faced by black males: "African American men have defined manhood in terms familiar to white men: breadwinner, provider, procreator, protector. Unlike white men, however, blacks have not had consistent access to the same means to fulfill their dreams of masculinity and success" (1992: 1).

Under advanced capitalism, the ability of poor black males to perform as breadwinners or providers is limited by wage and employment structures that marginalize them. They must, then, search elsewhere for the resources through which they can assert their manliness. Disempowered politically, economically, and socially, young black males must express their capacity, their power as males, through alternative means. Having been denied the typical avenues by which to establish masculinity, they must nonetheless constantly prove to themselves and to others that they are men. hooks (1992), Oliver (1988) and Majors and Billson (1992) all concur that for many, this is achieved through the performance of "compulsive masculinity" wherein "typical masculine values become a rigid prescription for toughness, sexual promiscuity, manipulation, thrill-seeking and a willingness to use violence to resolve interpersonal conflict" (Majors and Billson, 1992: 34). A central facet of this form of identity construction is adherence to a similarly "compulsive" and compulsory heterosexuality. We might contrast this to masculinity enacted through "patriarchal status" or a generalized assertion of power on the basis of maleness. The alternative "phallocentric masculinity" implies that "what a male does with his penis becomes a greater and certainly more accessible way to assert masculine status" (hooks, 1992: 94). For many young men, black masculinity demands the performance and policing of a narrowly defined version of manliness that requires heterosexuality. Combine this with the prescription for violence and control over others and you have a formula for anti-gay violence.

Violence against gay black men is a corollary of the cool pose. As such, it is "about how black males have created a tool for hammering masculinity out of the bronze of their daily lives" (Majors and Billson, 1992: 1). It is a means of asserting the perpetrator's identity for all to see and evaluate—he is a manly man, virile, strong, heterosexual, and in control of at least these aspects of his life. If he is to be held accountable to his gender identity—given the limits imposed by his racial identity— at least he can make the claim to have acted in accordance with the prerequisites of aggressive heterosexuality.

Conversely, violence against gay black males also shapes the victim's identity. James Baldwin once commented that being attacked by white people—on account of his refusal to be a "good Negro"—only made him angry, whereas being attacked by black people—on account of his refusal to be a "real man"—made him want to cry. Such victimization is a rejection, an ostracism, a penalty. This is echoed by West's observation that gay black men "reject the major stylistic option of black machismo identity, yet are marginalized in white America and penalized in black America for doing so. In their efforts to be themselves, they are not really 'black men,' not machismo-identified" (1994: 129).

The youth on the street who punishes the gay black male is holding his victim accountable to a particular racialized gender performance. He is seeking to police the boundaries of sexuality that are defined for him in the dominant black institutions. He is reading the script written by the African Methodist Episcopalian (A.M.E.) church, which has publicly denounced homosexuality, or the Howard University newspaper, which referred to black gay males as "freaks" engaged in "depravity." Having rejected these censures, gay black men are vulnerable to violent attempts to make them repent and realign themselves with their brothers. Failing this, anti-gay violence alternatively reminds gay black males that they are traitors to their race and their gender, and therefore reviled.

These tentative remarks were intended to draw attention to the reality of intercultural violence among and between oppressed groups. I have suggested that such intercultural violence may be seen as efforts to police boundaries between groups, thereby enhancing the solidarity and privilege of the perpetrator's reference community. The irony of this particular manifestation of identity construction is that the perpetrator and the victim often have experienced a similar (but not identical) oppression. In other words, blacks, Jews, Asians, homosexuals, and others not explicitly noted herein have all suffered various degrees of discrimination and victimization. Yet rather than acknowledging this and forming coalitions, they often have resorted to conflict among themselves. It appears as if they have so internalized the dominant aspects of white masculine supremacy that this is the only lens through which they can view one another.

## SIX

Hate Groups and Ideologies of Power

Yaweh's Children are like lambs being led to slaughter—This IS a battle, "The Children of Light vs. The Children of Darkness." Yes, a Racial Holy War.

—Posse Comitatus, online

The hate groups currently enjoying a renewed popularity would have no hesitation in supporting the contention of the extreme right-wing magazine *American Renaissance* that "it has been more than 30 years since the civil rights era but in many respects race relations are worse than ever. In the 1960s, Americans hoped to build a nation in which race would no longer matter, and people of all backgrounds would live together in harmony. *It is now clear that the assumptions of the civil rights movement were wrong*" (*American Renaissance*, online). Indeed, many would go further to say that not only the assumptions but the intentions of the civil rights movement were wrong, misguided, even destructive of the American way of life. Consequently, from their point of view, it is time to roll back the disastrous gains of the 1960s and 1970s and reassert the "true" American identity grounded in white, male, heterosexual hegemony. In essence, hate groups represent an extreme—but not aberrant—element of a broader cadre concerned with trimming the sails of the myriad counterhegemonic forces and ideologies that have arisen out of the civil rights decades. They represent a counter-counterhegemonic, or counterinsurgent force determined to rearticulate the racial and gender dynamics in the United States.

Cheryl Kerchis and Iris Marion Young briefly summarize the efforts of diverse social movements to claim group autonomy, political inclusion, and freedom from discrimination. What these movements shared was a commitment to the equal valuation and treatment of all social groups, "requiring each to recognize and respect the values of the experiences and perspectives of all other groups" (Kerchis and Young, 1995: 8). Such an approach challenged long-standing and deeply embedded ideologies and practices that consciously sought to devalue "otherness"—Jim Crow laws, job segregation, sodomy legislation, for example. In contemporary terms, it is precisely this form of inclusive and egalitarian politics that hate groups would seek to overturn. This is not an unexpected or surprising development, since hegemony and the practices of insurgency are inherently dynamic and unstable. It is the case that

> the insurgent process is one whereby subordinate group members introduce a particular tactic, the dominant group, over time, adjusts, counteracts, and often neutralizes that particular subordinate group strategy. . . . The end result of the struggle is often a reshaping of the existing stratification structure. (Roscigno, 1994: 112)

While I would argue that there is no ultimate "end result" of this ongoing process, Roscigno's point is well taken: counterhegemonic threats to the established racial and gendered order consistently are met with counter-mobilization on the part of the traditionally dominant groups(s). Extremist hate groups are explicitly organized to neutralize the threat—and occasionally the physical presence—represented by minority groups such as people of color, women, and gay men and women. Many, like the Church of Jesus Christ in Israel, are fully prepared for a Racial Holy War (RAHOWA) that would "return power to the white race" (Charles Scott, cited in "Merchants of Hate," online). Similar sentiments are to be found among adherents of the Montana Freemen who insist, "We are not to allow women or foreigners, colored people, jews, and/or citizens of the United States to rule over us" (cited in ADL, "The Freemen Network," online). Thus, these hate groups take it upon themselves to mobilize a force against what they perceive to be invalid usurpers.

In short, the contemporary reemergence of hate groups is grounded in a profound sense of dislocation motivated by the perceived "crisis of identity" spawned by the civil rights movement. As the Peoples' Resistance Movement sees it, "Political moves and social changes are now taking place which . . . are rapidly weakening our institutions and threaten to end in chaos and anarchy" (online). Jared Taylor, founder of the virulently racist *American Renaissance* magazine, is similarly explicit about the source of his hostility. Traditional arrangements in racial and gender relations, he argues, "served the country well, so long as . . . the two traditional minorities—Blacks and Indians—did not have voices. All this changed, beginning in the 1960s. The civil rights movement gave voices to Blacks and Indians, and changes in immigration law brought a massive influx of non-whites. It was the end of a certain kind of America" (cited in ADL, 1996a: 178). The "American" is no longer (as if it ever were) an uncontested vision. Instead, the very meaning of American identity, and especially the meaning of "whiteness" has been seriously thrown into question. Hate groups have mobilized in an effort to reassert a narrow, exclusive understanding of the national identity.

This chapter is an exploration of the renewal of the hate movement in the United States, and its role in the politics of difference that inform hate-motivated violence. In dramatic ways, hate groups threaten to extend their impact beyond the immediate membership. Their mantra of intolerance is gaining considerable legitimacy in light of the changing messengers and media that carry their message. In this chapter, I delineate the core ideological belief systems that undergird the movement, and I address the significance of contemporary hate group in terms of their connections to the political mainstream and to the growing militia movement. I also explore the implications of their strategic and recruitment use of modern communication. Together, these patterns facilitate hate groups' abilities to make some claim to legitimacy and, therefore, acceptance. Before I begin to trace these alignments, however, I present a brief descriptive overview of the current nature and activities associated with the hate movement.

SCOPE AND ACTIVITIES OF THE HATE MOVEMENT

The existing supremacist groups are a diverse lot, ranging from the contemporary incarnations of the traditional Ku Klux Klan (KKK), to the loosely organized skinheads. While these myriad groups are characterized by differences in age, class, and gender structures, as well as in ideologies, practices, and national visibility, what they share is a commitment to clean up the "cultural pollution"—however defined—that apparently has sullied the United States. The most prevalent manifestation of the pollution, from this perspective, are racial and ethnic minority groups. Thus, most hate groups are oriented around white supremacist and anti-Semitic platforms. Nonetheless, women, homosexuals, atheists, and other minority groups may also be on the "hit lists" of these groups. Increasingly, the liberal welfare state is becoming the focus of wrath: the state is to blame for the rising "impertinence" of minority groups. While anti-government militias are most commonly associated with the latter, Morris Dees (1996), James Ridgeway (1995), and the Anti-Defamation League (ADL) (1996) make clear that the boundaries between hate-motivated extremists and anti-state extremists are becoming more and more blurred. In his role as director of the Southern Poverty Law Center, Dees has marshaled substantial evidence supporting the notion that adherents of white supremacist organizations—such as Louis Beam of the Aryan Nations—are infiltrating militia groups.

Excluding militia groups, Milton Kleg (1993) suggests that it is possible to identify five distinct categories of hate groups operative in the

1990s: Identity Church adherents, neo-Nazis, skinheads, Ku Klux Klansmen/women, and Posse Comitatus members. It is important to bear in mind, however, that these too are far from distinct units—membership is fluid, with people moving in and out of groups, and maintaining memberships in several at once. Moreover, there is considerable interaction and cooperation between groups in terms of rallies, information sharing, and links on hate lines, for instance.

The first of the groups, the Identity Church movement incorporates some of the most active and violent organizations of the 1990s, including Aryan Nations; The Order (now defunct); the Covenant, Sword and Arm of the Lord; and Rev. Pete Peters's Church of Christ. Groups in this class ground their anti-Semitic and racist tenets in a scriptural reading that posits white Christians as God's "chosen" people, and Jews, especially, as the children of Satan. Neo-Nazi groups turn, not to the Bible, but to tracts of Germany's Third Reich to inform their "Americanism, Nazi-style—send the blacks to Africa and the Jews to the ovens" (cited in Kleg, 1993: 201). The "White Power" rhetoric of neo-Nazi groups such as the National Socialist White Peoples' Party (NSWPP) or the National Alliance is shared in a somewhat less orderly and consistent manner by the rising numbers of skinheads. Skinheads tend to be more loosely organized, but also more violent than many other hate groups. Sara Bullard (1991) claims that the skinheads of the 1990s are every bit as violent as was the KKK of the 1920s and 1950s. The KKK—currently in a state of fragmentation—addresses contemporary problems like AIDS, crime, welfare, or immigration "solely through the prism of race and offers not solutions but a licence to hate" (ADL, 1991: 2). In part, the resurgence in KKK membership can be explained by its change in tactics, toward mainstreaming, best exemplified by David Duke's smooth professional persona. Finally, the Posse Comitatus shares the anti-Semitism of other hate groups, alongside the anti-statism of the militia groups. Indeed, the two targets of opprobrium inherently are linked in the Posse Comitatus's belief in the Zionist Occupied Government (ZOG). From this perspective, the only legitimate form of government exists at the local level, since the federal government is orchestrated by Jewish financial interests.

The membership represented by hate groups in the United States is difficult to ascertain; estimates of the number of active group members vary widely. Erin Starr offers a conservative estimate of 25,000 Americans actively involved in hate groups, but also notes that an additional 150,000 may be "armchair racists" who receive literature and possibly attend rallies without necessarily taking any other action (1997, online). Feagin and Vera (1995) provide similar numbers for the early 1990s, suggesting 20,000–30,000 active white supremacists, representing 300 groups, and 150,000 "armchair" supremacists. Ridgeway's (1995) extensive review of the history of white supremacist groups in the United States identifies 25 major hate groups, with extensive offshoots of each. This appears to be a conservative estimate, in that Kleg (1993) and Bullard (1991) number Identity Churches alone at 40 and 150 respectively. Bullard's estimate of the total number of hate groups—350—is closer to that of Feagin and Vera. The Southern Poverty Law Center's (SPLC) Klanwatch project records evidence of 240 active hate groups in approximately 40 states in 1996 (Klanwatch, 1997). By the time the organization published its 1998 report, the number had jumped an astonishing 20 percent, up to 474 active groups nationwide (Klanwatch, 1998).

In terms of specific groups' memberships, Bullard asserts that in 1990, the KKK counted its numbers at only 5,000, the century's nadir. This corresponds with the ADL's estimate of 4,000–5,000 for 1995, as compared to a high of five million in 1925. In fact, by 1990, Identity Church membership had surpassed that of the KKK, with somewhere between 5,000 and 10,000 participants (Bullard, 1991); by 1998, Identity Churches could boast 81 chapters across the country (Klanwatch, 1998). Skinheads, too, probably outnumber the KKK, although these are even more difficult to count due to their lack of organizational structure. The ADL consistently puts their numbers at 3,500 in the 1990s (ADL, 1993; 1996), while Kleg's (1993) estimate ranges from 5,000 to 10,000. The SPLC (1997) tracks an alarming growth in the number of skinhead groups, from 30 in 1995 to 37 in 1996, and 42 in 1998 (Klanwatch, 1998).

With the possible exception of skinhead groups, the statistics cited above—which are undoubtably conservative—represent a decline both in numbers of groups and in group membership since the 1980s. For example, a Klanwatch *Intelligence Report* of 1997 shows a reduction in hate groups from 300 in 1992, to 240 in 1996. Consider also Bullard's (1991) evidence that, although the KKK enjoyed a growth in numbers over the late 1970s and early 1980s (from 9,000 in 1978 to 11,000 in 1981), by 1990 the various splinter groups included only about 5,000 members. This is also supported by the ADL (1996) figures of approximately 10,000 in 1981, 9,000 in 1982, 6,000 in 1984, 5,000 in 1988, and 4,000 in 1991. A Klanwatch (1997) analysis suggests several reasons for these declining numbers, including low unemployment (leading to lessened "scapegoating"), competition from Patriot and militia groups which may or may not have racist undertones, and changes in strategies from visible actions to more clandestine activities. The latter is related to the increased "mainstreaming" of hate groups and hate figures, as exemplified by the likes of David Duke. It also might be attributed to the success of federal and state actions taken against such groups (Klanwatch, 1996; 1997). For example, the quashing of The Order—

one of the most violent offshoots of Aryan Nations—was accomplished largely through the prosecution of its leaders. To be sure, the fact that hate group membership showed decline early in the decade seemed to be cause for celebration.

However, this optimism unfortunately must be tempered with later evidence that, as the decade and the century draw to a close, there seems to be a resurgence of hate group activity and membership. Brian Levin is quoted by Klanwatch as saying that "there are a growing number of apocalyptic thinkers . . . and the problem is that they're creating their own apocalypse. Some are committing suicide, and others are blowing up federal buildings or trying to initiate a race war that will lead to apocalypse" (1998: 6). Consequently, it is hardly the time to declare hate group violence dead. On the contrary, the earlier decline and the more recent regrowth in numbers seem to have been accompanied by corollary increases in the level of violence perpetrated by these groups (ADL, 1993). Here I refer to both the elevated brutality and scope of impact. This is most evident among skinhead groups, who by 1990 accounted for over one-half of violent racial assaults (Bullard, 1991). Klanwatch (1997) documented a dramatic jump in skinhead crimes from 29 in 1995 to 51 in 1996. Moreover, skinheads were responsible for 22 bias-motivated homicides between 1990 and 1993, compared to only 6 between 1987 and 1990 (ADL, 1996). One must look beyond the numbers to get a real sense of the impact of hate group violence. Consider once again skinhead activities. The violence perpetrated by these predominantly young haters is especially brutal. Their attacks on minorities—including racial minorities and gays—often consist of multiple skinheads besetting one or a few targets, armed with a range of lethal weapons. Their brutality is legend, as illustrated by the following incident which occurred near Boston in 1996:

> Amid shouts of "you're gonna' die," over a dozen members of the group invaded the party, wielding knives, chains, pipes, an ax handle and a broomstick. . . . The Skinheads directed most of their rage at 22 year old Jason Linsky. . . . The leader of the group . . . straddled the victim's beaten body and stabbed him nine times. (Klanwatch, 1997: 1)

Such extreme violence is not restricted to skinheads, as the next example from Jackson, Mississippi, reveals:

> A black man, D. Q. Holyfield, 49, was shot to death when a gunman opened fire at a restaurant in a predominantly black neighborhood. Ten others were injured during the shooting spree allegedly aimed at blacks. Larry Wayne Shoemaker, 55, a reported white supremacist, committed suicide after setting the restaurant

ablaze. During a search of his residence, police found two AK-47 assault rifles, 3 empty 30-round clips, a MAC-11 assault weapon, a 12-gauge shotgun, an AR-15 assault rifle, two handguns, white supremacist literature, and Nazi flags. (Klanwatch, 1997: 23)

The latter example also illustrates an important trait of contemporary hate groups: they are heavily armed. They are fully prepared for the much awaited "race war" in which they will defend the white race. A 1993 ad in the anti-Semitic Liberty Lobby's *Spotlight* newsletter offered for sale (under an alias often used by Timothy McVeigh), such items as an anti-tank weapon and ammunition. Militia members as well as hate group members have been found in possession of night vision equipment, automatic weapons, and explosives. They are learning how to use them in pseudo-military encampments, like Butler's Aryan Nations retreat at Hayden Lake. And they are utilizing their weapons and their lessons. At least six adherents of the Christian Identity group called the Phineas Priesthood are suspected of being responsible for a violent crime spree in Spokane, Washington. Three members have been charged with armed robbery of a bank, bombing of a newspaper office, and bombing of an abortion clinic. Such violence is considered both acceptable and necessary to cleanse the white race of the impurities introduced by minorities and "sexual deviates." Alarmingly, the Priests are not alone in their use of explosives in order to further their mission. Antiracist activists and law enforcement authorities agree that this particular form of domestic terrorism is on the upswing.

Similarly, intimidation by fire may be an attempt to cleanse the South of its black residents. A substantial minority of the church arsons currently occurring in the South appear to be the work of white supremacists. For example, four members of the Christian Knights of the Ku Klux Klan were arrested in 1996 on charges stemming from a series of arsons perpetrated against predominantly black churches in South Carolina. Some members face additional charges in connection with other racially motivated offenses (Klanwatch, 1996). Residences also have been targeted by white supremacist arsonists, as was the case in Crown Point, Indiana, where a self-proclaimed skinhead set fire to a rooming house within days of three Hispanics moving in. As is the case in hate crime generally, the message in such cases is clear: you're different, you don't belong, you should leave.

What emerges from this cursory overview of the scope and nature of hate group activity is that a relatively small number of people are engaging in a small—albeit vicious—number of violent acts perpetrated against minority groups and against the state. It is likely that organized hate groups are responsible for little more than 10 to 15 percent of all hate crime (Levin and McDevitt, 1993). This is not to downplay the seriousness of their actions, especially in light of the foregoing discussion of the nature of hate group violence. Nonetheless, it is clear that hate groups are not the primary perpetrators of bias-motivated crime. The vast majority is committed—singly or in groups—by people who are not directly connected to any organized form of hate. This raises the question of why it is important to examine hate groups. The answer is aptly summed up by Elinor Langer who states that "at the least, there appears to be a kind of multiplier effect whereby one thing leads to another and the mere existence of the movement acts as an enabling force for the open expression of racism" (1990: 85). And, as the ADL has recently observed, "The shootings in Los Angeles and Chicago and the synagogue burnings in Sacramento did not begin with a gun or a firebomb. They began with ugly, hateful words and ideas from racist, anti-Semitic groups, and from the extremist manifestos of white-supremacist hate-mongers" (1999: 1). Hate groups are but an extreme expression of the widespread racism, sexism, and homophobia that pervades United States culture. These groups lend voice, and perhaps some legitimatcy, to sentiments held by those unaffiliated with the Klan or skinheads, for example. The ideologies they endorse provide a framework within which others also can articulate and legitimate their own antipathies to potential minority victims. Moreover, it is my contention that hate groups facilitate the negative construction of difference in the United States. In particular, they provide a menu of ideologies that presume the hegemony of white, heterosexual, Christian male power.

IDEOLOGIES OF POWER

It is important to keep in mind that identity is constructed relationally, so that while hate activists construct themselves through rhetoric and violence, they are simultaneously shaping the identity of their opposites—the individual and collective victims (Frankenberg, 1993: 236). Thus, the process of doing whiteness or masculinity or heterosexuality or Christianity is fundamentally asymmetrical, since each of these terms "signals the production and reproduction of dominance rather than subordination, normativity rather than marginality, and privilege rather than disadvantage" (Frankenberg, 1993: 236). To the extent that hate groups define their collective identity as the norm, they necessarily engage in a politics of difference which seeks to negate, exclude, and repress those groups that are outside the norm—nonwhites, non-Christians, nonheterosexual, even nonmale. They do so by invoking ideological claims to superiority and power, which represent the ongoing struggle on the part of supremacists for the right to define the limits and boundaries of inclusion within the United States.

While the exercise of power may be backed by force, it is most effective if exercised in more "legitimate" or acceptable forms—through ideological means, in particular (Gramsci, 1971). Ideological constructs supportive of unequal power relations permeate society. They inform and are reinforced by myriad institutional forms: "power, privilege and the ownership of productive processes have always been unequally allocated in a social hierarchy stratified by" such dimensions as race, class, and gender (Marable, 1995: 363–364). Ideologies of racism, homophobia, and sexism condition human action, identity, and place in such a way as to maintain hierarchies of difference. Goldberg might refer to these mutually reinforcing structures as a "field of discourse," characterized by "racist expressions of principles, supposed justifications of difference, advantages, claims to superiority (whether considered "natural" or "developed") and of racist practices and institutions. These expressions have widely divergent forms: scientific, linguistic, economic, bureaucratic, legal, philosophical, religious, and so forth" (1990: 297).

It is these discursive forms that create a coherent hate movement. In particular, in this chapter, I examine the "supposed justifications" of difference and superiority to which Goldberg refers. Thus, for example, the National Alliance (online) insists on distinguishing between that which is "wholesome and natural," in other words, white Christian heterosexuality, and its opposite, that which is "degenerate and alien." As this example illustrates, it is apparent that many of the identified ideologies are constructed upon essentializing dualisms: Us versus Them; good versus evil; strong versus weak; superior versus inferior. Moreover, these dualities are interpreted as inherent in the groups in question and therefore a legitimate foundation for the marginalization of the Other, who is consistently the negative and subordinate half of the equation. I turn now to an examination of the central ideological forms associated with the contemporary hate movement.[1]

CHRISTIAN IDENTITY

The anti-Semitism and racism that characterize so many hate groups—and not just the Identity Churches—can be traced to the theocratic principle of Christian Identity. On the basis of a creative reading of biblical scripture, those advocating this perspective claim the white race to be the direct descendants of Ancient Israel, and therefore God's chosen people:

> WE BELIEVE that Adam, man of Genesis, is the placing of the
> White Race upon this earth. Not all races descend from Adam.
> Adam is the father of the White Race only. (Aryan Nations, online)

---

1. For the most part, I have used primary sources to unpack the discourses of hate. In particular, I have made significant use of the websites established by hate activists. These are readily accessible electronic documents that tend to emphasize the core beliefs of the groups in question.

Consequently, only the "White Race" truly is blessed and thereby part of God's kingdom in heaven. Frequent references are made to the assurances by God's law and natural law that the white race is the covenant race, and therefore to be jealously protected. The World Church of the Creator reminds its followers that

> what is good for the White Race is the highest virtue, and what is bad for the White Race is the ultimate sin. We have come to hold these views by observing the Eternal Laws of Nature. . . . The highest Law of Nature is the survival of one's own kind. . . . It is therefore logical and sensical [*sic*] to place supreme importance upon the Race and to reject all ideas which fail to do so. (online)

In contrast to the glorification of the white race, Jews are seen to be the source of all evil, spawned as they are by the Devil himself:

> WE BELIEVE that there are literal children of Satan in this world today. . . . WE BELIEVE that the Canaanite Jew is the natural enemy of our Aryan (White) Race. The Jew is like a destroying virus that attacks our racial body to destroy our Aryan culture and the purity of our race. (Aryan Nations, online)

It is the belief in this ongoing struggle between good (Aryans) and evil (Jews) that propels the anti-Semitic violence perpetrated by these groups. It is only in the name of God and God's will that activists lash out against the enemy. It was to preserve God's chosen race against the "lying Jew" that outspoken broadcaster Alan Berg was assassinated by the Aryan Nations offshoot, The Order. It is, from this perspective, the duty and mission of all Aryans to ensure the survival of the white race at any cost. This is evident in the Oath of The Order:

> I, as a free Aryan man, hereby swear an unrelenting oath upon the green graves of our sires, upon the children in the wombs of our wives, upon the thrones of God Almighty, sacred in his name, to join together in holy union with those brothers in this circle and to declare forthright that from this moment on I have no fear of death, no fear of foe; that I have a sacred duty to do whatever is necessary to deliver our people from the Jew and bring total victory to the Aryan Race. (cited in Ridgeway, 1995: 107)

Those subscribing to Christian Identity philosophy propose a litany of threats posed by Jews, in order to justify their paranoia. In general terms, Jews are perceived as the anti-Christ. According to Ellison, the founder of the Covenant, the Sword and the Arm of the Lord (CSA), the goal of all is to "destroy God's people and Christianity through its Talmudic teaching, forced interracial mixings, and perversions" (cited in ADL, 1996: 21). Through their domination of all cultural, financial, and political institutions, Jews are believed to have taken control of the United States, thereby redefining "American" culture in ways that are deemed offensive. Jews are blamed for the loss of racial purity, for economic downturns, and for spreading immorality in the name of Satan.

As a corollary of this, the anti-Semites often portray African Americans as the pawns of the Jewish conspiracy. It is blacks who are forced into interracial mixing at the behest of Jews seeking to defile the white race. Black-on-white crime also is seen as a phenomenon orchestrated by Jews as a means of cowing whites. CSA doctrine explicitly holds that "Jews are financing the training of Blacks to take over most of our major cities" (cited in ADL, 1996: 210). After Jews, blacks are perceived to be the greatest threat to the purity and safety of the white race:

> Today you cannot escape the terror of black ghettos and Brown Barrios. Your children and your children's children will have no refuge. The DEATH OF THE WHITE RACE is neither imaginary nor far off in the distant future. (Aryan Nations, online)

Nowhere is the racist sentiment more evident—and vicious—than in the second "bible" of the Identity movement, *The Turner Diaries*. Written by William Pierce under the pseudonym Andrew MacDonald, the book is a blueprint for racial violence. It is a fictional account of the long-hoped-for revolution against the "corruption of our people by the Jewish-liberal-democratic-equalitarian plague which afflicts us" (MacDonald, 1996: 42). Robert Matthews, founder of The Order, gave a copy of *The Turner Diaries* to each member of his organization. Consequently, it was used as a guide for a series of racially motivated robberies, arsons, and assassinations, and for the Oklahoma City bombing. Dees argues that there were many in the hate movement who viewed the book as prophetic and therefore "used its gruesome tale of genocide to justify criminal acts in the name of a holy crusade to save their race" (1996: 141).

That is the bottom line for Identity members: their belief system not only legitimates but calls for the violent repression, or even elimination, of minority groups. The identification of Jews and blacks, especially, as enemy of the white race evokes defensive justifications for the assaults carried out against them. I will return to this theme again, when I more explicitly address the "racial holy war."

WHITE SUPREMACY

A natural extension of Christian Identity ideology is that of white supremacy. Whether God-given or biologically derived, the white race is deemed inherently superior to all others. The creation of race categories and valuations represents a means of identity construction for both whites and other races. Race is seen as an "essence" that carries with it inherent differences between groups, differences that are claimed as justification for "natural" hierarchies. The National Alliance (online) summary statement of beliefs makes this apparent:

> We see ourselves as part of Nature, subject to Nature's law. We recognize the inequalities which arise as natural consequences of the evolutionary process. . . . We accept our responsibilities as Aryan men and women to strive for the advancement of our race in the service of Life. (online)

They go on to state that

> our world is hierarchical. Each of us is a member of the Aryan (European) race, which, like other races, developed its special characteristics over many thousands of years during which natural selection not only adapted it to its environment but also advanced it along its evolutionary path.

A similar claim is made by the KKK:

> Our main and fundamental objective is the Maintenance of the Supremacy of the White Race in this Republic. History and physiology teach us that we belong to a race which nature has endowed with an evident superiority over all other races, and that the Maker in thus elevating us above the common standard of human creation has intended to give us over inferior races a domination from which no human laws can permanently derogate. (cited in Sapp, Holden, and Wiggins, 1993: 123–124)

Inevitably, the white race is presumed to be at the top of this hierarchy, followed by the Jews and the "mud-people," that is, people of color. Blacks typically are placed on the lowest level. Ultimately, the ideology of white supremacy seeks to restore the white privilege that right-wing extremists claim has been lost.

There are no limits to the perception of the superiority of the white race. Whites assume their proper and natural place at the top of the pyramid because of the diversity of their talents. They are masters of all things creative and moral. An *American Renaissance* (online) magazine article claims that in "intelligence, law-abidingness, sexual restraint, academic performance, resistance to disease—whites can be considered 'superior' to blacks." Particular emphasis is often placed on the creative genius of the white race. Progress—narrowly defined as technical and technological advances—is argued to be derived from European innovation and intelligence. It is those of European descent who are responsible for the current shape of "civilization." The Aryan group ALPHA makes the claim that, historically, breakthroughs and advances were made, if not entirely then predominantly, by White men and their abilities. All other races hung on our coattails, learning from us but never leading our people. (online)

William Pierce, in an *American Dissident Voices* article, echoes this belief, saying that the "vital spark I'm talking about, the genius for order, the spirit of progress which built our civilization, is European."

For many white supremacists, the focus historically has been on the "inferiority" of the black race. Whether in Africa or America, blacks are deemed to be incapable of creativity, incapable of intellectual labor, incapable of constructing a "civilization" or "culture." Presumably, they lack that vital spark to which Pierce refers. White racialist Roger Roots offers "proof" of this in his online essay "Whites and Blacks: 100 Facts," in which he catalogs the "deficiencies" and "threats" posed by blacks. For example, he contends that "throughout 6,000 years of recorded history, the Black African Negro has invented nothing," nor have they cultivated anything, nor have they built anything of lasting value. Roots also devotes considerable attention to another favorite theme among white supremacists—IQ measures. He cites studies showing differences in brain size, intelligence, test performance, and so on, all of which are meant to show that blacks inherently are less intelligent than whites. Roots concludes his survey by favorably citing Robert E. Lee's declaration that "wherever you find the Negro everything is going down around him, and wherever you find the White man you see everything around him improving."

It is these presumed relationships of inferiority and superiority that underlie hostility toward the political, legal, and economic advances of minorities since the civil rights movement. Why should "inferior" races prosper and compete on the same level with the far more intelligent, moral, and advanced white race? Why should obviously less endowed peoples be privileged by affirmative action policies? Minorities, from this perspective, do not "deserve" to benefit from the labors of the white race, since they are unable to return the favor.

It is also these presumed relationships of inferiority and superiority which underlie the strident calls for "racial purity." It is bad enough that white people are forced to work with or—worse yet—for blacks, Hispanics or Asians. What is even more threatening is the possibility of miscegenation, that is, "race-mixing." Such practices inherently taint the white race, and infect it with the weaknesses of the other races. Senator Bilbo of Mississippi is often cited as the most articulate defender of this claim:

> But if the blood of our White race should become corrupted and mingled with the blood of Africa, then the present greatness of the United States of America would be destroyed and all hope for civilization would be as impossible for a Negroid America as would

be redemption and restoration of the Whiteman's blood which has been mixed with that of the Negro. (cited in Roots, online)

The rhetoric of antimiscegenation is common among white supremacists. How else could the white race maintain its "supremacy" other than by maintaining its purity? Any "contamination" by nonwhite blood introduces into the white bloodline all of those reviled deficiencies characteristic of the "mud people." Supremacists look with disgust and hostility on those race traitors who seek out nonwhite mates, as is the case for the Klansman overheard by Ezekiel (1995:10) at a Klan rally: "What is the worst, to see a couple—to see some white woman and some black man—ugh! It just turns my stomach."[2]

Strom's (online) *FREESPEECH* treatise on miscegenation provides ample evidence of this perspective. The title of the essay—"Racemixing—Worse Than Murder: Murder Is Homicide; Racemixing Is Genocide"—is indicative of the tone of his argument. It is Strom's fear that the increase in interracial births will ultimately lead to the elimination of the white race, and with it all hope for progress and civilization. For him and others of like mind, race mixing constitutes part of the genocidal agenda of nonwhite races. Strom (online) links the rhetoric of white supremacy with that of antimiscegenation, arguing that the white race's

> continued existence would undoubtedly be assumed by our
> superior intelligence and unmatched technology, if it were not
> for those who practice and promote the genocide of our people
> through racial mixing. By their actions they are killing us. . . .
> They kill infinite generations of our future. Their crime—the
> crime of racial mixture—is far, far worse than mere murder.

Race mixing is deemed to be yet another symptom of the loss of white power and identity, since it violates the sacred order of the established hierarchy. It muddies the boundaries between the races in such a way that the politicized superiority of whites is thrown into question. Consequently, miscegenation elicits calls for enforced racial purity as a means of correcting the emerging imbalance in the relationship between whites and nonwhites. The latter must be put back in "their place," by force, if necessary.

VILIFYING THE "OTHER"

One potent means by which supremacists are able to reaffirm the priority of the white race is by calling upon images which vilify the Other in their midst. Rhetors reconstruct minorities in threatening or unsym-

---

2. Antimiscegenation rhetoric also pulls together racist and sexist ideologies, as I will discuss in a later section.

pathetic terms, so that violence perpetrated against these minorities loses its malevolent connotations. They are presented as unworthy of the respect that might otherwise inhibit violent interactions.

The age-old tradition of dehumanizing one's victim has served hate groups well, especially with respect to their caricature of blacks and Jews. This portrayal of nonwhites as something less than human is readily apparent in cartoon images, for example, which paint blacks as ape-like, or Jews as spiders or serpents. Yet the technique is also exploited in the written and spoken words of the extremist groups. Racist derogation masquerades as humor on the White Racialist "Nigger Joke Center" webpage, where "nigger" is defined as

> an African jungle anthropoid ape of the primate family pongidae. Imported to the United States as slave labor in the late 1700s–1800s, these wild creatures now roam freely—while destroying the economic and social infrastructures of America and various other nations. These flamboyant sub-humans love to consume large quantities of greasy fried chicken and listen to fellow apes "sing" rhymes over def beats.

Similarly, Roots's "100 Facts About Blacks and Whites" makes consistent reference to the "simian-like" nature of Africans, with such phrases as "similar to an ape," "approximating the simian form," "like that of the gorilla," or "thus more characteristic of an ape." These characterization distance "Us" from "Them" in a very dramatic way, constituting the "Other" as unhuman and therefore not subject to the same respect, rights, and protections as their white counterparts. It releases the hate activists from the inhibitions and prohibitions that govern interactions between fully human beings.

If these "subhumans" can be shown to be a violent threat to the white race, then the potential white perpetrators can further distance themselves from their potential nonwhite victims. Thus, another common theme among hate groups is the inherent criminality of minorities. Nonwhites are portrayed as "egregiously anti-social elements, riot-prone minorities, dastardly criminals, homosexuals, drug-dealers, perverts" who pose a constant threat to the moral, peaceful, law-abiding white race (White Nationalists, online). White nationalist Yggdrasil favorably cites an Australian journalist who claims that crime statistics indicate that "a large segment of black America has waged a war of violent retribution against white America" (online). Strom (online) refers to unconstrained and ongoing rapes of white women and girls by "Black criminals." William Pierce (American Dissident Voices, online) suggests that, given the history of cannibalism in Africa, it is no surprise the African Americans engage in so much violent crime. Confederate White Pride (online) erroneously reports that minorities are responsible for over 85 percent of all violent crime. Given these contentions, then, persecution of minorities becomes justifiable: it is a noble pursuit, intended to free the nation of the menace represented by the minority rapists, murderers, and thieves. They must be eliminated before they overpower and eliminate the majority.

Supremacists are equally prone to make rhetorical appeals to the economic and cultural threats posed by minorities. The fear is not so much of the end of the European race as it is the end of European culture, which is assumed to be superior to all other cultural forms. Whatever rituals, beliefs, or practices others bring to America are believed to weaken this great white civilization. Minorities bring the United States' culture "down" to their level, rather than advancing it. Consequently,

> Our fellow country men wallow in the decadence and filth of materialism, self-gratification, homosexuality and drug use. The once beautiful cities of America lay in decay and ruin, after being over-run by the "so-called" "under-privileged minorities." (ALPHA, online)

How these flaws are derived from minority cultures and not the materialism and individualism associated with capitalism is unclear. What is clear is that supremacists seek to lay the demise of Western civilization at the feet of minority groups who insist on the recognition of their identity. Changes in the demographics and traditions of the United States lead supremacists to fear the loss of their identity, and more important, their privilege as the dominant sect. A White Aryan Resistance (WAR) online essay laments the fact that the white people of the United States "have become a people dispossessed." They exhort whites to recognize that "all about us the land is dying. Our cities swarm with dusky hordes. The water is rancid and the air is rank. Our farms are being seized by usurious leeches, and our people are being forced off the land." WAR, like other groups, is not reticent to call for the violent reclamation of the "natural" hierarchy. They call for a campaign of vengeance in which "blood will flow."

Also among the victims of this vengeance will be those whom hate groups have identified as the source of the economic malaise that has beset the United States. The culprits are twofold. On the one hand, Jews are held to be the "usurious leeches" who are bleeding the country dry, and who seek to control worldwide economies. On the other hand, minorities—and especially immigrants—are held to be draining the national economy: "Social welfare programs waste your tax dollars and pay countless numbers of minorities to sit at home, do drugs and make more babies that will eventually also jam the welfare roles [*sic*]" (ALPHA, online).

Thus, minorities are portrayed in a very unsympathetic manner, as either animals, criminals, destroyers of civilization, or financial liabilities. In this light, there is little to recommend them as worthy "country-men." On the contrary, they are seen as cancers that must be rooted out. The continuation and advancement of white society is presumed to depend on the removal of those groups that carry with them the seeds of destruction. Hate groups work to exclude and deny the rights of those who do not fit their model of what it is to be "American." Such rhetoric empowers white supremacists, while disempowering nonwhite minorities. It reaffirms the coveted hierarchy that relegates the "Other" to their position of inferiority.

XENOPHOBIA

While blacks and Jews are the predominant targets of the hostility of right-wing hate groups, many within the movement broaden their animosity to include a host of other racial and ethnic minority groups. This is most evident in the fervor of their anti-immigrant rhetoric, which seeks to construct immigrants as dangerous Others within. In fact, rhetors are fond of using the explicitly exclusionary term "alien" rather than "illegal immigrant," presumably to highlight the legally and culturally marginal status of these people, and their supposed nonhuman status. Immigration, too, represents a challenge to the white race. Unlike the cases of the previous three waves of immigration, the current arrivals are not predominantly European, are not even predominantly white. On the contrary, they are much more likely to be fleeing the violence and poverty of the Third World. Thus, they overwhelmingly are Asians, and Hispanics from South and Central America. On the basis of race alone, these immigrants are not as readily assimilable as their predecessors. And this makes people like David Duke nervous:

> The darkening of our nations mimics histories of many other nations. The nations of the Caribbean, Central and South America, are predictive example of the fate that awaits us. The Third World awaits our children. It is in our streets, in our tax-payer paid-for housing projects, in our jails, and in our mayor's chairs. . . . Our children grow up in an alien society that our fore-fathers would not recognize. (Duke, online, 1996b: 2)

The hegemonic bloc in the United States—white European males—are in a crisis of identity brought on by the increasing diversity engendered by the immigration patterns of the late twentieth century. Culturally, nonwhite, non-European immigrants are constructed as major contributors to the breakdown of United States' unity and stability. Heide Tarver (1994) provides an insightful analysis into the ways in which English-only initiatives argue an Us versus Them dichotomy, wherein immigrants carry with them customs, folkways, and language (derided as "gibberish") which make native-born English-speaking

Americans "strangers in their own land" (Tarver, 1994: 214). In the National Association for the Advancement of White People (NAAWP) newsletter, David Duke warned that immigration

> will make white people a minority totally vulnerable to the political, social and economic will of blacks, Mexicans, Puerto Ricans, and Orientals. A social upheaval is now beginning to occur that will be the funeral dirge for the American we love. I shudder to contemplate the future under non-white occupation: rapes, murders, robberies multiplied a hundred-fold, illiteracy such as in Haiti, medicine such as in Mexico, and tyranny such as in Togoland. (cited in Langer, 1990: 94)

In an address to the weekly radio show *American Dissident Voices*, William Pierce likewise observed that

> During the 50 years since the Second World War, America has been darkening, has been getting less and less white. Immigration from Europe was cut off after the war—except for Jews of course—and the flood gates from the non-white world were opened. Asians and mestizos have been pouring into the country, both legally and illegally. (online)

The outcome of this "browning" or "darkening" of the country, according to Pierce and others like him, is "more and more non-Whites, more and more crime and filth and disorder" (ibid.: 4). Immigrants—with their dark skin, their odd ways, and their foreign cultures and languages—will hasten the demise of the true, white Christian identity. They will overrun the white race and overturn the existing relations of power.

In addition to the cultural threats posed by immigrants, hate activists argue that they also bring with them economic problems. From their perspective, immigrants—especially Third World immigrants—come to this country for two reasons: to exploit the welfare system and to take Americans' jobs. In an environment already strained by corporate downsizing, such rhetoric plays on the fears of an economically insecure public. Consequently,

> Immigrant bashing is a popular activity in assigning blame for the nation's economic problems. When stagnation is evident in the national economy and unemployment exceeds seven percent, a pervasive fear that one's job is on the line often emerges. Anxiety triggers frustration and blame; resentment towards immigrants, documented and undocumented, becomes an ugly side of racism, nativism and xenophobia. (Ochoa, 1995: 227)

As hate groups would have it, the tide of immigration must be turned to minimize and reverse the flood of "mud people" onto United

States shores. Violence is perceived to be a legitimate strategy by which to eradicate that which has been constructed as evil and sinister.

SEXISM/HETEROSEXISM

To this point, the discussion has focused primarily on hate groups taking aim at racial and ethnic minorities. Increasingly, however, these groups have broadened their discourse to incorporate sexist and homophobic sentiment. While the rhetoric of sexism is often less strident than that of racism, it is nonetheless apparent that some supremacists "want to save the white race by controlling the behavior of white women—they attack interracial couples, lesbians and feminists. They join the antiabortion movement, believing they can prevent white women from getting legal abortions" (Center for Democratic Renewal (online).

From the perspective of some supremacists, women have one function that defines their station in life: childbearing. Just as the black civil rights movement led African Americans to "forget their place," so too has the women's movement distorted the proper and natural relationship between men and women. Too many women—especially feminists and lesbians—seem to no longer need or at least depend on men. This poses a threat to the supremacists' masculinity, certainly, but also to the white race as a whole. Women are forgoing childbearing for their careers; abortions reduce the white birthrate; white women are choosing to marry nonwhite men. Women are in the midst of constructing a feminine gender identity that does not conform to that with which white supremacists are comfortable.

Extremist conceptions of gender parallel those of race, to the extent that gender also is deemed essential. There are two natural and distinct sexes, each with biologically "wired" roles. This basic tenet informs subsequent sexist and homophobic ideological stances. Allen Sapp et al. cite a right-wing pamphlet on the topic of gender differences:

> There is the world of woman and the world of man. Nature has ordained that man should be the guardian of the family and the protector of the community. The world of contented womanhood is made of family: husband, children and home. (1993: 127)

Thus it falls to the white woman to ensure the physical and social reproduction of the white race. This is her role and responsibility. Any deviation is an inherent threat to the continuation of the race. This underlies the previously noted hostility toward interracial relationships. Miscegenation "taints" the white bloodline, thereby contributing to its demise. For Strom (online), race mixing is tantamount to white genocide. George Eric Hawthorne (online) contends that it spells death.

It is in the discourse of antimiscegenation that we see the intersection of the racism and sexism inherent in hate groups' rhetoric.

Strictures against interracial unions are an attempt to control and regulate both nonwhites and nonmales. The womb of the white woman must be preserved for the bearing of pure, white children. Black men must not be permitted to defile that vessel. Such logic resonates with the long-standing mythologies of the "black rapist" and the protection of white women: "Protection of white women reinforced femaleness and thus the notion of 'separate spheres' while simultaneously constructing racial boundaries between White and African American men" (Messerschmidt, 1997: 35). Antimiscegenation rhetoric similarly seeks to reaffirm the boundaries between genders and between races, to reaffirm the appropriate "place" of white women and nonwhite men.

Reinforcing this intersection of racism and sexism is the rhetoric of abortion politics as practiced by the hate groups. Again we see the insistence on the essence of the reproductive role that is to be played by white women. As the White Aryan Resistance position statement makes clear, it is not necessarily abortion in general that is problematic. Rather it is abortion by Aryan women—they would welcome nonwhite abortions:

> WAR supports birth control and abortion for non-whites living in North America. WAR encourages racially conscious White women to produce white children. . . . As the non-white races continue to breed with little control, White people have voluntarily destroyed millions of healthy, White babies. . . . Those who have bought into this suicidal way of thinking must at some point receive future Aryan justice. (online)

White abortion tips the racial balance—this is what white racialists fear. They fear not only the loss of control of "their women" but of their own place in American politics and culture. If nonwhite minorities are allowed to become a mathematical majority, the assumption is that they will also become dominant in sociopolitical terms as well. The hegemonic position of white men would be in question.

That is the predominant reason for hate groups' opposition to abortion. Yet they also challenge it on the basis of the freedom it permits women. Abortion is an issue of control and autonomy. And these are "rights" that extremists are reluctant to allow women. The denial of women's control over their own bodies becomes an attempt to maintain their subordination to and dependence on men. This is a crucial exercise in the wake of thirty years of the women's movement, in which the gender line was blurred and the absolute dominance was questioned. Anti-abortion politics, then, is an important means of reaffirming that essentialist gender line. It reasserts the sanctity of traditional gender relations of power, which place women on the "private" domestic side and men on the "public" political side. In an interview in *FREESPEECH*, Pierce refers to the sexual division of labor as consisting of "fundamentally different roles for men and women: men are the providers and protectors, and women are the nurturers. Men bring home the bacon and they guard the den; women nourish the children and tend the hearth" (online).

In this conservative vision of woman-as-mother, women are to be fulfilled only through the institution of motherhood. The problem is that "this image of 'mother' is not an image of a real woman with real children, or of a real woman active in the public world of work—let alone of a real woman who controls her own sexual behavior. It is instead, an objectified image of a 'woman' as a disembodied vessel of domestic nurturance" (Karst, 1993: 54). But, according to hate groups, this is as it should be. Too many women have rejected the responsibility of domestic nurturance. And access to abortion has facilitated this:

> Today greater numbers of White children are being killed in the womb than ever before. And when we are speaking of killing our own offspring, if we are true to the instincts that ensure our survival and make us what we are, we must recognize that we are speaking of a particularly horrifying kind of killing. There is something almost unbelievably depraved about women committing this obscene act for no other reason than convenience. (Strom, online)

The depravity to which Strom refers is not to be blamed on individual women. Rather the culprit behind the loss of traditional gendered identities is feminism. As a philosophy and as a practice, feminism represents, to hate groups, a "destructive aberration," "a sickness with deep emotional roots" (Pierce, online). It is held to be destructive to the extent that it has contributed to an unnatural racial and gender balance:

> At the racial level it is destructive because it divides the race against itself, robbing us of racial solidarity and weakening us in the struggle for racial survival, and because it reduces the White birthrate. . . . It also undermines the family by taking women out of the home and leaving the raising of children to television and day-care centers. (Pierce, online)

It is feminism which has eroded the traditional relationship between men and women, by encouraging women to seek fulfillment outside the family in a "traditionally male role," that is, through education, employment, and political activism. Feminism encourages an "arrangement between men and women which goes against Nature. Biologically, a man is a man in every cell of his body and his brain . . . and a woman is a woman to the same degree" (Pierce, online). When women go against nature, they upset this delicate balance, assuming "unfeminine" qualities and roles. This is a potent challenge to the assumption of masculine superiority since feminism constructs women as politically and economically capable in their own right.

Concomitant with the threat posed by feminism is the emergence of a visible and vocal gay identity politics. Since, it is assumed, homosexuals do not reproduce, they too represent a threat to the continued survival of the white race: "Those who recruit for homosexual sodomy are a factor in pushing us ever closer to the edge of racial suicide. Every recruit for them is how many White children never born?" (Strom, online).

Yet the hostility extends beyond this. In some respects, hatemongers appear more frightened by the specter of homosexuality than feminism. It certainly is seen as an even more aberrant and unnatural phenomenon: "America should not accept homosexual activity as normal behavior. . . . Nature intended for a man and a woman to interact sexually, not members of the same sex" (National Socialist Movement, online). As this quote suggests, the homophobic rhetoric tends to be highly charged, referring to "perversions," "defectives," "nature freaks," and "degeneracy." Like autonomous women, homosexuals are represented as distortions of the natural order. More so than women even, homosexuals challenge essentialist gendered boundaries. They are, in fact, "gender traitors," in that they refuse to be forced into the binary categories of feminine or masculine.

Gender constitutes a hierarchical structure of domination not only between but also within genders. This structure of power is also constitutive of the broader pattern of sexual power relations, in which heterosexual masculinity comes to the fore. The hierarchy of masculinities valorizes this narrow, hegemonic form of masculinity, while denying or limiting the power of "lower" forms. Because male homosexuality challenges the fundamental assumptions of what it is to "be a man," it is inevitably assigned an inferior—and hateful—status, leaving gays vulnerable to practices intended to maintain their subordination.

The rhetoric of many hate groups also reaffirms the moral culpability of gays. Just as they vilify nonwhites, they portray gays as a menace to society on many levels. For example, there is a concern that homosexuals seek to pervert white youths by recruiting them to their "lifestyle": "They want to teach that this perversion is proper. They want to teach our kids in school this is normal" (Rev. White's Christian Politics, online). More than that, however, gays presumably victimize youth, through child pornography, or molestation. According to American Christian Nationalist CyberMinistries, "The simple fact is that gays moleste [*sic*] children much more than straight people. In Maryland state prisons, 70% of the child molesters in prison, molested boys, i.e., *homosexual by definition*" (online, emphasis added). From this perspective, homosexuality is synonymous with pedophilia.

Additionally, gays are held to blame for the spread of AIDS, a phenomenon equally threatening to their "recruits" and the white race in general. The Knights of the Ku Klux Klan point to a correlation between the repeal of sodomy legislation and the "plague of AIDS now ravaging our land" (online). Strom proclaims that those who are lured into homosexuality get "anal sodomy, death by infectious disease, and an anti-life philosophy" (online). Given these multiple threats, the ultimate conclusion reached by hate activists is that homosexuality must be eliminated. For some, the answer is to help gays find God so that they might see the error of their ways. For others, however, there is no salvation for gays. They must be physically eliminated. Thus, it is not uncommon for hate groups to engage in violence against gays, or to call for the death penalty for known homosexuals. In other words, "suffer not the sodomite to live."

PERSECUTION PARANOIA

As noted previously, the context and impetus for much of the contemporary hate movement is a profound sense of unease as a result of the nominal gains associated with the civil rights movement. Hate groups articulate the belief that white Americans have suffered as a consequence of a shifting balance of power. Where once white privilege was relatively uncontested, it now is constantly challenged. The conclusion that hate activists reach is that it is not minorities who are oppressed and persecuted, but the shrinking white majority. Consequently, hate groups lead the way in bemoaning the contemporary plight of the "angry white male" who presumably is being displaced by equally angry, even vengeful "mud people" and "femi-Nazis." It is, from this perspective, "the blacks and browns who are racist. It is the blacks and the browns who are exploiting the race issue for advantage" (Yggdrasil, online). It is now the "blacks and browns" who seek to exclude the whites from power that is thought to be rightfully theirs. It is the "blacks and browns" who are engaging in an "agenda to destroy the white race" (Knights of the KKK, online), leaving the "White people of the World . . . in a state of chaos (Hawthorn, online). A recent *American Dissident Voices* online radio program entitled "It's Genocide" goes so far as to contend that

> the people of European descent of this world are the targets of a
> constant, consistent, systematic, sustained campaign of genocide,
> with the intention of humiliating, subjugating and eventually elim-
> inating our people.

European Americans are thought to face extinction on many levels, both literally and figuratively. Black crime and immigrant crime, for example, are taken as evidence of a conspiracy to physically eliminate white Americans. And the justice system is complicit in this since "the guilty often go unpunished or the innocent are persecuted, not on the basis of any evidence, but based upon the racial composition of the jury" (*American Dissident Voices*, online). This is a sentiment shared by the National Alliance's Kevin Strom, who asks

> How often are White people the victims of diverse juries who decide against the White accused or for the non-White accused because of a perception that we Whites have got it coming to us? . . . The lack of justice, the racial group think of hate Whitey, the non-White crime, the increase in the population of non-Whites, and the decrease and aging of the White population are all going to accelerate and reinforce each other. (online)

White Americans are presumably defenseless in the face of these ongoing physical assaults that threaten the very survival of the race. There is nowhere to turn for assistance and sympathy, since even the courts contribute to this loss of control. Consistently, then, the retaliatory argument is made that the best defense is a good offense. It is only in racial self-defense that white supremacist groups lash back with violence against their attackers. It is racial loyalty that underlies the Northern Thunder group's assertion that the "White race faces certain extinction in the near future, *unless we identify and destroy our executioners*" (online, emphasis added).

While a substantial number of hate activists envision the literal death of the white race, many more emphasize the loss of identity and place of the white race. For some, this is manifest in the apparent vilification of whites by the "liberal media." Skinhead George Eric Hawthorne contends that "judgement has been passed" on white America, and whites have been found to be "evil people" (Resistance Records online). The extreme right-wing Heritage Front asks us to

> pity the poor white man, blamed for everything—past and present. He's depicted by the media as a beer swilling idiot or brutal swine—about to be clubbed into submission by the noble Wesley Snipes. The white man has been so relentlessly trashed that many have abandoned traditional values and courtesies for fear of REPRISAL. (online)

The price for the white man's sins, according to hate group rhetoric, has been the loss of his proper place through the undermining of white rights and subsequent discriminatory treatment. Persecution on the streets is accompanied by persecution in the classroom, the workplace, the boardroom: "Aryans are being killed and murdered in the cities and streets of this nation. White patriots are being rounded up. What's left of our rights are almost gone" (National Socialist Movement of Illinois, online).

There is a sense among extremists that their rights as citizens have been sacrificed—illegitimately—to vocal minorities. Permeating the rhetoric is a sense that the gains of the civil rights movement inevitably represent a loss for the traditional hegemonic bloc of white European males. There is talk of whites being "displaced" by nonwhites, of "anti-white measures," of "reverse discrimination." White Nationalist Yggdrasil argues that the "political struggles for preferences and groups advantages that take place in the legislatures always favor organized minorities over complacent majorities" (online). Jared Taylor of *American Renaissance* magazine concurs: "A White majority has already established laws and regulations that discriminate against Whites" (online). As evidence of discriminatory treatment, rhetors point to affirmative action policies, immigration policy and practice, even hate crime legislation. Together, they argue, these sorts of initiatives protect minorities while vilifying and, in fact, punishing the white majority. Strom makes this argument explicit in a *FREESPEECH* article:

> We are legally forbidden to favor our own people in hiring, educating and the disbursement of tax money. We are forbidden, on pain of being fired or ostracized, to make public statements in support of the survival of White Americans. We are told not to note that White Americans are being oppressed and vilified . . . Do White Americans have any politicians in Washington explicitly standing up for our interests and concerns? How absurd. Of course not! (online)

What underlies this sentiment is anger at the loss of traditional privilege. The "angry white males" of the hate movement mourn the loss of authority that allowed them carte blanche to oppress the "Other." Now they must give up the "right" to wield unquestioned power to discriminate, a situation they see as "reverse discrimination." For them, the recognition of minority rights is one more symptom of the crisis of identity experienced by European Americans.

ANTI-STATISM

Who is to blame for the crisis in white America? Almost unanimously, hate groups would identify the state—specifically the Zionist Occupied Government (ZOG)—as the culprit. The United States' government embodies the Jewish- and communist-inspired liberalism that lies at the root of the threats to the white race. Many, like Louis Beam, would identify the government as the premier enemy of "the people." So great is the hostility toward the government that groups like Aryan Nations have established a point system for assassinations of government agents and civil rights activists.

According to the hate movement, the government has overextended its reach. It is conspiring to construct a "new world order" in which those of European descent would play a minor role. As evidence of this, they point to international trade agreements, extensive law enforcement bodies such as the FBI, ATF, and INTERPOL, "black heli-copters," and specific incidents such as those at Waco and Ruby Ridge. The Posse Comitatus, for example, claims that

> the federal government has grossly overstepped it's [*sic*] bounds. It's [*sic*] agencies (alphabet soup gangs) have committed atrocities and murders against "We the People," and are out of control. (online)

White fears are hung on two key axes of anti-statism: minority advantages and Jewish control. Recall the previous discussion of the "persecution paranoia" that permeates the hate movement. As members see it, the government has capitulated to the vocal—and unreasonable—demands of civil rights activists, at the expense of white male privilege. No longer does the state represent "We the People." As hate activists see it, the state now represents "Them" rather than "Us." Foreigners, gays, and feminists call the shots in such a way as to deny traditional rights and values. NAAWP refers to the "rape" of the White majority, whereby "minorities have, thru (sic) their concentrated voting power, bribed the government into taking civil rights away from un-organized Whites and giving them to minorities" (online).

In addition to "giving away" civil rights, the government has further compromised the supremacy of White Americans by opening the doors to excessive immigration. Immigrants represent yet another special interest group with which whites must compete. Additionally, as dis-cussed earlier, the increasing numbers of "mud people" represent an economic and cultural threat as well, since

> the population are [*sic*] being poisoned by an un-natural [*sic*] stream of mud people. Critics to this are kept silent, their youth abuses drugs, the native population culture and way of life have to stand back. (Fourth Reich, online)

White racialists feel they have been abandoned by the state, that their folkways, traditions, and interests have been sacrificed to the "God of multiculturalism." The state and its related agencies seek only to pre-serve and promote "diversity," which, to the hate movement, means nonwhite interests. The egalitarian initiatives introduced since the 1960s have resulted in a pendulum swing too far to the left. The out-come has been seen as a racially *unjust* society.

This conspiracy to subordinate and oppress the white race is believed to be spearheaded by a cabal of international Jews—hence the reference to the Zionist Occupied Government. Many hate activists have grown disillusioned and distrustful of the federal government, in light of their belief that it is being manipulated by foreign and domes-tic Jewish interests. The civil rights advances previously alluded to are deemed part of this conspiracy. Minority groups are exploited as wedge to use against the white majority. They are used as a battering ram with which to weaken the defenses of the "master race." Freeman Dale Jacobi, for example, blames Jews with having imported black slaves into the United States in order to destroy, not strengthen the nation and its economy. And this orchestration continues today:

> The very Christian foundation, its economic structure, its philosophy and its moral [*sic*] today are being attacked by foes WITHIN—working for masters WITHOUT. There are alien-minded organized minorities, all bound to the racist-Zionistic masonic order of the B'Nai B'Rith. (People's Resistance Movement, online)

WAR shares this perception:

> Not by accident but by design these terrible things have come to pass. . . . Evidence abounds that a certain vile, alien people have taken control of our country. . . . The Capitalists and the Communists pick gleefully at our bones while the vile hook-nosed masters of usury orchestrate our destruction. (online)

According to this rhetoric, Jews have gained such control over the U.S. government that they are freely able to manipulate all areas of policy and practice. Pierce sees evidence of this conspiracy in President Clinton's national defense team—which is 100 percent Jewish. He claims that the Jews have Clinton "exactly where they want him. He dare not disobey them" (Pierce, online). Thus, Jews are in a position to extort financial favors from the U.S. government. The CyberNationalist Group is similarly convinced of the heavy infiltration of government by Jews: "In these positions, he has enriched himself through lack of principle, corrupting our Culture, perverting justice, and destroying our economy in his quest for lucre" (online). From the perspective of the hate movement, then, ZOG represents the ultimate threat to the survival of the white race. It encourages the "browning" of the population; it gives up the nation's autonomy to Jewish economic interests; and it contributes to the devaluation of European-inspired culture. The only viable response to such a trend is the creation of

> a strong centralized government spanning several continents to coordinate many important tasks during the first few decades of a White world: the racial cleansing of the land, the rooting out of racially destructive institutions, and the reorganization of society on a new basis. (National Alliance, online)

This is the starting point for the white racialist agenda for change—revolutionary change that will restore the privilege and prominence of the white race.

The overlapping belief systems documented herein lead many hate groups to the sort of conclusion noted above: through organized action, the white race must reverse the trends represented by the myriad forms of white racial "suicide" and "genocide." Moreover, the goal of this action is fairly consistent from group to group. It is best summarized by the "14 Word" principle shared by many Christian Identity groups: "We must secure the existence of our people and a future for White children." The means by which to achieve this goal, however, differ somewhat. For some, the first step is relatively simple: take back the state; legislate against miscegenation, sodomy, or abortion; or close the borders in order to halt the darkening of the United States. Pierce suggests one mechanism by which to stop illegal immigration from Mexico: shoot anyone attempting to cross illegally. He assures us that "Two or three shootings in the first night . . . and the word would be out: Don't cross the border unless you want to die" (online). He justifies this approach by resorting to the rhetoric of vilification, in which the "alien" is constructed as criminal: "Fewer immigrants would have to be shot trying to come across the border that first night than law-abiding Americans are now being murdered each year by illegal-alien criminals in California and Texas." Hence, the most extreme violence can be justified by re-creating the "Us" versus "Them" opposition, which portrays "Them" as even more violent and therefore deserving of execution. The same logic would apply to homosexuals, who are deemed worthy of execution because of their role in spreading AIDS, or victimizing children.

Another common theme—shared by hate groups and the militia movement—is the idea of racial segregation, generally in geographical terms. According to this position, the white race can survive only if it is isolated from the biological and cultural influences of the non-Aryan races. The most effective way to keep the bloodline pure is to establish—or reestablish, as they see it—autonomous racial nations. For some, this would mean deporting non-Europeans to their country or continent of origin: Africans to Africa, Asians to Asia, Hispanics to Mexico, Cuba, Haiti, or wherever. The National Socialist Vanguard claims that the "Black folks in the large or small cities will have no way to survive except repatriation" (online). Strom agrees:

> Since Farrakhan and other Black Nationalists want a nation of their own, let them have one. That means that we can have a nation of our own. Since Black Nationalists want to go to Africa, let them go. That means that we can have our America back. (online)

For others, racial separation can be established within the existing borders of the United States. A white racialist online newsletter, *The*

National Observer, suggests "strict geographical separation, devoid of racial conflict or oppression," in which each ethnic group would establish its own political territory. Groups like the NAAWP, some cells of the KKK, and Aryan Nations have long called for a white racial homeland in the northwestern United States, leaving the rest of the nation to diverse minority groups. The NAAWP has designed an elaborate "relocation" strategy, consisting of nine ethnically based regions. The "White Bastion" would cover the extreme northwest. "Navahona" would contain all Native Americans in the area currently known as New Mexico. "Alta California," the twenty-mile-wide band along the United States–Mexico border, would be home to Mexican Americans—illegal immigrants would be shot on sight. Hawaii would become "East Mongolia," the nation of all Asians and Pacific Islanders. African Americans would be "regrouped" in the deep South, in what is now Florida, southern Alabama, and part of southern Mississippi, and would be called "New Africa." However, Miami, Miami Beach and Dade County—"New Cuba"—would be reserved for Cubans. "West Israel"— the U.S. homeland of the Jews—would take up Manhattan and Long Island, while the remainder of the New York metropolitan area, or "Minoria," would be set aside for "unassimilable minorities," including Puerto Rican and Mediterranean immigrants. Finally, French Canadian immigrants would remain in "Francia," the extreme northern portions of Maine, New Hampshire, Vermont, and New York states. Of course, groups advocating such measures recognize that such strategies would involve "difficulty and temporary unpleasantness." It might even require the use of force. Nonetheless, it is in the best long-term interests of all groups in question. It is especially important to the NAAWP, however, that the whites regain "a nation":

> We must have White schools, White residential neighborhoods and recreation areas, White workplaces, White farms and countryside. We must have no non-Whites in our living space, and we must have open space around us for expansion. (National Alliance, online)

Only in this way can white society purge itself of the "alien" and "dangerous" hordes that threaten to destroy Aryan culture in the United States.

However, an alarming number of supremacist groups—especially those within the Christian Identity movement—argue that separation is not a sufficient means by which to preserve the white race. For them, all traces of the nonwhite presence must be erased from the United States. It is inevitable that the trajectories of world history will lead to RAHOWA—*RAcial HOly WAr*—in which whites must be victorious. According to Aryan Nations' Richard Butler, it is God's will, since "As his Divine Race, we have been commissioned to fulfil His Divine purpose and plan, the restitution of all things" (cited in Kleg, 1993: 190). Only by winning the battle against evil—whether defined as Jew, black, or "mud races"—can supremacists restore the divine order as given by God. This is an order in which the chosen white race prevails.

Representatives of the various hate groups are explicit in their call to arms. They do not shrink from violence. Consider the following illustrative exhortations:

> War is upon the land. The tyrants blood will flow. . . . This is war. . . . We declare ourselves to be in full unrelenting state of war with those forces seeking and consciously promoting the destruction of our faith and race. (WAR, online)

> WE BELIEVE that the White Race, its Biological and Cultural Heritage, is now under attack by our mortal racial enemies: Jews, niggers and the mud races. WE BELIEVE that RAHOWA (RAcial HOly WAr) . . . is the only road to the resurrection and redemption of the White Race. (World Church of the Creator, online)

> WE BELIEVE that due to the Jew-instigated demographic explosion of the mud races, we must (as a matter of life and death!) not only start but also win the worldwide White Racial Holy War in this generation. (World Church of the Creator—Maryland Chapter, online)

It is this call to RAHOWA that puts minorities most at risk, since it attempts to justify violence by appealing to God's will. According to the rhetoric, Jews and their allies have distorted the word of God, and in so doing, they threaten the white race. When it is believed that these "sub-human" and "soul-less" races are closer to Satan than to God, it becomes acceptable to attack them in the name of ridding the world of evil. Supremacists claim a moral right to engage in violence as a means of restoring God's law, and the white race to its rightful place in the United States' racial hierarchy. This is the ultimate discursive attempt to marginalize and disempower the perceived threats posed by women, homosexuals, and all people of color. I will conclude with a musical version of the call to arms, found in the lyrics of the skinhead group Operation Ghetto Storm:

> You have slept too long,
> Come and join the chase,
> Slaughter the beasts that would darken our race
> Don helmet and sword and pin on thy shield . . ."
> Kill the dark cloud and drive it to flight,
> All cowards and faggots will tremble with fright,
> Look well upon your kindred who are proud to be white,

Let your blood boil with anger,
Let your heart swell with pride,
You must fight in this battle,
You must fight side by side . . .

THE METAMORPHOSIS OF THE HATE MOVEMENT

The history of the hate movement is lengthy. It finds its roots in racist
and misogynistic theories, ideologies, and practices that are centuries
old. However, the contemporary hate movement faces something of a
dilemma. The legacy of the civil rights movement means that both the
vicious rhetoric and the historically effective means of responding to
the threat of Otherness—lynching, genocidal practices, and legal exclusion—have less resonance and feasibility today. They are as likely to be
condemned as applauded. To a certain extent, this is a "kinder, gentler
nation" than it was at the beginning of the twentieth century. Consider
the public outcry and condemnation of the murderers of James Byrd
and Matthew Shepard. The savvy, organized hatemongers of today are
not ignorant of this limitation and so are forced to alter their tone and
tactics. If they are to recruit, if they are to establish public credibility,
they must distance themselves from the likes of John William King—as the
Klan did when it, too, denounced the dragging death of Byrd in Jasper,
Texas. This does not mean that racial or religious or gender violence is
no longer a part of their arsenal. Rather, it means that such violence is
increasingly contextualized within a more contemporary, sanitized
"look" and "feel," intended to render the appearance of moderation. In
short, the hate movement is in the midst of a metamorphosis.

In dramatic ways, hate groups threaten to extend their impact
beyond the immediate membership. Their mantra of intolerance is
gaining considerable legitimacy in light of the changing messengers
and media that carry their message. In what follows, I address the significance of contemporary hate groups, in terms of their connections to
the political mainstream, and to the growing militia movement. I also
explore the implications of their strategic and recruitment use of modern communication technologies. Together, these patterns facilitate
hate groups' abilities to make some claim to legitimacy, and therefore,
acceptance.

"BUTTON-DOWN TERROR": HATE GOES MAINSTREAM

The uncertainty that characterizes contemporary identity politics leaves
the most fearful and most alienated elements of white society vulnerable to the recruitment efforts of the hate movement, which provides
"easy answers" to America's woes. They share with white supremacist
organizations one of the elements Doug McAdam (1982) insists is crucial to the development and cohesiveness of any social movement: a

shared consciousness or perception of unjust conditions. Betty Dobratz and Stephanie Shanks-Meile (1997), for example, found the "white man's struggle" and "fear of falling" to be important bases for white supremacists' decisions to become part of the movement. Significantly, an increasing proportion of the hate movement's membership seems to be characterized by nontraditional demographics, as more middle-income, white-collar workers become drawn to the message of salvation (Klanwatch, 1998; Dobratz and Shanks-Meile, 1997; Ferber, 1998). The hate movement becomes an effective beacon because

> it is diverse in its expression, which can provide a haven for those seeking an explanation of the social conditions of white disenfran-chisement along with a call to action. The "new rural ghetto" con-sists of formerly middle-class people who had achieved "American cultural goals" and lost it. Often forgotten, they are filled with rage as they "watch in hunger" as others eat at tables that not long ago were their own. (Dobratz and Shanks-Meile, 1997: 279)

Moreover, slight modifications in the presentation of intolerance have made the contemporary hate movement more palatable, more acceptable to a public sensitized by a generation of discourse of equal-ity, multiculturalism, and diversity. In a word, hate is increasingly "main-stream" and thus increasingly legitimate. In part, this has been accomplished by toning down the rhetoric and engaging in symbolic racism. This "new racism" couches the old hostilities in abstract, ideo-logical terms or "code words" that appear to have rational rather than emotive connotations.

The KKK has been at the forefront of the movement toward a more moderate appearance. Grand Wizard Thomas Robb, for example, asserted that Klan leaders would be "taught to avoid statements that sound hateful and turn people off" (cited in Kleg, 1993: 216). He and others of like mind speak of love of the white race, rather than hatred of others; they speak of preservation of a way of life, and other such mantras. In their search for respectability, some hate groups have rejected explicitly racist terms for more "subtle" code words that act as proxies for traditional rhetoric. Primary among these is the assurance that they don't hate blacks or Jews or gays; rather they simply love their own race. ZOG becomes "government interference"; White Christian becomes "average citizen"; cross burnings become "illuminations"; African Americans become "welfare cheaters." Don Black, for example, eschews the pejorative connotations of "racist" in favor of the term "White Nationalist." Revisionist historians focusing on Holocaust denial are perhaps the most gifted at couching their anti-Semitism in euphemisms. Rather than speaking of the "holohoax" or Jewish con-spiracies, they artfully phrase their appeals in terms of scientific evidence, such as aerial photography, or DNA evidence. Whatever the rhetoric, the message remains the same: the Other is not to be trusted; the Other threatens the white, Christian, heterosexual hegemony.

Moreover, the paraphernalia long associated with the Klan are also—at least temporarily—a thing of the past. Nazi symbols have been eliminated, and "the white sheets and hoods are being replaced by the security uniform, consisting of a white shirt, black tie, Klan emblem (a cross with a drop of blood in the center), black trousers and black boots" (Kleg, 1993: 216). In spite of his persistence in using racist and homophobic rhetoric, Tom Metzger is largely in agreement with this more professional presentation. He urges his colleagues and followers to opt for suit and tie, rather than Army fatigues. Moreover, it is not surprising that hate groups have used the media to disseminate this new image, appearing well dressed and articulate on television interviews, for example.

Such tactics have proven successful already. Nowhere is this more evident than in the political success enjoyed by David Duke, former Louisiana KKK grand wizard. Duke's recognition that legitimacy could come only with moderation and respectability is apparent in his exhortation for Klan members to "get out of the cow pasture and into hotel meeting rooms" (ADL, 1996a: 36). So smooth was his self-presentation that Duke's often-imitated style became known to journalists as "rhinestone racism" or "button-down terror." Rejecting the in-your-face aggression of traditional white supremacists, Duke instead adopted what Ridgeway refers to as "the persona of the boyishly good-looking white rights activist" (1995: 166). Who could be threatened by this benevolent and compassionate seeker of justice?

To further solidify his new identity, Duke publicly disavowed his Klan membership in 1980, only to reemerge as the founder of the National Association for the Advancement of White People (NAAWP). Through this "white rights" organization, Duke continued to promote racial segregation. His efforts to mainstream his racist visions are apparent in his exhortations—similar to Robb's—to "never refer to racial superiority or inferiority; only talk about racial differences, carefully avoiding value judgements" (cited in Ridgeway, 1995: 38). Duke reformed his own rhetoric along these lines once he turned to legitimate politics. While leader of the Populist Party in 1989, Duke made the following argument:

> I wouldn't say Hitler was right on race, but I do believe that there are genetic differences between races and that they profoundly affect culture. . . . I think that, for instance, there's differences in physical ability, there's differences in musical abilities, there's differences in IQ. (cited in Ridgeway, 1995: 172)

Notice how Duke carefully avoids evaluating racial diversity, focusing instead on "difference" as though that were a neutral term. But in light of the cultural tendencies to evaluate difference in negative terms, and in light of the stereotypes implied by the references to physical, musical, and intellectual disparities, the connotations are indeed negative.

Duke's political campaigns, whether as a Populist or a Republican, exploited these toned-down racial messages in his handling of such bread-and-butter issues as welfare, immigration, affirmative action, and crime. Consistently, these were used as code words to denigrate racial minorities without using the terms "black" or "Hispanic," for example. Early on, at least, he struck a chord among voters. In March 1988, his run for president garnered him one-twentieth of the votes cast. In January 1989, he narrowly won a Louisiana state legislature seat. In 1990, he barely lost a bid for a United States Senate seat but received 60 percent of the white vote. And, in 1991, Duke lost a bid for the Louisiana governor's position, while nonetheless managing to win 700,000 votes. Duke's political fortunes have continued to decline since 1991, yet he continues to pursue this line. The fact that he has been able to gain victory and later a significant number of votes speaks volumes to the effectiveness of his methods of delivery. As such, Duke lends legitimacy to an albeit muted ideology of intolerance that continues to lay the blame for cultural, moral, and economic decay squarely at the feet of minorities.

Duke's explicit association with the hate movement follows historical precedent, to the extent that numerous presidents, senators, representatives and governors of both the Democratic and Republican parties throughout the nineteenth and early twentieth centuries were quite open about their exclusionary politics. In fact, politics was an arena in which "whiteness" was to be constructed: "Participating in politics . . . was an essential practice for defining white men (hegemonic masculinity) in relation to black men (subordinate masculinity) and to all women. Indeed, political parties were fraternal organizations that bonded white men through their whiteness—it bound men to others like themselves" (Messerschmidt, 1997: 18). There was no shame, then, in incorporating white supremacist values into the political party platform. In fact, local political party membership often mirrored the local Klan membership. Even into the 1950s, there is evidence of the open relationship between politics and white supremacy. The year 1955, for example, witnessed the birth of the "Federation for Constitutional Government," which was committed to resisting integration: "This was no fringe group of beer-bellied bigots and Ku Klux Klansmen. Two United States senators, six United States representatives, and five serving or former governors were elected to its advisory board. The federation was 'a great crusade [for] un-tainted racial heritage, culture and institutions of the Anglo-Saxon race,' according to Democratic Senator James O. Eastland of Mississippi" (Stern, 1992: 2). The contemporary links between the racist right and mainstream politicians is also consistent with the nation's history of right-wing populism, which consists of "strong themes of social injustice, exclusion and resentment . . . directed at . . . racial minorities, the blacks, the 'yellow peril,' and so on" (Winant, 1994: 34). According to Omi and Winant (1994), the current era of "authoritarian populism" found its origins in George Wallace's rearticulation of racial politics in the 1960s. Wallace's appeals to law and order and other racial codes resurrected the historical link between general electorate fears and the agendas of diverse hate groups (Dobratz and Shanks-Meile, 1997).

While the United States is typically a two-party nation, fringe parties often attempt to insert themselves into the political process. More often than not, these historically have been parties motivated by extremist ideologies. The Populist Party, founded in 1983, promoted the anti-Semitism of the Liberty Lobby. Prominent among its leadership were members of the KKK and other hate groups. It also coordinated the launch of David Duke's national political career, as well as that of Bo Gritz. Throughout the 1980s and 1990s, the Populist Party remained committed to an openly racist, sexist, and homophobic agenda. In 1995, the party changed its name to the National Union, and decided not to run its own candidate. However, it continues to play a significant role in national politics by supporting and financing "appropriate" candidates, those who espouse similarly exclusive ideologies.

In the absence of viable third-party alternatives, white supremacists turn to the Republican or Democratic parties as a platform for their particular brand of politics. Many have been more than a little successful. Klansman Tom Metzger, who later went on to form White Aryan Resistance, ran in the 1980 Democratic primary in California. He won the primary by 318 ballots but was later defeated by the Republican candidate. The same year, the leader of the National Socialist Party, Harold Covington, ran for attorney general in the Republican primary. Covington lost, but did manage to garner 43 percent of the ballots and to win 45 percent of the counties. In 1990, Ralph Forbes ran in the Arkansas Republican primary for the office of lieutenant governor. Forbes had a long history of involvement with the Nazi party, the Klan, and the Identity movement. He won 40 percent of the first ballot, though he was defeated in a later run-off.

No less disturbing than Duke's or Forbe's involvement in politics are the links forged between legitimate politicians and hate activists by Larry Pratt. On the one hand, Pratt is a former Virginia state legislator, head of a political action committee with ties to the Republican Party, and a former cochair of Pat Buchanan's presidential campaign. On the other hand, he is also director of Gun Owners of America and the Committee to Protect the Family Foundation (an antiabortion organization), founder of English First, and a frequent speaker at white supremacist and militia gatherings. He successfully has blended his political career with his right-wing activism. Dees remarks that "Pratt is equally at home with individuals who prefer combat boots to Gucci's, camouflage uniforms to three-piece, tailored suits, and the practice of guerrilla warfare tactics to the playing of politics. As a result, he frequently serves as a bridge between the two groups—the mainstream politicians, at both the federal and state levels, and far-right elements—by bringing them together at fund-raisers, dinners and other social events" (1996: 54–55).

That Pratt sympathizes with the hate movement is evident in his relationship with extremist Pete Peters and his speaking engagements with white supremacist groups. The most infamous of these was his appearance at Estes Park, Colorado, at a gathering held in response to the shooting of Randy Weaver's wife and son at Ruby Ridge. However, it is also evident in his political stance on gun ownership and the formation of militias, both of which he interprets as legitimate constitutional rights. The goal of these militias would be to reverse the ills facing the United States: they could be used in the war on drugs, or against illegal immigrants, for example. Here we see the connection to the hate movement. Both of these themes are heavily endowed with racial undertones. The conclusion: militias are necessary to achieve victory in the inevitable race war.

Paradoxically, then, at the same time that some extremists are attempting to tone down their image, space is opening up in political forums for their intolerant views. Duke and Pratt have not been alone in diffusing the rhetoric of hate throughout the cultural landscape. What enabled their success were openings created first by the Reagan administration and then the Bush administration. Republican policies and rhetoric in the 1980s and 1990s have signaled a concerted effort—at the federal and state levels—to rearticulate the racial and gender balance that many felt had swung too far to the left (Omi and Winant, 1994). Leonard Weinberg explicitly argues that "the GOP has become a "big tent" under which a variety of ERGs [extreme right-wing groups] and individual right-wing racists have come to feel at home. The tie-in seems related to at least three themes central to the party's outlook: ardent anticommunism, opposition to the welfare state, and defense of "traditional" values" (1998: 20). The intersection of the ideological positions of right-wing extremists and the Republican Party has proven fortunate for both. Senator Trent Lott of Mississippi and Congressman Mel Hancock rode this crest to office, either in spite of or because of their association with the far-right organization Council of Conservative Citizens. Pat

Buchanan brings his own brand of racial and gender politics to the national arena. The ADL tracks and reports the involvement of political leaders in Jubilee Celebrations sponsored by *Jubilee* magazine, the voice of Identity Churches, neo-Nazis, and skinheads. Through such involvement, the ADL maintains, "mainstream political forces have, knowingly or unknowingly, lent their legitimacy to this force of bigotry. . . . 'Jubilation 1994' caused a furor because two of the scheduled speakers were Republican state Senators" (online).

While the electoral success of these extremists has been limited, they nonetheless have made their mark at the level of political discourse. They were successful in injecting a note of intolerance into political debate, since "any success pushes mainstream candidates to imitate them. If [they] win even a minor election, they gain credibility, access to the system, and the ability to do better by raising funds from other extremists and those across the country who are too easily taken in by scapegoating" (Stern, 1992: 11).

As part of the official political apparatus, such extremists have the appearance of legitimate actors with valid interpretations of the state of economic and cultural relations throughout the country. They are the visible and audible presence of right-wing extremism and intolerance within the machinery of the state.

"THE MILITIA PROJECT"

In addition to penetrating mainstream political culture, hate groups have made inroads into the militia movement. Given the broader appeal, audience, and membership of the militia movement relative to the hate movement, it is alarming that hate activists are beginning to infiltrate these organizations, where they can add their racial and sexist animosities to the militia's distrust of the state.

Recognizing a golden opportunity to extend their rhetoric of hate beyond traditional hate group membership, some leading hate activists quickly have joined ranks with the growing militia movement. Dees (1996) provides a rough estimate that there are over 440 active militia groups and over 360 patriot groups nationwide, with cells in every state. The CDR (n.d.) suggests that by 1995, the militia movement boasted at least 100,000 members. Events like the Waco and Ruby Ridge sieges and the Oklahoma City bombing seem to have stimulated membership. However, much of the recent growth also can be attributed to the movement of supremacists from traditional hate groups into the militias. The CDR claims that, while militias are not exclusively made up of supremacists, "the line becomes blurred as one out of five active white supremacists have not only become involved but have become national leaders" in the movement (1995: 4). Increasingly, the distinctions between the two types of organizations are becoming muted in terms of membership and ideology. Louis Beam, a longtime Klansman and virulent racist, is the architect of the militia movement's strategy of "leaderless resistance." Beam learned from his experiences with the Klan the danger of traditional lines of leadership and communication. "Leaderless resistance" advocates phantom cells and individual action as a means of defeating state tyranny. Ongoing dissemination of information through newsletters, computer online services and leaflets would keep members informed and allow them to design viable strategies for attack. Beam also hosts an annual Aryan World Congress, where he takes the opportunity to encourage the formation of militias, and to encourage Aryan Nation members to join these anti-government organizations.

As a guide to action for the militia, Beam's leaderless resistance is second only to William Pierce's *Turner Diaries*. Pierce, too, has assumed a leadership role within the militia movement. The role of his *Diaries* as a blueprint for action is most tragically illustrated by the Oklahoma City bombing, which followed to the letter the fictional account of the bombing of a federal building found in the *Diaries*. More recently, Pierce has launched a "Militia Project," the goal of which is to forge strong alliances with the militia movements. Specifically, Pierce argues that the militias "are being badly misled in the ideological realm and are in need of some Alliance input" (cited in Dees, 1996: 204).

Pierce is concerned that the focus of the militia movement is too narrow. He seeks to extend the "ideological realm" beyond anti-statism, to incorporate his own brand of racism and anti-Semitism. Already it is apparent that the militia movement has embraced traditional supremacist ideologies. However, in order to ensure their welcome within the movement, supremacist ideologues first had to seek common ground. In this context, the glue that first bound the two movements together was anti-statism: the belief that the state was excessively interventionist, and illegitimate. This was the hook upon which Beam and Pierce, for example, were able to hang their racism. One means by which this is accomplished is by exploiting the strict constitutionalism of many of the militia groups. The militia movement had long rejected the legitimacy of the Thirteenth through the Fifteenth amendments. Their claim is that the Constitution guarantees rights only to the white "founding" race of the United States. Thus, only white Americans are considered "true" citizens—all others are relegated to the status of "Fourteenth Amendment citizens" with "alienable" rights. Robert Wangrud of an Oregon Christian Patriot group claims that

> there is only one race that founded this country and that is the White Race. The Constitution recognizes this and clearly states that only white people can be citizens of this country. The 14th

Amendment changed all that, but we feel it became law illegally and as such is not binding. (*Christian Patriot jam line*)

From here, it is no great stretch to condemn nonwhite races as inferior, or justify their relegation to second-class status. For example, Aryan Nations leader Richard Butler, in league with Militia of Montana founder John Trochmann, forged a code of conduct that reflects this ideology. It reads in part:

Article I: Only Aryans (White Race) are allowed citizenship of the nation and only citizens can:
1) vote and own property within the nation's borders.
2) conduct business, possess (keep) and bear arms.
3) hold office in government, industry or society.
4) comprise military or law enforcement personnel . . .

Article II: Non-citizens can live in the Republic but only under the custodianship of a citizen.

Article III: All hybrids called Jews are to be repatriated from the Republic's territory, all their wealth redistributed to restore our people . . .

Such policies suit the hate movement's goals of excluding and disempowering the minorities that they claim threaten the survival of the white race. Yet that also correspond to the militia movement's attention to the original Constitution.

Because racism within the militias often is presented in sanitized form—as patriotism or constitutionalism—it has the face of legitimacy. The violence and intolerance are downplayed and hidden behind questions of "rights" and "rights violations." This is what accounts for the broader appeal of the militia movement. It provides an apparently benign arena for dissatisfied citizens. Anyone from tax protesters to racists to bankrupt farmers to unemployed workers can voice their hostility without necessarily being labeled as sexist or homophobic or racist. By crossing the line into the militia movement, hate groups are able to open themselves up to people who would otherwise resist joining a neo-Nazi or KKK organization. As Klanwatch director Joe Roy observes, "militias, common law courts and other Patriot organizations allow members to vent their anger in a manner that is more acceptable to mainstream America" (Klanwatch, 1997: 17).

Beyond the dangers of increased numbers and the broader appeal of the militia movement lies the danger that inheres when you mix open-ended hostility with paramilitary activity. More so than the traditional hate groups, militias are heavily armed and trained to use the arms—as is their presumed right according to the Second Amendment.

In a letter of warning to Attorney General Janet Reno, Dees clearly stated his fears in this context: "We have substantial evidence that white supremacists are infiltrating the leadership of these organizations. In our view, this mixture of armed groups and those who hate is a recipe for disaster" (1996: 107). Similarly, Dees's associate Danny Welch concluded in a report on the militia movement that "it is a movement fuelled by religious fanaticism and racism, fully armed and willing to kill. Its members are capable of becoming Americanized versions of the kind of extremists you read about in other countries, a full-scale terrorist underground" (cited in Dees, 1996: 105).

This potential is explicit in Beam's strategy of "leaderless resistance." He is very much in favor of a nationwide network of invisible cells armed and ready to engage in an all-out assault against the "menacing horde" of minorities and against the state. And it is explicit in the rhetoric of militia adherents across the country. All are ready to "take back" their country and disarm the federal state.

Even this cursory examination of the links between the militia and hate movements—and the implications thereof—suggests that the danger posed by supremacist ideologies and actions is growing. It has expanded into a dangerously armed and trained set of organizations that tend to have a broader public appeal. Ultimately, both the audience and potential harm derived from intolerance are extended by this intersection.

CYBERHATE

While many purveyors of hate are content to spread their rhetoric of intolerance in the "real" community, there are those who prefer to hold their conversations in "cyberspace" or in the context of "virtual communities." Consistent with the shifting demographics (that is, increasingly middle-class membership) and sophistication of the hate movement is an increasing willingness to take advantage of the Internet as a tool for both recruitment and unification. Traditionally, the primary means by which hate groups recruited members or spread their message of intolerance has been by word of mouth, or by pamphleteering. However, several current factors have combined to change this. On the one hand, cheaper, faster, and more accessible means of transmission and communication have emerged—telephone messaging and computer messaging, to name just two. On the other hand, hate group leadership has become much more sophisticated to the extent that it is in a position to take advantage of these developing technologies.

WAR founder and continued leader, Tom Metzger, has a particular genius for exploiting new, high-tech communication options. He and his counterparts in other hate groups have been blessed with a novel marketing gift in the form of the Internet. This particular form of communication is superior to all others as a means of widely and quickly disseminating hate propaganda. Computers are increasingly affordable. At the very least, they easily can be accessed through work, local schools, universities, and colleges. Websites are easily and cheaply maintained. Best of all, from the perspective of hate groups, the Net remains unregulated. In short, readiness and ability to exploit the Internet ensures effective communication between current and potential movement membership, which, according to McAdam (1982) is also vital to movement solidarity.

A special ADL report entitled *The Web of Hate: Extremists Exploit the Internet*, directs detailed attention to the use of the Internet by hate-mongers: "As computers become less expensive, simpler to use and consequently more common in American homes (and workplaces), as the barriers to disseminating information through computers fall, bigots of all kinds are rushing to use the power of modern technology to spread their propaganda" (ADL, 1996b: 3). The origins of "cyberhate" generally are traced to white supremacist Donald Black. Ironically, Black became proficient at using the computer while serving time for conspiracy to overthrow the government of Dominica. Upon release, he put his new skills to work by creating a webpage, *Stormfront*, in 1995. Black refers to his homepage as the "White Nationalist Resource Page," or, alternatively, as "a resource for those courageous men and women fighting to preserve their White Western culture, ideals and freedom of speech and association—a forum for planning strategies and forming political and social groups to ensure victory" (*Stormfront*, online). The site includes news items, letters, the Canadian white racialist magazine *Up Front*, neo-Nazi graphics and symbols, current and archived "articles of interest to White Nationalists," mailing lists, news groups, and electronic bulletin boards. In addition, it provides links to myriad other white nationalist sites.

Black's initiatives have been followed by the construction of hate-oriented and "White Power" sites at such a rate that it is virtually impossible to estimate the number of such websites. The online Hate Directory professes to identify and monitor all existing hate pages. Yet its estimate of approximately 120 (as of May 1997) appears conservative in light of the fact that one Aryan Nations site (Plunder and Pillage) provides 128 "White Pride" links, each of which leads to dozens more not noted by either the Hate Directory or Aryan Nations. It probably is not an exaggeration to say that there are thousands of domestic and international websites marketing various brands of hatred and intolerance. The ADL remarks on the consequences: "Few Americans would willingly welcome hate groups such as neo-Nazis or the KKK into their homes to spread their pernicious message of hate. Yet, as a result of the fast spreading technology of the Internet, and the World Wide Web, many people have, through inadvertence or curiosity, encountered hate-filled messages and images on the screens of their home computers (ADL, 1996b: 3). For many who may encounter these webpages, the ideas and images are antithetical to their understanding of American ideals of democracy and equality. As such, they are quickly dismissed. Yet for others, they reinforce or implant tolerance and hostility. Thus, those with embedded biases may find affirmation on the Net. Others—uncertain about "American" identity, or feeling dislocated by economic or cultural change—may find a prepackaged answer to their questions.

Young people are especially vulnerable to the lure of the Internet. It is largely high school and college students, along with young professionals, who take advantage of the Net. ADL National Director Abraham Foxman notes that "high tech haters are all the more pernicious because they are targeting the television-reared, multi-media, computer literate generation: our youth" (ADL, 1997a). Consider this example: A ninth-grade student who is researching weather systems on the Net enters "Stormfront" as her keyword for searching. While she probably will find some information on how weather systems develop, she is likely to happen upon the white nationalist–sponsored webpage by the same name. This has one of the most extensive sets of cyberhate links available on the Internet. Its letters link, as well as many of the essay links, contain virulent racist, sexist, and homophobic messages and images. One such link is Resistance Records, which may have particular appeal to a young person. Her curiosity piqued, the student might link to the *American Renaissance* webpage (of course, someone studying the Renaissance might also inadvertently find this page as well). There she could read an article that professes the following: "If massive non-white immigration continues, and welfare keeps encouraging high birth rates among blacks and Hispanics, whites will soon become a minority in the United States" (*American Renaissance*, online). The ALPHA link would lead her to the message that "our fellow countrymen wallow in the decadence and filth of materialism, self-gratification, homosexuality and drug use. The once beautiful cities of America lay in decay and ruin, after being over-run by the so-called 'underprivileged minorities'" (ALPHA, online).

These are powerful messages that could be discovered quite accidentally. The impact would be heightened should the youths seek them out explicitly. Ideas gleaned from the Web solidify, if not mold, the perceptions of identity, difference, and culture that the individuals may or may not already bring to the site.

Additionally, there are many sites that would seem to be especially alluring to the MTV generation—those sites that feature music. Resistance Records, mentioned above, is North America's largest distributor of White Power music. Its website offers audio excerpts of dozens of such CDs. Moreover, it includes downloadable album covers, and online ordering. Operation Ghetto Storm goes one step further. In addition to all of the above, this White Power band site provides written lyrics of its music. Consider this example that highlights its readiness to engage in a race war:

> In order for Jews to control us all,
> All that oppose them, must—PERISH AND FALL.
> Armed with the media, the cops and feds,
> Never resting until the white movements dead [*sic*],
> When the time comes to stand and fight,
> You'll be marked the enemy because you're white.
> (From "Perish and Fall," Operation Ghetto Storm, online)

Whether couched in the pseudoscientific arguments of Holocaust deniers, or the more virulent messages of Metzger or Aryan Nations, cyberhate is a powerful force. It goes largely unregulated and unchallenged. Given the reification of technology in this culture, those who access computer-based sites often take the data and arguments for literal truth. We have encouraged our youth to use this resource, to become Net-literate, without necessarily reminding them that what appears online is not all fair, accurate, or favorable. This is not at all unsatisfying to the hate groups:

> This is the hope of the haters: use the media to create an alternative channel to spread the word, to reach the impressionable, reinforce the beliefs of the converted, and create a community of the like-minded. On the Web, they preach on an easy-to-use, powerful and far-reaching platform that confers special legitimacy and filters out opponents. (ADL, 1996b:34)

It is this conferring of legitimacy that makes the use of the Net by hate groups particularly troubling. It places the rhetoric of these groups on an equal footing with all other forms of discourse. It confers validity on the messages delivered, in spite of their potential harm to the groups demonized in the electronic literature. Moreover, as the above quote suggests, the use of the Internet enhances communication between the "converted," that is, within the movement itself. This is vitally important in light of the earlier discussion of the diversity within the hate movement. While there are obvious points of convergence across the various Klan groups or Identity Churches or skinhead organizations, the hate movement historically has been varied and, in fact, fractured. Internet communication facilitates the creation of the collective identity that is so important to movement cohesiveness (McAdam, 1982). As a recent Klanwatch report observes, increasing reliance on email, webpages, and electronic chat rooms "give(s) racists an empowering sense of community. Even lone racists, with no co-religionists nearby, feel they are part of a movement" (1998: 25).

Internet communication helps to close the social and spatial distance that might otherwise thwart efforts to maintain a collective identity. Given the geographical dispersal of hate groups across the country, the medium of cyberspace allows members in Maine, Mississippi, and Idaho to engage in real-time conversations, to share the ritual and imagery that bind the individuals to the collective without having to travel great distances or incur great costs. Virtual conversations and ready access to webpages aggressively asserting the shortcomings of the Other strengthen the resolve of individual members by creating the framework for a shared sense of both peril and purpose.

Moreover, Internet communication knows no national boundaries. Consequently, it allows the hate movement to extend its collective identity internationally, thereby facilitating a potential "global racist subculture" (Back, Keith, and Solomos, 1998). There is no reason to expect that processes of globalization affecting commerce, politics, and demographics will not also affect the realm of identity politics, played out by the hate movement (Weinberg, 1998). Weinberg argues that the Internet will in fact provide the vehicle for the construction of a "common racial identity reaching across the Atlantic" (79). Regardless of national affiliation, Internet communiction allows white people across the globe to share in the celebration of a common race. Thus, for example, cyberhate sites are increasingly multilingual. They tend to exploit (white) multicultural symbols drawn from Nordic, Celtic, or Nazi mythology. And such sites facilitate the importation of outlawed documents and rhetoric so that all can share in the discourses of hate. For example, while Germany and many other European nations have criminalized the publication and dissemination of racist propaganda, these nations have yet to establish an effective means of regulating the virtual border crossing of cyberhate. In short, the potential of the Internet for creating an enhanced sense of unity among the computer-mediated community of haters is vast and, in fact, global.

The hate movement has taken on a new, modern face. It is no longer the preserve of uneducated bigots from the backwoods—if indeed it ever was. On the contrary, as the foregoing analysis suggests, it is now increasingly crossing into the mainstream. The strength of the contemporary hate movement is grounded in its ability to repackage its message in ways that make it more palatable, and in its ability to exploit the points of intersection between itself and the prevailing ideological canons. As I argue in the following chapter, those points of intersection are readily identified in the rhetoric, policy, and practices of the state.

## SEVEN

Permission to Hate:
Ethnoviolence and the State

Through the political and juridical sides of its activity, the state secures a certain kind
of political order, enforces a certain kind of legal order, maintains a certain kind of
social order.

—Hall, Critcher, Jefferson, Clarke, and Roberts, *Policing the Crisis*

Writing of the murder of a young gay man in Bangor, Maine, John
Preston pondered the context of the perpetrators' acts. He wondered if
they "had heard members of the state legislature as they stood in the
House and Senate and described gay men and lesbians as less than
human" (1995: 74–75). This question should not be easily dismissed,
since hate-motivated violence can flourish only in an enabling environment. In the United States, such an environment historically has been
conditioned by the activity—and inactivity—of the state. State practices,
policy, and rhetoric often have provided the formal framework within
which hate crime—as an informal mechanism of control—emerges.
Practices within the state—at an individual and institutional level—that
stigmatize, demonize, or marginalize traditionally oppressed groups
legitimate the mistreatment of these same groups on the streets. This
chapter examines the ways in which state rhetoric, policy, and practice
provide the context for violence against minorities.

Before proceeding, it is important to define what I understand as
"the state." William Chambliss offers a useful starting point, in which
the state is seen as

> a set of interrelated institutions with specific roles and role occu-
> pants who make decisions. The decisions of the role occupants in

the structures that create laws are a response to events external to the state. The passage of law creates a response from groups external to the state, which stimulates further law making. (1988: 121)

Included among the role occupants are those who have a voice, a platform, that intersects with the machinery of government. This obviously includes politicians (whether in office or running for office), legislators, bureaucrats, and others specifically "within" the governing body; but it also includes those "outside" of that machinery who nonetheless touch the essence of the political apparatus through their role as lobbyists or activists, for example. Thus, the state is "peopled" by both politicians and mobilized sectors of the public.

But the state is further conditioned by other elements of society. At a minimum, it is constituted of and by culture, ideology, political economy, internal apparati of the legislature and administration, and, as noted above, the public (Wonders and Solop, 1993). It is these elements that condition "events external to the state" and that subsequently motivate state action and discourse. Thus, the state is best seen as a dialectical formation "aimed at the resolution of contradictions, conflicts, and dilemmas that historically are grounded in time and space" (Chambliss, 1993: 9). Of particular interest in this chapter are the ways in which the state is implicated in identity discourses and how these discourses consequently condition the environment for hate crime.

The role of the state in legitimating hate crime is inextricably linked to its role in the politics of identity making and the construction of difference. In particular, it facilitates a negative politics of difference, wherein that which is "different" is deemed "deviant," "dangerous," "inferior." For Iris Marion Young, this "always implies a good/bad opposition; it is always a devaluation, the naming of an inferiority in relation to a superior standard of humanity" (1990: 208). This essentialist and dichotomized understanding of cultural boundaries undergirds the subsequent articulation of discourses around race, ethnicity, gender, and sexual orientation. In this context, hate speech and hate acts construct a hierarchy of identities in which the hegemonic form is affirmed simultaneously with the marginalization of others.

With this understanding of the state in mind, I utilize a Gramscian framework to examine the role of the state in facilitating the creation of cultural tendencies in which hatred and bigotry against specified Others can be exercised through the use of violence. Connell points to the potential limitations of Gramsci's work, particularly its relevance to analyses of cultural and political forms other than capitalism and its attendant class relations (1987: 184). Gramsci's focus on class struggles led him to minimize the importance of race, gender, religion, and other cultural forms of social relations. I contend that it is nonetheless possible to extend his analysis to encompass these alternative dimensions of difference. Indeed Gramsci's frequent references to the intellectual and moral components of hegemony leave considerable room for cultural interpretations.

The utility of Gramsci's general framework for understanding non-class differences is recognized explicitly in the work of Omi and Winant (1994). For them, hegemony is applicable beyond class, since class, race, and gender "share certain obvious attributes in that they are all 'socially constructed' and they all consist of a field of projects whose common feature is their linkage of social structure and signification." Similarly, Chantal Mouffe's (1988) analysis of "new political subjects" reminds us that "each social agent is inscribed in a multiplicity of social relations . . . thus, someone inscribed in the relations of production of a worker is also a man or a woman, white or black, Catholic or Protestant, French or German and so on" (1988: 89). Moreover, each of these "sides" of identity represents a form of power and subordination. Thus hegemony is variously constructed around this diversity of subject positions and antagonisms, so that struggles are grounded not only in economics, but in politics and culture as well. In other words, we cannot artificially separate our class identity from our race or gender identity. We can speak only to the contextual and situational salience of each dimension.

So, for example, Omi and Winant (1994) make the argument that the state is increasingly the preeminent site of racial conflict. The state is implicated in constructing popular notions of identity in racialized terms. Ascendancy—or domination—"which is embedded in religious doctrine and practice, mass media content, wage structures, the design of housing, welfare/taxation policies and so forth" applies as much to the construction of hierarchies of race and ethnicity as it does to class (Connell, 1987: 184). West and Fenstermaker remind us that race, along with class and gender, acts as a "mechanism for producing social inequality" (1995: 9). Of course, Jim Crow laws are the strongest historical example of this racial ordering. But the banning of affirmative action legislation—on the grounds that quotas are unjust—is a more contemporary expression of the "proper" place of minorities. The state not only holds us accountable to race, but plays a critical role in shaping what it means to "do race." Thus, the state serves to both define and maintain what it is to "do difference."

This also can be seen in efforts to construct gender, as illustrated in Messerschmidt's *Masculinities and Crime* (1993). In this work, he characterizes the construction of hegemonic and subordinate forms of masculinity as a social practice: "Depending upon the setting, practices attempt to define and sustain specific conceptions of hegemonic masculinity, which express and reproduce social divisions of labor and power as well as normative heterosexuality" (Messerschmidt, 1993: 83). The state is an integral site for these struggles around definitions of what constitutes hegemonic masculine identities. Messerschmidt explicitly argues that the state is a site for the mobilization of hegemonic masculinity, because it serves as a primary location wherein "institutionalized practices define and sustain specific conceptions of masculinity that express and reproduce social divisions of labor and power as well as of normative heterosexuality" (Messerschmidt, 1993: 156, 174). It is, in part, the role of the state to "keep the gender line bright and clear, so that women can be women and men—white men especially—can be men" (Karst, 1993: 31). The state polices this gender line through, for example, sodomy legislation, which favors heterosexuality (that is, "true" manhood), or through restrictions on gays in the military, which silence male and female homosexuals. Similarly, proposals that would deny Aid to Families with Dependent Children (AFDC) benefits to single mothers aim to force unmarried mothers into dependency on a male—either husband or father—thereby restoring the all-important "father role" (Karst, 1993).

This chapter focuses specifically on the role of the state in constructing an "intellectual and moral unity" around race, ethnicity, gender, and sexuality. I am concerned with the ways in which the state supports the "hegemonic bloc" associated with white, heterosexual male dominance. Indeed the state infuses civil society with ideals representative of this bloc, referred to by bell hooks (1994; 1995) as the "white supremacist, patriarchal, capitalist" bloc. To the extent that this is so, there emerges a climate that bestows "permission to hate." As this chapter illustrates, the mechanisms through which this can be accomplished are manifold—rhetoric, legislation, policy, the arbitrary use of "legitimate violence," activities of particular agents (such as membership in an organized hate group), and secondary victimization.

HEGEMONY AND THE RHETORIC OF HATE

Omi and Winant characterize the bulk of the United States' history of racial relations as a "war of manoeuvre" in which subordinate groups have been forced into a defensive role, oriented around self-preservation—against the threat of lynching, for example (1994: 81). Moreover, the state has been deeply embedded in this "war" since it is in fact a racial state, structured by and constitutive of racial politics. To continue the Gramscian analysis, they argue that "the racial order is equilibrated by the state—encoded in law, organized through policy making, and enforced by a repressive apparatus" (Omi and Winant, 1994: 84). In other words, the state is embedded in the processes of legitimating and defining difference, and of constructing a racialized and gendered hegemonic formation.

Recent years, however, have upset the equilibrium of racialized as well as gendered politics. Contemporary social movements—representative of a transition to the "war of position"—have placed both the state and the "warring factions" in qualitatively new roles. In the face of challenges from women, people of color, and gays, to name but a few, the state has been placed in a position of having to resolve a cultural "crisis of legitimacy" every bit as painful as the corresponding fiscal crisis. It is ironic that "by challenging the racial verities of the past and revamping the old political terrain, the racial [and gender] minority movements set the stage for the racial reaction" of the 1970s, 1980s, and 1990s (Omi and Winant, 1994: 117).

The egalitarian changes wrought by the civil rights initiatives of the 1960s and 1970s were perceived by a large bloc as a dramatic threat to their social and economic well-being. Already in the 1970s, racial subtexts were informing discourse around the economic woes of the nation, as Asian imports and Hispanic immigrants took the blame for job and profit loss in the United States, as well as for the dilution of the United States' cultural hegemony. The national identity, "who 'we' were as a nation—seemed to be moving under their feet, and the tremors called into question not just the authority of traditional values, but the identities bound up with those values" (Karst, 1993: 8). To maintain legitimacy, and to restore any semblance of equilibrium, the state is faced with the task of absorbing the reactionary challenge, just as it had previously absorbed the egalitarian challenges of an earlier era.

To facilitate this enterprise, the state can call upon existing public sentiment around race and gender. The political rhetoric of hate does not fall on deaf ears. Consider Gramsci's assertion that hegemony must begin with or incorporate prevailing sentiments. Degradation of the Other is on fertile ground in a culture with a history of—indeed origins in—a world view that saw nonwhites as heathen savages, for example. The United States is itself a legacy of centuries of persecution of minorities, whether they be Native Americans, immigrants, women, or "sexual deviants." Such a history normalizes mistreatment of those who do not conform appropriately to the preconceived hierarchies. That leaves us with a culture reflected in bitter letters to the editor, opinion polls that seem to tap deep divisions and resentments, and, ultimately, hate-motivated violence.

Feagin and Vera (1995) present ample survey data to support the contention that individual Americans subscribe to a range of intolerant and bigoted attitudes and stereotypes. Whatever the questions tapped— beliefs about criminal activity, industriousness, welfare dependency, interracial marriages—white respondents tended to characterize ethnic and racial minorities in negative terms. For example, a NORC survey in 1990 found that a majority of white respondents evaluated blacks at the high end of the scale with respect to tendencies toward both violence and welfare dependency. A 1993 Gallup poll further confirms this issue. When asked which racial group was responsible for the bulk of crime (among blacks, Hispanics, Asians, and whites), respondents rated blacks at the upper end of the continuum and whites at the lowest end (Gallup, 1993a).

The public position on gays is somewhat more ambiguous and in fact contradictory. On the one hand, a large proportion of respondents indicated in a Gallup poll that gays were demanding "special rights," rather than the same rights as others. Nonetheless, the majority surveyed did feel that gays should be protected from discrimination in employment (Gallup, 1993b). However, while public support for gay rights—with respect to housing and jobs at least—seems to be increasing, this does not necessarily reflect acceptance of homosexuality per se. In line with the stereotypical image of gays as pedophiles, many respondents continue to resist the notion of gay men and women as high school (49 percent) and elementary school (54 percent) teachers (Gallup, 1992). More generally, 57 percent of those surveyed in 1992 considered homosexuality an unacceptable "alternative lifestyle" (Gallup, 1992).

A backlash against immigrants is also reflected in public sentiments. In general, the majority (65 percent) of those polled feel that immigration levels should be decreased (Gallup, 1993c). When asked whether "too many," "too few," or "about the right amount" of people from specific countries were entering the United States, Arab, Latin American, and Asian immigrants were most often in the "too many" category (64, 62, and 62 percent, respectively). Unpacking these positions, we find rationales that speak to perceived threats associated with immigrants: Fifty-five percent of respondents felt that immigration "threatened American culture"—in fact, 82 percent of those who felt immigration should be decreased felt so threatened. Fifty-six percent of respondents indicated their belief that immigration was a drain on the U.S. economy. For example, 60 percent agreed that Latin American immigrants end up on welfare, and 64 percent agreed that immigrants hurt the economy by "driving wages down" (Gallup, 1993c). In somewhat more general terms, respondents revealed dramatic prejudices in their response to the following question: "For each [nationality] please tell me whether you believe their presence has generally benefitted the country or generally created problems for the country" (Gallup, 1993c: 14). Irish, Poles, Chinese, and Koreans were seen by the majority to have benefited the United States. In contrast, Mexicans, Cubans, Iranians, and Haitians overwhelmingly were perceived as problematic. No more than 29 percent of respondents supported any of these groups. Corresponding to this are the findings from another Gallup poll

(1993a): twenty-nine percent of those surveyed feared that immigrants were more likely than other groups to commit crime.

Such are the sentiments that the state absorbs and reflects back onto the public. The state gives weight to the concerns expressed by the public. Public expressions of sexism or homophobia or racism by state actors are constituted of and by public sentiments of intolerance, dislike, or suspicion of particular groups. Thus, the state seems to reaffirm the legitimacy of such beliefs, while at the same time giving them public voice. Political rhetoric simultaneously evokes and exploits fears of this erosion of identity boundaries and the threats posed by the Other. In so doing, the state rhetors play on cultural symbols that differentiate "Us" from "Them": good versus evil; the "savage" versus the "civilized"; the "unnatural" Other versus the "natural" conformist. For example, they may draw on the age-old mythology of black-man-as-rapist to support contemporary images of the black-man-as-criminal.

Political discourse reaffirms and legitimates the negative evaluations of difference that give rise to hate crime. Thus, I accept Teun van Dijk's thesis that discourse is central to the "enactment, expression, legitimation and acquisition" of bigotry of all types, including hate-motivated violence (1996: 2). The state is a contested site, wherein the "deliberate use of hate by rhetors is an overt attempt to dominate the opposition by rhetorical— if not physical—force" (Whillock and Slayden, 1995: xiii).

Political expressions of hate and bigotry are to be located at any number of different sites. Press releases and related sound bites, judicial decisions, congressional debates, commission hearings, and certainly single-issue and electoral political campaigns are laden with images and language—both implicit and explicit—representative of the dominant ideologies of race and gender. The demonization of minority groups is reinforced by the racialized and gendered discourse of other politicians, judges, political lobbyists, and more. And the targets are diverse: independent women, welfare recipients, Arab Americans, to name a few. However, to illustrate my argument, I have chosen to explore the rhetoric that shapes the environment of intolerance toward three of the most vilified groups: African Americans, homosexuals, and recent immigrants (especially people of color).

THE BLACK MENACE

Black males historically have been presented as the "villain"—first as the dreaded rapist of white women and currently as "the criminal" in much broader terms. The race-crime nexus is inescapable in a culture that defines black males as predators, whether in sexual, physical, or material terms. An *Atlantic Monthly* cover story explicitly referred to the racialized state, with a cover headline that read: "When The Official Subject Is Presidential Politics, Taxes, Welfare, Crime, Rights Or Values, The

Real Subject Is RACE" (May 1991). There is a tendency to use racial themes as the framework for comprehending major social problems, whether they be social or economic woes (Omi and Winant, 1994: 115). This is certainly the case with respect to crime.[1] Ronald Reagan's oft-quoted image of the "typical" criminal is illustrative: "a stark, staring face, a face that belongs to a frightening reality of our time—the face of a human predator, the face of the habitual criminal. Nothing in nature is more cruel and more dangerous" (cited in Reiman, 1995: 52). While Reagan veils his rhetoric in the popular code words of "predator" and "habitual criminal," David Duke is explicit in his characterizations of interracial threats of violence when he refers to the "plague of rapes and murders of White women by blacks" (Duke, online). He even goes so far as to suggest that the phenomenon of hate crimes against blacks are a myth constructed to divert attention from the "real" problem of black violence against whites: "In the media and history books, we constantly read about European-American violence toward African-Americans. But what the average European-American actually sees in everyday life is the opposite—attacks on European-Americans by African-Americans" (Duke, online). Similar pictures were evoked in the trial of the officers accused of beating Rodney King, during which the defense exploited the imagery of "jungles" and of the "brute strength" of King. King became the epitome of the dangerous, savage black male who was to be feared, and therefore repressed. However, the equation whereby black males are the sum of crime perhaps reached its pinnacle in the 1988 presidential election campaign, wherein "Willie" Horton became the political icon of the menacing black male. In this case, the portrait was all the more powerful in that it revolved around the age-old mythology of not just the black criminal but the black rapist. Ostensibly, the ad was intended as a critique of the Massachusetts furlough policy and Democrat Michael Dukakis's apparent "softness" on crime. Nonetheless, the use of Horton's rape of a white woman while on furlough played on racial fears that have a history as old as the nation. Dukakis's campaign manager clearly recognized this effect:

> Whether it was intended or not, the symbolism was very powerful . . . you can't find a stronger metaphor, intended or not, for racial hatred in this country than a black man raping a white woman. And that's what the Willie Horton story was. (Estrich, cited in Runkle, 1989: 115–116)

---

1. Keep in mind that while black males are overrepresented in the UCR arrest statistics, white males still account for the bulk of all recorded crime. Young (1996) discusses at length the erroneous tendency to equate disproportionality with the relative involvement of blacks and whites in crime.

The impact of the ad was later heightened by Maryland's GOP committee, which mailed thousands of letters which included the following warning:

> By now, you have heard of the Dukakis/Bentsen team. But have you heard of the Dukakis/Willie Horton team? . . . You, your spouse, your children, your parents and your friends can have the opportunity to receive a visit from someone like Willie Horton if Mike Dukakis becomes president. (cited in Feagin and Vera, 1995: 116)

The letter affirmed what white America already suspected: the "someone like Willie Horton" is the evil and predatory black male—not "someone like us." He is different and threatening and violent. He is the ultimate threat to our personal safety.

This demonization of black America was accomplished in the same campaign on yet another dimension. Horton's aunt—Millie Horton—was portrayed in subsequent discussion as the prototypical "welfare queen" who was no doubt "swindling the American people" (Owens, cited in Feagin and Vera, 1995: 122). Clarence Thomas likewise exploited the legend of black welfare queens, pointing to his own sister's draining of the nation's resources. Even before the confirmation hearings, Thomas had shown his willingness to manipulate racial and gender stereotypes by comparing his own personal and political success—earned by dint of hard labor, according to him—to his sister's failure, that is, her status as a welfare cheat. Thomas was quoted by the *New York Times*: "She gets mad when the mailman is late with her welfare check. That's how dependent she is. . . . What's worse is how her kids feel entitled to the check" (*New York Times*, July 7, 1991). In an address to The Federalist Society, Thomas berates welfare recipients for revelling in their "victim status." He contrasts our "cultural heroes" who, like himself, succeed against all odds, with those who "choose" poverty, crime, and welfare. Not only do they accept their plight, they welcome it, and especially the welfare check, as a special right. Wahneema Lubiano (1992) makes the argument that Anna Mae Thomas's economic dependence—and that of other welfare recipients—becomes constructed as a moral failure, thereby occluding the realities of power and opportunity structures.

The "welfare queen" is held morally responsible for the loss of family and the American way of life, for the economic woes of the country, and for the decline in personal responsibility. As Lubiano expresses it, the "welfare mom" is the demon characterized by "the lack of a job and/or income (which equals degeneracy in the Calvinist United States); the presence of a child or children with no father and/or husband; and finally, a charge on the collective U.S. treasury—a human debit" (1992: 337–338). Thus, these "welfare queens" are guilty not only of bilking the nation of its resources, but for all manner of additional sins. Duke blames the government for having "supported and financed (with our own tax money) a massive non-White welfare birthrate that is producing chronic crime, degenerated schools and cities, huge costs in welfare, medical care, education, housing, policing, courts and incarceration" (Duke, online).

So while black males represent a threat to the nation's physical security, their female counterparts pose a parallel economic threat. Both depictions communicate to white America that black America is not only different, but something to be feared and reviled. Such assertions both reflect and reinforce popular stereotypes and concerns, urging the community to define race relations in terms of "Us" versus "Them" dichotomies. Significantly, they also give public voice to anti-black sentiment. White middle-class Americans—feeling assaulted by the twin threats of crime and economic malaise—welcome a tangible "enemy" to blame. The "Black Menace" is one such demon. The racist rhetoric of U.S. politicians condones and encourages intolerance, even hostility, toward African Americans. Coming as they do from political leaders, these messages attain a degree of legitimacy, thereby supporting a hegemonic racial order in which black men and women are "rightfully" relegated to the bottom of the hierarchy. Such vilification represents black Americans as valid victims of derogation and, potentially, violence.

THE UNGODLY GAYS

Much the same can be said of the political discourse surrounding gay and lesbian identities. The yearly reports of the National Gay and Lesbian Task Force, for instance, include myriad examples of state officials publicly voicing their disdain and repulsion for gay men and lesbians. Their assessment of gays is stated in ways even more explicit than the discourse around race. Even those who would shrink from explicitly racist discourse do not have the same tremors of insecurity when assailing gays. Among the recent offerings:

> Al Boris, a [Wilkes-Barre, Pennsylvania] city council member asserted at a December 21 city council meeting that gay men should be shot and that AIDS research should be cut because gay men "are getting what they deserved." After a public outcry, Boris apologized for his remarks at a January council meeting. Then he claimed that homosexuals recruit people with mental retardation for sex and that the media hides gay men's "deadly activities" behind civil rights.

> A member of the San Diego City Council stated that he would "like to see all gays put in a gas chamber."

[Oklahoma City] Representative Bill Graves said he, like the "majority" of people, know that "gays are the reason for the AIDS plague." Graves added, "It is not the city's place to subsidize immorality. The next thing you know, why, we'll have pedophiles in day care." (NGLTF, 1994: 31–34)

Graves's statement is perhaps the most concise synopsis of contemporary anti-gay and -lesbian sentiment. It contains references to the three most egregious sins for which gays are held accountable: the spread of AIDS, ungodliness, and pedophilia. What is even more dramatic about these accounts are the explicit calls for the "elimination" of a whole class of people, as in Boris's claim, for example. This appeal goes beyond the marginalization of gays to suggest very strongly that they be executed. It is no less than the advocacy of homicidal violence against gays. The Philadelphia Lesbian and Gay Task Force voices valid concerns about the inherent dangers of such expressions:

When the President's men use the bully pulpit of a national convention as a forum for hate-mongering, it is no wonder that the bigoted and the hate-filled feel free to violate our rights and to attack us. (1992: 2)

Nor is it beyond the courts—presumably the ultimate "neutral arbiter"—to engage in rhetoric invalidating gay and lesbian identities. Such speech abounds in judicial decisions (Dressler, 1992; Goldyn, 1981). It is still possible to find evidence of publicly expressed sentiments that mirror the generations-old words of William Blackstone, who set precedents for British and U.S. interpretations of sodomy. In the early 1800s, and still in the late 1900s, there are public figures who would describe sodomy as "the infamous crime against nature," "a crime not fit to be named" (Blackstone, 1811: 215). A 1973 Arkansas district court decision reiterated Blackstone's sentiments in much more graphic terms:

It will be unnecessary for us to set out the sordid testimony about the (alleged homosexual) act, which appeared so revolting to one of the two deputies sheriff . . . that he vomited thrice during the evening. (cited in Goldyn, 1981: 34)

This was reinforced in 1993 when an Ohio Supreme Court judge—in a case of a gay man's parole violation—railed against the "evils" and "immorality" of homosexuality (NGLTF, 1994: 34). And it is reinforced regularly by Dallas District Court judge Jack Hampton, whose views on homosexuality are no secret:

I don't care for queers cruising the streets picking up teen-age boys. . . . I've got a teen-age boy. . . . Those two guys wouldn't have been killed if they hadn't been cruising the streets picking up teen-age boys. (cited in Bissinger, 1995: 82)

But Hampton is best known for his quip that "I put prostitutes and queers at the same level . . . and I'd be hard put to give somebody life for killing a prostitute" (cited in Berrill and Herek, 1992: 294).

Like Graves, cited earlier, Hampton and his peers perpetuate the most virulent expressions of hatred and bigotry. From their privileged positions as agents of the state, they publicly express private sentiments of morality. An immutable stigma is applied to gay identity, which is perceived as a moral and physical threat to the public's well-being. Like the young black males, homosexuals of both sexes may be predatory and are certainly menacing. Yet the unspoken threat is that which gays pose to the gendered hierarchy. They are gender traitors: gay men because they have broken ranks with dominant males; lesbians because they have rejected their wifely roles. Carefully arranged gender boundaries are uncomfortably blurred by homosexuality.

Consequently, the denial of gays on the basis of their sexuality resounds in the rhetoric of family values, so aptly summed up by a premier spokesperson, Jesse Helms:

> Think about it. Homosexuals and lesbians, disgusting people marching in the streets demanding all sorts of things, including the right to marry each other. How do you like them apples? (cited in Karst, 1993: 18)

And in the words of Newt Gingrich,

> It is madness to pretend that families are anything other than heterosexual couples. Over time, we want to have an explicit bias in favor of heterosexual marriages. If you look at the pathologies and weaknesses in America today, re-establishing the centrality of marriage and the role of a male and a female in that relationship is a very central issue of the next 20 years. (cited in NGLTF, 1995: 20)

So, according to the rhetoric, not only do gay men and lesbians threaten "our" families (our "teenage sons"), so too do they threaten the very moral fiber of society—a fiber that is bound up with the heterosexual family. All the social ills of the nation are to be laid at the feet of gay men and lesbians whose "lifestyle choice" has led to the disintegration of a decidedly conservative Christian moral order (never mind the pathologies that inhere in many traditional families). Pat Buchanan's stance on this is aptly representative: "I do not believe this is a valid, legitimate, moral lifestyle. Period. Paragraph" (NBC *Meet the Press*, February 11, 1996).

Nationwide, recent anti-gay ballot initiatives have played on all of these fears—of sexual predators, of disease carriers, of destroyers of families—in their calls for the denial of civil protections for gays. Oregon, Maine, Arizona, and Florida are among those states that have been the sites of bitter political campaigns oriented around the prevention or repeal of what far-right representatives have inaccurately termed "special rights" for gay men and lesbians. The anti-gay rhetoric at the heart of these explicitly political campaigns has fanned the flames of homophobia:

> Far Right operatives created an atmosphere of loathing and contempt for lesbian, gay and bisexual people by poisoning communities with rhetoric and misinformation that vilify and demonize lesbians, gay men and bisexuals as sexual predators and undeserving of basic human rights and protections against discrimination. . . . [They] portrayed gay people as degenerate, un-American, privileged, sexually perverse and subhuman. (NGLTF, 1994: 16–17)

The first of such campaigns was perhaps the most vicious in its assaults on gays. The 1992 Oregon measure explicitly defined homosexuality as "abnormal, wrong, unnatural, and perverse" (Moritz, 1995: 57). Moreover, its very title, "Minority Status and Child Protection Act," openly equates homosexuality with pedophilia. During Colorado's campaign in the same year, Pastor Pete Peters—on the basis of his scriptural interpretation—called for the death penalty for gays. Concerned Maine Families (CMF), the primary sponsor of the Maine anti-gay initiative, explicitly vilified homosexuals as pedophiles and as the transmitters of AIDS. In addition to these moral accusations, more recent efforts have introduced the novel idea of presenting gays as an economic threat as well. In supporting the Maine ballot measure, for example, CMF consistently portrayed gays as a privileged minority seeking special rights that would infringe on the basic rights of others:

> Homosexual militants are coming to Maine to *BUY* your vote. Be prepared for an expensive TV advertising blitz to convince you that gays are an oppressed minority group. . . . To grant gay extremists special "minority" status would be to legalize a radically unfair scheme that would destroy civil rights practice as we know it and rob from the poor to give to the rich. (CMF, 1994: 1)

According to the political rhetoric, awarding gays "special rights" would mean heterosexuals could lose their jobs, employers would be sued unjustly by gay employees, gays would consume tax dollars in the form of block grants, and the free speech of all would be infringed upon.

There is ample evidence that some citizens took these threats seriously. The NGLTF (1994) documented a frightening increase in violence against gays corresponding to Colorado's November 1992 initiative. Similarly, Maine's attorney general logged elevated numbers of attacks on homosexuals in that state, leading up to the November 1995 vote (Maine attorney general office, personal communication, February 1996).

In part, the elevated rates of violence against gays during such campaigns are a response to their activism and visibility. When they mobilize to defend or press for their rights, they are seen to be overstepping the boundaries of propriety. Visibility of gays also has become a politicized issue in the context of the ongoing debate about gays in the military. In particular, the message of the "don't ask, don't tell" policy is that gays should be rendered *invisible* and *silent*. An anonymous Navy admiral wrote in a letter to the *New York Times*, "We know we have a certain number of gays performing extremely well, but they're in the closet, and as long as they stay there, we're fine" (cited in the *New York Times*, February 15, 1993). In this context, however, a new threat is implied. There are those who use this debate to voice the traditional concerns about the sexually predatory and promiscuous gay soldier and the threat he or she poses to individual heterosexual victims. The additional and more far-reaching threat implied by the recent debate over homosexual men and women in the military extends to the whole nation: they pose a national security risk. Indeed, in *Watkins v. United States Army* (1986), the Army defended its exclusionary policy with reference to worries about emotional relationships between gay soldiers of different ranks, and the vulnerability of gay soldiers to blackmail.

Senator Dan Coates, as late as 1993 reiterated the fear that the presence of homosexuals was risky business. He demanded that Clinton "prove to the nation that increased sexual tension in military units will not undermine their effectiveness" (cited in *New York Daily News*, March 25, 1993). The underlying assumption? That gay soldiers would prey on their pitiable heterosexual comrades, leaving the latter weak and incapable of functioning as "manly soldiers." At heart, the message is that the acknowledgment of homosexuality within the armed forces would significantly lower efficiency by lowering morale—upstanding heterosexuals would be so dismayed by their association with gay colleagues that they would be incapable of performing their duties. The presence of homosexuals challenges the core of the military institution: the celebration of an idealized, therefore unswervingly heterosexual, masculinity.

THE IMMIGRANT THREAT

It is ironic that the United States armed forces—which have traditionally excluded women, men of color, and homosexuals—were constructed to defend a nation that includes among its mantras "Give me your tired, your hungry, your poor, your huddled masses yearning to breathe free." In contrast to this mythology, we see resurrected a political discourse that seeks also to construct immigrants as dangerous Others within, as in the use of the term "alien" rather than "illegal immigrant." This reflects the historical ambivalence toward immigrants in a nation of immigrants, a notion reinforced by the former governor of Colorado and his coauthor:

> Immigration policy was once an asset to this country, helping to make us strong. But its current uncontrolled state will seriously harm this country and its institutions. (Lamm and Imhoff, 1985: 49)

Now, the United States is faced by an "immigration crisis." As is often the case, the public looks to its political leaders for a cue on how to interpret the real and perceived impact of the dramatic demographic and cultural changes associated with immigration. The most vocal of discourses tend not to paint a favorable portrait. The ghosts of the 1920s have returned to haunt us. Then, as now, there was a widespread fear that unbridled immigration would destroy the moral, economic and (mono)cultural fiber of the United States. In allegorical style, Lothrop Stoddard painted a frightening picture:

> If America is not true to her own race-soul, She will inevitably lose it, and the brightest star that has appeared since Hellas will fall like a meteor from the human sky, its brilliant radiance fading into the night. (1986: 64; orig. 1920)

More than seventy years later, Florida's governor Lawton Chiles bemoaned a similar risk:

> As surely as the winds and rains of Hurricane Andrew assaulted south Florida in a crisis that forever changed it, there is another storm, illegal immigration, that is battering our shores today. (cited in Isbister, 1996: 6)

Note the analogies offered: in both statements, immigrants are associated with the "forces of nature." This is reminiscent of the Nativist ideologies that place non-Anglos, and especially nonwhites, closer to nature, that is, more primitive than white Anglos. This also informs Buchanan's rhetoric of the inherent cultural inferiority of immigrants. Thus, his infamous statement echoes this sentiment in less flowery, more direct terms: "immigration is helping fuel the cultural breakdown of our nation" (cited in Zeskind, 1996: 23). He more explicitly enumerates his fears elsewhere: "I believe the explosion in illegal immigration is causing massive crime, social disruption and an enormous drain on government services" (Buchanan, online).

In the current round of identity politics, rhetoric revolves around the preferred model of assimilation and cultural integration. The problem arises, for a state favoring this model, from the shape and character of the current wave of immigration. Unlike the cases of the previous three waves of immigration, the current arrivals are not predominantly European, are not even predominantly white. On the contrary, they are much more likely to be fleeing the violence and poverty of the Third World. Thus, they overwhelmingly are Asians and Latin Americans. On the basis of race alone, these immigrants are not as readily assimilable as their predecessors. Consequently, the hegemonic bloc in the United States—white European males—are in a crisis of identity brought on by the increasing diversity engendered by the immigration patterns of the late twentieth century. Culturally, nonwhite, non-European immigrants are constructed as major contributors to the breakdown of U.S. unity and stability.

Bette Hammond, president of Stop the Out of Control Problem of Immigration Today (STOP IT), fears that "We have so many groups wanting to be in America, but not wanting to be American" (cited in Isbister, 1996: 183). Instead, so goes the argument, these "foreigners" seek to reap the advantages of the United States' economy while contributing to the demise of United States' culture by insisting on the integrity of their own cultural heritage—which, of course, is presumed to be inferior to that of the United States. This is echoed in Pat Buchanan's assertion that

> if no cutoff is imposed on social benefits for those who breach our
> borders and break our laws, the message will go out to a desperate
> world: America is wide open. . . . If America is to survive as "one
> nation, one people" we need to call a "time-out" on immigration
> to assimilate the tens of millions who have lately arrived.
> (Buchanan, online)

Lamm is similarly forthright in his position: "I believe that America's culture and national identity are threatened by massive levels of legal and illegal immigration" (Lamm and Imhoff, 1985: 77).

The underlying assumption is that Anglo culture of the United States (whatever that is), is inherently superior to all others. Peter Brimelow enters the political debate on immigration with his observation that

> it should not be necessary to explain that the legacy of
> [the Zulu kings] Shaka and Cetewayo—overthrown just over
> a century ago—is not that of Alfred the Great, let alone
> Elizabeth II *or any civilized society.* (cited in Fukuyama, 1994:
> 153; emphasis added)

This cultural upset is similarly decried by a conservative think tank, the Rockford Institute, in an article that insists that immigrants have no more intention of shucking the third world they've lugged across the border than they have of leaving after they make their millions. Once here, they're here for good, disrupting our institutions, like public schools, with foreign languages, pagan religions, and oddly spiced foods. (cited in Miles, 1994: 134)

Immigrants, it seems, are an affront and a danger to the Anglo-Christian way of life established in this land.

The particular fear underlying such assertions seems to be the potential strength that new immigrant groups might choose to wield. Richard Lamm and Gary Imhoff refer to a "new splintering of our society that results directly from large and continuing immigration"; and again, "growing immigrant ethnic groups have the potential to be ethnic power bases for splinter groups" (Lamm and Imhoff, 1985: 79, 95). The very choice of terms is intriguing. Symbolically, the authors invoke the painful notion of "splinters," of a festering wound, rather than a term that would lend legitimacy to ethnic collectives—terms like "interest groups" or "political action groups," for example. The implication of this warning is that the increasingly diverse pool of immigrants is a "thorn in one's side." Whose side? That of the dominant white majority. Racial and ethnic immigration threatens to challenge the privileged position of European Americans, who for so long have been unquestionably in control.

Concomitantly, part of this perceived danger also involves the invocation of the theme of immigrant criminality. Even Clinton has jumped on this bandwagon. In response to reports that a suspect in the World Trade Center bombing might have been admitted—fraudulently—on political asylum, Clinton quipped, "We must not—we will not surrender our borders to those who wish to exploit our history of compassion and justice" (cited in Mills, 1994: 14–15). Immigrants are presented as the "partners in crime" to the black native-born male. California governor Pete Wilson drew out this implication in a speech at Los Angeles Town Hall: "As we struggle to keep dangerous criminals off our streets, we find that 14 percent of California's prison population are illegal immigrants—enough to fill eight state prisons to capacity" (April 25, 1994). Has it not been ever thus? Clifford Shaw, Henry McKay, and their colleagues of the Chicago school noted in the first half of the century the tendency of politicians to assign delinquent labels to immigrants, as if this were part of their genetic make-up, or part of their cultural ethos. The same stigma is attached to immigrants in the latter half of the century.

Lamm and Imhoff devote a full chapter to the crime-immigrant nexus. They foreshadow Wilson's comments, arguing that

as far as we are from solving our own crime problem, we cannot afford to ignore the lawlessness that comes with the breakdown of our borders. Our immigration policies are exacerbating our national epidemic of crime. (1985: 49)

Following this warning, the authors introduce three pages of anecdotal evidence to "prove" the contributions of (especially illegal) immigrants to the violent crime rate in this country. In fact, in spite of their assurances to the contrary, Lamm and Imhoff imply that immigrants are inherently criminal (1985: 53). They support this contention, first, by generalizing their observation that illegal immigrants are by definition criminal. Additionally, however, they marshal evidence from the case of the Mariel boatlift. Relying solely on the arguments of an investigating officer by the name of Detective Alvarez, Lamm and Imhoff suggest that since so many of these (illegal) immigrants were *probably* criminals, then it is reasonable to assume that, in general, many immigrants are also *probably* criminals.

From the perspective of a democratic state, anti-immigrant rhetoric couched in cultural terms is dangerous. It is too easily identified as racist or, at least, as ethnocentric. The more moderate course, then, is to emphasize the economic distress caused by immigrants. Just as the cultural message marginalizes immigrants as permanent outsiders, or demonizes them as inherently criminal, economic messages vilify them as a serious drain on the nation's resources.

California Governor Pete Wilson arguably has been one of the foremost spokespersons arguing for immigration reform on explicitly economic grounds. His infamous Proposition 187 and the rhetoric surrounding it are clear evidence of his stand on immigration. However, like Lamm, Wilson's particular fear of Hispanic immigration is belied by his emphasis on illegal (that is, Mexican) immigrants who are responsible for the fact that "we're forced to spend $1.7 Billion each year to educate students who are acknowledged to be in the country illegally. In total, California taxpayers are compelled by federal law to spend more than $3 Billion to provide services to illegal immigrants—it is approaching 10 percent of our state budget" (Wilson, 1994). If the abstract allusions to cultural difference and diversity don't attract the public's attention, emphasizing the impact of immigration on their wallets certainly will. To shift the debate from values to dollars is to promote fears of economic instability in an already unstable environment. And to lay the blame on the "immigrant threat" is to displace attention from government mismanagement. Presenting immigrants as a financial drain on state resources constructs them as enemies of all "hardworking" Americans. Wilson recognizes the value of such a project when he assures his public that he is aware of their pain: "It is a slap in the face of the tens of thousands who play by the rules." Again, we see the game of Us versus Them, in which "They" are the villains.

From this perspective, immigrants—especially Third World immigrants—come to this country for two reasons: to sack the welfare system and to take the jobs of Americans. The former belief underlies Wilson's Proposition 187, which would have excluded illegal immigrants and their children from most state social services, and recent proposals, which would exclude even legal immigrants from social security payments. Presumably, immigrants are getting rich off the United States' welfare system; it is catapulting them into the middle class, over the heads of long-suffering native-born Americans. I, for one, would like to see the computations that place welfare recipients in a middle-income bracket.

Immigrants are in a double bind. On the one hand, they are berated for their presumed exploitation and plundering of the social safety net. Yet on the other hand, should they turn instead to legitimate employment—as the vast majority do—they then are reviled for stealing "American" jobs. Meldren Thomas Jr., former governor of New Hampshire, levies both charges in one very direct statement:

> One tax expert estimates that right now the average tax payer pays $259 a year just to support illegal aliens now in the United States. Illegal aliens cost you tax dollars when they get food stamps, welfare benefits, medical and medicare payments, free bilingual public schooling and social security benefits—illegal immigrants take 3.5 million jobs from Americans. (cited in Simon and Alexander, 1993: 259)[2]

Whether framed in economic, cultural, or criminal terms, the underlying message is that war must be declared on the invading force of immigrants. Lamar Alexander, for example, would have us introduce a new branch of the armed forces intended to root out and eliminate the invaders by force. Ultimately, to frame a problem in such terms and to call for an armed response plants the seeds of violence in the broader culture. Immigrants are constructed as the "enemies" of the American way of life, who present a threat than can be contained only by extreme means.

LEGAL HEGEMONY AND HATE CRIME

Political rhetoric all too often becomes institutionalized in state policy and legislation. This has dual implications, in that law has both material and ideological effects. On the one hand, the law itself effectively can

---

2. Oddly enough, even the AFL-CIO recognizes the fallacy of immigrant responsibility for job loss. In a statement on "Immigration and the American Dream," the executive council explains, "The facts are these: immigrants are not the cause of America's declining wages and the export of good jobs overseas. Immigrants are not responsible for the 'downsizing' that is sweeping through many U. S. industries and throwing millions of Americans out of work" (1995).

exclude or restrict the participation of particular groups in the ongoing activities and processes of society—just as immigration and naturalization law historically have prevented many Asians from entry, or from attaining citizenship. Law can also—by its silences—exclude groups from protections afforded others, such as in the failure to include gays or women in hate crime or civil rights legislation. The latter examples have the material effects of leaving the unnamed groups vulnerable to bias-motivated attacks and the ideological effect of indicating that they are unworthy of protection, and therefore legitimate victims. In other words, law is a dramatic form of political and cultural expression that "draws the boundaries that divide us into groups, with momentous effects on our individual identities" (Karst, 1993: 2). Law and legal ruminations are discursive practices by which Self and Other are constructed. They are an integral part of the field in which difference is constructed and reaffirmed.

There is an endless array of examples of legislation and policy that support my contention about the role of law in conditioning the environment for hate crime: sodomy legislation criminalizes gays; "immigration sweeps" stigmatize and victimize Latinos, in particular; antiabortion policies limit women's autonomy; social security restrictions endanger and exclude immigrants; Federal policy marginalizes Native American populations; the military's "don't ask, don't tell" policy silences gays. In their own way, each of these pieces serves to marginalize or subordinate the groups in question. Each raises questions about the particular group's legitimacy and place in U.S. society; in some cases, they explicitly define their "outsider" status. Such legislation and policy reflect and entrench a "public mood [which] has become a nationalistic jingoism that justifies the institutionalization of discrimination and rejects moral obligation to the poor" (Shepherd, 1991: 4). In order to uncover more clearly the dynamics of law within the context of identity politics, I turn now to a closer examination of three illustrative legal fields: immigration and naturalization law; social welfare policy; and hate crime legislation.

IMMIGRATION AND NATURALIZATION

Perhaps more than any other legal realm, that of immigration and naturalization designates "insider" and "outsider" status. It denotes inclusion and exclusion, and specifies who is worthy of acceptance. Conversely, it also specifies those who are to be excluded lest they "defile" or "threaten" the purity of the American soul. The United States has a lengthy history of discriminatory immigration policy, the aftershocks of which remain in both symbolic and material terms. Moreover, the recent resurgence of nativist and anti-immigrant sentiment indicates that such policies are not only historical artifacts, but part of the contemporary landscape as well.

Like the public rhetoric that marginalizes and often stigmatizes subordinate ethnic groups, the effect of the legal order is to coconstruct relative identities (van Dijk, 1995). As Ruth Frankenberg (1993) observes, racist discourses—of which law is a part—play a fundamental role in designating "difference" and inferiority. In particular,

> Whiteness and Americanness seemed comprehensible to many
> only by reference to Others excluded from these categories. . . .
> One effect . . . is the production of an unmarked, apparently
> autonomous white/Western self, in contrast with the marked,
> Other racial and cultural categories with which the racially and
> culturally dominant category is co-constructed. (1993: 17)

Historically, changing immigration and citizenship policies have been effective means by which to delimit both "whiteness" and "Americanness." Such policies have enabled white males, in particular, to sustain a dominant identity and, along with that, a precariously balanced series of cultural hierarchies. In other words, the politics of immigration has long facilitated the construction of whiteness by "drawing boundaries, engaging in boundedness" (Weiss, Proweller, and Centrie, 1997: 214). Here I speak of the physical "boundaries" guarded by immigration exclusions, as well as the symbolic "boundaries" guarded by immigration rhetoric.

Nowhere has this marking of difference been more apparent than in the historical discrimination against Asians under the immigration laws. Widespread racial animus from labor leaders, temperance activists, and agricultural interests in the latter part of the nineteenth century finally pressed the federal government to react to the perceived threats that Asians were thought to represent to employment (for example, wage deflation), morality (for example, opium use), and hygiene (for example, prostitution). This agitation—which grew violent at times—was accompanied by increasingly restrictive immigration and naturalization policies. As a complement, many western states established a series of nuisance ordinances, including head taxes and state entry inspections. Together, these policies served to reinforce the "foreignness" of Asian immigrants and the stereotypes associated with them: immorality, drug addiction, prostitution, fiendish competition, and so one. Michael Olivas paints a picture in which we see how Asians initially were "imported for their labor and not allowed to participate in the society they built; or expelled when their labor was no longer considered necessary" (1995: 10).

As early as 1875, the U.S. Congress passed the first immigration act restricting Asian entry. Mirroring public and political perceptions that Chinese women, in particular, were lewd and depraved, the legislation effectively halted their entry into the United States. The Page Law sought to bar felons, contract laborers, and prostitutes. Since it was "common knowledge" at the time that all Chinese women were prostitutes, most were not accepted into the country. Between 1881 and 1885, there followed a flurry of acts and revisions (for example, Chinese Exclusion Act of 1882) that increasingly restricted Chinese entry so that by 1885, only twenty-two Chinese men were admitted. The 1882 Chinese Exclusion Act was renewed for ten years in 1892 and extended indefinitely in 1902. Restrictions remained in place until the 1952 McCarran-Walter Act.

The early decades of the twentieth century extended these exclusions to most Asians. The 1917 Immigration Act barred immigration from virtually all of Asia; the 1924 National Origins Act barred the entry of Japanese wives, even those whose husbands had already attained citizenship. The same act reinforced the foreign identity of Asians by denying entry to those ineligible for citizenship. According to the 1790 United States Naturalization Act and subsequent Supreme Court decisions, this meant that no Asians were to be allowed to immigrate, since citizenship was restricted to "free white persons."[3] *Ozawa v. United States* (1922) and *United States v. Thind* (1924) found that neither Japanese nor Asian Indians, respectively, were considered to be white. This definition of Asians as perpetual foreigners on the basis of race alone would hold until the 1960s, carrying with it the imputation of Otherness. Cases like those noted above "show that whites fashion an identity for themselves that is the positive mirror image of the negative identity imposed on people of color" (Lopez, 1995: 548).

Scattered among these anti-Asian policies were a number that also painted a cadre of southern and eastern Europeans as "not quite white." While Europeans continued to dominate among immigrants throughout the first part of the twentieth century, all were not equally welcome. The southern and eastern Europeans—such as Poles, Jews, Greeks—were thought to be of inferior, filthy, and immoral stock. Based on the assumption that they were illiterate and unassimilable races, a 1921 immigration reform included a literacy test for potential immigrants. This was accompanied by immigration quotas equal to 3 percent of a given country's population in the United States. Clearly, this favored the majority northern European population. The disparity was reinforced by 1924 legislation that reduced the quotas to 2 percent of the population represented in the 1890 Census. The message was clear: these scurrilous Europeans were not wanted and would be admitted only sparingly, as needed to fill the need for cheap labor in an industrializing country.

Under the 1965 Immigration and Naturalization Act, quotas and exclusions were largely lifted. The legislative emphasis shifted from

---

3. In 1868, this legislation had been modified to extend citizenship to those of African descent. As low as African Americans were in the U.S. cultural hierarchy, Asians sat even lower.

nation-based preferences to class- and family-based preferences. Family reunification policies still ensured a steady stream of predominantly northern Europeans. The alternative emphasis on job skills continued to favor those professional and highly skilled laborers from Europe, but also began to draw well-educated Asians. For the first time since the mid-1800s, the United States had relatively open doors. However, with the liberalization of immigration policy came unanticipated—and, to some, threatening—shifts in the demographics of immigration. As noted previously, the immigrants at the close of the twentieth century overwhelmingly are people of color from Asia, Africa, and South and Central America. They are "not like us."

In the absence of restrictive immigration laws, the border wars have come to be fought by other means. Especially during the Reagan and Bush administrations, attention was drawn to securing the United States–Mexico border against the "dark swarm" of Mexican immigrants. An America's Watch (1992) report acknowledges the extent to which changes in law and policy have created a climate of mistrust, suspicion, and violence along the border. Similarly, Timothy Dunn (1996) documents what he refers to as the militarization of this space.

The militarization of the border zone can be traced to the Immigration Reform and Control Act of 1986. The act offered amnesty to undocumented immigrants already in the United States. Yet it also called for stricter Immigration and Naturalization Service (INS) enforcement mechanisms along the United States–Mexico border as a means of stemming the "tidal wave," the "invasion" of illegal immigrants. The "war against immigrants" escalated in 1996 with the Illegal Immigration Reform and Immigration Responsibility Act. The most dramatic element of this policy was the restriction of public benefits for aliens and immigrants. Coming as it did on the heels of Pete Wilson's infamous anti-immigrant initiatives in California, the policy further stigmatized and marginalized immigrants. Some advocates in states like Texas have sought—unsuccessfully—to bar children of illegal immigrants from public education. The material effect of such initiatives would be to restrict the services available to families of recent immigration—and thereby threaten their quality of life, if not very survival. It would leave them with little power or resources to resist victimization. Symbolically, these policies define immigrants as outside the community and therefore outside the protections of the U.S. polity.

While I have emphasized the racial and ethnic discrimination historically inherent in U.S. immigration and naturalization policy, it is also important to recognize the gender politics of such policies. The restrictions on public benefits, for example, are most threatening to women and children. While a small proportion of immigrants in the United States live in female-headed households (Miller and Moore, 1997), it is these households that are most likely to use such services as AFDC. To limit access is thus to limit living standards. Moreover, immigration policy continues to exclude prostitutes, without any apparent recognition of the economic and social oppression that has conditioned such "employment." Similarly, the United States has been slow to recognize the refugee status of women fleeing gender persecution in their home countries, reinforcing the conviction that sexual or domestic violence, for example, is private and personal rather than public or political (Wilets, 1997).

Another controversial arena in this context is the legal status of gay men and lesbians with respect to immigration. Beginning with the Immigration and Naturalization Act of 1917, homosexuals were to be denied entry. Both the INS and the Public Health Service (following the edict of the American Psychological Association) concurred at the time that gay men and women could be classified as "mentally defective" or suffering from a "constitutional psychopathic inferiority." A 1947 Senate investigation further recommended that an addition be made to the categories of excludable aliens: "homosexuals and other sex perverts." The revision was rejected, but only because the Senate Judiciary Committee concluded that "the provision for the exclusion of aliens afflicted with psychopathic personality or a mental defect . . . [was] sufficiently broad to provide for the exclusion of homosexuals and sex perverts" (cited in Fowler and Graff, 1985: 626–627). The courts continued to hold that gay men and lesbians were legally excluded for medical reasons. Such policy and practice maintains the stigmatized identity of homosexuals, constructing them as "defective" and "sick" individuals.

Collectively, the net effect of this nation's discriminatory immigration and citizenship policies has been to disempower those seeking inclusion. At the extreme, this has been accomplished through legislation explicitly denying entry to those deemed a threat—in physical, political, economic, moral, or cultural terms. However, it also has been accomplished by strictly delimiting the civil, political, and social rights claimed by "foreigners." And this in turn has created an unsympathetic environment for immigrants. It designates immigrants as inherently inferior and less worthy of protections. The legislation has reinforced the political and public imagery of "foreigners" as threatening or predatory. In demonizing immigrants, policy sets the stage for "immigrant bashing" as a means of reminding the victims of their precarious position in this "community."

SOCIAL WELFARE POLICY

One of the pre-eminent domestic equivalents of the "foreigner" in the contemporary era is the welfare recipient. Proposition 187, for example, is informed by equally derogatory visions of both immigrants and those in need of social support. Like their immigrant counterparts, the "welfare slobs" are assumed to be unlike "us"; they are outside of "our" community; they represent all that "we" are not. They are irresponsible, promiscuous, drug addicted, slovenly. And they are therefore worthy targets of our moral opprobrium. They are the symbolic victims of the "Mean Season" to which Fred Block, Richard Cloward, Barbara Ehrenreich, and Francis Fox Piven (1987) have referred. Typically, it has been women and people of color who have been vilified as such drains on our national coffers, and as morally degenerate.

Law and social policy are doubly complicit in these constructions, since they serve both to create and to maintain the marginality of affected groups. In other words, welfare policy "reproduces gender (and racial) stratification structurally by replicating a gendered (and racialized) division of labor and culturally by inculcating an ideological framework that sustains the division of labor" (Quadagno and Fobes, 1997: 257). Policy in this area reinforces the racism and sexism that underlie hate-motivated violence, by representing welfare recipients as inferior beings.

California's Proposition 187 is one of the most dramatic contemporary illustrations of the impact of public benefits policy. Kevin Johnson speaks of its "quadruple whammy," which "besides affecting persons with a certain immigration status, has a disparate impact on people of color (especially Mexican immigrants against whom many of the efforts to reduce benefits are specifically directed), women (who are disproportionately affected by limitations on public assistance), and the poor (who are most in need of public benefits and services)" (1995: 1516). Those apt to be most adversely affected by restrictions such as those proposed by Proposition 187 are precisely those people who are already vulnerable to social, economic, and physical violence—immigrant women and men of color. The additional burdens imposed by limitations on public aid leaves them with even fewer resources by which to insulate themselves from assaults.

Proposition 187 exploits broadly based fears of the threats posed by immigrants. Section one explicitly makes the claim that the people of California have "suffered and are suffering economic hardships caused by the presence of illegal aliens in this state. That they have suffered and are suffering personal injury and damage caused by the criminal conduct of illegal aliens in this state." Section five declares the act's intent to be to "diligently protect public funds from misuse." If upheld, the act would preclude undocumented immigrants from receiving such public provisions as social services, health care, and education.[4]

---

4. Undocumented immigrants have long been denied access to such federal programs as AFDC.

Proposition 187 vilifies both illegal aliens and welfare recipients. It portrays both as public burdens, and aliens, especially, as criminals. "They" cost "us" liberty and wealth. More specifically, given the demographics of California's immigrant population, it generally is assumed that "they" are ethnically identifiable as Latinos (and to a lesser extent, Asians):

> There is an equation now in California that goes: Illegal
> Immigrants, equal to Mexicans, equal to criminals, equal to some-
> one who wants social services. (Johnson, 1995: 1533, citing the
> Mexican ambassador to the United States)

In this equation, immigration status, ethnicity, and the tendency toward violent and fraudulent behavior are conflated, such that "they," the outlaws, once again are constructed in negative relational terms to "us," the victims. Immigrant and Latino bashing thus becomes a legitimate means of self-defense. Having crossed geopolitical boundaries, immigrants of color are feared to be similarly intent on transgressing economic, moral, and cultural borders as well.

In addition to its ideological effects, Proposition 187 would have concrete—and disparate—material effects as well. The provision calling for verification of immigrant status would escalate the already dramatic problem of law enforcement harassment of "foreigners," in other words, people of color and those who speak with an accent. Moreover, the proposition would put immigrant women of color at particular risk of impoverishment, risky pregnancies, and even heightened violence. To the extent that county domestic violence shelters are state funded, they too, would be off limits to undocumented immigrants. In general, exclusion from public aid signals exclusion from the protections afforded others, leaving undocumented residents with few political or social resources with which to defend themselves against discriminatory treatment.

The multiple marginalization represented by Proposition 187 is reproduced in an array of social security provisions. In particular, race, class, and gender oppression are at the core of recent welfare state retrenchment policies. Just as Proposition 187 would have a disproportionate impact on women and men of color, so, too, do recent reversals of the U.S. commitment to welfare state initiatives. And again, such moves have both material and symbolic effects.

The material effects of the social safety net backlash are made obvious by the socioeconomic indicators revealing worsening conditions for "underclass" minorities and women. Indeed, there is a consensus among contributors to a recent volume edited by Greg Shepherd and David Penna (1991) that there is a strong connection between state policy and the creation and maintenance of an "underclass" constituted largely by minorities. Specifically, Shepherd asserts that "the rapid rise in poverty levels in the inner city, the number of homeless who are minorities, the amount of single women with dependents, and the unemployment of minorities in urban areas all correspond to the rapid decrease in government assisted programs" (1991: 7).

To the extent that blacks and Hispanics are overrepresented in the welfare and state assistance rolls, they are disproportionately affected by the ongoing attack on the welfare state. Restrictions on eligibility and on payments deepen the level of poverty, rather than resolve it. Consequently, by the middle of the 1990s, increasing numbers of blacks and Hispanics lived below the poverty level, were unemployed, and were concentrated in menial low-paying jobs. Children and single mothers were particularly hard hit by these rollbacks; in 1997, 40 percent of black children, 38 percent of Hispanic children and 13 percent of white children were living in poverty (National Center for Children in Poverty, 1999). According to the Census Bureau (online), in 1996, 40.8 percent of black single mothers and 43.7 percent of Hispanic single mothers lived below the poverty level, compared to 24.9 percent of their white counterparts. The increasingly popular "workfare" programs will only exacerbate the problem, by forcing jobless women and minorities to accept menial low-paying jobs that leave them below the poverty line. In other words, the states' tendencies to manipulate social policy along race, class, and gender lines "not only perpetuate racism and sexism, but guarantee the continued unequal distribution of economic resources" (Lubiano, 1992: 350).

Even before the most recent cuts in welfare provisions, Michael Tonry (1995) documented the impact that such impoverishment had on the income reporting practices of welfare recipients. The combination of below-poverty benefits and severe restrictions on additional income create the context for the criminalization of the poor. In the effort to provide for their families, many welfare mothers feel compelled and morally justified in turning to the underground economy (Tonry, 1995; Young, 1993). Contrary to the popular belief, however, this is more likely to involve under-the-table work for pay than it is to involve selling drugs or their own bodies. It is one of the tragic ironies of the contemporary structure of welfare provisions that welfare recipients live the stereotype of fraud.

Connected to welfare eligibility is the question of bureaucratic oversight of recipients' behavior. Although we have moved beyond the days of "man-in-the-house" rules and midnight raids to ascertain the sexual behavior of welfare recipients, those receiving benefits continue to be subject to "patronizing, punitive, demeaning and arbitrary treatment by the people employed to 'serve' them" (Young, 1990: 54). The lives of welfare recipients are not their own. As Young asserts,

People who depend on public subsidy or private charity to meet some or all of their needs must often submit to other people's judgements about their lives and actions. . . . Contemporary rhetoric and policy proposals seem determined to deprive them further of their autonomy. (1990: 126–127)

The loss of autonomy that such surveillance and derogation engenders constructs the "welfare queen" as a second-class citizen, therefore outside the protections afforded full citizenship. In return for the meager allotment, s/he must give up an array of rights, including privacy, integrity, and credibility. Journalist Rita Henley Jensen describes her experiences as a single mother supporting her education through welfare:

I had to prove every statement was not a lie. Everything had to be documented . . . the procedure was a subtle and constant reminder that nothing I said was accepted as truth. Ever. (1998: 247)

Jensen also acknowledges the fear with which all welfare mothers live, that

any neighbor can call the authorities about a welfare mother, making a charge of neglect, and that mother, *since she is less than nothing*, might not be able to prove her competency. (1998: 248)

In spite of the best efforts of the majority of mothers on welfare to care for their children, seek employment, or perhaps even educate themselves, the process of degradation that is the welfare system nonetheless portrays them generically as undeserving of the privileges of citizenship. They are constructed as not belonging to—and therefore not privy to participation in—the community of hardworking, self-sacrificing "normal" people. Thus marginalized, recipients are both practically and symbolically vulnerable to attack. Welfare recipients are worthy only of "our" contempt, given their antisocial "refusal" to work (Fraser and Gordon, 1994; Handler, 1990).

Indeed, Joel Handler (1990) views the history of welfare policy in the United States as an institutionalized effort to deviantize the gendered and racialized subjects who, in the public rhetoric, have become synonymous with welfare: the African-American welfare queen and her illegitimate children. Moreover, "These two groups have come to be equated with joblessness, drugs, and crime. Thus the stereotypical AFDC recipient is considered a prime contributor to this new scourge" (Handler, 1990: 925). Like immigration policy, then, welfare policy re-creates the dual racial threats of crime and economic strain alluded to previously.

Regardless of the color of the recipient, welfare policy also reinforces gender stratification and the disempowerment of women. The escape from familial patriarchy that often underlies women's welfare applications is an empty venture when it is only replaced by state patriarchy (Eisenstein, 1994; Jensen, 1998). So, for example, whereas married, middle-class women are (unrealistically) encouraged not to work outside the home, to stay home with the children, and be supported by the male breadwinner, the poor single mother is (unrealistically) coerced to work outside the home to support herself and her family. She is stigmatized for her failure to live within the bounds of a traditional heterosexual marriage. The eligibility restrictions, the surveillance, the degradation ceremonies are meant to send women running back to their husbands, or perhaps fathers. Consider Arizona Representative Anderson's proposal that encourages programs for single female welfare recipients who are "interested in pursuing a career track in home management"—in other words, marriage (*Arizona Republic*, 1998: A1). Nationwide, most states have proposed and enacted legislation requiring teenage mothers to remain with their families in order to receive state support. Given the reassertion of the "appropriate" family and gender roles, women outside these boundaries become deviant—they are "dependent" on the wrong entity. Had they been "dependent" on a male partner or guardian, this would have been acceptable. But to be "dependent" on the state is to turn one's back on one's proper place.

HATE CRIME LEGISLATION

It is not only legal actions that signify the worth and value of individuals and communities. It is not only legal proscriptions that construct membership and belonging in the imagined community. The inaction of law is likewise a mechanism by which people are valuated. In other words,

> The places where law does not go to redress harm have tended to be the places where women, children, people of color and poor people live. This absence of law is itself another story with a message, perhaps unintended, about the relative value of different human lives. (Matsuda, 1993: 18)

The recent spate of hate crime legislation, for example, is remarkable for its silences. These statutes recognize a particular class of victims whose victimization is motivated by prejudice and bias. In so doing, hate crime legislation also signifies who constitutes a "legitimate" victim and who does not. The failure to acknowledge the threats posed by hate crime directed toward the powerless in U.S. society "tells a story" with the moral that it is acceptable to assault the unnamed victim. Consequently, in many states the violence perpetrated against gay men and lesbians and against women is rendered invisible, if not normative by their exclusion from the legislation.

Robert Kelly, Jess Maghan, and Woodrow Tennant capture the ambiguous place of gays and lesbians in the context of hate crime legislation: "Whereas Asians are often considered the "model minority," gays and lesbians might be considered the "marginal minority." Their inclusion under hate crimes legislation has been sporadic, based generally on political rather than rational considerations" (1993: 32). All but three states[5] have implemented some variant or combination of hate crime legislation, including penalty enhancement statutes, bias-motivated violence and intimidation statutes, or institutional vandalism statutes. Yet only fourteen of these states and the District of Columbia include sexual orientation as a protected class.[6] Passage of the federal Hate Crime Statistics Act (HCSA), signed in 1990 and renewed in 1996, consistently was held up through the 1980s by the fierce opposition of Senator Jesse Helms and similarly anti-gay senators. When it passed, it did include sexual orientation, along with the less controversial categories of race, religion, and ethnicity.

These exclusionary practices extend a powerful message and a legislative justification for the violent marginalization of gay men and lesbians. They suggest that "lesbians and gay men do not deserve full legal protection and justice. It also signals to perpetrators, criminal justice personnel and the rest of society that anti-gay hate crimes will not be punished" (Berrill and Herek, 1992: 293). That the opponents of gay and lesbian inclusion intended the stigmatization of this community is exemplified by Jesse Helms's strident fight against the HCSA, on the basis that it offered unwarranted protection, and worse, respectability to homosexuals. It was his contention that to include sexual orientation would be to put homosexuality on a par with traditional protected classes such as race and religion. To his mind, this was morally and politically unsound and unacceptable. Initially, he offered a compromise amendment to the bill, which read as follows:

It is the sense of the Senate that—

(1) the homosexual movement threatens the strength and the survival of the American family as the basic unit of society;

(2) state sodomy laws should be enforced because they are in the best interest of public health;

(3) the Federal government should not provide discrimination protections on the basis of sexual orientation; and

(4) school curriculums should not condone homosexuality as

---

5. South Carolina, Nebraska, and Wyoming.

6. California, Connecticut, Florida, Illinois, Iowa, Minnesota, New York, New Hampshire, New Jersey, Oregon, Utah, Vermont, Washington, and Wisconsin. Some states have, at various times, amended their legislation, or deleted sexual orientation from existing legislation (e.g., Maine).

an acceptable lifestyle in American society. (cited in Fernandez, 1991: 277)

Helms's proposed amendment draws upon and lends legitimacy to the abundant cultural myths of homosexuality: that homosexuals "recruit" and therefore threaten traditional family values; that their sexuality is deviant and worthy of criminalization; that they are a public health menace; that their sexual orientation is a choice, or lifestyle, rather than an inherent part of their identity. Helms reapplies the stigma of homosexuality.

The amendment was too extreme, even for a relatively conservative Senate and Congress. Owing largely to the efforts of the NGLTF and the coalition of Senators Paul Simon, Orrin Hatch, and Robert Dole, the amendment was toned down so that the nonetheless incongruent clause read:

Sec. 2. (a) Congress finds that—

(1) The American family life is the foundation of American society;

(2) Federal policy should encourage the well-being, financial security, and health of the American family;

(3) Schools should not de-emphasize the critical value of American family life.

(b) Nothing in this Act shall be construed, nor shall any funds appropriated to carry out the purpose of the Act be used, to promote or encourage homosexuality.

The message remains the same. The legislation privileges heterosexual relations and a very narrow definition of family. It continues to imply that homosexuality represents an impending threat to the moral, economic, and physical well-being of the United States. And it reaffirms Helms's position that homosexuality ordinarily should not be considered worthy of state protections against discrimination.

If the efforts of the gay and lesbian movement to have sexual orientation recognized in legislation have been met with vicious opposition, then it can be said that similar efforts to recognize gender have been met with ambivalence. The former has marginalized gay men and lesbians, the latter has rendered invisible the violence perpetrated against women qua women. Even the Anti-Defamation League, which has led the development of hate crime legislation, long excluded gender from its model legislation, referring only to crimes "where the victims are intentionally selected by reason of their actual or perceived race, color, religion, national origin, or sexual orientation" (ADL, 1994: 3). It was not until 1996 that the ADL added gender to its model legislation, "after coming to the conclusion that gender-based hate crimes could not be easily distinguished from other forms of hate motivated violence" (ADL, 1997: 3).

State legislators have followed the lead of the ADL. Like the ADL, states were slow to acknowledge the parallels between gender-motivated violence and other forms of bias crime. Consequently, by 1990, only seven states included gender in their hate crime provisions; by 1997, the number had grown to seventeen—still a minority. Most dramatically, the HCSA continues to pass over gender-motivated violence. It is tragically ironic, in fact, that the HCSA was passed—without the inclusion of gender—in the same year that Marc Lepine murdered fourteen female engineering students at Montreal's Ecole Polytechnique.

The exclusion of gender from hate crime protections occludes the nature and extent of gender-motivated violence daily perpetrated against women. It renders invisible and somehow less dramatic the violence experienced by women. It denies the reality that patterned abuse at the hands of a lover or father or stranger share a systemic grounding in the gendered hierarchy: "The exclusion of sex-hate as a form of hate violence is not only a profound denial of the most pervasive form of violence in the United States, but an attempt to deny the reality of patriarchal/sexist oppression" (Sheffield, 1995: 439).

By leaving gender out of the hate crime equation, legislators are re-creating the myth that gendered violence is an individual and privatized form of violence, unequal to the public and political harm suffered by racial or religious minorities, for example. This interpretation portrays women as less needy of legislative redress, since they are seen as individual rather than collective victims. Yet as demonstrated in chapter 4, oftentimes the violence experienced by women is conditioned by broader cultural and political patterns of gender inequality, not simply the dynamics of a particular relationship.

Consequently, in concrete material terms, the silence of hate crime legislation on the question of gender "renders any act or threat designed to intimidate, harass, cause fear, or use force against a woman based on hostility or underlying misogynistic feeling invisible and beyond the scope of redress provided by hate crime penalties" (Miller, 1994: 230). Women persecuted because of their gender are unable to turn to the law for legal protection. In spite of the generalizability of their experiences, they do not have the same recourse to the civil or criminal prosecution of offenders motivated by misogyny, as opposed to racism or anti-Semitism, for example. Nor do they have access to the symbolic power implied in hate crime legislation. They cannot make the claim to victim status in this context. As with gay men and lesbians, women are left with no legitimate voice with which to proclaim their victimization. If, as Wolfe and Copeland contend, legislation that effectively punishes hate crime declares that hate motivation will not be tolerated, then the converse is also true: legislation that fails to punish the violence perpetrated against particular groups declares that it will be tolerated (1994: 204). Moreover, "failing to recognize some crimes against women as the bias crimes they are only perpetuates the pathology that gives rise to the crime" (Nestelrode, 1995: 21).

As a corrective to this situation, Senator Biden first proposed the Violence Against Women Act (VAWA) in 1990. Signed into law in 1994, the act does in fact equate violence against women with other forms of hate crime. It recognizes that women are victimized and terrorized for no other reason than that they are women. Such an acknowledgment has broad symbolic appeal. Moreover, it is accompanied by mechanisms intended to punish offenders and protect and support the victims. Yet to embed violence against women within a discrete piece of legislation is to perpetuate the myth that such violence is somehow different from other forms of hate-motivated violence. In spite of best intentions, VAWA sets women separate and apart from other victims experiencing similar violence on the basis of their identities. It therefore disguises the shared patterns of systemic discrimination and violence.

POLICING DIFFERENCE:
LAW ENFORCEMENT VIOLENCE AND THE OTHER
The legal exclusion and marginalization of the Other through law and social policy leaves its subjects vulnerable to other forms of social and physical violence at the hands of agents of the state. Law enforcement agents enact the power of law—and its identity-making capacities— through their actions on Others. State personnel construct identity through ongoing practices that institutionalize specific and normative forms of gender and race. In particular, they engage in "derivative deviance," or violence perpetrated on the marked Others who are "presumed unable to avail themselves of civil protection" (Harry, cited in Berrill and Herek, 1992: 290). In other words, the state itself acts as a victimizer, thereby validating the persecution of gender and racial minorities through its example.

POLICING GENDER AND SEXUALITY
As the professional embodiment of masculinity, law enforcement agencies are crucial sites for reconstructing gender and the attendant boundaries between masculinity and femininity, between heterosexuality and homosexuality. Consequently, it is important to examine the institution of law enforcement as an arena in which male police officers, in particular, construct their own hegemonic masculinity, while reaffirming the subordinate and marginal status of women and homosexuals. In this way, they in fact facilitate the re-creation of gendered boundaries that contribute to broader social practices of ethnoviolence. In short, "the police have the

capacity to regulate gendered power relations as a whole, while in the process of constructing gender themselves" (Messerschmidt, 1993: 176). In what follows, I emphasize how sexual harassment and "gay bashing" within police organizations reconstitute masculine power and normative heterosexuality, thereby supplementing and legitimating similar activities of civilian perpetrators of hate crime.

Police work embodies the ideals of aggressive masculinity: toughness, bravery, strength. Consequently, women are deemed unfit for such work, "since traditionally they are viewed as weak, indecisive, emotionally unstable and timid" (Erez and Tontodonato, 1992: 241). When women enter the world of law enforcement, the masculinity of the role becomes questionable. Susan Martin's work has aptly demonstrated the threat posed to men's status and self-image as women increasingly enter the traditional male stronghold of policing. Some males may choose to enforce their masculinity and their power by subordinating women. Sexual harassment within the police force is one resource for this work of doing gender. It allows men to reassert the gendered and sexualized distinction between men and women.

Sexual harassment offers some form of protection against the perceived threat of the "feminization" of policing. Masculine solidarity is reinforced by patterns of behavior that "superimpose their sexual identities and male status superiority on coworker equality" (Martin, 1992: 295). Men distance themselves from women by emphasizing the sexuality of the latter through offensive sexual jokes and innuendo, references to women's physical appearance, groping women, and making sexual advances. Gratch (1995: 57) recounts a case in Oklahoma: "the hostile work environment was established when officers told obscene jokes, posted pornographic photographs with a female officer's name on them, wrote derogatory comments and epithets next to her name on the posted work and leave schedules, and filed false misconduct claims" (1995: 57). Such behavior accomplishes gender work in three ways: it asserts the "healthy" heterosexuality of the male offenders, thereby affirming that they are in fact "real men," while subsequently castigating women for having stepped outside their appropriate gender boundaries.

Women who enter policing are perceived to be violating the code of "femininity." A police academy training officer is reported to have told a female recruit that "this is my personal opinion; I don't think you should be in this job. You should go home and have babies" (Wexler and Lojan, 1983: 50). This sentiment is shared by another male officer who asserted that "a woman can't be refined and be a police officer too. Women give up some of their femininity to work this job" (Martin, 1992: 294). There is some "essence" assigned to women that demands adherence to a very narrow conception of how femininity is to be enacted— and engagement in policing is not part of it. Rosabeth Kanter's (1977) work in organizational cultures has relevance here. Women are held to be accountable to three primary modes of femininity: mother, sex object, kid sister. Should they refuse any of these, and adopt alternative gendered identities, they are assigned the identity of "iron maiden" and thus denigrated and harassed.

In response, women police officers attempt to reconstruct their femininity. Susan Martin (1992) draws an interesting distinction between police*women* and *police*women as a means of characterizing the different femininities female police officers typically enact. Police*women* attempt to maintain accountability to traditional femininity "by acquiescing to stereotypic feminine roles and seeking sex-typed assignments" (Martin, 1992: 293). These women re-create traditional femininity within the masculine field by engaging in "women's work" (domestic violence cases and juvenile offenders, for example) and by exploiting their own sexuality.

In contrast, *police*women construct something of an oppositional femininity by which they assert traits associated with the police culture: aggression, professionalism, and toughness, for example (Martin, 1992). However, this too is often met with further harassment and defamation ("dyke," "bitch"). Rather than interpret this as femininity, male officers fear that such a construction of identity by a woman further erodes the boundaries between men and women.

The consequence of these adaptive constructions of gender on the part of male officers is that the differences between men and women are forcibly reaffirmed. Specifically, the harassment "consistently create(s) and maintain(s) gender differences that reproduce the gender divisions of labor, gendered power, and normative sexuality" (Messerschmidt, 1993: 182). Moreover, these patterns parallel those of other perpetrators of hate crime. The violent subordination of women thus is condoned, if only implicitly, by deed rather than by word. When they, too, derogate, harass, and sexually assault women, police lend validity to the predatory victimization of women. They confirm the "essential" weaknesses and inferiorities that are assumed to be associated with femininity. In this sense, then, the state is complicit in perpetuating violence against women rather than constraining such activity.

Just as police regulate the gendered relations of power between men and women so too do they regulate the gendered relations of power between men. This too reflects the rigidly held perceptions that policing is a "hypermasculine" profession, which must purge itself and society at large of the challenges posed by alternative masculinities, and homosexuality in particular. In this context, "homosexuality would appear to represent part of the societal disorder that the police officer has dedicated his or her life to eradicating" (Burke, 1994: 193). Consequently, rather than defending gay men and lesbians against hate crime, too often police officers themselves are perpetrators. Berrill's (1992) summary of hate crime victims reveals that, on average, 20 percent of gay men and lesbians report victimization at the hands of police and that a significant proportion of reported violence against gays is perpetrated by police (see also Comstock, 1991; NGLTF, 1993, 1994, 1995, 1996, 1997).

The most visible incidents of police efforts to regulate and contain homosexuality historically have been the harassment and raids on gay establishments: bars, bathhouses, and parks, for example. In his assessment of police harassment of gays and lesbians in New York City, Rosen (1992: 161) defines the term as

> active police conduct for reasons unrelated to individual or public safety, directed at persons believed by police to be homosexual, which has the effect of annoying, impeding, embarrassing, injuring, threatening, or intimidating such persons. (1992: 161)

This definition is very much in line with the guiding definition of ethnoviolence adopted in this volume: violence intended to marginalize through behavior which is threatening or intimidating. Police persecution of gay establishments facilitates their further stigmatization.

The most infamous of such campaigns was the series of raids on bars and baths throughout New York City, and especially in Greenwich Village, in the late 1960s. Inspired by Mayor Lindsay's admonition to rid New York City of "honky tonks, promenading perverts . . . homosexuals and prostitutes," the New York Police Department mounted a sweep of gay businesses. Their activities frequently included false charges, verbal harassment, and beatings (Comstock, 1991; Rosen, 1992). Ironically, the raids, culminating with the Stonewall Rebellion of 1969, had the unintended consequence of mobilizing gay activism against such harassment and oppression nationwide. However, to every action there is a reaction. Increased activism was met by different forms of persecution. Gay organizations and events have been targeted so that throughout the 1970s and 1980s and to this day, police have attacked numerous demonstrations and meetings celebrating gay pride. In 1991, for example, police apparently provoked a confrontation with demonstrators protesting against Governor Wilson's veto of a gay rights bill: "Multiple arrests were made and numerous injuries resulted. Protesters were subject to beatings and anti-gay slurs" (Burkhe, 1996: 6). So persistent and demoralizing were the assaults on a New York City chapter of the Daughters of Bilitis that the organization ultimately folded (Rosen, 1992). In that particular case, police were tangibly successful in "managing" out of existence an activist lesbian association.

Individualized acts of police violence perform the same functions at a more localized level. While harassment or assaults are intended to remind their victims of their subordinate "place," such acts also serve to validate the normative heterosexuality of the officers to the audience of their peers. A lesbian officer in Washington, D.C., observed, "The guys were kind of macho when you got them together. . . . Together, they have this macho crap going on. I'd hear them talk once in a while, and I'd hear derogatory comments like 'Faggot'" (in Burkhe, 1996: 55). It is not uncommon for verbal slurs to escalate into physical violence, as occurred in a recent case in Minneapolis. A group of police officers called a young cross-dressed man a "fag" and then beat him with clubs as the man tried to break up a fight. The victim, who required medical attention, was charged with disorderly conduct. Adding insult to injury, the officers threatened to charge him with "falsely impersonating a woman" (NGLTF, 1995: A–7). In this example, it is evident that the officers were intent on "policing" the boundaries of sexuality and gender simultaneously. Like their civilian counterparts, they engage in violence as a display of their own aggressive heterosexuality, as well as a display of the victim's subordinate and deviant performance of gender. Police thus frequently use their position to enforce the rigid hierarchies that marginalize non-heterosexuals. Gay men and lesbians who forget "their place" are forcibly reinserted into the lower reaches of the "natural" order. Again this leaves them vulnerable to public violence, since they have been "officially" designated as valid and legitimate victims of animosity and violence. By their violent actions, police officers provide imitable models for the enforcement of gender boundaries.

Moreover, police officers set the stage for anti-gay ethnoviolence by acts of omission, or failure to act on behalf of gay victims. Anti-gay violence is explicitly condoned when police fail to investigate or lay charges when victims report assaults motivated by anti-gay bias. A New York City executive reported:

> I was attacked by two kids while walking alone in the Ramble last month. Miraculously, I found a patrolman and told him what had happened, as blood streamed down my cheek from a cut over my left eye. You know what he said? "Serves you right, faggot." (cited in Rosen, 1992: 187)

An even more blatant act of police advocacy occurred during a Gay Activists Alliance dinner at which many activists were attacked by attendees. One witness testified that in the presence of a police officer,

> he saw Maye "grind his heel" into Manford's groin "four or five times." Another witness saw Maye lift and shake one of the victims. The *New York Times* reported that witness's reaction. "He said he was 'shocked' that the police had 'adamantly refused to take any action whatsoever, loudly proclaiming their protective feelings for Mr. Maye.'" (Rosen, 1992: 179)

While the assailant symbolically castrated the "sexual deviant," the officers stood by, not just in mute compliance but in vocal support.

It is little wonder, in light of police action and inaction, that gay victims of hate crime are reluctant to report victimization. Typically, less than 20 percent of such victimizations are ever reported to police, largely because the victims anticipate some form of secondary victimization (Berrill and Herek, 1992; Comstock, 1991; Dean, Wu, and Martin, 1992). As shown above, this might take the form of hostility, further abuse, or inaction. This disempowers victims. They perceive themselves to be without legal redress. Conversely, it empowers perpetrators, by signifying the validity and acceptability of their actions. Police abuse and police neglect are enabling; they communicate to the public at large that, by virtue of their gender and sexual transgressions, gay men and lesbians forfeit civil protections. Like all women, then, gay men and lesbians are implicitly and explicitly designated "assailable" by agents of the law.

POLICING RACE

Many of the police patterns and mechanisms that regulate sexuality also are employed as a means of policing racial boundaries. Messerschmidt draws a similar comparison when he states that the repression of men of color, in particular,

> parallels the status of gay men, in the sense that such men represent subordinated masculinities. In this way, then, the police construct a white, heterosexual form of hegemonic masculinity through the authorized practice of controlling "deviant" behavior of "inferior" men. (1993: 184)

Law enforcement agents are often the "front line" in efforts to keep the racialized Other within the boundaries of cultural definitions applied to them. The exercise of aggressive masculinity on the part of white police officers sustains the cultural and institutional marginalization of men of color, in particular, as subordinate masculinities. Perhaps this is not surprising, in light of Herbert Williams and Patricia Murphy's (1990) observation that the modern U.S. police force emerged out of slave patrols. The legacy of this historical association is that police still carry out the role of keeping people of color "in their place."

The cultural myths that have come to signify people of color inform police violence against minorities. They provide the context within which law enforcement officers can rationalize their own relational enactment of white masculinity through brutal acts. Skin color alone marks the "other" as deviant, criminal, potentially violent. That race matters to police in their efforts to manage identity is apparent in an experience recounted by Cornel West:

Years ago, while driving from New York to teach at Williams College, I was stopped on fake charges of trafficking cocaine. I told the police officer I was a professor of religion, he replied, "Yeh, and I'm the Flying Nun. Let's go, nigger." (1994: xv)

There is no room for positive imagery of blacks when "black men, by their very existence, are valid suspects" (Watts, 1993: 241).

Judith Butler's (1993) examination of the Rodney King beating reveals the normativity of the assumption of black pathology. The black body is already and always inscribed as a threat to the safety and sanctity of whiteness. People of color may, at any time, cross the appropriate physical and social boundaries that otherwise insulate them from whites. This is where the police enter; they are situated as guardians of these borders, charged to "protect whiteness against violence, where violence is the imminent action of that black male body" (Butler, 1993: 18). Police violence is legitimate in this schema—it is a defensive act. Such violence is a safe display of both the "whiteness" and the "aggressive masculinity" of the perpetrator. While police violence against minorities recasts the latter in demonized terms, it attests to the perpetrators' solidarity with their white male peers.

Consequently, police violence is especially likely to occur where the victims have forgotten their "appropriate" place in the racial order. The loss of place may be geographical as well as social, hence the likelihood of police harassment of people of color in predominantly white neighborhoods. Minority women are not immune, either, as is evident in Laura Fishman's experiences:

> I was deemed suspicious enough to be stopped simply because I was a black woman. This form of police harassment always occurred whenever I walked in white, affluent neighborhoods. Not only was I rudely questioned about my purpose for walking in these neighborhoods, frequently I was required to give proof that I was not a prostitute, heroin addict or maniac. (1998: 116)

Police brutality is most likely in situations wherein minority individuals or communities are attempting to construct oppositional racial identities. These efforts challenge the marginal or subordinate position that has been assigned to them and that is expected of them. Ethnoviolence becomes a means to restore the balance.

On the street, these dynamics play themselves out in conflicts between police and minority individuals who assume an antagonistic or resistant stance. It is not surprising that in communities where minority youth are routinely stopped, searched, and questioned, for no reason other than the color of their skin, these same youth are hostile toward police. In an attempt to empower themselves relative to the uniformed force of white racism, they do away with the deference that is expected of them as members of subordinate races. The legacy of indifference, hostility, and brutality toward minority communities "breeds consequences. When any minority group experiences injustice at the hands of the dominant society, anger, frustration and agony are bred" (Boldt, 1993: 60). So, too, are the roots of resistance sown. Minority youth respond to the context of brutalization with attempts to gain both racial and gender recognition through challenging or confrontational behavior. On the one hand, such behavior serves notice to police that the individual in question does not accept his or her subordination. On the other hand, for males especially, it is a peer display of one's toughness, fearlessness, and solidarity. While this may gain respect from one's peers, it may enrage police officers who see resistance as a threat to their (racial) authority. Consequently, they believe that their use of force is justified in the interest of showing the "suspect" his "place." Rodney King's "resistance" to police apprehension, for example, was read as justification enough for his beating. So begins the deadly cycle in which racial politics gives rise to oppositional and reactionary confrontations. Each "side" is consumed with enacting a racial identity that is empowered and recognized.

Collective challenges to the authority of "whiteness" also are likely to elicit violence on the part of law enforcement agencies. This has been especially apparent since the emergence of the civil rights challenges of the 1960s and 1970s.

As minority legal oppression became increasingly unbearable, particularly when minority members were literally denied control of their own communities, many rebelled. The ensuing racial protests, or as they were viewed by the dominant majority, "riots," and their suppression led to a shocking series of brutal, violent and lawless acts by law enforcement representatives throughout the country. (Mann, 1993: 127)

The civil rights movements spearheaded by people of color initiated a series of challenges and reforms that tested the limits of the prevailing racial order. However, this profound insertion of difference into the currents of political and social life is not without resistance of its own. On the contrary, "strong opposition arose to confront the new-found assertiveness and proliferation of cultural difference that the movement had fostered" (Winant, 1997: 30). While much of the opposition and corresponding violence sprang from the grass-roots level, state law enforcement agents also played an integral role. Images of police "dispersing crowds" with fire hoses or tear gas are an indelible part of U.S. history. Missing and murdered civil rights workers—black, white, Jewish, Native American, and Latino—are also part of this legacy of resistance to civil rights advances. In 1967 alone, 83 people, mostly black, were killed, and hundreds more injured at the hands of police.

At the forefront of state harassment and violence against minorities throughout the 1960s and 1970s was the FBI's Counter Intelligence Program, COINTELPRO. This institutional policy was initiated in 1941, largely to eliminate communists. However, in the 1960s it was relaunched with the expanded mandate to disrupt and neutralize "dissident" groups, specifically, those of Native Americans, blacks, and Puerto Rican *independentistas* (Churchill, 1997; Messerschmidt, 1983; Churchill and VanderWall, 1990). A 1968 memorandum, for example, encouraged COINTELPRO agents to

> prevent the coalition of militant black nationalist groups . . .
> prevent militant black nationalist groups and leaders from
> gaining respectability . . . prevent the rise of a black "messiah"
> who could unify and electrify the militant black nationalist
> movement. Malcolm X might have been such a "messiah";
> he is the martyr of the movement today. (cited in Churchill
> and VanderWall, 1990: 58)

In short, COINTELPRO was designed to prevent or eliminate the construction of collective oppositional racial identities. With respect to black activists, this meant that the Black Panther Party and the Nation of Islam were singled out for special attention. Late in 1969, for example, agents broke into the home of Panther activist Fred Hampton, killed two members, and injured several others. This was typical of the COINTELPRO activities, with the result that "during the Nixon era, and during its adjunct Ford administration, hundreds of black organizers were murdered, destabilized or imprisoned. Nearly every case is now traceable to government intelligence sources and outright assassination and frame-ups. . . . The attack on Indian demonstrators and particularly on American Indian Movement activists was brutal and grisly, with a far greater ratio of deaths and imprisonments than any other movement" (Ortiz, 1981: 12).

As Roxanne Dunbar Ortiz reports, the American Indian Movement (AIM) was also a favored target of police repression. Organized to resist the allocation and exploitation of Native American lands, and in general the oppression of Native peoples, AIM was fated to be seen as a dissident group that threatened the racial order. Nowhere did the campaign turn more deadly than on the Pine Ridge Reservation in South Dakota. AIM took a leading role in challenging a proposed transfer of mineral-rich land back to the federal government. In response, local police departments, the FBI, and a tribal ranger group—the GOONsquad (Guardians of the Oglala Nation)—mustered massive resources and ammunition against the Native American organizers. In the end, dozens of Native Americans had been killed, hundreds more injured by gunfire, beatings, and cars forced off the road (Messerschmidt, 1983). This contemporary "Indian war" took a tremendous toll:

> Even if only documented political deaths are counted, the yearly murder rate on the Pine Ridge Reservation between 1 March 1973 and 1 March 1976 was 170 per 100,000. By comparison, Detroit, the reputed "murder capital of the United States," had a rate of 20.2 per 100,000 in 1974. The U.S. average was 9.7 per 100,000. (Johnson and Maestas, 1979: 83–84).

What these patterns of police brutality illustrate is that violence is an appropriate means with which to confront counterhegemonic racial mobilization. When blacks or Native Americans or Puerto Ricans organize to upset the racial balance, it is acceptable to put them back in their place quite forcibly. Those who cross the political, social, or cultural boundaries are legitimate victims of racial violence. So, too, are those who cross geographic boundaries. Those who "don't belong" are subject to the coercive actions of law enforcement agents, in a way that parallels the localized "move-in" violence perpetrated by other offenders.

Consequently, border violence, wherein legal and illegal immigrants are victimized by vigilantes and by Border Patrol agents alike, has reached an alarming rate. Undocumented immigrants are at a heightened risk of victimization and revictimization because of their particular fears of reporting abuses by civilians and state agents. INS and Border Patrol agents have a job to do: stop illegal border crossings. However, buoyed by a climate of anti-immigrant hostility, officials can be overzealous in their policing of the border. Excessive use of force and unwarranted abuses do occur. A report issued by the American Friends Service Committee of Los Angeles documented fifty-five incidents of brutality and misconduct by INS agents (a mere fraction of what is suspected), one of which ended in death. Of these, ten of the complainants were U.S. citizens, twenty-seven were legal residents or visitors (Southern Poverty Law Center, 1997f). An America's Watch report documents several such cases, including that of Francisco Ruiz and his pregnant wife, Evelyn. When Ruiz attempted to protect his wife from an attack by a Border Patrol agent (which included him pressing his foot on her abdomen), he was shot once in the stomach and once in the buttock (Nuñez, 1992: 1574–1575).

The border violence experienced by Mexican immigrants in particular is an extension of the broader sense—noted above—that the United States is in the midst of an "immigration crisis," that the nation has lost control of the flow of disruptive newcomers. All too often, reports of misconduct are thus met with official indifference, if not support.

An important basis for the apparent failures of law enforcement to protect the rights of the Other often can be traced to the connection between state agencies and white supremacist organizations. The investigation that followed the taped beating of Rodney King revealed extensive organized white supremacist activity within the rolls of police agencies. These findings were symptomatic of a broader national trend that reveals intimate links between state actors and groups explicitly organized to target those designated as the Other. The pattern holds throughout the apparatuses of the state: within law enforcement agencies, the military, corrections, and within the ranks of political parties and leaders. Hate activists have inserted themselves into the official layers of the state bureaucracies, thereby enhancing their ability to shape public policy and to engage in ethnoviolence with relative impunity. Many of the politicians cited earlier in the discussion of political rhetoric, for example, have documented ties with white supremacist groups. This was argued explicitly in chapter 6. Consequently, agents of the state carry with them into the political or legal realm the ideologies and practices associated with the hate groups—ideologies that legitimate ethnoviolence, practices that include ethnoviolence.

The demographics and ideologies of police and white supremacist groups are strikingly similar. Both are predominantly white male institutions; both are committed to maintaining the established order. In short, the two entities share

> the "us" against "them" mentality which . . . makes the police susceptible to white supremacist preachings. The police . . . carry out a commitment to suppress threats to the hierarchy of the state and society which leaves Black people and other people of color at the bottom. (Novick, 1995: 83)

Certainly the links are not as intimate or as extensive as in the past, when local sheriffs and their deputies were often Klan members. Nonetheless, monitoring organizations like the ADL and SPLC's Klanwatch have documented a tendency for white supremacist cells and individuals to once again emerge inside police departments. Moreover, these activists are doing more than spreading the message. They are acting out their ideologies in violent ways. They assault colleagues and citizens alike in their efforts to reconstruct a "white man's world," or as Omi and Winant (1994) put it, to rearticulate whiteness.

In its least extreme manifestation, the relationship between law enforcement and the white supremacist movement has been passive, in the sense that law enforcement officers fail to act against those organizations. This even has been the case where police, including FBI agents, have infiltrated white supremacist organizations (Churchill and

VanderWall, 1990; Novick, 1995). A particularly dramatic case occurred in Greensboro, North Carolina, in 1979. Five members of the Communist Workers Party (CWP) were killed at an anti-Klan rally by Klan members. What makes the case even more significant is the role played by ATF and FBI agents. It is believed that the names of the CWP members to be shot were provided by an ATF agent, and that "the hit squad itself seems to have been recruited, organized and led on its lethal mission by an FBI infiltrator" (Churchill and Vander Wall, 1990: 181).

In recent years, police complicity with white supremacist activities also has taken the form of implicit or explicit support for Klan rallies and similar gatherings. This is manifest in a variety of ways: failure to police such rallies; off-duty police providing security for the rallies; police cordoning of Klan parades and activities; and, at the extreme, the forcible suppression of anti-Klan demonstrators. Across the country, law enforcement agents have made their sympathies apparent by aiming their brutality at those resisting white supremacist activity. Given the tendency for the Klan or Aryan Nations rallies, for example, to lead to violence, this failure to prevent Klan activities is ultimately enabling. It clears the way for hate groups to engage in cross burnings, harassment, and assaults with little fear of police reprisals.

Some officers of the state are so much in agreement with the ideologies of the supremacists that they become members themselves. Some—threatened by change and by difference—see this as an active means by which to recover the hegemonic place of white, heterosexual males. Their joint status as part of the repressive arm of the state and as a white supremacist provides affirmation—to them and to their peers—that they are true American patriots, ready to engage in violence in order to stem the tide of civil rights advances for minorities. Consequently, these officers are as likely to engage in violence themselves as they are to condone the ethnoviolence engaged in by others. Consider the following examples of white supremacist activity within law enforcement and military operations:

- 1979, U.S.S. Concord, America, and Independence — Klans of the Invisible Empire are active on all three ships, as evidenced by cross burnings, white robes, and racial attacks.
- 1983, Richmond, California—The white supremacist group Cowboys operating in the police department is exposed when two of its members are involved in the murders of two black men.
- 1985, Louisville, Kentucky—A fifteen–year veteran of the Jefferson County Police Department is revealed as a long-term Klansman who had used police computer files to assist Klan activity. He also revealed the identities of other members of COPS—Confederate Officers Patriot Squad—within the police department.
- 1986, St. Paul's, North Caroline—Marines from Camp Lejeune

and soldiers from Ft. Bragg engage in paramilitary training with the KKK and White Patriot Party.
- 1990, Cambridge, Massachusetts—A technical sergeant in the Army National Guard is arrested with 500 weapons, 500,000 rounds of ammunition, an anti-tank gun, a rocket launcher, a swastika poster, and other Nazi propaganda.
- 1992, Boynton Beach, Florida—A police officer is fired for flashing a swastika tattoo at a Jewish officer. He defends himself by arguing that racism and white supremacy are prevalent and accepted in the police department.

Given that these agents carry both arms and ideologies of hate, they pose the same threat as the civilian white supremacists. They contribute to a climate in which intolerance and its concomitant violence are normalized. Moreover, they pose a very real physical threat, as evidenced from the above examples. These are the very people entrusted with the "equal protection" of all people. Yet, in light of their white supremacist affiliations, and their racist and homophobic activities, it is apparent that they are failing in this.

The identity politics addressed herein are contested terrain. The "hatemongers" like Lamm or Duke touch the nerves of a threatened populace. Yet their rhetoric has not gone unchallenged. There are also those within the state who seek to reverse the trends toward intolerance. This is the impetus behind Rev. Jesse Jackson's Rainbow politics, for example, or President Clinton's call for a national dialogue on race. However, as Clinton's critics have been quick to point out, symbolic gestures must be accompanied by practical policies that empower minorities so that they are in a position to speak back to their detractors in such a way that their multiple identities—not the stereotypes—are recognized and valued. As I argue in the following chapter, the agenda for change will require the collective engagement in a positive politics of difference that combines short-term responses as well as long-term transformative practices which disrupt institutionalized structures of inequality.

| EIGHT | Conclusion: Doing Difference Differently |

You may shoot me with your words,
You may cut me with your eyes,
You may kill me with your hatefulness,
But still, like air, I'll rise.

—Maya Angelou, *Still I Rise*

I wrote at the outset that the end of the twentieth century was much like its beginning—steeped in racism, bigotry, and violence. Yet something on the landscape has changed by the close of the century. That is, there is strong evidence of unprecedented and committed resistance to ethnoviolence. The communities bearing the brunt of hate-motivated crime have not been passive victims of the varied forms of violence they experienced. On the contrary, many have been very active in asserting the legitimacy of their identities, challenging heterosexism, patriarchy, racism, and bigotry, and resisting the cultural and individual forms of violence to which they are subjected.

From the perspective of this text, it is not surprising that such challenges have emerged in response to hate crime. As I noted in chapter 2, hegemonic formations are subject to ongoing crisis tendencies that open up space for counterhegemonic strategies. In other words, hegemony implies its own potential demise, since any hegemonic formation is subject to strain, resistance, and transformation. It is a process of struggle. It is in this space that campaigns against the negative and violent politics of difference must be waged in order to transform current patterns into a positive politics of difference. The perceived threats to which hate crimes are a response are themselves indicative of the crisis tendencies that constantly throw the hegemonic order into question.

Civil rights movements, wage and employment gains, political empowerment—all these and more represent the thin end of the wedge that holds the potential for further rending the fabric of a racist, sexist culture. I remain optimistic that the structures and images underlying hate crime can be mitigated through a positive politics of difference.

Writing of anti-gay violence, for example, David Wertheimer (1992), Gregory Herek (1992b), and Kevin Berrill and Herek (1992) all point to institutional and policy-oriented ways in which gay bashing can be challenged. Barry Adam (1992) and Michael Nava and Robert Dawidoff (1994) call for education and publicity, leading to enhanced tolerance, as solutions to homophobia. Levin and McDevitt (1993) and the ADL tend to emphasize the role of legislation in combating hate crime generally. While all of these responses are valuable and perhaps useful in the short term, they lack the transformative capacity that would release us all from the chains of bigotry. Connell (1992), on the other hand, refers to the "practical politics" of difference, which includes educational and institutional initiatives, as well as deeper structural changes that are intended to begin breaking down the hierarchical and dichotomous structures of difference. In what follows, then, I offer an array of strategies that may combine to remove the boundaries which separate "us" from "them." Until we are able, as culture, to celebrate difference rather than denigrate it, until we dismantle those boundaries, we will continue to force people into rigid categories of male/female, straight/gay, white/not-white, normal/deviant—often through violence. What we seek to create through these long- and short-term initiatives is a culture in which we are not forced to "choose" an identity on the basis of reified and privileged categories. However, "the goal should not be to transcend race," or difference in general, but "to transcend the biased meanings associated with" difference (Dyson, 1991). In other words, we must begin to think of and enact difference differently.

RECLAIMING THE STATE: PUBLIC POLICY AND SOCIAL JUSTICE

It would be anomalous to argue here that the state will be a major player in reconstituting difference in positive terms. As I argued in chapter 7, the state is itself deeply implicated in the politics of difference, and not usually in progressive ways. In light of the exclusionary rhetoric and practices highlighted throughout that chapter, it is evident that actual and potential victims cannot always count on the state to defend them from bias-motivated violence. It is in the context of a perceptibly racialized and gendered state that those public attitudes and actions emerge. The rhetors of the state reinforce and often create images of the Other that portray them as deviant or menacing; moreover, state policy often leaves the Others outside the protections afforded "us." Thus, it is imperative that alternative voices and images be disseminated. It is vital that civil rights organizations like the NGLTF and the ADL continue to expose and raise their voices against those who would demonize the nation's minorities. If political rhetoric fuels the flames of hatred, then it is also clear that a positive politics of difference expressed at the level of the state can temper, if not extinguish, those flames.

First and foremost, politicians must assume a leadership role in condemning rather than embracing organized hate groups. Winant (1994) argues for a politics of *left-wing populism* as an antidote to the spread of the hate movement's right-wing populism. Such an initiative would call for an ethical commitment to social justice grounded in justice rather than injustice, inclusion rather than exclusion, respect for rather than resentment of difference. Just as the hate movement has piggy-backed on the reactionary politics of the Republican Party, so too might a progressive movement exploit the windows opening up within the Democratic Party: Reagan has his counterpart in Clinton, David Duke in Jesse Jackson. While recognizing the inherent limitations of Clinton's agenda, Michael Eric Dyson acknowledges that

> it's infinitely better than shooting or stabbing or killing one another. It's better than black men killing each other in the streets of Detroit or Chicago. It's better than black people being beaten and killed by white policemen in New York or Los Angeles. It's better than Latinas being victimized by the ideology and institutional expressions of anti-immigrant sentiment. Conversation certainly is superior to destroying one another and our nation.
> (Dyson, interview with Chennault, 1998: 312).

Giving oppressed communities an opportunity to have a voice in such conversations is a first step in realizing social justice. As defined by Kerchis and Young (1995) and by Anna Coote (1998), social justice revolves around participation and democratic representation in the home, the workplace, and in political arenas. It involves "the realization of institutions that allow all people to develop and exercise their capacities, express their experiences, and participate in determining their actions and the conditions of their actions" (Kerchis and Young, 1995: 16). In other words, social justice consists of the ability to "do difference" without fear of violent reprisal. It frees women to make household decisions without fear of being beaten; it frees people of color to pass through or live in any neighborhood without fear of attack; it frees gay men and lesbians to demand equal treatment and recognition without fear of violence.

In a just society, difference would not be the foundation of criminalization, marginalization, or victimization. On the contrary, difference would be the foundation of inclusion and equity in all areas of social life. This reconstruction will require that all of those means of bridging difference discussed throughout this chapter be embedded in social, economic, and cultural practices that empower rather than disempower difference. Coincident with social action for reform of legislation, education, and victim services, we also have a responsibility to work toward social change which mitigates the negative effects of difference. Access to adequate housing and medical care, education, full-time employment, income support, child care, and other crucial social services should be acknowledged as the inalienable rights of all rather than the privilege of a few. Ultimately, "the goal should be to make sure that every child, whoever his or her parents and whatever their race or class, has a reasonable chance to live a satisfying, productive and law-abiding life" (Tonry, 1995: 208). Only then can we say that this is a truly just society in which difference is not denigrated.

Recognition of social and economic rights also need to be accompanied by efforts to include and integrate difference into our cultural repertoire. The values and practices of alternate cultures must be recognized for what they contribute:

> Black Americans find in their traditional communities, which refer to their members as "brother" and "sister," a sense of solidarity absent from the calculating individualism of white, professional, capitalist society. Feminists find in the traditional female values of nurturing a challenge to a militarist world-view, and lesbians find in their relationships a confrontation with the assumptions of complementary gender roles in sexual relationships. From their experience of a culture tied to the land, American Indians formulate a critique of the instrumental rationality of European culture that results in pollution and environmental destruction. (Young, 1990: 205)

LAW AS A MECHANISM OF EMPOWERMENT

An important first step in empowering Others is to interrogate the role of the legal structure in perpetuating unequal relations of power. As noted in chapter 7, the law itself effectively can exclude or restrict the participation of particular groups in the ongoing activities and processes of society—just as immigration and naturalization law historically have prevented many Asians from entry, or from attaining citizenship. Law can—by its silences—exclude groups from protections afforded others, such as in the failure to include gays or women in hate crime or civil rights legislation. Law can also marginalize and stigmatize others. Law is implicated in the shaping and valuing of difference. It is an integral part of the field in which difference is constructed and reaffirmed, an integral mechanism by which the boundaries between Us and Them are policed.

However, the law is not an immutable behemoth. It is vulnerable to the impact of ongoing struggles between groups. It is itself a site at which raced and gendered relations of power are enacted. Recent reversals on issues such as affirmative action and bilingual education are evidence of its limitations. Nonetheless, law has been used effectively to extend the rights and protections afforded women, people of color, gays, and ethnic and religious minorities. The Violence Against Women Act has dramatically expanded the protections and services available to battered women. Successive Civil Rights Acts—nationally and at the state level—have been crucial to the recent political and economic advances of people of color in particular. It is not unreasonable, then, to consider legislative reform as a means of addressing the negative and exclusionary effects of difference. Consequently, a useful starting point would be the elimination of the types of exclusionary legislation illustrated by the discussion in chapter 7. For example, as long as the sexuality of gay men and women continues to be criminalized, they will be beyond the protection of the criminal justice system. Thus, the primary mechanism for eliminating legal and, indirectly, illegal victimization of gay people will be to decriminalize sodomy, same-sex solicitation, and same-sex sexual activities. However, this will not occur in a vacuum, but within the context of broader initiatives intended to ensure the realization of the civil and legal rights of all people. Coincident with the elimination of discriminatory legislation, then, is the need for inclusive legislation addressing hate crime specifically.

This is the traditional response to the emergence of social problems in the United States—to provide a statute to manage the perceived crisis. And there may be some symbolic value to opting for legislation as a means of responding to ethnoviolence. Just as hate crime is an expressive act, so too is hate crime legislation. It sends a message to its intended audience(s) about what is to be tolerated.

However, hate crime legislation is not without serious limitations. As I argued in chapter 7, there are significant disparities in hate crime legislation (see Appendix I). Foremost among these are inconsistencies in protected classes. Where traditionally oppressed groups are excluded from the legislation—as is often the case with women and gay men and lesbians—the implication is that they are not worthy of the same protections afforded racial minorities. Moreover, the groups that are protected vary dramatically across jurisdictions, so that there is no shared national vision of whom should be extended the protections of the law. In a similar vein, the nature of hate crime legislation is itself disparate. At the federal level, hate crime may be confronted through the Hate Crime Statistics Act, the Hate Crime Sentencing Enhancement Act, the Violence Against Women Act, the Hate Crimes Prevention Act, the Church Arsons Prevention Act, or the Civil Rights Act. At the state level, some jurisdictions address bias-motivated violence and intimidation, some account for institutional vandalism, and some allow for penalty enhancement for bias-motivated crime. However, the states are by no means consistent in their inclusion or invocation of such criminal legislation.

The ambiguity of the law is apparent in the latter case. On the one hand, the lack of consistency in defining and responding to hate crime by statute prohibits a coherent vision of the problem. On the other hand, the fact that there are multiple jurisdictions and multiple actions available may in fact work to the advantage of victims. Where criminal law fails, civil injunctions invoking the language of rights are readily available at the federal level, if not the state level. Rights claims can be powerfully transformative discourses, since

> they articulate a vision of entitlements, of how things might be, which in turn has the capacity to advance political aspiration and action. . . . Whilst rights-in-isolation may be of limited utility, rights as a significant component of counter-hegemonic strategies provide a potentially fruitful approach to the prosecution of transformatory political practice. (Hunt, 1990: 18)

Hunt's final point is the crux: while law can be and has been used effectively to advance the place and protections afforded long-disadvantaged groups, its limitations mean that law alone is an insufficient field of discourse.

This may be especially relevant in the context of hate crime legislation, which is, ironically, a point of convergence for both progressive and reactionary forces. Terry Maroney (1998) identifies hate crime legislation as a tool of appeasement for minority communities that has few political drawbacks. Like Valerie Jenness and Kendal Broad (1998), Maroney acknowledges that the hate crime movement arose out of the successes and rhetoric of the civil rights and victims' rights movements. While the former clearly corresponds with liberal politics, the latter is closely aligned with conservative "get tough" crime policies. Consequently, hate crime legislation is a curious blend of progressive and conservative sentiment. It cleverly embeds both a "caring" approach with respect to crime victims, as well as a punitive approach to perpetrators. In short, argues Maroney, anti–hate crime measures have been institutionalized in such a way as to abrogate protection of minority victims to the very state authorities that have so frequently and so long contributed to their subordination:

The fact that anti-hate measures have been assimilated so easily into the very criminal justice system they seek to challenge indicates that they fit squarely within its dominant ideology. This raises questions about those measures' capacity for changing that system. (Maroney, 1998: 597)

An immediate question that arises is that of the role of police in invoking hate crime legislation. As noted in chapter 7, police officers themselves are frequent perpetrators of violence and brutality against people of color, gay men, and lesbians. In addition to outright bias, many officers remain insensitive or poorly trained—either of which can contribute to inadequate enforcement of hate crime measures. Add to that, prosecutorial reluctance to proceed with hate crime charges, and the limitations of hate crime legislation are readily apparent (Maroney, 1998; Hernandez, 1990; Padgett, 1984). Consequently, it is vital that legislative initiatives be embedded in a broadly based politics of difference that operates at multiple levels, in multiple sites.

ANTIPREJUDICE/ANTIVIOLENCE PROGRAMMING

The legal regulation of difference is shaped by broader social and cultural perceptions of difference. Across the country, we have seen time and again how the Other is demonized, and subsequently victimized. Stereotypes of the "promiscuous woman," for example, consistently have served to enable violence against women, just as stereotypes of gay men as pedophiles have consistently served to enable violence against them. In each of these cases, the stereotypes disempower those who are different, since their difference is assumed to be immutable and deviant. Consequently, one key to empowerment is to eliminate the discriminatory and/or privileging effects of difference.

Equally important, however, is the need to (re)connect diverse communities as a means of reducing hate crime, in particular. If this divisive form of violence is to be minimized, differences between groups must also be bridged. It is not enough to provide services for the victims of such hostility. The other side of the equation also must be addressed, so that the pool of offenders is reduced through treatment and prevention strategies. As a condition of probation, some judges across the country have attempted to prevent secondary offenses by helping the offender to see the humanity of the victim's community. This often is accomplished by requiring that the offender engage in community service with the victim community: an anti-Semite might work with the ADL; a gay-basher may work with a local gay and lesbian advocacy group (Levin and McDevitt, 1993).

As a means of preventing hate crime, antiprejudice and antiviolence projects have begun to spring up across the country, especially in elementary and secondary schools. This is an initiative that federal, state, and local governments must continue to support through promotional and funding activities. For example, the Office of Juvenile Justice and Delinquency Prevention (OJJDP) sponsored the development of a Healing the Hate curriculum directed toward youthful hate crime offenders. Similarly, the Department of Education is mandated by the Safe and Drug Free Schools and Communities initiative to support the development of hate crime prevention curricula, as well as training programs for teachers and administrators. Together, the OJJDP and the Department of Justice fund the National Center for Hate Crime Prevention. Working in partnership with such agencies as the ADL, the Center for Democratic Renewal, and the International Association of Chiefs of Police, the Center is dedicated to interventions for youth, in particular. The Center provides training, workshops, technical support, interventions, and information for youth, practitioners, and communities.

The ADL has worked closely with local and national educators. In fact, it was a federal Safe and Drug Free Schools grant that allowed the creation of the ADL's Stop the Hate program, which by now has been adopted by hundreds of schools nationwide. This is a multidimensional antibias program that offers peer training to secondary school students. Additionally, recognizing the extent to which hate crime is shaped by broader community sentiment, Stop the Hate extends diversity training not only to teachers and school administrators, but also to parents and the community. The SPLC—another partner in antibias programming—has developed a similarly impressive model through its Teaching Tolerance project. This preventive initiative assists educators in designing curricula that encourage students to recognize, understand, and value difference.

To generalize on the content and structure of antiviolence curricula is a difficult task. However, a recent manual jointly published by the Department of Education and the Department of Justice (n.d.)—Preventing Youth Hate Crime—identifies seven elements of effective school-based hate prevention programs. The criteria address an array of issues, from the identification and measurement of hate crime in every school to potential responses to hate crime offenders. The emphasis, however, is placed on educational initiatives that attempt to disrupt the boundaries that separate Us from Them. Specifically, the stated elements are:

1. Provide hate prevention training to all staff.
2. Ensure that all students receive hate prevention training through age-appropriate school-based activities.
3. Develop partnerships with families, community organizations, and law enforcement agencies.

4. Develop a hate prevention policy to distribute to every student, every student's family, and every employee of the school district.

5. Develop a range of corrective actions for those who violate school hate prevention policies.

6. Collect and use data to focus districtwide hate prevention efforts.

7. Provide structured opportunities for integration.

It is to be hoped that such interventions break the connections between difference and intolerance, so that subsequent generations will be less vulnerable to the messages of hate propagated by both the mainstream and the hate movement. To the extent that educational activities—in the schools and in the community—are able to deconstruct damaging and divisive stereotypes, they will continue to be effective mechanisms by which to counteract prejudice and discrimination. While not all educators or students will be receptive to the alternative messages of tolerance, "for every school child and young adult that we can and do reach, we shall be influencing a world beyond our own." (Kleg, 1993: 260)

CRIMINAL JUSTICE IN THE INTERESTS OF SOCIAL JUSTICE

Brian Ogawa succinctly describes the quandary facing victims who have come in contact with the criminal justice system:

> All victims of crime are susceptible to being mistreated by uncaring, misinformed or antagonistic individuals and/or an overburdened, ponderous and jaded criminal justice system. These are insensitivities or injustices that victims of every race and ethnicity have endured. (1994: 4)

The task of the criminal justice system, then, is not only to mitigate the negative effects of difference for communities but for individual victims of those communities. The experience of victimization is traumatic for all people; however, it can be doubly, triply so for those whose difference leaves them even more vulnerable and at the mercy of a "jaded criminal justice system."

As argued previously, hate crime victims legitimately fear the risk of secondary victimization. Criminal justice personnel are not immune to the tendency to violently construct their own identities to the detriment of those Others with whom they come in contact. This trend must be turned around through positive action on the part of the state.

Criminal justice agencies that are representative of the communities they serve almost invariably will be more aware of the particular problems of these communities. However, minority groups are dramatically underrepresented as service providers in the criminal justice system. As the United States becomes even more diverse, it will become increasingly important for agencies to recruit those who are "different."

It is these recruits who will bring with them an understanding of their clientele, as well as slightly different approaches to their jobs. Latino/a police officers, for example, will bring insights into the specificity of domestic violence among Latinos/as; women may bring dialogic rather than aggressive tactics into emotional confrontations; physically challenged persons bring attention to the barriers implied by the physical environment. In other words, hiring those who are different is a way to celebrate and take advantage of diversity.

Nonetheless, hiring and promoting Others within criminal justice agencies is no guarantee that those agencies necessarily will be more sensitive to cultural diversity. There are gay men who are racist, women who are sexist, Latinos who are classist. Ignorance and prejudice cut across difference. Consequently, regardless of the make-up of criminal justice agencies, cultural awareness training will have a crucial role to play in sensitizing its members to the experiences, values, and needs of the communities they serve. While this must take place within criminal justice academies and agencies, it also must be integrated into criminal justice curricula at community colleges and universities. A strong exemplar is my own Department of Criminal Justice at Northern Arizona University. As Marianne Nielsen and Phoebe Stambaugh (1998) have articulated in a recent article, this department explictly addresses diversity issues across the curriculum. Indeed, the department requires a junior level course, Human and Cultural Relations in Criminal Justice. So committed are the faculty to enhancing student awareness of the implications of difference for criminal justice that they recently published a textbook for this and similar courses, entitled *Investigating Difference: Human and Cultural Relations in Criminal Justice.* The inclusion of such courses in all Criminal Justice degree programs would be a fine start in ensuring that students and future practitioners are cognizant of the cultural dynamics that give rise to hate crime.

Similarly, criminal justice practitioners must be made aware that different communities may in fact experience the trauma of victimization in different ways. A recent Office for Victims of Crime report observes,

> Different concepts of suffering and healing influence how
> victims experience the effects of victimization and the process
> of recovery. . . . Methods for reaching culturally diverse
> victims must include resources that are specific to their needs.
> (1998: 157)

The criminal justice response to serving the needs of victims has been varied and broad, ranging from legislation (such as the Federal Victim and Witness Protection Act of 1982 and the Victims of Crime Act of 1984), to the establishment of victim's bills of rights such as that developed by the International Association of Chiefs of Police in 1983, to the array of services known as Victim-Witness programs. These services cross the boundaries of difference. They serve the general needs of victims, regardless of what "category of difference" they may occupy. However, those victimized because of their difference, or those who experience victimization differently because of their difference, or those who are uncomfortable with the criminal justice system because of their difference often require culturally specific services. The Violence Against Women Act acknowledges this. It is an exploitable resource for victims, offering legal redress as well as funding for programs, services, and shelters intended to confront violence against women. Hate crime legislation and antiviolence projects similarly offer protections, advocacy, and aftercare for victims of ethnoviolence.

Awareness and knowledge of how hate crime affects its victims allows criminal justice actors to implement services that are appropriate to localized dynamics. For example, communities experiencing high rates of victimization of women may implement nighttime transportation services, or short- and long-term shelter programs. None of these would be an appropriate response, however, where the paramount problem is violence against gay men and lesbians. In those cases, media and educational campaigns against homophobia, or the creation of a local gay and lesbian advocacy panel would be effective interventions. Ultimately, the key to effective delivery of victim services is sensitivity to the cultural needs of the victim's community in a way that empowers victims and potential victims.

THE POSITIVE POLITICS OF DIFFERENCE

The last decade of the twentieth century has seen a flurry of hate crime legislation and other state activities, none of which have had an appreciable effect on the frequency, or certainly the severity, of hate crime. Such initiatives are insufficient responses to bias-motivated violence, in that they do not touch the underlying structures that support hate crime. Abdicating responsibility for countering such violence to the state, then, will not be a sufficiently effective long-term strategy. Rather, the responsibility must be shared and distributed across institutional and interactional levels. Moreover, the ultimate goal is not only to attack hate crime but to disrupt the institutional and cultural assumptions about difference that condition hate crime. West and Zimmerman's observations on gender are equally applicable to difference grounded in religion, race, or ethnicity:

> Doing gender furnishes the interactional scaffolding of social structure along with a built-in mechanism of social control. . . . Social change, then, must be pursued both at the institutional and cultural level of sex category and at the interactional level of gender. (1987: 147)

One of the themes that underlies my conceptualization of hate crime is that it is a mechanism for constructing difference. Moreover, this violence is legitimated and accompanied by an array of facilitative mechanisms, such as stereotypes, language, legislation, and job segregation. It is apparent, for example, that stereotyping Native Americans as "savages," or criminalizing the sexuality of gay men and lesbians, or excluding Asians from citizenship have served to maintain the stigmatized outsider identity of these Others. It is also apparent that these Others have been defined negatively in terms of their relationship to some dominant norm—that is, that "black" is defined as inherently inferior to "white," Jewish to Christian, gay to straight. Nonetheless, there is reason for hope. To the extent that difference is socially constructed, it also can be socially reconstructed. In other words, as a society, we can redefine the ways in which difference "matters." We can strive for a just and democratic society in which the full spectrum of diversity addressed here is reevaluated in a positive and celebratory light.

In other words, an insurgent politics of difference must reconstruct both the cultural and institutional supports for particular ways of doing and valuing difference. Such changes, of course, will not occur magically or out of the beneficence of the state or some imagined hegemonic bloc. On the contrary, they will require the concentrated efforts of grassroots mobilizations. The new social movements that have done the transformative labor of the last half of the twentieth century must continue to extend the early gains in the workplace, in the home, and in the public imagination. Hate violence must be undercut indirectly through movements oriented around the positive politics of difference, but also directly through community efforts against hate crime specifically.

We would do well to heed Young's (1990) advice that we embrace a positive politics of difference. This would involve much more than efforts to assimilate Others, or merely "tolerate" their presence. Rather, it challenges us to celebrate our differences. Of course, this requires that much of our current way of ordering the world be radically altered. It means that we must cease to define "different" as inferior and see it instead as simply not the same. As Minow states so elegantly,

> Changing the ways we classify, evaluate, reward, and punish may make the differences we had noticed less significant . . . irrelevant or even a strength. The way things are is not the only way things could be. (1990: 377)

This pursuit of a positive politics of difference is not an abolitionist project. Nor should it be allowed to become one. The heart of the agenda is not oriented around "color (or gender) blindness" or "neutrality." Both the liberal assimilationist and radical abolitionist models run the risk of occluding the persistent reality of oppression and disadvantages that accrue to difference. Only by acknowledging difference can we recognize its effects. Consequently, our goal must be a transformative politics that empowers difference:

> I am just what they say I am—a Jewboy, a colored girl, a fag, a dyke, or a hag—and proud of it. No longer does one have the impossible project of trying to become something one is not, under circumstances where the very trying reminds one of who one is. (Young, 1990: 166)

This is doing difference differently, under different ground rules where enacting one's identity is not an occasion for potential rebuke. Rather, doing difference becomes a risk-free expression of one's culture, perspectives, and insights.

To engage in such a powerful politics is to resist the temptation to ask all individuals to conform to an artificial set of norms and expectations. It is to reclaim and value the "natural" heterogeneity of this nation rather than force a false homogeneity. It is to refuse to denigrate the culture and experiences of black people, women, or gay men, for example. It is to learn and grow from the strength and beauty that other cultures have to offer.

Given the historical and contemporary processes uncovered in this book, reconstructing the meaning and value associated with difference will be no easy task. It will require dramatic changes in attitudes and behavior throughout society. The remainder of the chapter is devoted to a consideration of policies and practices that will facilitate the creation of an alternative vision of difference, which will preclude the violent exclusion and disempowerment of the Other.

Connell (1990, 1992) provides a useful model for what he calls the "practical politics" involved in eliminating gender inequality. We would do well to mimic this approach in setting the agenda for a broader "practical politics" of difference, one that may provide alternative ways of doing difference and give rise to choice rather than to violence. Consider the following a "different" bill of rights and freedoms:

> *In the context of labor:* equity of wages across race and gender categories; freedom from workplace harassment; elimination of job segregation patterns; democratic decision making in the workplace; equitable distribution of household labor; affordable and available child care.

> *In the context of power:* democratic and equitable representation and participation in state, workplace, and household politics; freedom to voice dissent; autonomy of thought and action; freedom from public and private forms of violence; freedom to live in the place and conditions of one's choice.

In the context of sexuality: control over one's sexuality and reproductive capacity; freedom to choose sexual partners and activities; freedom from sexual violence.

In the context of culture: freedom from stereotypical imagery and expectations; ability to respond to and overturn negative imagery; freedom to define one's own individual and collective identity.

In achieving these ends, the foundations that support hate violence will be weakened, so that such violence becomes anomalous, rather than characteristic of U.S. culture.

Ultimately, the mobilizations around these four axes must provide the basis for collective struggle in the interests of social justice. Put another way, they represent an emancipatory politics concerned with overcoming what Young (1995) refers to as the "five faces of oppression" that characterize the experiences of minority groups: exploitation, marginalization, powerlessness, cultural imperialism, and violence. Much of the "indirect" labor in countering hate crime revolves around the first four dimensions noted above. However, this broad, long-term agenda must be accompanied by efforts in the direct service of staunching the tide of hate.

Valerie Jenness's work on antiviolence projects reveals that widespread ethnoviolence has in fact mobilized identifiable social movements. In particular, she draws attention to the success of feminist and gay and lesbian organizations in developing "collective action frames" that have redefined hate crime as a legitimate social problem. In fact, Jenness and Broad conclude that "anti-violence projects across the United States have provided and continue to provide the structural basis for the mobilization around violence and victimization" (1998: 174) Such bodies serve two primary roles: lobbying for the elimination of discriminatory law and practice; and monitoring and responding to hate crime.

For example, Wertheimer (1992: 229) observes that the gay and lesbian community has assumed the tasks of "identifying and defining the problem of violence against its members, providing appropriate services to individuals in need, and working to heal the injuries that violence can create in the larger community" (1992: 229). More specifically, the National Gay and Lesbian Task Force actively has been gathering data on the extent, nature, and dynamics of hate crime since 1973. Moreover the organization acts as a clearinghouse for information on anti-gay violence. As the NGLTF mission statement asserts, this body confronts a full array of anti-gay activities, including violence:

Since its inception, NGLTF has been at the forefront of every
major initiative for lesbian, gay, bisexual and transgender rights . . .

NGLTF is the front line activist organization in the national gay and lesbian movement. As such, it serves as the national resource center for grassroots lesbian, gay, bisexual and transgender organizations that are facing a variety of battles at the state and local level — such as combating anti-gay violence, battling Radical Right anti-gay legislative and ballot measures, advocating an end to job discrimination, working to repeal sodomy laws, demanding an effective governmental response to HIV and reform of the health care system and much more. (NGLTF, online)

A similar organization representing the interests of Asian Americans is the National Asian Pacific American Legal Consortium (NAPALC) yearly audit. The NAPALC provides summary counts of anti-Asian violence, synopses of cases, information on legal action taken by NAPALC, analyses of regional and national trends, extensive policy recommendations, and direct assistance to communities at risk. American Citizens for Justice originally was founded in 1983 in protest of the lenient sentences given to Vincent Chin's murderers. It continues to fight for the civil rights of all Americans, and especially Asian Americans, by engaging in legal consultations, the monitoring of anti-Asian violence, and the provision of educational services. The Asian American Legal Defense and Education Fund similarly is committed to promoting the civil rights of Asian Americans. It has established an Anti-Asian Violence Project, which litigates and provides counseling for victims of hate crime and police brutality. The Asian Immigrant Women Advocates recognizes and addresses the particular problems of immigrant women who often are exploited and subjugated by both their originating culture and that of the United States. AIWA seeks to empower these women by providing job training and counseling, as well as education on their rights in their new home.

In response to the harassment and violence often suffered by immigrants, many antiviolence and civil rights groups have emerged in recent years. Some, like the Coalition Against Asian Violence and the California Border Violence Delegation Project, serve regionally and ethnically specific interests by monitoring and publicizing violence against them. Others, like the American Friends Service Committee's Immigration Law Enforcement Monitoring Project, have a broader mandate to address violence experienced by all immigrants regardless of country of origin. These are just a few of the existing bodies that serve as useful models in building a politics of resistance within particular communities. Such organizations must continue to play a pivotal role in monitoring and responding to hate crime. However, such constituent-based bodies will benefit greatly from the parallel work of broader antiviolence/antibias organizations, like the Southern Poverty Law Center (SPLC), the Anti-Defamation League (ADL), and the Prejudice Institute. Each of these perform an invaluable service for the public in their roles as monitors, litigators, and educators. Since 1979, the SPLC Klanwatch project has closely monitored hate groups and hate crime nationwide, consequently unearthing evidence that has proven useful in the prosecution of civil rights suits against white supremacist groups. Similarly, the ADL (established in 1913) effectively has monitored and responded to anti-Semitic activity. In recent years, it has extended its scope to encompass hate and bias crime more generally. Like Klanwatch, the ADL publishes and distributes the data it collects.

Equally important are the activities of the antiviolence projects in responding to hate groups and hate crimes directly. The Prejudice Institute, for example, supplements its research activities with direct technical assistance to communities that have been victimized, and with program and policy design. The ADL has been instrumental in shaping public policy responses to hate crime and hate groups. In fact, most states have adopted legislation inspired by the ADL's model hate crime legislation. Klanwatch is also directly involved in community responses to hate group activity, both through litigation and the organization of local antiprejudice events and rallies.

These sorts of organizations play a critical educational role as well. Many regularly publish and distribute newsletters to members, police departments, and educational institutions. Whether monthly, quarterly, or yearly, these resources highlight the threats posed by hate group activities and what can be done to dilute the threats. These regularly scheduled publications are supplemented by more specialized documents, such as the ADL's *Hate Crimes: Policies and Procedures for Law Enforcement Agencies*, Klanwatch's *Ten Ways to Fight Hate*, or the Prejudice Institute's *The Traumatic Effects of Ethnoviolence*.

These organizations are especially important in mobilizing communities in response to the contemporary hate movement. As I argued in chapter 6, the movement has taken on a new, modern face. It is no longer the preserve of uneducated bigots from the backwoods—if indeed it ever was. On the contrary, it now increasingly is crossing into the mainstream. Consequently, at the same time that the overt violence associated with these groups has declined, their impact on public sentiments and—more ominously—public policy has grown. As Ezekiel concludes on the basis of his interviews with hate group members,

> The white racist movement is stronger . . . when respected leaders pander to racism (the Willie Horton ads in the Bush campaign) or encourage the white population to conceive of people of color as welfare cheats and criminals. The white racist movement is part of

America, not an alien presence; it grows and wanes as general American racism grows and wanes. (1995: 323)

Because the hate movement has shifted its place to the mainstream, it is there that it must be challenged. Perhaps the most effective means of confronting these groups is through the maintenance and support of antiviolence projects that do battle against them—in the courts, in the media, in public fora.

CROSSING BOUNDARIES/BRIDGING DIFFERENCE

The social movements and organizations referred to above will continue to affect change for the communities for which they speak. However, it is becoming increasingly important that they recognize their shared objectives and engage in coalition building. Chapter 5 explicitly highlights the multiethnic and multicultural dynamics of hate crime. It is, indeed, more than a black/white issue. Moreover, differences are themselves overlapping and intersecting. That is, each of us occupies multiple identities, as a woman, and a Latina, and a Catholic, for example. Or, in the words of Audre Lorde,

> As a Black, lesbian feminist comfortable with the many different ingredients of my identity, and a woman committed to racial and sexual freedom from oppression, I find that I am constantly being encouraged to pluck out some one aspect of myself and present this as the meaningful whole, eclipsing or denying other parts of self. But this is a destructive and fragmenting way to live. My fullest concentration of energies is available to me only when I integrate all the parts of who I am, openly. (1995: 449)

So it is with communities, whether locally or globally. Only by acknowledging and overcoming the "fragmentation" of community can collective action be an effective brake against hate crime. Given the intersection and multiplicity of individual identities, each of us has an interest in bridging difference.

Moreover, the groups of which I have written in this volume often have experienced a similarity (but not sameness) of oppression. In other words, blacks, Jews, Asians, homosexuals and others all have suffered various degrees of discrimination and victimization. We have seen how racial, ethnic, and gender communities alike have been marginalized and victimized in the context of the four axes of labor, power, sexuality, and culture. Yet rather than acknowledging this and forming coalitions, they often have resorted to conflict among themselves. It appears as if they have so internalized the dominant aspects of white masculine supremacy that this is the only lens through which they can view one another. Intercultural coalitions must challenge the essentialist assumptions about identity that insist on irreconcilable differences between races, between genders, between race and gender. As I suggested earlier, all groups share some similarities as well as some differences. Thus, the key to transcending oppression and violence is to transcend the boundaries that artificially divide us. Social change will require that we see race, class, gender, and sexuality as "categories of connection" rather than as categories of opposition. Angie Chung and Edward Taehan Chang speak to the need to recognize the intersectionality of identities:

> Biracial and multiracial coalitions that focus on women of color in the workplace or gay/lesbian non-whites are other forms of multiple oppression politics that strengthen the intersectionality of race, gender and sexuality politics. Furthermore, the latter types of movements hold great promise because they inherently require flexibility in the boundaries of racial identity, as demonstrated by the paradigms proposed by Black feminists and lesbians. (1998: 96)

One of the most dramatic examples of this philosophy is to be found in Patricia Hill Collins's (1990) call for the recognition of race, class, and gender as interlocking systems of oppression. Such a conceptualization moves beyond identifying the similarities and differences that characterize oppressions grounded in each of these, toward an analysis that looks for points of connectedness. It is the latter that will allow collective resistance to multiple and cross-cutting structured relationships through coalition building.

The multi- and intercultural alliances necessary to minimize interethnic violence rest on practices that empower all minority groups. In other words, such strategies must be "transformative rather than simply effective in reducing tensions or addressing particular problems" (Okazawa-Rey and Wong, 1996: 35). Such coalitions will find strength in building bridges that challenge the institutional and cultural supports for hate violence. Energies must be devoted to the identification and acknowledgment of what these communities share—across the axes of identity construction that inform this analysis—rather than what divides them. African Americans, Jews, Latinas, and gay men would find that they each in their own way have suffered exclusionary political practices, workplace discrimination, sexual stereotyping, and of course, violence. For example, Bacon (1996) suggests that immigrant status is a potentially unifying point for people of color, women and men, and those who practice diverse languages and religions. In spite of their differences, most immigrants share the experience of discrimination and economic exploitation. The commonality of oppression and the concomitant willingness to resist can draw diverse communities together. We have seen some evidence of this already, in Southern California for example, where typically Latino-led labor movements have embraced the interests of non-Latino workers as well (Anner, 1996; Chung and Chang, 1998; Ortiz and Timmerman, 1995). Here, class-based organizations have united communities that are otherwise separated by ethnicity, race, or culture.

The contemporary literature on crosscutting coalitions strongly suggests that effective organizing must be grounded in the tangible experiences of the prospective communities (Chung and Chang, 1998; Regalado, 1994). That is, such coalitions are most likely to coalesce and survive if they are based in common substantive, practical issues. Chung and Chang make the point that, in light of current economic restructuring and its consequent hardening of racial conflict, intercultural organizing must "move beyond the humanistic ideologies of cross-cultural communication and racial harmony to address the substantive issues of the different racial and economic life situations that make up contemporary society" (1998: 96). This might include collective struggles against wage disparities, housing segregation, or any of the other "rights and freedoms" mentioned earlier.

However, in the present context, an obvious point of convergence for disparate communities is the hate-motivated violence that afflicts them all. This volume has argued that bias-motivated violence crosses all boundaries of race, gender, sexuality, religion, and ethnicity. Moreover, it has become evident in my analyses of violence against women and against lesbians in particular that the motivations for violence against each of these groups is often indistinguishable. That is, women and lesbians often are victimized because they are perceived to be enacting both gender and sexuality inappropriately. In addition, lesbians of color tend to be at a very high risk of victimization, suggesting the simultaneity of the effects of race, gender, and sexual oppression. Chapter 5 also made explicit how gay men of color experience similar violence at the intersection of race/ethnicity and sexual orientation. These few examples underscore the importance of similarly crosscutting responses to hate crime.

Flavio Francisco Marsiglia (1998) explicitly argues that this very integration of identities can provide the foundation for a politics of resistance and confrontation, as lesbians of color, for example, struggle against their simultaneous racial and sexual marginalization. Jenness and Broad (1998) argue that existing antiviolence projects themselves represent the convergence of four social justice movements around a shared problematic. The civil rights movement, women's movement, gay and lesbian movement, and victims' rights movement share a commitment to countering discrimination and its related forms of violence. The antiviolence projects of which Jenness and Broad write reflect not only localized social movements, but also the power of collective action that consciously crosses boundaries. Despite the different interests, perspectives, tactics, and strategies, these projects nonetheless coalesce around shared experiences of "violence, victimization, civil rights, and compensation in light of symbolic and material discrimination" (Jenness and Broad, 1998: 174). Such coalitions do not force its members to "pluck out" one part of their identities; they resist the fragmentation that otherwise alienates people from their multiple communities and from the rich variation of their own identities.

However, the antiviolence organizations featured in Jenness's work have been severely limited in consciously recognizing and acting upon these "shared experiences." Alliances formed to combat anti-gay violence or anti-woman violence or anti-black violence too often have been based on narrow, even competitive visions of oppression and violence. This is an extension of the historical limitations of contemporary social movements. The gay and lesbian movement and the women's movement have long been criticized for their failure to attend to the distinct experiences and interests of people of color in particular (Collins, 1990; hooks, 1989; Harris, 1995; Jenness and Broad, 1994). Similarly, the black civil rights movement has been charged with nurturing rather than confronting sexism and homophobia (hooks, 1989; Lorde, 1984; Rhue and Rhue, 1997).

Nonetheless, there is reason for hope as more individuals and collectives recognize and act on the intersectionality of oppressions (Lerner and West, 1996; Reyes and Yep, 1997). While insisting that the gay and lesbian movement, for example, largely has been a "white person's movement," Jenness and Broad also acknowledge that there is a growing tendency to attend to the "intersection between multiple sources of bias" (1998: 55–56). Thus, they describe several gay and lesbian antiviolence organizations that explicitly have addressed the relationships between communities, through such strategies as conscious acknowledgments of multiculturalism in mission statements; formation of coalitions with other organizations grounded in race, religion, or ethnicity; publication of articles in newsletters; and sponsorship of community events supporting shared opposition to discrimination and violence.

Among the gay and lesbian organizations that seem to be most committed to combating the full array of violence is the Spokane Gay and Lesbian Community for Dignity and Human Rights, which acknowledges the multiplicity of oppressions in the following way:

> As we organizers networked with groups targeted for oppression, challenges arose among us—to identify and acknowledge the *hidden barriers* to ending oppression in our own community. . . . We stretched ourselves enough to recognize that oppression touched us

all. Oppression is *exclusive;* thereby, creating solutions to end oppression meant utilizing *inclusive* tactics to end crimes of hate, bias and oppression. The Spokane Gay and Lesbian Community for Dignity and Human Rights has a vision that a climate for the intolerance of violence and oppression in the Spokane community can be shaped by our united effort to stand together in the spirit of equity. We are committed to taking the leadership in this task of building a common alliance. (cited in Jenness and Broad, 1998: 58)

There are other examples of multidimensional organizing that might serve as models for coalitions around hate crime as a generalized phenomenon. Many of these are local or regional, and therefore able to respond to local needs. One such body is the Northwest Coalition Against Malicious Harassment (NWC). The NWC is truly a "mosaic of members." Both its general membership and its board of directors are drawn from gay and lesbian, Jewish, Christian, Latino/a, African-American, Asian-American, and Native American communities; civil rights activists; human rights commissions; law enforcement agencies; labor organizations; businesses; and many others. The organization's mission statement is similarly inclusive:

> The NWC works to foster communities free from malicious harassment, violence, and bigotry based on race, religion, gender, sexual orientation, and national origin and ancestry (ethnicity). Recognizing that growing social conflict has led to an increase in and the mainstreaming of organized bigotry, the NWC is committed to being an integral part of the movement to end bias crime and organized bigotry.

The NWC seeks to achieve these goals through monitoring and responding to hate crime and to groups advocating bigotry and violence, as well as through general education and lobbying for effective legislation.

Similar bodies have begun to emerge nationwide, often in response to perceived increases in hate crime locally, or to particularly dramatic cases. In Montgomery County, Maryland, the Network of Neighbors/Network of Teens was established in 1982 as a response to an increase in reported hate crime against youths. Like the NWC, Network members represent a cross-section of the local community. The Network is intended to

- offer support to victims by listening and offering resistance and reassurance;
- help create a sense of community among those who live near each other;
- keep citizens informed of hate activities occurring in the county; and

- help keep the human relations commission and the county police informed of incidents and of tensions in communities that could lead to incidents.

One of the most compelling examples of local community organizing across cultures emerged in Billings, Montana, in 1993 where a local group of white supremacists initiated a campaign of violence and intimidation. The group harassed members of a black church, distributed KKK fliers, desecrated Jewish graves, and spray-painted swastikas and racial epithets on Native American homes. The culminating event for the community came when a brick was thrown through a window displaying a lighted menorah. Refusing to be intimidated and separated by the efforts of the Aryan organization, community members instead engaged in strategies of resistance and solidarity. Civil rights and religious groups held vigils and demonstrations. The local Painters' Union repainted the vandalized homes. And thousands of homes—Jewish and non-Jewish—displayed pictures of menorahs that had been printed in the local newspaper.

So effective was this spontaneous coalition that the local supremacist group ceased its efforts and apparently moved on. However, equally important is the fact that Billings set an emulable example for other communities, thereby inspiring a "tolerance movement." Thanks to a PBS documentary, the Not In Our Town message has spread to over thirty states. A series of videos produced and distributed by the California Working Group encourages local community mobilization against all forms of bigotry and oppression.

Whether mobilizing around difference and the hate crime that difference currently inspires takes the form of narrow or broad, local or national coalitions, the common factor will be attention to the ways in which the structural and cultural context shapes our interpretations and enactment of difference. The many different models described here will have only limited impact if they do not include in their efforts strategies that also challenge the foundations of hate crime. These organizations, coalitions, and movements must also recognize and challenge the limited definitions and models that currently exist for "doing difference." It will continue to be the role of diverse and united social movements to struggle against the rigid, essentialist social constructs that insist on particular ways of being and doing. By everyday practice, and by formal organizing, social movements can shatter the mythologies of difference, as well as the structural patterns that have so long limited options for labor, empowerment, and sexuality. In short, ongoing resistance can allow the next generation to do difference differently.

APPENDIX I States' Hate Crime Statutes

	AL	AK	AZ	AR	CA	CO	CT	DC	DE	FL	GA	HI	ID
Bias-Motivated Violence and Intimidation	✓	✓	✓		✓	✓	✓	✓	✓	✓			✓
Civil Action				✓	✓	✓	✓	✓		✓			✓
Criminal Penalty	✓	✓	✓		✓	✓	✓	✓	✓	✓			✓
Race, Religion, Ethnicity	✓	✓	✓		✓	✓	✓	✓	✓	✓			✓
Sexual Orientation			✓		✓		✓	✓	✓	✓			
Gender		✓	✓		✓			✓					
Disability	✓	✓	✓		✓			✓	✓				
Interference with Religious Worship					✓			✓		✓			✓
Institutional Vandalism	✓		✓	✓	✓	✓	✓	✓	✓	✓	✓	✓	
Data Collection[1]			✓		✓		✓	✓		✓			✓
Training for Law Enforcement Personnel			✓		✓								

1. States with data collection statutes which include sexual orientation are: AZ, CA, CT, DC, FL, IL, IA, MD, NV, OR and WA; those which include gender are: AZ, DC, IL, IA, MN, WA.

	IL	IN	IA	KS	KY	LA	ME	MD	MA	MI	MN	MS	MO
Bias-Motivated Violence and Intimidation	✓		✓			✓	✓	✓	✓	✓	✓	✓	✓
Civil Action	✓		✓			✓		✓	✓	✓			✓
Criminal Penalty	✓		✓			✓	✓	✓	✓	✓	✓	✓	✓
Race, Religion, Ethnicity	✓		✓			✓	✓	✓	✓	✓	✓	✓	✓
Sexual Orientation	✓		✓			✓	✓		✓		✓		
Gender	✓		✓			✓	✓	✓	✓	✓			
Disability	✓		✓			✓	✓		✓		✓		
Interference with Religious Worship								✓	✓	✓	✓	✓	✓
Institutional Vandalism	✓	✓		✓	✓	✓	✓	✓	✓	✓	✓	✓	✓
Data Collection	✓		✓			✓	✓	✓	✓	✓	✓		
Training for Law Enforcement Personnel	✓	✓			✓	✓			✓		✓		

	MT	NE	NV	NH	NJ	NM	NY	NC	ND	OH	OK	OR	PA
Bias-Motivated Violence and Intimidation[2]	✓	✓	✓	✓	✓		✓	✓	✓	✓	✓	✓	✓
Civil Action		✓	✓		✓					✓	✓	✓	✓
Criminal Penalty	✓	✓	✓	✓	✓		✓	✓	✓	✓	✓	✓	✓
Race, Religion, Ethnicity	✓	✓	✓	✓	✓		✓	✓	✓	✓	✓	✓	✓
Sexual Orientation		✓	✓	✓	✓							✓	
Gender		✓		✓	✓		✓		✓				
Disability		✓	✓	✓	✓		✓				✓		
Interference with Religious Worship			✓			✓	✓	✓			✓		
Institutional Vandalism	✓		✓		✓	✓	✓			✓	✓	✓	✓
Data Collection		✓	✓		✓						✓	✓	✓
Training for Law Enforcement Personnel												✓	

2. New York state law provides penalty enhancement limited to the crime of aggravated harassment.

	RI	SC	SD	TN	TX	UT	VT	VA	WA	WV	WI	WY
Bias-Motivated Violence and Intimidation[3,4]	✓		✓	✓	✓	✓	✓	✓	✓	✓		
Civil Action	✓		✓	✓			✓	✓	✓			
Criminal Penalty	✓		✓	✓	✓	✓	✓	✓	✓	✓		
Race, Religion, Ethnicity	✓		✓	✓			✓	✓	✓			
Sexual Orientation	✓						✓	✓				
Gender	✓						✓	✓				
Disability	✓						✓	✓				
Interference with Religious Worship	✓	✓	✓	✓				✓		✓		
Institutional Vandalism	✓	✓		✓	✓			✓	✓			
Data Collection	✓				✓			✓	✓			
Training for Law Enforcement Personnel	✓								✓			

Source: Anti-Defamation League, 1999, *Hate Crime Laws* (www.adl.org/99hatecrime/provisions.html).

3. The Texas statute refers to victims selected "because of the defendant's bias or prejudice against a person or group."

4. The Utah statute ties penalties for hate crimes to violations of the victim's constitutional or civil rights.

APPENDIX II States' Hate Crime Data

NUMBER OF HATE CRIME INCIDENTS BY STATE, 1991–1998

	1991	1992	1993	1994	1995	1996	1997	1998
Alabama	**	4	5	**	**	0	0	**
Alaska	**	**	24	9	8	9	10	**
Arizona	48	172	208	205	220	250	330	283
Arkansas	10	37	13	9	7	1	0	3
California	5	75	364	354	1,751	2,052	1,831	1,749
Colorado	128	258	178	173	149	133	113	128
Connecticut	69	62	117	68	87	114	113	109
Delaware	29	47	33	42	45	67	58	19
District of Columbia	**	14	10	2	4	16	6	2
Florida	**	334	239	214	164	187	93	179
Georgia	23	66	75	51	49	28	45	34
Hawaii	**	**	**	**	**	**	**	**
Idaho	33	54	70	117	114	72	46	58
Illinois	133	241	724	19	146	333	339	277
Indiana	0	19	82	89	35	36	62	50
Iowa	89	36	39	226	29	43	55	0
Kansas	6	3	0	**	**	28	55	54
Kentucky	0	5	13	5	81	109	48	45
Louisiana	0	13	23	92	7	6	4	10
Maine	**	19	32	5	75	58	57	57
Maryland	431	484	404	150	353	387	321	282
Massachusetts	200	424	343	**	333	454	441	431
Michigan	**	122	247	252	405	485	461	384
Minnesota	225	411	377	**	285	268	214	248
Mississippi	1	0	0	6	6	3	0	3
Missouri	136	158	168	139	135	150	157	118

continued

NUMBER OF HATE CRIME INCIDENTS BY STATE, 1991–1998

	1991	1992	1993	1994	1995	1996	1997	1998
Montana	**	**	21	0	11	10	15	22
Nebraska	**	**	**	**	**	3	3	52
Nevada	16	23	12	16	68	44	45	60
New Hampshire	**	**	0	3	24	1	**	16
New Jersey	895	1,114	1,101	895	768	839	694	757
New Mexico	0	**	4	4	24	44	24	31
New York	943	1,112	934	911	845	903	853	776
North Carolina	**	1	10	7	52	34	42	39
North Dakota	**	1	1	5	3	1	2	2
Ohio	80	105	260	357	267	234	265	172
Oklahoma	99	147	60	20	37	83	41	57
Oregon	296	376	237	177	152	172	105	93
Pennsylvania	277	432	391	278	282	205	168	168
Rhode Island	**	48	62	37	46	40	43	29
South Carolina	**	4	27	30	26	42	71	94
South Dakota	**	**	4	1	5	3	34	19
Tennessee	1	4	2	20	25	33	46	58
Texas	95	486	418	364	326	350	333	300
Utah	**	12	45	93	107	59	49	66
Vermont	**	**	1	12	10	4	3	13
Virginia	53	102	100	95	51	92	105	160
Washington	196	374	457	281	266	198	190	221
West Virginia	**	**	**	**	**	4	3	21
Wisconsin	41	67	19	40	45	43	50	**
Wyoming	**	0	10	6	19	4	6	6

** indicates that the states did not report

Sources: Federal Bureau of Investigation, 1991; 1992; 1993; 1994; 1995; 1996; 1997; 1998; 1999.

Acker, Joan. 1992. "Gendering Organizational Theory," in *Gendering Organizational Analysis*, ed. A. J. Mills and P. Tancred. Newbury Park, CA: Sage, 248–260.

Adam, Barry. 1995. *The Rise of a Gay and Lesbian Movement*. New York: Twayne Publishers.

———. 1992. "The Construction of a Sociological Homosexual in Canadian Textbooks," in *Sociology of Homosexuality*, ed. Wayne Dynes and Stephen Donaldson. New York: Garland Publishers, 19–32.

Adams, Peter, Alisa Towns, and Nicole Garvey. 1995. "Dominance and Entitlement: The Rhetoric Men Use to Discuss Their Violence Towards Women." *Discourse and Society*. 6(13): 387–406.

Adelaide Institute: www.adam.com.au

Adisa, Opal Palmer. 1997. "Undeclared War: African American Women Writers Explicating Rape," in *Gender Violence: Interdisciplinary Perspectives*, ed. Laura O'Toole and Jessica Schiffman. New York: New York University Press, 194–208.

AFL-CIO. 1995. "Statement on Immigration and the American Dream." Bal Harbor, FL, February 23.

Aguirre, Alberto, and Jonathan Turner. 1997. *American Ethnicity*. Boston: McGraw-Hill.

Aho, James. 1994. *This Thing of Darkness: A Sociology of the Enemy*. Seattle: University of Washington Press.

———. 1990. *The Politics of Righteousness: Idaho Christian Patriotism*. Seattle: University of Washington.

Almaguer, Tomás. 1995. "Chicano Men: A Cartography of Homosexual Identity and Behavior," in *Men's Lives*, ed. Michael Kimmel and Michael Messner. Boston: Allyn and Bacon, 418–431.

ALPHA: www.alpha.org/whyalpha

American Dissident Voices, *Stormfront*: www.org/immigrant/adv_immi.html

American Renaissance: www.amren.com

America's Watch. 1992. *Brutality Unchecked: Human Rights Along the U.S. Border with Mexico*. New York: America's Watch.

Anderson, Margaret, and Patricia Hill Collins. 1995. "Preface to Part IV," in *Race, Class and Gender: An Anthology*, ed. Margaret Anderson and Patricia Hill Collins. Belmont, CA: Wadsworth, 350–362.

Anner, John. 1996. "Having the Tools at Hand: Building Successful Multicultural Social Justice Organizations," in *Beyond Identity Politics: Emerging Social Justice Movements in Communities of Color*, ed. John Anner. Boston: South End Press, 153–166.

Anti-Defamation League. 1999. *Frontline*. New York: ADL.

———. 1998. *Explosion of Hate: The Growing Danger of the National Alliance.* New York: ADL.

———. 1997. *Hate Crime Laws.* New York: ADL.

———. 1996a. *Hate Groups in America.* New York: ADL.

———. 1996b. *Danger: Extremism.* New York: ADL.

———. 1996c. *Web of Hate: Extremists Exploit the Internet.* New York: ADL.

———. 1994. *Hate Crime Laws.* New York: ADL.

———. 1993. *Young Nazi Killers: The Rising Skinhead Danger.* New York: ADL.

———. 1991. *The KKK Today: A 1991 Status Report.* New York: ADL.

———. 1989. *Combatting Bigotry on Campus.* New York: ADL.

———. n.d. *Hate Crimes: Policies and Procedures for Law Enforcement Agencies.* New York: ADL.

———. www.adl.org

Anti-Violence Project, 1998, *Anti-LGBTH Violence in 1997.* New York: New York City Gay and Lesbian Anti-Violence Project.

———. 1997, *Anti-LGBTH Violence in 1996.* New York: New York City Gay and Lesbian Anti-Violence Project.

Apple, Michael. 1997. "Consuming the Other: Whiteness, Education and Cheap French Fries," in *Off White: Readings on Race, Power and Society,* ed. Michelle Fine, Lois Weis, Linda Powell, and L. Mun Wong. New York: Routledge, 121–128.

Arizona Republic. 1998. "Welfare Moms Should Marry," February 15: A1.

Aryan Nations: www.stormfront.org/an.html

Atlantic Monthly. 1991. "When the Official Subject Is . . .," May.

Bachman, Ronet, and Linda Saltzman. 1995. *Violence against Women: Estimates From the Redesigned Survey.* Washington, DC: Bureau of Justice Statistics.

Back, Les, Michael Keith, and John Solomos. 1998. "Racism on the Internet: Mapping Neo-Fascist Subcultures in Space," in *Nation and Race,* ed. Jeffrey Kaplan and Tore Bjørgo. Boston: Northeastern University Press, 73–101.

Bacon, David. 1996. "Contesting the Price of Mexican Labor: Immigrant Workers Fight for Justice," in *Beyond Identity Politics: Emerging Social Justice Movements in Communities of Color,* ed. John Anner. Boston: South End Press, 97–118.

Bailey, Frankie. 1991. "Law, Justice and 'Americans': An Historical Overview," in *Race and Criminal Justice,* ed. Michael Lynch and Britt Patterson. Albany, NY: Harrow and Heston, 10–21.

Bain, Christian Arthur. 1995. "Anti-Gay Violence in the Workplace." *The Advocate,* June 13: 31–32.

Barker, Rodney. 1992. *The Broken Circle.* New York: Simon and Schuster.

Barnes, A. S. 1985. *The Black Middle Class Family.* Bristol, IN: Wyndham Hall Press.

Bart, Pauline, and Eileen Moran, eds. 1993 *Violence against Women.* Newbury Park, CA: Sage.

Becker, Howard. 1963. *Outsiders: Studies in the Sociology of Deviance.* New York: Free Press.

Belknap, Joanne. 1996. *The Invisible Woman: Gender, Crime and Justice.* Belmont, CA: Wadsworth.

Bem, Sandra Lipsitz. 1998. "In a Male-Centered World, Female Differences Are Transformed into Female Disadvantages," in *Race, Class and Gender in the United States* (4th ed), ed. Paula Rothenberg. New York: St. Martin's Press, 48–52.

Bensinger, Gad. 1992. "Hate Crime: A New/Old Problem." *International Journal of Comparative and Applied Criminal Justice* 16: 115–123.

Berk, Richard, Elizabeth Boyd, and Karl Hamner. 1992. "Thinking More Clearly about Hate-Motivated Crimes," in *Hate Crimes: Confronting Violence against Lesbians and Gay Men,* ed. Gregory Herek and Kevin Berrill. Newbury Park, CA: Sage, 123–143.

Berrill, Kevin. 1993. "Anti-Gay Violence: Causes, Consequences and Responses," in *Bias Crime: American Law Enforcement and Legal Responses,* ed. Robert Kelly. Chicago: Office of International Criminal Justice, 151–164.

———. 1992. "Anti-Gay Violence and Victimization in the United States: An Overview," in *Hate Crimes: Confronting Violence against Lesbians and Gay Men,* ed. Gregory Herek and Kevin Berrill. Newbury Park, CA: Sage, 19–45.

———, and Gregory Herek. 1992. "Primary and Secondary Victimization in Anti-Gay Hate Crimes: Official Response and Public Policy," in *Hate Crimes: Confronting Violence against Lesbians and Gay Men*, ed. Gregory Herek and Kevin Berrill. Newbury Park, CA: Sage, 289–305.

Biden, Joseph. 1993. *Statement on Introduction of the "Violence Against Women Act of 1993."* Washington, DC.

Bissinger, H. G. 1995. "The Killing Trail." *Vanity Fair*, February: 84–88; 142–145.

Black, Donald, and Albert Reiss. 1970. "Police Control of Juveniles." *American Sociological Review* 35: 63–77.

Blackstone, William. 1811. *Commentaries on the Laws of England, Vol. 4*. London: William Reed.

Block, Fred, Richard Cloward, Barbara Ehrenreich, and Frances Fox Piven. 1987. *The Mean Season: The Attack on the Welfare State*. New York: Pantheon.

Boldt, Menno. 1993. *Surviving as Indians: The Challenge of Self-Government*. Toronto: University of Toronto Press.

Bowling, Benjamin. 1993. "Racial Harassment and the Process of Victimization." *British Journal of Criminology* 33(2): 231–250.

Browne, Angela. 1995. "Fear and the Perception of Alternatives: Asking 'Why Battered Women Don't Leave' Is the Wrong Question," in *The Criminal Justice System and Women*, ed. Barbara Price and Natalie Sokoloff. New York: McGraw-Hill, 228–245.

———, and Kirk Williams. 1993. "Gender Intimacy and Lethal Violence: Trends from 1976 Through 1987." *Gender and Society* 78.

Brownmiller, Susan. 1974. *Against Our Will*. New York: Simon and Schuster.

Brownworth, Victoria, 1991. "An Unreported Crisis," *The Advocate*, November 5: 50, 52.

Buchanan, Patrick. "Letter from Pat Buchanan on Immigration": www.buchanan.org/pimmgt.html

———. "Immigration Time-out" www.buchanan.org/timeout.html

Bullard, Sara. 1991. *The Ku Klux Klan: A History of Violence and Racism*.

Montgomery, AL: Southern Poverty Law Institute.

Bureau of Justice Assistance. 1997. *A Policy Maker's Guide to Hate Crimes*. Washington, DC.

Bureau of Justice Statistics. 1996. *Non-Citizens in the Federal Criminal Justice System, 1984–94*.

Burke, Marc. 1994. "Homosexuality as Deviance: The Case of the Gay Police Officer." *British Journal of Criminology* 34(2): 192–203.

Burkhe, Robin. 1996. *A Matter of Justice: Lesbians and Gay Men in Law Enforcement*. New York: Routledge.

Butler, Judith. 1993. "Endangered/ Endangering: Schematic Racism and White Paranoia," in *Reading Rodney King, Reading Urban Uprisings*, ed. Robert Gooding-Williams. New York: Routledge, 15–22.

Caputi, Jane. 1993. "The Sexual Politics of Murder," in *Violence against Women*, ed. Pauline Bart and Eileen Moran. Newbury Park, CA: Sage, 5–25.

———, and Diana Russell. 1992. "Femicide: Sexist Terrorism against Women," in *Femicide: The Politics of Woman Killing*, ed. Jill Radford and Diana Russell. New York: Twayne Publishers, 13–21.

Carrigan, Tim, Bob Connell, and John Lee. 1987. "Toward a New Sociology of Masculinity," in *The Making of Masculinities: The New Men's Studies*, ed. Harry Brod. Winchester, MA: Allen and Unwin, 63–100.

Center for Democratic Renewal. n.d. *Militias: Exploding into the Mainstream*. Atlanta: CDR.

———. 1995. *1994: A Year of Intolerance*. Atlanta: CDR.

Chaiken, Jan. 1998. *Violence by Intimates: Analysis of Data on Crimes by Current or Former Spouses, Boyfriends and Girlfriends*. Washington, DC: Bureau of Justice Statistics, NCJ 167237.

Chambliss, William. 1993. "On Lawmaking," in *Making Law: The State, the Law, and Structural Contradictions*, ed. William Chambliss and Marjorie Zatz. Bloomington: Indiana University Press, 3–35.

———. 1988, *Exploring Criminology*. New York: Macmillan.

Chang, Robert. 1997. "A Meditation on Borders," in Juan Perea. *Immigrants Out.* New York: New York University Press, 244–253.

———. 1995. "Toward an Asian American Legal Scholarship: Critical Race Theory, Post-Structuralism and Narrative Space," in *Critical Race Theory,* ed. Richard Delgado. Philadelphia: Temple University Press, 322–336.

Chennault, Ronald. 1998. "Giving Whiteness a Black Eye: An Interview with Michael Eric Dyson," in *White Reign: Deploying Whiteness in America,* ed. Joe Kincheloe, Shirley Steinberg, Melson Rodriguez, and Ronald Chennault. New York: St. Martin's Press, 298–328.

Cho, Sumi. 1993. "Korean Americans vs. African Americans: Conflict and Construction," in *Reading Rodney King, Reading Urban Uprisings,* ed. Robert Gooding-Williams. New York: Routledge, 196–211.

Christian Patriots: www.ORCHRISTPAT.org

Chun, Jennifer. 1996. "Color of Racism." *WE Magazine* (online): www.asiandir. com/we.march96/color.html

Chung, Angie, and Edward Taehan Chang. 1998. "From Third World Liberation to Multiple Oppression Politics: A Contemporary Approach to Interethnic Coalitions." *Social Justice* 25(3): 80–100.

Churchill, Ward. 1997. "The Bloody Wake of Alcatraz: Political Oppression of the American Indian Movement During the 1970s," in *American Indian Activism,* ed. Troy Johnson, Joane Nagel, and Duane Champagne. Chicago: University of Illinois Press, 242–284.

———. 1996. *From a Native Son.* Boston: South End Press.

———. 1994. *Indians Are Us?* Monroe, ME: Common Courage Press.

———, and Jim Vander Wall. 1990. *Agents of Repression.* Boston: South End Press.

Coleman, Wanda. 1993. "Blacks, Immigrants and America." *The Nation,* February 15: 187–191.

Collins, Michael. 1992. "The Gay-Bashers," in *Hate Crimes: Confronting Violence against Lesbians and Gay Men,* ed. Gregory Herek and Kevin Berrill. Newbury Park, CA: Sage, 191–200.

Collins, Patricia Hill. 1993. "The Sexual Politics of Black Womanhood," in *Violence against Women,* ed. Pauline Bart and Eileen Moran. Newbury Park CA: Sage, 85–104.

———. 1990. *Black Feminist Thought: Knowledge, Consciousness and the Politics of Empowerment.* New York: Routledge.

Coltrane, Scott. 1995. "Stability and Change in Chicano Men's Family Lives," in *Men's Lives,* ed. Michael Kimmel and Michael Messner. Needham Heights, MA: Allyn and Bacon, 469–484.

Comstock, Gary. 1991. *Violence against Lesbians and Gay Men.* New York: Columbia University Press.

Concerned Maine Families. 1994. *STOP Special Gay Rights Status.* Newsletter.

Congressional Caucus for Women's Issues. 1992. *Violence against Women.* Washington, DC.

Connell, Robert. 1995, *Masculinities.* Berkeley: University of California Press.

———. 1992. "Drumming Up the Wrong Tree." *Tikkun* 7(1): 31–36.

———. 1990. "The State, Gender and Sexual Politics: Theory and Appraisal." *Theory and Society* 19(4): 507–544.

———. 1987. *Gender and Power.* Stanford, CA: Stanford University Press.

Cook, Dee. 1993. "Racism, Citizenship and Exclusion," in *Racism and Criminology,* ed. Dee Cook and Barbara Hudson. London: Sage, 136–157.

Cook, John. 1993. "Collection and Analysis of Hate Crime Activities," in *Bias Crime: American Law Enforcement and Legal Responses,* ed. Robert Kelly. Chicago: Office of International Criminal Justice, 143–150.

Coote, Anna. 1998. "Bridging the Gap between Them and Us," in *Social Policy and Social Justice,* ed. Jane Franklin. Cambridge, England: Polity Press, 182–197.

Corley, Charles, and Geneva Smitherman. 1994. "Juvenile Justice: Multicultural Issues," in *Multicultural Perspectives in Criminal Justice and Criminology,* ed. James Hendricks and Bryan Byers.

Springfield, IL: Charles C. Thomas, 259–290.

Cornell, Stephen, and Douglas Hartmann. 1998. *Ethnicity and Race: Making Identities in a Changing World.* Thousand Oaks, CA: Pine Forge Press.

Craven, Diane. 1996. *Female Victims of Violent Crime.* Washington, DC: Bureau of Justice Statistics.

Crenshaw, Kimberlé Williams. 1994. "Mapping the Margins: Intersectionality, Identity and Violence Against Women of Color," in *The Public Nature of Private Violence,* ed. Martha Albertson Fineman and Roxanne Mykitiuk. New York: Routledge, 93–118.

Criminal Justice Collective of Northern Arizona University. 2000. *Investigating Difference: Human and Cultural Relations in Criminal Justice.* Needham Heights, MA: Allyn and Bacon.

Curran, Dan, and Claire Renzetti. 1994. "Introduction: Gender Inequality and Discrimination on the Basis of Sexual Orientation," in *Contemporary Societies: Problems and Prospects,* ed. Dan Curran and Claire Renzetti. Englewood Cliffs, NJ: Prentice Hall, 204–209.

Cybergrrl, online. 1996. *Domestic Violence Statistics*: www.cybergrrl.com

Daniels, Jessie. 1997. *White Lies: Race, Class, Gender and Sexuality in White Supremacist Discourse.* New York: Routledge.

Dean, Laura, Shanyu Wu, and John Martin. 1992. "Trends in Violence and Discrimination against Gay Men in New York City: 1984–1990," in *Hate Crimes: Confronting Violence against Lesbians and Gay Men,* ed. Gregory Herek and Kevin Berrill. Newbury Park, CA: Sage, 46–64.

Dees, Morris. 1996. *Gathering Storm: America's Militia Threat.* New York: Harper Perennial.

de la Garza, Rodolfo, Angelo Falcon, Chris Garcia, and John Garcia. 1994. "Mexican Immigrants, Mexican Americans, and American Political Culture," in *Immigration and Ethnicity,* ed. Barry Edmonston and Jeffrey Passel. Washington, DC: Urban Institute Press, 227–250.

Dinnerstein, Leonard. 1994. *Anti-Semitism in America.* New York: Oxford University Press.

Dobash, R. Emerson, and Russell Dobash. 1998. "Cross-Border Encounters: Challenges and Opportunities," in *Rethinking Violence against Women,* ed. Rebecca Dobash and Russell Dobash. Thousand Oaks, CA: Sage, 1–22.

———. 1997. "Violence against Women," in *Gender Violence: Interdisciplinary Perspectives.* ed. Laura O'Toole and Jessica Schiffman. New York: New York University Press, 266–278.

Dobratz, Betty, and Stephanie Shanks-Meile. 1997. *"White Power, White Pride!" The White Supremacist Movement in the United States.* New York: Twayne Publishers.

Dollard, John. 1937. *Caste and Class in a Southern Town.* New Haven, CT: Yale University Press.

Donat, Patricia, and John D'Emilio. 1997. "A Feminist Redefinition of Rape and Sexual Assault: Historical Foundations and Change," in *Gender Violence: Interdisciplinary Perspectives,* ed. Laura O'Toole and Jessica Schiffman. New York: New York University Press, 184–193.

Doob, Christopher. 1993. *Racism: An American Cauldron.* New York: HarperCollins.

Dressler, Joshua. 1992. "Judicial Homophobia: Gay Rights Biggest Roadblock," in *Homosexuality, Discrimination, Criminology and the Law,* ed. Wayne Dynes and Stephen Donaldson. New York: Garland, 79–87.

Duberman, Martin. 1993. *Stonewall.* New York: Penguin Books.

Duke, David. 1996a Untitled: www.duke.org/object.html

———. 1996b "Why I am Running for United States Senator": www.duke.org/MISSION.html

———. 1996c "A Campaign Fragment: Sergeant Bilko": www.duke.org/bilk-mov.html

———. 1996d "David Duke for Senate": www.duke.org/intro1.html

Dunn, Timothy. 1996. *The Militarization of the U.S. Mexico Border, 1978–1992.* Austin, TX: Center for Mexican American Studies Press.

Dyson, Michael Eric. 1991. *Reflecting Back: African American Cultural Criticism.* Minneapolis: University of Minnesota Press.

Editors of the *Harvard Law Review*, 1990, *Sexual Orientation and the Law.* Cambridge: Harvard University Press.

Ehrlich, Howard. 1998. *Perspectives 6.* Baltimore: The Prejudice Institute.

———. 1994. "Campus Ethnoviolence," in *Race and Ethnic Conflict*, ed. Fred Pincus and Howard Ehrlich. Boulder, CO: Westview, 279–290.

———, Barbara Larcom, and Robert Purvis. 1994. *The Traumatic Effects of Ethnoviolence*. Towson, MD: The Prejudice Institute.

Eisenstein, Zillah. 1994. *The Color of Gender.* Berkeley: University of California Press.

Erez, Edna, and Pamela Tontodonato. 1992. "Sexual Harassment in the Criminal Justice System," in *The Changing Roles of Women in the Criminal Justice System*, ed. Imogene Moyer. Prospect Heights, IL: Waveland, 227–252.

Espiritu, Yen. 1997. *Asian American Women and Men.* Thousand Oaks, CA: Sage.

Ezekiel, Raphael. 1995. *The Racist Mind.* New York: Penguin.

Faludi, Susan. 1991. *Backlash.* New York: Anchor Books.

Fanon, Frantz. 1990. "The Fact of Blackness," in *Anatomy of Racism*, ed. David T. Goldberg. Minneapolis: University of Minnesota Press, 108–126.

Farrakhan, Louis. 1996. "Black Muslims Are Telling the Truth about Jews," in *Race Relations: Opposing Viewpoints*, ed. Paul Winters. San Diego, CA: Greenhaven Press, 50–54.

Feagin, Joe. 1997. "Old Poison in New Bottles: The Deep Roots of Modern Nativism," in *Immigrants Out*, ed. Juan Perea. New York: New York University Press, 13–43.

———, and Clairece Booher Feagin. 1996. *Racial and Ethnic Relations.* Upper Saddle River, NJ: Prentice Hall.

———, and Hernán Vera. 1995. *White Racism.* New York: Routledge.

Fenstermaker, Sarah, Candace West, and Don Zimmerman. 1991. "Gender Inequality: New Conceptual Terrain," in *Gender, Family and Economy: The Triple Overlap.* ed. Rae Lesser Blumberg. Newbury Park, CA: Sage, 289–307.

Ferber, Abby. 1998. *White Man Falling: Race, Gender and White Supremacy.* Lanham, MD: Rowman and Littlefield.

Fernandez, J. 1991. "Bringing Hate Crimes into Focus." *Harvard Civil Rights and Civil Liberties Law Review* 26: 261–292.

Fernandez, John. 1996. "The Impact of Racism on Whites in Corporate America," in *Impacts of Racism on White Americans*, ed. Benjamin Bowser and Raymond Hunt. Thousand Oaks, CA: Sage.

Ferree, Myra Marx. 1987. "She Works Hard for a Living: Gender and Class on the Job," in *Analyzing Gender*, ed. Beth Hess and Myra Marx Ferree. Newbury Park, CA: Sage, 322–347.

Fierman, Jaclyn. 1994. "Is Immigration Hurting the U.S.?" in *Arguing Immigration: The Debate over the Changing Face of America*, ed. Nicolaus Mills. New York: Touchstone, 67–75.

Fine, Michelle. 1997. "Witnessing Whiteness," in *Off White: Readings on Race, Power and Society*, ed. Michelle Fine, Lois Weis, Linda Powell, and L. Mun Wong. New York: Routledge, 57–65.

———, Lois Weis, and Judi Addelston. 1997. "(In)Secure Times: Constructing White Working Class Masculinities in the Late Twentieth Century." *Gender and Society* 11(1): 52–68.

Fishman, Laura. 1998. "The Black Bogeyman and White Self Righteousness," in *Images of Color, Images of Crime*, ed. Coramae Richey Mann and Marjorie Zatz. Los Angeles: Roxbury, 109–125.

Flowers, Ronald Barri, 1990. *Minorities and Criminality.* Thousand Oaks, CA: Sage.

Fowler, Peter, and Leonard Graff. 1985. "Gay Aliens and Immigration: Resolving the Conflict between *Hill* and *Longstaff*." *University of Dayton Law Review* 10(3): 621–644.

Frankenberg, Ruth. 1993. *White Women, Race Matters: The Social Construction of Whiteness.* Minneapolis: University of Minnesota Press.

Franklin, Karen, 1998. "Unassuming Motivations: Contextualizing the Narratives of Anti-Gay Assailants," in *Stigma and Sexual Orientation*, ed.

Gregory Herek. Thousand Oaks, CA: Sage.

Fraser, Nancy, and Linda Gordon. 1994. "A Genealogy of *Dependency*: Tracing a Keyword of the U.S. Welfare State." *Signs* 19(2): 309–336.

French, Marilyn. 1992. *The War against Women.* New York: Summit Books.

Frontline. *Is LA Burning?* April 27. 1993.

Fukuyama, Frances. 1994. "Immigrants and Family Values," in *Arguing Immigration: The Debate over the Changing Face of America*, ed. Nicolaus Mills. New York: Touchstone, 151–168.

Gallup. 1993a. "Americans Feel Threatened by New Immigrants." *Gallup Poll Monthly*, July: 2–96.

———. 1993b. "Racial Overtones Evident in Americans' Attitudes about Crime." *Gallup Poll Monthly*, December: 37–42

———. 1993c. "Public Polarized on Gay Issues." *Gallup Poll Monthly*, April: 30–34.

———. 1993d. "Americans Feel Threatened by New Immigrants." *Gallup Poll Monthly*, July: 2–96.

———. 1992. "Public Opinion Divided on Gay Rights." *Gallup Poll Monthly*, June: 2–6.

Gardner, Carol Brooks. 1995. *Passing By: Gender and Public Harassment.* Berkeley: University of California Press.

Giddens, Anthony. 1992. *The Transformation of Intimacy.* Oxford: Polity.

Gilroy, Paul. 1982. "The Myth of Black Criminality." *Socialist Register, 1982.* London: Merlin Press.

———. 1990. "One Nation under a Groove: The Cultural Politics of 'Race' and Reason in Britain," in *Anatomy of Racism*, ed. David T. Goldberg. Minneapolis: University of Minnesota Press, 263–282.

Goffman, Erving. 1963. *Stigma: Notes on the Management of Spoiled Identity.* New York: Touchstone Books.

Goldberg, David Theo. 1995. "Afterword: Hate or Power?" in *Hate Speech*, ed. Rita Kirk Whillock and David Slayden. Thousand Oaks, CA: Sage, 267–276.

———. 1990. "The Social Formation of Racist Discourse," in *Anatomy of Racism*, ed. David T. Goldberg. Minneapolis: University of Minnesota Press, 295–318.

Goldyn, Lawrence. 1981. "Gratuitous Language in Appellate Cases Involving Gay People: 'Queer-baiting' from the Bench." *Political Behavior* 3(1): 31–48.

Gramsci, Antonio. 1971. *Selections from the Prison Notebooks.* New York: International Publishers.

Gratch, Linda. 1995. "Sexual Harassment among Police Officers," in *Women, Law and Social Control*, ed. Alida Merlo and Jocelyn Pollock. Needham Heights, MA: Allyn and Bacon, 55–77.

Grau, Günter. 1993. *Hidden Holocaust?* London: Cassell.

Greene, Beverly. 1997. "Ethnic Minority Lesbians and Gay Men: Mental Health and Treatment Issues," in *Ethnic and Cultural Diversity among Lesbians and Gay Men*, ed. Beverly Greene. Thousand Oaks, CA: Sage, 216–239.

Hacker, Andrew. 1995. *Two Nations: Black and White, Separate, Hostile, Unequal.* New York: Ballantine Books.

Hall, Stuart, C. Critcher, T. Jefferson, T. Clarke, and B. Roberts. 1978. *Policing the Crisis*, London: Macmillan Publishers Ltd.

Hall, Stuart, and Phil Scraton. 1981. "Law, Class and Control," in *Crime and Society: Readings in History and Theory*, ed. M. Fitzgerald, G. McLennan, and J. Pawson. London: Routledge and Kegan Paul, 460–497.

Hamm, Mark. 1994a. *American Skinheads: The Criminology and Control of Hate Crime.* Westport, CT: Praeger.

———, ed. 1994b. *Hate Crime: International Perspectives on Causes and Control.* Cincinnati: Anderson.

Handler, Joel. 1990. "'Constructing the Political Spectacle': The Interpretation of Entitlements, Legalization and Obligations in Social Welfare History." *Brooklyn Law Review* 56: 899–974.

Harris, Angela. 1995. "Race and Essentialism in Feminist Legal Theory," in *Critical Race Theory*, ed. Richard Delgado. Philadelphia: Temple University Press, 253–267.

Harry, Joseph. 1992. "Conceptualizing Anti-Gay Violence," in *Hate Crimes: Confronting Violence against Lesbians and Gay Men*, ed. Gregory Herek and Kevin Berrill. Newbury Park, CA: Sage, 113–122.

———. 1982. "Derivative Deviance: The Case of Extortion, Fag-Bashing and Shakedown of Gay Men." *Criminology* 19: 546–564.

Hate Directory: www.dpscs.state.md.us.80/hatedir.htm

Hate Watch: www.hatewatch.org

Hearles, John. 1993. *Politics in the Lifeboat.* Boulder, CO: Westview.

Heer, David. 1996. *Immigration in America's Future.* Boulder, CO: Westview.

Heger, Heinz. 1980, *The Men with the Pink Triangles.* Boston: Alyson Publications Inc.

Heise, L. 1989. "International Dimensions of Violence against Women." *Response* 12(1): 3–11.

Herdt, Gilbert. 1997, *Same Sex, Different Cultures.* Boulder, CO: Westview.

Herek, Gregory. 1992. "The Social Context of Hate Crimes: Notes on Cultural Heterosexism," in *Hate Crimes: Confronting Violence against Lesbians and Gay Men,* ed. Gregory Herek and Kevin Berrill. Newbury Park, CA: Sage, 89–104.

———, and Kevin Berrill. 1992. "Introduction," in *Hate Crimes: Confronting Violence against Lesbians and Gay Men,* ed. Gregory Herek and Kevin Berrill. Newbury Park, CA: Sage, 1–10.

Hernandez, Tanya Kateri. 1990. "Bias Crimes: Unconscious Racism in the Prosecution of Racially Motivated Violence." *Yale Law Journal* 99: 832–864.

Hesse, Barnor, Dhanwant Rai, Christine Bennett, and Paul McGilchrist. 1992, *Beneath the Surface: Racial Harassment.* Aldershot, England: Avebury Press.

Hirschi, Travis. 1969. *Causes of Delinquency.* Berkeley: University of California Press.

Hochschild, Arlie. 1995. "The Second Shift: Employed Women Are Putting in Another Day of Work at Home," in *Men's Lives,* ed. Michael Kimmel and Michael Messner. Needham Heights, MA: Allyn and Bacon, 443–447.

Hodge, John. 1990. "Equality: Beyond Dualism and Oppression," in *Anatomy of Racism,* ed. David T. Goldberg. Minneapolis: University of Minnesota Press, 89–107.

Holmes, Steven. 1994. "Survey Finds Minorities Resent One Another Almost as Much as They Do Whites." *New York Times,* March 3, 1994: B8.

hooks, bell. 1995. *Killing Rage: Ending Racism.* New York: Henry Holt and Company.

———. 1994. *Outlaw Culture.* New York: Routledge.

———. 1992. *Black Looks.* Boston: South End Press.

———. 1990. *Yearning.* Boston: South End Press.

———. 1989. *Talking Back.* Boston: South End Press.

———. 1981. *Ain't I A Woman: Black Women and Feminism.* Boston: South End Press.

Hopkins, Patrick. 1992. "Gender Treachery: Homophobia, Masculinity, and Threatened Identities," in *Rethinking Masculinity: Philosophical Explorations in Light of Feminism,* ed. Larry May and Robert Strikwerda. Landham, MD: Rowman and Littlefield, 111–131.

Hudson, Barbara. 1993. "Racism and Criminology: Concepts and Controversies," in *Racism and Criminology,* ed. Barbara Hudson. London: Sage, 1–27.

Hunt, Alan. 1990. "Rights and Social Movements: Counter-Hegemonic Strategies." *Journal of Law and Society* 17(3): 1–20.

Hurtado, Aída. 1989. "Relating to Privilege: Seduction and Rejection in the Subordination of White Women and Women of Color." *Signs* 14: 833–855.

Ikemoto, Lisa. 1995. "Traces of the Master Narrative in the Story of African American/Korean American Conflict: How We Constructed Los Angeles," in *Critical Race Theory,* ed. Richard Delgado. Philadelphia: Temple University Press, 305–315.

Immigration and Naturalization Service (n.d.). *Illegal Alien Resident Population*: www.ins.usdoj.gov/stats/illegalalien/index.html

Institute for Historical Review: www.kaiwan.com/~ihrgreg

Interagency Task Force on Immigration Policy. 1979. *Staff Report.*

Isbister, John. 1996. *The Immigration Debate: Remaking America.* West Hartford, CT: Kumarian Press.

Jenness, Valerie. 1995. "Social Movement Growth, Domain Expansion, and Framing Processes: The Gay/Lesbian Movement and Violence against Gays and Lesbians as a Social Problem." *Social Problems* 42(1): 145–170.

———, and Kendal Broad. 1998. *Hate Crimes: New Social Movements and the Politics of Violence.* New York: Aldine de Gruyter.

———, and Kendal Broad. 1994. "Anti-Violence Activism and the (In)Visibility of Gender in the Gay/Lesbian Movement and the Women's Movement." *Gender and Society* 8: 402–423.

Jensen, Rita Henley. 1998. "Welfare: Exploding the Stereotypes," in *Race, Class and Gender in the United States* (4th ed.), ed. Paula Rothenberg. New York: St. Martin's Press, 242–248.

Jo, Moon H. 1992. "Korean Merchants in the Black Community: Prejudice among the Victims of Prejudice." *Ethnic and Racial Studies* 15(3): 395–411.

Johnson, Bruce, and Roberto Maestas. 1979. *Wasi'chu: The Continuing Indian Wars.* New York: Monthly Review Press.

Johnson, Kevin. 1995. "Public Benefits and Immigration: The Intersection of Immigration Status, Ethnicity, Gender and Class." *UCLA Law Review* 42: 1509–1575.

Kanter, Rosabeth. 1977. *Men and Women of the Corporation.* New York: Basic Books.

Karst, Kenneth. 1993. *Law's Promise, Law's Expression.* New Haven, CT: Yale University Press.

Kaufman, Michael. 1992. "The Construction of Masculinity and the Triad of Men's Violence," in *Men's Lives,* ed. Michael Kimmel and Michael Messner. New York: Macmillan, 28–49.

Kelly, Robert, ed. 1993. *Bias Crime: American Legal Responses* (2nd ed.). Chicago: Office of International Criminal Justice.

———, Jess Maghan, and Woodrow Tennant. 1993. "Hate Crimes: Victimizing the Stigmatized," in *Bias Crime: American Law Enforcement and Legal Responses,* ed. Robert Kelly. Chicago: Office of International Criminal Justice, 23–47.

Kerchis, Cheryl, and Iris Marion Young. 1995. "Social Movements and the Politics of Difference," in *Multiculturalism from the Margins,* ed. Dean Harris. Westport, CT: Bergin and Garvey, 1–28.

Kim, Elaine. 1993. "Home Is Where the *Han* is: A Korean American Perspective on the Los Angeles Upheavals," in *Reading Rodney King, Reading Urban Uprisings,* ed. Robert Gooding-Williams. New York: Routledge, 215–235.

Kinsman, Gary. 1992. "Men Loving Men: The Challenge of Gay Liberation," in *Men's Lives,* ed. Michael Kimmel and Michael Messner. New York: Macmillan, 483–496.

Klanwatch. 1998. *Intelligence Report.* Montgomery, AL: Southern Poverty Law Institute.

———. 1997. *Intelligence Report.* Montgomery, AL: Southern Poverty Law Institute.

———. 1996a. *Intelligence Report.* Montgomery, AL: Southern Poverty Law Institute.

———. 1996b, *False Patriots: The Threat of Anti-government Extremists.* Montgomery, AL: Southern Poverty Law Institute.

———. 1994. *Ten Ways to Fight Hate.* Montgomery, AL: Southern Poverty Law Center.

Kleg, Milton. 1993. *Hate Prejudice and Racism.* Albany: State University of New York Press.

Kleinberg, Seymour. 1992. "The New Masculinity of Gay Men, and Beyond," in *Men's Lives,* ed. Michael Kimmel and Michael Messner. New York: Macmillan, 80–94.

Lamm, Richard, and Gary Imhoff. 1985. *The Immigration Time Bomb.* New York: Truman Tally Books.

Langer, Elinor. 1990. "The American Neo-Nazi Movement Today." *The Nation,* July 16/23: 81–107.

La Rossa, Ralph. 1995. "Fatherhood and Social Change," in *Men's Lives* (3rd Ed.), ed. Michael Kimmel and Michael Messner. Needham Heights, MA: Allyn and Bacon, 448–460.

Lehne, Gregory. 1992. "Homophobia among Men: Supporting and Defining the Male Role," in *Men's Lives*, ed. Michael Kimmel and Michael Messner. New York: Macmillan, 381–394.

Lerner, Michael, and Cornel West. 1996. *Jews and Blacks: A Dialog on Race, Religion and Culture in America.* New York: Penguin.

Lester, Julius. 1994. "The Lives People Live," in *Blacks and Jews: Alliances and Arguments*, ed. Paul Berman. New York: Delta, 164–177.

Levin, Jack, and McDevitt. 1993, *Hate Crimes: The Rising Tide of Bigotry and Bloodshed.* New York: Plenum.

López, Ian Haney. 1995. "The Social Construction of Race," in *Critical Race Theory*, ed. Richard Delgado. Philadelphia: Temple University Press. 191–203.

Lorber, Judith. 1994. *Paradoxes of Gender.* New Haven, CT: Yale University Press.

Lorde, Audre. 1995. "Age, Race, Class and Sex: Women Redefining Difference," in *Campus Wars: Multiculturalism and the Politics of Difference*, ed. John Arthur and Amy Shapiro. Boulder, CO: Westview, 191–198.

———. 1984. *Sister Outsider.* Trumansburg, NY: Crossing Press.

Los Angeles County Office of Education, 1995: www.LACOE.gov

Lubiano, Wahneema. 1992. "Black Ladies, Welfare Queens, and State Minstrels: Ideological War by Narrative Means," in *Race-ing Justice, En-Gendering Power*, ed. Toni Morrison. New York: Pantheon, 323–363.

Lugones, María, and Joshua Price. 1995. "Dominant Culture: *El Deseo por un Alma Pobre*," in *Multiculturalism from the Margins*, ed. Dean Harris. Westport, CT: Bergin and Garvey, 103–128.

Lynch, Michael, and Byron Groves. 1989. *A Primer in Radical Criminology.* Albany, NY: Harrow and Heston.

MacDonald, Andrew. 1996. *The Turner Diaries.* New York: Barricade Books.

MacKinnon, Catharine. 1991. "Reflections on Sex Equality under Law." *Yale Law Journal* 100: 1281–1319.

Majors, Richard, and Janet Mancini Billson. 1992. *Cool Pose.* New York: Touchstone Books.

Mann, Coramae Richey. 1993. *Unequal Justice.* Bloomington: Indiana University Press.

Manning, Marable. 1995. "Beyond Racial Identity Politics: Towards a Liberation Theory for Multicultural Democracy," in *Race, Class and Gender: An Anthology*, ed. Margaret Anderson and Patricia Hill Collins. Belmont, CA: Wadsworth, 363–366.

Maroney, Terry. 1998. "The Struggle against Hate Crime: Movement at a Crossroads," *New York University Law Review* 73: 564–620.

Marovitz, William. 1993. "Hate or Bias Crime Legislation," in *Bias Crime*, ed. Robert Kelly. Chicago: Office of International Criminal Justice, 48–53.

Marsiglia, Flavio Francisco. 1998. "Homosexuality and Latino/as: Towards an Integration of Identities," in *Violence and Social Injustice against Lesbian, Gay and Bisexual People*, ed. Lacey Sloan and Nora Gustavsson. New York: Haworth Press, 113–126.

Martin, Patricia Yancey, and Robert Hummer. 1995. "Fraternities and Rape on Campus," in *Race, Class and Gender: An Anthology*, ed. Margaret Anderson and Patricia Hill Collins. Belmont, CA: Wadsworth, 470–487.

Martin, Susan. 1992. "The Changing Status of Women Officers: Gender and Power in Police Work," in *The Changing Roles of Women in the Criminal Justice System*, ed. Imogene Moyer. Prospect Heights, IL: Waveland, 281–305.

———, and Nancy Jurik. 1996. *Doing Justice, Doing Gender.* Thousand Oaks, CA: Sage.

Martinez, Elizabeth. 1997. "Scapegoating Immigrants," in *Immigration: Debating the Issues*, ed. Nicholas Capaldi. Amherst, NY: Prometheus, 237–234.

Mathabane, Mark, and Gail Mathabane, 1992, *Love in Black and White: The Triumph of Love over Prejudice and Taboo.* New York: HarperCollins.

Matsuda, Mari. 1993. "Public Response to Hate Speech: Considering the Victim's Story," in *Words That Wound*, ed. Mari

Matsuda, Charles Lawrence III, Richard Delgado, and Kimberlé Williams Crenshaw. Boulder, CO: Westview, 17–51.

McAdam, Doug. 1982. *Political Process and the Development of Black Insurgency, 1930–1970.* Chicago: University of Chicago Press.

McCarthy, John, and Mark Wolfson. 1992. "Consensus Movements, Conflict Movements, and the Cooptation of Civic and State Infrastructures," in *Frontiers in Social Movement Theory,* ed. Aldon Morris and Carol McClurg Mueller. New Haven, CT: Yale University Press, 273–297.

McClain, Paula, and Joseph Stuart. 1995. *Can We All Get Along? Racial and Ethnic Minorities in American Politics.* Boulder, CO: Westview.

McIntosh, Mary. 1968. "The Homosexual Role." *Social Problems* 16: 182–192.

Meet the Press (NBC), February 11, 1996.

Messerschmidt, James. 1997. *Crime as Structured Action.* Thousand Oaks, CA: Sage.

———. 1993. *Masculinities and Crime.* Lanham, MD: Rowman and Littlefield.

———. 1983. *The Trial of Leonard Peltier.* Boston: South End Press.

Michalowski, Ray. 1985. *Order, Law and Crime.* New York: Random House.

Miles, Jack. 1994. "Blacks vs. Browns," in *Arguing Immigration: The Debate over the Changing Face of America,* ed. Nicolaus Mills. New York: Touchstone, 101–142.

Miller, Jean Baker. 1995. "Domination and Subordination," in *Race, Class and Gender in the United States* (3rd ed.), ed. Paula Rothenberg. New York: St. Martin's Press, 57–63.

Miller, John, and Stephen Moore. 1997. "The Index of Leading Immigration Indicators," in *Immigration: Debating the Issues,* ed. Nicholas Capaldi. Amherst: Prometheus, 306–323.

Miller, Neil. 1995. *Out of the Past: Gay and Lesbian History from 1969 to the Present.* New York: Vintage Press.

Miller, Susan. 1994. "Gender-Motivated Hate Crimes: A Question of Misogyny," in *Contemporary Societies: Problems and Prospects,* ed. Dan Curran and Claire Renzetti. Englewood Cliffs, NJ: Prentice Hall, 229–240.

Miller, Susan, and Kären Hess. 1998. *The Police in the Community: Strategies for the 21st Century.* Belmont, CA: West/Wadsworth.

Mills, Nicolaus. 1994. "Introduction," in *Arguing Immigration: The Debate over the Changing Face of America,* ed. Nicolaus Mills. New York: Touchstone, 11–30.

Minow, Martha. 1990. *Making All the Difference: Inclusion, Exclusion and American Law.* Ithaca, NY: Cornell University Press.

Moraga, Cherrie. 1996. "Queer Aztlán: The Reformation of Chicano Tribe," in *The Material Queer,* ed. Donald Morton. Boulder, CO: Westview, 297–304.

Moritz, Marguerite J. 1995. "The Gay Agenda: Marketing Hate Speech to Mainstream Media," in *Hate Speech,* ed. Rita Kirk Whillock and David Slayden. Thousand Oaks, CA: Sage, 55–79.

Mouffe, Chantal. 1988. "Hegemony and New Political Subjects: Toward a New Concept of Democracy," in *Marxism and the Interpretation of Culture,* ed. Cary Nelson and Lawrence Grossberg. Urbana: University of Illinois Press, 89–105.

———. 1979. "Hegemony and Ideology in Gramsci," in *Hegemony and Ideology in Gramsci,* ed. Chantal Mouffe. London: Routledge and Kegan Paul, 169–207.

National Alliance: www.natall.com

National Asian and Pacific American Legal Consortium. 1995. *Audit of Violence Against Asian and Pacific Americans.*

———. 1999. Email correspondence re: Audit of Anti-Asian Violence.

National Center for Children in Poverty. 1999. "Young Children in Poverty Fact Sheet": cpmcnet.columbia.edu/dept/nccp/main4.html

National Gay and Lesbian Alliance. 1995. *Anti-Gay/Lesbian Violence, Victimization and Defamation in 1994.* Washington, DC: NGLTF Policy Institute.

National Socialist White People's Party: www.capecod.net/~ndemonti

Nava, Michael, and Robert Dawidoff. 1994. *Created Equal: Why Gay Rights Matter to America.* New York: St. Martin's Press.

Nestelrode, Jana. 1995. "Bias Crimes: the Issue of Gender," paper presented at the annual meetings of the Academy of Criminal Justice Sciences, Boston, MA.

New Republic. 1993. "Arms and the Men," February 15.

New York Daily News. 1993. "Gays in the Military and Wavering Bill," March 25.

National Gay and Lesbian Task Force. 1999. *Anti-Gay/Lesbian Violence, Victimization and Defamation in 1998.* Washington, DC: NGLTF Policy Institute.

———. 1998. *Anti-Gay/Lesbian Violence, Victimization and Defamation in 1997.* Washington, DC: NGLTF Policy Institute.

———. 1997. *Anti-Gay/Lesbian Violence, Victimization and Defamation in 1996.* Washington, DC: NGLTF Policy Institute.

———. 1996. *Anti-Gay/Lesbian Violence, Victimization and Defamation in 1995.* Washington, DC: NGLTF Policy Institute.

———. 1995. *Anti-Gay/Lesbian Violence, Victimization and Defamation in 1994.* Washington, DC: NGLTF Policy Institute.

———. 1994. *Anti-Gay/Lesbian Violence, Victimization and Defamation in 1993.* Washington, DC: NGLTF Policy Institute.

———. 1993. *Anti-Gay/Lesbian Violence, Victimization and Defamation in 1992.* Washington, DC: NGLTF Policy Institute.

Nielsen, Marianne, and Phoebe Stambaugh. 1998. "Multiculturalism in the Classroom: Discovering Difference from Within." *Journal of Criminal Justice Education* 9(2): 281–291.

Note. 1995. "Racial Violence against Asian Americans." *Harvard Law Review.* 106: 1926–1943.

Novick, Michael. 1995. *White Lies, White Power.* Monroe, ME: Common Courage Press.

Nuñez, Michael. 1992. "Violence at Our Border: Rights and Status of Immigrant Victims of Hate Crimes and Violence Along the Border between the United States and Mexico." *Hastings Law Journal* 43: 1573–1605.

Ochoa, Albert. 1995. "Language Policy and Social Implications for Addressing the Bicultural Experience in the United States," in *Culture and Difference: Critical Perspectives on the Bicultural Experience in the United States,* ed. Antonia Dander. Westport, CT: Bergin and Garvey, 227–253.

Office for Victims of Crime. 1998. *New Directions from the Field: Victims Rights and Services for the 21st Century.*

Ogawa, Brian. 1999. *Color of Justice: Culturally Sensitive Treatment of Minority Crime Victims.* Boston: Allyn and Bacon.

Okazawa-Rey, Margo, and Marshall Wong. 1996. "Organizing in Communities of Color: Addressing Interethnic Conflicts." *Social Justice* 24(1): 24–39.

Olivas, Michael. 1995. "The Chronicles, My Grandfather's Stories, and Immigration Law: The Slave Traders Chronicles as Racial History," in *Critical Race Theory,* ed. Richard Delgado. Philadelphia: Temple University Press, 9–20.

Oliver, Melvin, and James Johnson. 1984. "Interethnic Conflict in an Urban Ghetto: The Case of Blacks and Latinos in Los Angeles." *Research in Social Movements, Conflict and Change* 6: 57–94.

Oliver, W. 1988. "The Symbolic Display of Compulsive Masculinity in the Lower-Class Black Bar." Unpublished manuscript. University of Delaware, Newark.

Omi, Michael, and Howard Winant. 1994. *Racial Formation in the United States* (2nd ed.). New York: Routledge.

Omi, Michael, and Howard Winant. 1993. "The Los Angeles 'Race Riots' and Contemporary U.S. Politics," in *Reading Rodney King, Reading Urban Uprisings,* ed. Robert Gooding-Williams. New York: Routledge, 97–114.

Operation Ghetto Storm: www.whitepower.com/ghettostorm

Ortiz, Isidro, and Paula Timmerman. 1995. "Contemporary Chicano Struggles," in *Multiculturalism from the Margins,* ed. Dean Harris. Westport, CT: Bergin and Garvey, 87–102.

Ortiz, Roxanne Dunbar. 1981. "Foreword," in *Native Americans and Nixon: Presidential Politics and Minority*

Self Determination, ed. Jack Forbes. Los Angeles: American Indian Studies Center.

O'Sullivan, Chris. 1998. "Ladykillers: Similarities and Divergences of Masculinities in Gang Rape and Wife Battery," in *Masculinities and Violence*, ed. Lee Bowker. Thousand Oaks, CA: Sage, 82–110.

O'Toole, Laura, and Jessica Schiffman. 1997. "Introduction to Part I, Section 2," in *Gender Violence: Interdisciplinary Perspectives*, ed. Laura O'Toole and Jessica Schiffman. New York: New York University Press, 67–73.

———. 1997. "Introduction to Part II, Section 1," in *Gender Violence: Interdisciplinary Perspectives*, ed. Laura O'Toole and Jessica Schiffman. New York: New York University Press, 131–137.

Padgett, Gregory. 1984. "Racially Motivated Violence and Intimidation: Inadequate State Enforcement and Federal Civil Rights Remedies." *Journal of Criminal Law and Criminology* 75: 103–138.

Painter, Nell Irvin. 1992. "Hill, Thomas and the Use of Racial Stereotype," in *Race-ing Justice, En-Gendering Power*, ed. Toni Morrison. New York: Pantheon, 200–214.

Pendo, Elizabeth. 1994. "Recognizing Violence against Women: Gender and the Hate Crimes Statistics Act." *Harvard Women's Law Journal* 17: 157–183.

People's Resistance Movement—The Christian Alternative: www.powertech. no/aolsen/txt/forside.html

Perry, Barbara. 1999. "Defenders of the Faith: Hate Groups and Ideologies of Power," *Patterns of Prejudice* 32(3): 32–54.

———. 1996. "The State of Hate: The Impact of Policy, Practice and Rhetoric on Hate Crime." Annual Meetings of the American Society of Criminology, Chicago; November 1996.

Pham, Mai. Online. "Another Senseless Hate Crime": www.avl.umd.edu/staff/nowk/hate_crime.html

Pharr, Suzanne. 1995. "Homophobia as a Weapon of Sexism," in *Race, Class and Gender in the United States* (3rd ed.), ed. Paula Rothenberg. New York: St. Martin's Press, 481–490.

———. 1988. *Homophobia: A Weapon of Sexism*. Inverness, CA: Chardon Press.

Philadelphia Lesbian and Gay Task Force. 1992. *Discrimination and Violence against Lesbian Women and Gay Men in Philadelphia and the Commonwealth of Pennsylvania*. Philadelphia: PLGTF.

Pinkney, Alphonso. 1994. *White Hate Crimes*. Chicago: Third World Press.

Plant, Richard. 1986. *The Pink Triangle: The Nazi War against Homosexuals*. New York: Henry Holt and Company.

Pleck, Joseph. 1987. "The Theory of Male Sex Role Identity: Its Rise and Fall, 1936 to Present," in *The Making of Masculinities: The New Men's Studies*, ed. Harry Brod. Winchester, MA: Allen and Unwin, 21–38.

Plunder and Pillage: www.excaliber.com/thor

Pogrebin, Letty Cottin, and Earl Ofari Hutchinson. 1994. "A Dialogue on Black-Jewish Relations," in *Race and Ethnic Conflict*, ed. Fred Pincus and Howard Ehrlich. Boulder, CO: Westview, 219–226.

Prejudice Institute. 1994, *The Traumatic Effects of Ethnoviolence*. Towson, MD: Center for the Applied Study of Ethnoviolence.

Preston, John. 1995. *Winter's Light: Reflections of a Yankee Queer*. Hanover, NH: University of New England Press.

Quadagno, Jill, and Catherine Fobes. 1997. "The Welfare State and the Cultural Reproduction of Gender: Making Good Girls and Boys in the Job Corps," in *Race, Class and Gender in a Diverse Society*, ed. Diana Kendall. Boston: Allyn and Bacon, 253–273.

Quina, Kathryn. 1997. "The Victimization of Women," in *Gender Violence: Interdisciplinary Perspectives*, ed. Laura O'Toole and Jessica Schiffman. New York: New York University Press, 165–171.

Rasche, Christine. 1995. "Minority Women and Domestic Violence: The Unique Dilemmas of Battered Women of Color," in *The Criminal Justice System and Women*, ed. Barbara Price and Natalie Sokoloff. New York: McGraw-Hill, 246–261.

Regalado, James. 1994. "Community Coalition-Building," in *The Los Angeles*

Riots, ed. James Regalado. Boulder,
CO: Westview Press, 205–235.

Regan, Leo, 1993, *Public Enemies.*
London: André Deutsch Limited.

Reiman, Jeffrey. 1995. *The Rich Get Richer
and the Poor Get Prison* (4th ed.).
Boston: Allyn and Bacon.

Republican National Committee. 1996.
"America: Welcome Mat or Door Mat?"
Press release, March 18, 1996.

Resistance Records: www.resistance.com

Reskin, B. 1993. "Sex Segregation in the
Workplace." *Annual Review of Sociology*
19: 241–270.

Reyes, Eric Estuary, and Gust Yep. 1997.
"Challenging Complexities: Strategies
with Asian Americans in Southern
California Against (Heterosex)Isms,"
in *Overcoming Heterosexism and
Homophobia*, ed. James Sears and
Walter Williams. New York: Columbia
University Press, 91–103.

Rhue, Sylvia, and Thom Rhue. 1997.
"Reducing Homophobia in African
American Communities," in *Overcoming
Heterosexism and Homophobia*, ed. James
Sears and Walter Williams. New York:
Columbia University Press, 117–130.

Richards, Jeffrey. 1991. *Sex, Dissidence and
Damnation: Minority Groups in the
Middle Ages.* London: Routledge.

Ridgeway, James. 1995. *Blood in the Face.*
New York: Thunder's Mouth Press.

Roscigno, Vincent. 1994. "Social
Movement Struggle and Race, Gender,
Class Inequality." *Race, Sex and Class*
2(1), 109–126.

Rosen, Steven. 1992. "Police Harassment
of Homosexual Women and Men in
New York City 1960–1980," in
*Homosexuality: Discrimination,
Criminology and the Law*, ed. Wayne
Dynes and Stephen Donaldson. New
York: Garland, 505–536.

Rosenfeld, R. A., and A. L. Kalleberg.
1991. "Gender Inequality in the Labor
Market: A Cross-National Perspective."
Acta Sociologica 34: 207–225.

Rothenberg, Paula. 1998. "Introduction,
Part II," in *Race, Class and Gender in the
United States* (4th ed.), ed. Paula
Rothenberg. New York: St. Martin's
Press, 110–114.

———. 1995. "Introduction," in *Race,
Class and Gender in the United States*

(3rd ed.), ed. Paula Rothenberg. New
York: St. Martin's Press, 1–12.

———. 1992. "The Construction,
Deconstruction and Reconstruction of
Difference," in *Bigotry, Prejudice and
Hatred*, ed. Robert Baird and Stuart
Rosenbaum. Buffalo, NY: Prometheus,
47–64.

Rothschild, Eric. 1993. "Recognizing
Another Face of Hate Crimes: Rape as
a Gender-Bias Crime." *Maryland
Journal of Contemporary Legal Issues* 4(2):
231–285.

Runkle, D. R. 1989, *Campaign for
President: The Campaign Managers Look
at '88.* Westport, CT: Auburn House.

Russell, Diana. 1990. *Rape in Marriage.*
Bloomington: Indiana University
Press.

Sabbaugh, Suha. 1990. *Sex, Lies and
Stereotypes: The Image of Arabs in
American Popular Fiction.* Washington,
DC: American-Arab Anti-
Discrimination Committee.

Sacks, Karen Brodkin. 1997. "How Jews
Became White," in *Race, Class and
Gender in the United States* (4th ed.), ed.
Paula Rothenberg. New York: St.
Martin's Press, 100–115.

Sanday, Peggy. 1998. "Pulling Train," in
*Race, Class and Gender in the United
States* (4th ed.), ed. Paula Rothenberg.
New York: St. Martin's Press, 497–503.

Sapp, Allen, Richard Holden, and
Michael Wiggins. 1991. "Value and
Belief Systems of Right-Wing
Extremists: Rationale and Motivation
of Bias-Motivated Crimes," in *Bias
Crime: American Law Enforcement and
Legal Responses*, ed. Robert Kelly.
Chicago: Office of International
Criminal Justice, 105–131.

Schmid, A. P., and E. U. Savona. 1996.
"Migration and Crime: A Framework
for Discussion," in *Migration and Crime*,
ed. A. P. Schmid. Milan, Italy:
International Scientific and
Professional Advisory Council of the
United Nations Crime Prevention and
Criminal Justice Program.

Schneider, Beth. 1993. "Put Up and Shut
Up: Workplace Sexual Assaults," in
Violence against Women, ed. Pauline Bart
and Eileen Moran. Newbury Park, CA:
Sage, 57–72.

Schur, Edwin. 1997. "Sexual Coercion in American Life," in *Gender Violence: Interdisciplinary Perspectives*, ed. Laura O'Toole and Jessica Schiffman. New York: New York University Press, 80–91.

Scully, Diana, and Joseph Marolla. 1993. "Riding the Bull at Gilley's: Convicted Rapists Describe the Rewards of Rape," in *Violence against Women*, ed. Pauline Bart and Eileen Moran. Newbury Park, CA: Sage, 26–46.

Senate Committee on the Judiciary. 1990. *Women and Violence: Hearings on Legislation to Reduce the Growing Problem of Violent Crime against Women* (Part 2), 101st Congress, 2nd Sess. 79.

Shaw, Clifford, and Hanry McKay. 1942. *Juvenile Delinquency and Urban Areas*. Chicago: University of Chicago Press.

Shasta, Robert. 1995. *Multicultural Law Enforcement: Strategies for Peacekeeping in a Diverse Society*. Englewood Cliffs, NJ: Prentice Hall.

Sheffield, Carole. 1995. "Hate Violence," in *Race, Class and Gender in the United States* (3rd ed.), ed. Paula Rothenberg. New York: St. Martin's Press, 432–441.

———. 1989. "Sexual Terrorism," in *Women: A Feminist Perspective*, ed. Jo Freeman. Mountain View, CA: Mayfield, 3–19.

———. 1987. "Sexual Terrorism: The Social Control of Women," in *Analyzing Gender*, ed. Beth Hess and Myra Marx Ferree. Newbury Park, CA: Sage, 171–189.

Shepherd, George. 1991. "Backlash in the American Dream: Resurgence of Racism and the Rise of the Underclass," in *Racism and the Underclass*, ed. George Shepherd and David Penna. New York: Greenwood Press, 3–12.

Simon, Rita, and Susan Alexander. 1993. *The Ambivalent Welcome*. Westport, CT: Praeger.

Smith, George. 1988. "Policing the Gay Community: An Inquiry into Textually Mediated Social Relations." *International Journal of the Sociology of Law* 16: 163–187.

Smith, Robert. 1995. *Racism in the Post-Civil Rights Era*. Albany: State University of New York Press.

Smith, Susan. 1989. *The Politics of "Race" and Residence: Citizenship, Segregation, and White Supremacy in Britain*. Cambridge, England: Polity Press.

Southern Poverty Law Center.

———. 1999. *Intelligence Report* 93. Montgomery, AL: SPLC.

———. 1998a. *Intelligence Report* 89. Montgomery, AL: SPLC.

———. 1998b. *Intelligence Report* 90. Montgomery, AL: SPLC.

———. 1998c, *Intelligence Report* 91. Montgomery, AL: SPLC.

———. 1998d, *Intelligence Report* 92. Montgomery, AL: SPLC.

———. 1997a. *Intelligence Report* 85. Montgomery, AL: SPLC.

———. 1997b. *Intelligence Report* 86. Montgomery, AL: SPLC.

———. 1997c. *Intelligence Report* 87. Montgomery, AL: SPLC.

———. 1997d. *Intelligence Report* 88. Montgomery, AL: SPLC.

———. 1997e. *SPLC Report*. Montgomery, AL: SPLC.

———. 1997f. "Anti-Immigrant Violence," in *Experiencing Race, Class and Gender in the United States*, ed. Virginia Cyrus. Mountain View, CA: Mayfield, 223–228.

Spelman, Elizabeth. 1988. *Essential Woman: Problems of Exclusion in Feminist Thought*. Boston: Beacon Press.

Stanko, Elizabeth. 1985. *Intimate Intrusions*. London, England: Routledge and Kegan Paul.

Stannard, David. 1992. *American Holocaust*. New York: Oxford University Press.

Starr, Erin: www.darkwing.uoregon.edu/~bfmalle

State of Maine, Attorney General's Office. Personal communication, February 1996.

Steele, Shelby. 1994. "Breaking Our Bond of Shame," in *Blacks and Jews: Alliances and Arguments*, ed. Paul Berman. New York: Delta, 178–180.

Stern, Kenneth. 1996. *A Force upon the Plain:* New York: Simon and Schuster.

———. 1992. *Politics and Bigotry*. New York: American Jewish Committee.

Stiffarm, Lenore, and Phil Lane. 1992. "The Demography of Native North America," in *The State of Native America,* ed. Annette Jaimes. Boston: South End Press, 23–54.

Stoddard, Lothrop. 1986. "Selective Immigration Is Essential," in *Racism: Opposing Viewpoints*, ed. Bruno Leone. San Diego, CA: Greenhaven, 62–65.

Stormfront: www.stormfront.org

Strom, Kevin Alfred: www.com/FREESP

Subcommittee on Human Rights and International Organizations of the Committee on Foreign Affairs. 1990. *Allegations of Violence along the United States–Mexico Border.* 101st Congress, 2nd Sess., April 18.

Tafoya, Terry. 1997. "Native Gay and Lesbian Issues: Two Spirited," in *Ethnic and Cultural Diversity among Lesbians and Gay Men*, ed. Beverly Greene. Thousand Oaks, CA: Sage, 1–10.

Takaki, Ronald. 1992. "Reflections on Racial Patterns in America," in *From Different Shores: Perspectives on Race and Ethnicity in America*, ed. Ronald Takaki. New York: Oxford University Press, 24–36.

———. 1989, *Strangers from a Different Shore: A History of Asian Americans.* Boston: Little, Brown and Co.

Tannenbaum, Frank. 1938. *Crime and the Community.* Boston: Ginn.

Tanton, John, and Wayne Lutton. 1993. "Immigration and Criminality in the USA." *Journal of Social, Political and Economic Studies* 18(2): 217–234.

Tarver, Heide. 1994. "Language and Politics in the 1980s: The Story of U.S. English," in *Race and Ethnic Conflict*, ed. Fred Pincus and Howard Ehrlich. Boulder, CO: Westview, 206–218.

Taub, Nadine, and Elizabeth Schneider. 1990. "Women's Subordination and the Role of Law," in *The Politics of Law*, ed. David Kairys. New York: Pantheon, 151–176.

Thomas, Clarence. 1996. "Victims and Heroes in the 'Benevolent State,'" in *ColorClassIdentity*, ed. John Arthur and Amy Shapiro. Boulder, CO: Westview.

Thorne, Barrie. 1994. *Gender Play: Boys and Girls in School.* New Brunswick, NJ: Rutgers University Press.

Time. 1997. "Rocky Mountain Hate." December 1.

Tjaden, Patricia and Nancy Thoennes. 1998. *Stalking in America: Findings from the National Violence against Women Survey.* Washington, DC: Centers for Disease Control and Prevention.

Tolnay, Stewart, and E. M. Beck. 1992. "Toward a Threat Model of Southern Black Lynchings," in *Social Threat and Social Control*, ed. Allen Liska. Albany: State University of New York Press, 33–52.

Tonry, Michael. 1995. *Malign Neglect.* New York: Oxford University Press.

U.S. Census Bureau: www.census.gov/ hhes/www/poverty.html

U.S. Commission on Civil Rights. 1992a. *Civil Rights Issues Facing Asian Americans.*

———. 1992b. *Racial and Ethnic Tensions in American Communities: Poverty, Inequality and Discrimination.*

———. 1990. *Intimidation and Violence: Racial and Religious Bigotry in America.*

———. n.d. *Recent Actions against Citizens and Residents of Asian Descent.*

U.S. Department of Commerce. 1993. *Statistical Abstract of the United States.* Washington, DC.

U.S. Department of Education and U.S. Department of Justice. n.d. *Preventing Youth Hate Crime.* Washington, DC.

U.S. Department of Labor. 1991. *Employment and Earnings.* Washington, DC.

U.S. Federal Bureau of Investigation. 1999. *Hate Crime Statistics. 1998.* Washington, DC.

———. 1998. *Hate Crime Statistics. 1997.* Washington, DC.

———. 1996. *Hate Crime Statistics. 1995.* Washington, DC.

———. 1995. *Hate Crime Statistics. 1994.* Washington, DC.

———. 1994. *Hate Crime Statistics. 1993.* Washington, DC.

———. 1993. *Hate Crime Statistics. 1992.* Washington, DC.

———. 1992. *Hate Crime Statistics. 1991.* Washington, DC.

U.S. Merit Systems Protection Board. 1995. *Sexual Harassment in the Federal Workplace.* Washington, DC.

Vander Wall, Jim. 1992. "A Warrior Caged: The Continuing Struggle of Leonard Peltier," in *The State of Native America*, ed. Annette Jaimes. Boston: South End Press, 291–310.

van Dijk, Teun. 1995. "Elite Discourse and the Reproduction of Racism," in

Hate Speech, ed. Rita Kirk Whillock and David Slayden. Thousand Oaks, CA: Sage, 1–27.

Vaughan, Alden. 1995. *Roots of American Racism*. New York: Oxford University Press.

von Schulthess, Beatrice. 1992. "Violence in the Streets: Anti-Lesbian Assault and Harassment in San Francisco," in *Hate Crimes: Confronting Violence against Lesbians and Gay Men*, ed. Gregory Herek and Kevin Berrill. Newbury Park, CA: Sage, 65–75.

Warsaw, Robin. 1994. *I Never Called It Rape*. New York: HarperPerennial.

Watts, Jerry. 1993. "Reflections on the Rodney King Verdict and the Paradoxes of the Black Response," in *Reading Rodney King, Reading Urban Uprisings*, ed. Robert Gooding-Williams. New York: Routledge, 236–248.

Websdale, Neil. 1998. *Rural Woman Battering and the Justice System*. Thousand Oaks, CA: Sage.

———, and Meda Chesney-Lind. 1998. "Doing Violence to Women: Research Synthesis on the Victimization of Women," in *Masculinities and Violence*, ed. Lee Bowker. Thousand Oaks, CA: Sage, 55–81.

Weigman, Robyn. 1993. "The Anatomy of Lynching," in *American Sexual Politics*, ed. John Fout and Maura Shaw Tantillo. Chicago: University of Chicago Press, 223–245.

Weinberg, Leonard. 1998. "An Overview of Right-Wing Extremism in the Western World: A Study of Convergence, Linkage and Identity," in *Nation and Race*, ed. Jeffrey Kaplan and Tore Bjørgo. Boston: Northeastern University Press, 3–33.

Weis, Lois, Amira Proweller, and Craig Centrie. 1997. "Re-examining 'A Moment in History: Loss of Privilege inside White Working-Class Masculinity in the 1990s,' " in *Off White: Readings on Race, Power and Society*, ed. Michelle Fine, Lois Weis, Linda Powell and L. Mun Wong. New York: Routledge, 210–226.

Weisburd, Steven Bennett, and Brian Levin. 1994. "On the Basis of Sex: Recognizing Gender-Biased Bias Crimes." *Stanford Law and Policy Review*, spring: 21–47.

Weiss, Joan. 1993. "Ethnoviolence's Impact Upon and Response of Victims and the Community," in *Bias Crime*, ed. Robert Kelly. Chicago: Office of International Criminal Justice, 174–185.

———, Howard Ehrlich, and Barbara Larcom. 1991–1992. *Ethnoviolence at Work*. Baltimore: National Institute Against Prejudice and Violence.

Weissman, Eric. 1992. "Kids Who Attack Gays," in *Hate Crimes: Confronting Violence against Lesbians and Gay Men*, ed. Gregory Herek and Kevin Berrill. Newbury Park, CA: Sage, 170–178.

Wellman, David. 1993. *Portraits of White Racism*. Cambridge, England: Cambridge University Press.

Wertheimer, David. 1992. "Treatment and Service Intervention for Lesbian and Gay Male Crime Victims," in *Hate Crimes: Confronting Violence against Lesbians and Gay Men*, ed. Gregory Herek and Kevin Berrill. Newbury Park, CA: Sage, 227–240.

West, Candace, and Sarah Fenstermaker. 1995. "Doing Difference." *Gender and Society* 9(1): 8–37.

———. 1993. "Power, Inequality and the Accomplishment of Gender: An Ethnomethodological View," in *Theory on Gender/Feminism on Theory*, ed. Paula England. Hawthorne, NY: Aldine de Gruyter, 151–174.

West, Candace, and Don Zimmerman. 1987. "Doing Gender." *Gender and Society* 1(2): 125–151.

West, Cornel. 1994. *Race Matters*. New York: Vintage.

———. 1993. "Learning to Talk Race," in *Reading Rodney King, Reading Urban Uprisings*, ed. Robert Gooding-Williams. New York: Routledge, 255–260.

Whillock, Rita Kirk. 1995. "The Use of Hate as a Stratagem for Achieving Political and Social Goals," in *Hate Speech*, ed. Rita Kirk Whillock and David Slayden. Thousand Oaks, CA: Sage, 28–54.

———, and David Slayden. 1995. "Introduction," in *Hate Speech*, ed. Rita Kirk Whillock and David Slayden. Thousand Oaks, CA: Sage, ix–xvi.

White Nationalist: www.nationalist.org

Wildman, Stephanie, and Adrienne Davis. 1995. "Language and Silence: Making Systems of Privilege Visible," in *Critical Race Theory*, ed. Richard Delgado. Philadelphia: Temple University Press, 573–579.

Wilets, James. 1997. "Conceptualizing Private Violence against Sexual Minorities as Gendered Violence: An International and Comparative Law Perspective." *Albany Law Review* 60(3): 989–1050.

Williams, Hubert, and Patricia Murphy. 1990. *The Evolving Strategy of Police: A Minority View*. Washington, DC: U.S. Department of Justice.

Wilson, Pete. 1994. "Securing Our Nation's Borders." Speech presented at Los Angeles Town Hall, April 25, 1994.

Winant, Howard. 1998. "Racial Dualism at Century's End," in *The House That Race Built*, ed. Wahneema Lubiano. New York: Vintage, 87–115.

———. 1997. "Where Culture Meets Structure," in *Race, Class and Gender in a Diverse Society*, ed. Diana Kendall. Boston: Allyn and Bacon, 27–38.

———. 1994. *Racial Conditions*. Minneapolis: University of Minnesota Press.

Wolfe, Leslie, and Lois Copeland. 1994. "Violence against Women as Bias-Motivated Hate Crime: Defining the Issues in the USA," in *Women and Violence*, ed. Miranda Davies. London: Zed Books, 200–213.

Wonders, Nancy, and Fred Solop. 1993. "Understanding the Emergence of Law and Public Policy: Toward a Relational Model of the State," in *Making Law: The State, the Law, and Structural Contradictions*, ed. William Chambliss and Marjorie Zatz. Bloomington: Indiana University Press, 204–228.

Wright, Richard, 1945, *Black Boy*. New York: Harper and Row.

Yggdrasil: www.netcom.com/pub/yg/ygg

Young, Iris Marion. 1995a. "Social Movements and the Politics of Difference," in *Campus Wars: Multiculturalism and the Politics of Difference*, ed. John Arthur and Amy Shapiro. Boulder, CO: Westview. 199–225.

———. 1995b. "Five Faces of Oppression," in *Multiculturalism from the Margins*, ed. Dean Harris. Westport, CT: Bergin and Garvey, 65–86.

———. 1990. *Justice and the Politics of Difference*. Princeton, NJ: Princeton University Press.

Young, Vernetta. 1996. "The Politics of Disproportionality," in *African-American Perspectives on Crime Causation, Criminal Justice Administration, and Crime Prevention*, ed. Anne Sultan. Boston: Butterworth-Heinemann, 69–81.

Zellner, William, 1995, *Countercultures: A Sociological Analysis*. New York: St. Martin's Press.

Zeskind, Leonard. 1996. "White Shoed Supremacy." *The Nation* 262(23): 21–24.

Zion, James, and Elsie Zion. 1996. "Hazko's Sokee'—Stay Together Nicely: Domestic Violence under Navajo Common Law," in *Native Americans, Crime and Justice*, ed. Marianne Nielsen and Robert Silverman. Boulder, CO: Westview, 96–112.

INDEX

abortion clinic violence, 34, 141
adaptation, modes of, 35–36
African Americans, violence against, 1, 3, 43, 137–65, 183–85, 216–23
African Methodist Episcopal Church, 133
AIDS, demonization of, 156–57, 162, 191–92
Aid to Families with Dependent Children (AFDC), 182, 205, 206
alcohol use, 45, 100–101
ALPHA group, 146–47, 150, 176
American Citizens for Justice, 239
American Dissident Voices, 77, 147, 152, 157
"American" identity, 57–65, 135–37
American Indian Movement (AIM), 219–20
American Renaissance magazine, 135–37, 146, 159, 176
anomie, 35, 45
Anti-Asian Violence Project, 239
Anti-Defamation League, 4, 18–19, 137, 175–77, 209–10, 226, 232, 240
antimiscegenation rhetoric, 147–48, 153–54, 157
anti-Semitic violence, 18–19, 15–29, 143–47, 159–62, 175–77
antiviolence: coalitions, 243–46; projects, 231–33, 238–39; regional organizations, 20, 26, 245–46
Anti-Violence Project of NGLTF (AVP), 13, 21–23
Arab American Anti-Discrimination Committee, 20–21
Aryan Nation, 36, 138, 140–41, 144, 163–64, 172–73, 175
Asian Immigrant Women Advocates, 239
Asian American Legal Defense and Education Fund, 239
Asian Americans, violence against, 62, 72, 122–25, 239

Baldwin, James, 133
ballot initiatives: anti–gay, 191–92; anti–immigrant, 196–97
battering of women, 28, 93–95, 104
Beam, Louis, 172, 174
Berg, Alan, 144
Biden, Joseph, 28, 211
Bilbo, Senator, 147–48
Billings, Montana antiviolence movement, 246
Black, Donald, 175
Black Panther Party, 219
Blackstone, William, 189–90
Blood in the Face (Ridgeway), 32
Blue Boys, the, 108–109
Border Patrol, 220
Boris, Al, 188

boundary: crossing, 241–46; drawing, 199
Bowers v. Hardwick, 111
Bowling, Benjamin, 8–9
Brimelow, Peter, 194
Broad, Kendal, 243–44
Brownworth, Victoria, 116
Buchanan, Pat, 169–71, 190, 193–94
Burger, Warren, 111
Bush, George, 7
Butler, Richard Girnt, 38, 163–64, 173
Byrd, James, 1, 165

Carrigan, Tim, 113
Cato, Gavin, 128–29
Chambliss, William, 42, 179–80
Chang, Edward Taehan, 242
Chiles, Lawton, 193
Chin, Vincent, 79
Chinese Exclusion Act of 1882, 70, 200
Christian Identity, 34, 138–39, 141, 143–45, 162, 163–64, 169
Christopher Commission, Los Angeles, 39
Chung, Angie, 242
church arsons, 141
Church Arsons Prevention Act, 230
citizenship, restrictions on, 70–74
Clark, Kenneth, 69
class, social, 36–39, 41–46, 61–62, 74–80, 180–83, 204–205
Clinton, Bill, 28, 161, 195, 223, 227
Coalition for Navajo Liberation, 73
Colorado 1992 ballot initiative, 191–92
Communist Workers Party (CWP), 222
Concerned Maine Families (CMF), 191
Confederate White Pride, 149–50
control theories, 4, 33–35
Copeland, Lois, 9–10
Cornell, Stephen, 49
Council of Conservative Citizens, 170–71
Covenant, the Sword, and the Arm of the Lord (CSA), 138, 144–45
Covington, Harold, 169
Cowboys, the, 222
crime, definition of, 8–9
criminalization of minorities, 107, 111–12, 198, 205
criminology: critical, 41–46; failure to account for hate, 4, 31
Crown Heights riots, 119, 128–29
culture: embedded structures in, 1–2; and institutionalized difference, 51–52; permission by, 103–105; and practical politics, 238; of racism, 59–65